BEHIND PAUL SCOTT'S
Raj Quartet
A Life in Letters

BEHIND PAUL SCOTT'S

Raj Quartet

A Life in Letters

THE EARLY YEARS
(1940–1965)

VOLUME I

COMPILED AND EDITED BY

Janis Haswell

CAMBRIA
PRESS

Amherst, New York

Requests for permission should be directed to:
permissions@cambriapress.com, or mailed to:
Cambria Press
20 Northpointe Parkway, Suite 188
Amherst, NY 14228

Library of Congress Cataloging-in-Publication Data

Scott, Paul, 1920–1978.
    [Correspondence. Selections]
    Behind Paul Scott's Raj quartet : a life in letters / [edited by] Janis Haswell.
        p. cm.
    Includes bibliographical references and index.
    ISBN 978-1-60497-749-3 (v. 1: alk. paper)—ISBN 978-1-60497-750-9 (v. 2: alk. paper) 1. Scott, Paul, 1920–1978—Correspondence. 2. Authors, English—20th century—Correspondence. I. Haswell, Janis Tedesco. II. Title.

    PR6069.C596Z48 2011
    821'.914—dc22
    [B]

2011000397

To Carol and Rob,
Sally and Peter,
and in memory of Penny Scott

TABLE OF CONTENTS

LIST OF FIGURES

PREFACE

When novelist Paul Scott was teaching creative writing at the University of Tulsa in 1976, he arranged to sell his letters to the archives at McFarlin Library, thus making available to the public what had been—and what might have remained—a private record of his life. Yet, one might argue that Scott's personal life was deliberately documented. His meticulous duplication of his business and personal correspondences (via typed carbon copies) suggests that many years before, as his reputation as a writer was taking root and developing, he wrote his letters with the assumption that such material would one day be made publically available.

These letters will be of interest to several different audiences. There are the growing number of scholars worldwide who will find this collection illuminating in terms of Scott's purpose and scope as a writer, his process, and his choices about style and structure. Admirers of the *Raj Quartet*, whether the books themselves or the Granada series, will enjoy these insights into a creative and reflective master. Writers (both aspiring and published) will find a window into the painstaking process of drafting, revising, editing, and publishing as well as the give-and-take business of getting one's name into print.

For all audiences, these letters reveal a person who is not accessible through the novels themselves. In his correspondence that is published in this book, Scott is unmasked (to the degree that any writer is unguarded who habitually produces texts with an audience in mind) in ways that never disappoint. He narrates his daily activities in his voluminous correspondence with his family, friends, clients, fellow writers, editors, agents, and readers. These letters, in fact, tell his life story. They work like a sequence of mininarratives that, viewed together, allow the reader to better envision the author of the *Raj Quartet*.

In a speech during National Book Week in March of 1967, Scott remarked, "Authors on the whole are not very interesting people" (*My Appointment* 41). When he was forced to summarize his life (at the requests of a publisher or, in later years, of scholars who wanted to write about his novels), those autobiographical sketches were deliberately understated. For instance, in April of 1970, Scott wrote the following summary for the Northwest Arts Association:

> Paul Scott was born in London in 1920, into a family of immigrant artists from Leeds who maintained throughout their lives a belief in the superiority of the North over the South. They claimed connexion with the naturalist and engraver, Thomas Bewick, whose surname was often used as a middle name for elder sons. A younger son, Paul Scott was given the middle name of Mark, after his great-uncle, Mark Scott of Selby, who was three times Mayor and had a road named after him. He thinks he was named Mark in the hope that he would prosper in business and be immune from the claims and uncertainty of an artist's life. Educated at one of those private schools that used to be described as for the sons of gentlemen, he was withdrawn when funds ran out and at the age of sixteen set to work in the office of an accountant with a small but fascinatingly diverse practice. He continued his purely academic education at night school and by correspondence, to reach the matriculation standard necessary for the preliminary accountancy exams. This achieved, he seemed set for the commercial career his mildly Bohemian family had such a romantic view of.

He had, however, already decided to write. In his study were a three-act play, short stories, poems and one chapter of a novel called "Rachel" about a young man coming from the North to live in a bed sitter in Bloomsbury. The North and the bed sitter were imaginary. Only Bloomsbury was real—but not very.

The war provided him with the perfect excuse to suspend the uninteresting study of auditing and mercantile law. He served in the army at home, in India, Assam and Malaya from 1940 until 1946. His interest in India dates from this period. He has been back there twice, since independence.

Married in 1941, he now began life as a householder. He had had poems published in broadsheets and war-time anthologies. A three-act play was placed in the first four in an international competition, was published but not performed. Intending to continue as a writer he looked for a job in the book world and entered publishing on the business side. By 1950 he was secretary to four associated publishing companies but in that year he resigned and accepted the offer of a job with a leading firm of authors' agents.

In this same year he wrote a radio play, which was produced by Donald McWhinnie for the BBC. The play provided him with the theme for his first novel, which won the Eyre & Spottiswoode Literary Award in 1951. He continued as an agent, writing novels, radio and television plays in his spare time, until 1960 when he resigned his directorship in the firm and with the backing of his American publisher, devoted himself entirely to his own work.

Since 1960 he has published six novels, and has contributed reviews of fiction and nonfiction to a number of national newspapers and periodicals. In 1963 he was elected Fellow of the Royal Society of Literature. He is presently at work on the third novel in his trilogy about the last days of British rule in India and in 1969 received an Arts Council award to assist him in this, his major project to date. His wife has published several novels under the name of Elizabeth Avery. They have two daughters, the younger in her final year at York University, the elder with the National Touring company of "Hair", as deputy stage manager. (McFarlin 15:12)[1]

These facts—education, employment, service in the war, family, publications—are the bare bones of Scott's life.[2] This collection of letters
fleshes out the life of Scott the writer, which was all he ever wanted to
be—not just a writer but a great one.

What do the letters add to one's understanding of Scott's life? Most
fundamentally, they reveal the drive to be a writer as the seminal force
of his life from his boyhood on. Scott's sense of purpose as a human
being was grounded in the act of writing. While his preferred genre
changed over time—beginning with poetry, then changing to drama, and
ultimately ending with novels—his sense of purpose consciously and
continually revolved around writing. That drive prompted him to resign
as one of the directors of David Higham Associates Literary Agency
in 1960 in order to write full-time. Scott's holographs, typescripts, and
hundreds of reviews constitute a voluminous body of work, but just as
substantial are his business and personal correspondences—an inte-
gral part of Scott's writing career. His letters served various purposes:
to advise his clients, to sell an idea for a new novel to his publishers,
to work through a problem in a plot or theme with his editors, and to
maintain bonds with his family and friends. As early as the mid-1960s,
Scott declined to sell his papers piecemeal (despite having an increasing
need to supplement his royalties). Instead, he kept the material intact as
"something worth preserving."[3]

Readers of this collection will find in the following pages a full-
dimensional human being who, without a doubt, was driven to realize
his creative potential, but who was also devoted to his family and his
friends, tormented by his own failings, desperate (at times) because of
financial pressures, dedicated as an agent and a mentor to his fellow
writers, and at the end of his life, gifted as a teacher. These letters tell
the story of Paul Scott's life in a more complete, candid, and complex
way than any chronological narrative could do, revealing not only biographical details and literary commentary but also a compendium of the
literary/publishing scene over two decades. The style of these letters will
never disappoint; their contents will instruct and frequently move their
readers. It is my pleasure to make them accessible to readers who would

otherwise not be able to access this material and so never encounter Scott's voice—this life in letters.

PRINCIPLES OF SELECTING AND EDITING

I initially approached these letters purely as a scholar who was interested in Scott's novels—books I admire, reread, teach, and study. My primary principle of selection, then, was to transcribe the correspondence that reveals the working life of an author—his process of conceiving his novels, his search for the right form for his narratives, and his intentions in terms of his subject matter and themes. Practiced readers of the *Raj Quartet* know how difficult it is to extricate Scott's position from the innumerable perspectives he dramatizes. His letters (along with his speeches and lectures) provide evidence of clear, explicit, and unequivocal authorial intent—an indispensible component of any scholarly analysis.

This primary focus—to document Scott's life as an author—soon took me in a second direction. Scott's creative process assumed a complex dynamic. The drafting stage of his writing was always done in seclusion. But the revision stage often involved input from multiple sources. His wife Penny was very often his initial reader of a completed draft, but the letters exchanged between Scott and his editors, agents, and friends—Peter Green, John Willey, Adèle Dogan Horwitz, Maurice Temple Smith, Dorothy Olding, Roland Gant, and David Higham— show how they acted as sounding boards through the revision process. There is often an animated give-and-take in these discussions, with Scott accepting his correspondents' advice only if it made sense in terms of the lives and psychology of his characters and the integrity of his plot. Whether he accepted or rejected the advice he was given, however, the exchange of views helped Scott articulate for himself what each novel was trying to say.

Ultimately, it makes little sense to talk about Scott the author apart from Scott the man, and this became my third focus. In the process of my research, I discovered the private content of Scott's letters to be as compelling as the professional content, but more problematic. Scott was a caring, sensitive, humorous man who passionately loved his family and friends. But, as he poured his life into his art, he become more isolated from those he loved. His drinking became obsessive. Financial pressures made him desperate to complete the longer, more demanding novels of the *Quartet* even as crises on the home front slowed his progress. There is, then, a contradiction in what these letters reveal. On the one hand, they act as release valves in terms of Scott's reaction to the praise and criticism from his reviewers and readers, his need to write the kind of novels he wanted to write, his increasing desperation when those novels wouldn't sell as he hoped they would, his reflection with his fellow writers about the artistic process, his commiseration with them about the publishing industry, and his pride in the achievements of his wife (and fellow novelist) and of his talented daughters. On the other hand, as pressures mounted in the last decade of his life, Scott's correspondence became a vehicle whereby he could impose order on situations that seemed to be out of his control. On those occasions, rather than providing an accurate portrayal of events, the letters in fact create a deceptive sense of order and contentment.

I have, therefore, provided contextual information in the introductions as well as footnotes that may help readers to understand which letters are self-revelatory and which are self-concealing. It is not my place (or desire) to "correct" Scott. Nor do I want to impose my own interpretations on the readers of this collection. But a careful reading of these letters will (I hope) set the record straight in terms of previous literary and biographical scholarship. Still, there shouldn't be a heavy-handed editorial voice here. These letters give a voice to Paul Scott—writer, husband, father, and friend—and his perceptions and narratives about his world.

There are gaps of various sorts in the letters. Because Scott did not retain copies of his correspondence during his years in the army, only those letters that were retained by their recipients are available. Most notable from the early years are Scott's letters to Clive and Ruth Sansom (the neighbors of his parents, Tom and Frances Scott, on Bourne Hill). As Clive was a fellow poet, many of his and Scott's conversations were about writing and art, not (unfortunately) about Scott's first impressions and experiences on his posting to India. There are silences in the correspondence between 1946 and 1949 because there are few extant letters. There are also understandable gaps in the correspondence between Paul and Penny Scott, as Paul wrote to his wife only when they were separated by his travels.

Finally, there are gaps that are produced in the process of reducing the letters to a publishable number. Scott often wrote about the same topic to several people, repeating similar information to (for instance) both his publishers and/or both of his agents. Often, such repetition reveals the issues he thought were important or pressing. In reducing the number of pages that are published, that emphasis is diminished. A worse loss, perhaps, is in the coherence of the *petit récits*, the mininarratives that emerge over extended conversations with specific correspondents (Kay Dick, M. M. Kaye, Gerald Hanley, Peter Green, and E. M. Almedingen). The process of selecting and reducing the letters to a manageable number disrupts the flow of those conversations.

As a transcriber of these letters, I faced other challenges. In much of his correspondence, Scott used a manual typewriter—a now-archaic technology that required several steps to correct an error. He knew all the tricks of the trade from having to generate clean typescripts of his novels and book reviews; those tricks make working from carbons difficult. For instance, if he mistyped a letter (e.g., typing an *e* instead of a *d*), he would either correct it with a typewriter eraser or later "white it out" by retyping the incorrect letter using a correction sheet that overlaid a white powder over the *e*. Then he would cover the "erased" letter with the correct one. The carbon, as a result, shows the incorrect letter *e* typed twice (bolded in that sense), covered faintly by the correct letter *d*. In the case of letters and words, I have included the correction without a reference to the original error.

Changes in punctuation posed a more difficult problem. For instance, on the carbon there may be an incorrectly placed comma which Scott presumably corrected with a period. Or, perhaps he had first typed a semicolon, then typed a colon over it to correct it; this appears on the carbon as a semicolon with a darker comma. In such cases, I have opted to use the version that is closest to conventional use. In rare cases, I have also added punctuation to aid the reader in navigating some of Scott's longer sentences.

I have omitted strikeouts (either words that were deleted by typing *xxxx* through them or single letters with a diagonal marked through them) and corrected obvious errors in typing, spelling, and punctuation when Scott's intent was clear. Oftentimes, Scott neglected to underline the titles of books, newspapers, or magazines; I have added those. I have retained Scott's practice of considering the names of publishing houses as a collective and therefore using verbs in the plural rather than the singular, as in "Heinemann are planning publication in March" or "Penguin have taken a different position."

I have marked by [...] my own deletions within the letters of material that is repetitive or of little interest to readers. Occasionally, Scott would end a sentence or thought with a series of periods, which I have made uniform as four periods without brackets. Scott also was inconsistent in his use of single or double quotation marks. I have changed his single quote marks to double but have maintained the British convention of placing commas and periods outside the quote marks, along with the British spelling of words. One final editorial change: I have also adopted the more standard use of hyphens in words such as *subcontinent* (not *sub-continent*), *bookkeeping* (not *book-keeping*), and *freelance* (not *free-lance*).

WORKS CITED

Correspondence from the Paul Scott Papers, 1979.003, Department of Special Collections and University Archives, McFarlin Library, University of Tulsa, Tulsa, Oklahoma. Cited by box and folder number.

Scott, Paul. *My Appointment with the Muse*. Ed. Shelley Reece. London: Heinemann, 1986. Print.

ENDNOTES

1. Archival sources in the introductory materials are cited by their collection, box, and folder numbers.
2. For additional letters containing autobiographical sketches, see the following from the Tulsa archives: the letter to Hugh Corbett (18 September 1969), the letter to David Pease (3 April 1970), and the letter to Francine Weinbaum (19 July 1975). See also Scott's letter to Ralph King (17 July 1975), which is not included in this collection.
3. Scott's comment to Dr. Howard B. Gotlieb at Boston University, 15 February 1965 (McFarlin 5:15).

ACKNOWLEDGMENTS

I am grateful to Richard Workman and his staff at the Harry Ransom Humanities Research Center, University of Texas at Austin, and to Marc Carlson and his staff at the University of Tulsa for their invaluable assistance. My thanks also to Professor Thomas Staley, director of the Harry Ransom Humanities Research Center at Austin, and to Stephen Wood, for making available their correspondence.

My deepest gratitude goes to Sally and Carol Scott, whose guidance and faith in this project brought it to fruition. They have been most generous in allowing me to use previously unpublished family letters and in sharing their own stories.

Paul Scott's letters in the Special Collections at the McFarlin Library, University of Tulsa, and in the Harry Ransom Humanities Research Center, University of Texas–Austin, are © 2011 Carol and Sally Scott and reproduced by permission of David Higham Associates, Ltd.

My thanks to the College of Liberal Arts at Texas A&M University–Corpus Christi, which helped to support this project.

ABBREVIATIONS OF HOLDINGS

DHA-HRC | Scott's business correspondence while he was a literary agent for Pearn, Pollinger and Higham, later David Higham Associates, London. This large collection of many thousands of letters is held in the Harry Ransom Humanities Research Center at the University of Texas at Austin, Texas. Cited by box and folder numbers.

Harold Ober –Princeton | Dorothy Olding's professional correspondence from the Harold Ober Special Collection, Princeton University. Cited by box and folder numbers.

HRC | Private correspondence held by the Harry Ransom Humanities Research Center at the University of Texas at Austin, Texas, catalogued under the Paul Scott Collection, Series 1, Box 38, folders 3 and 4. Cited by box and folder numbers.

McFarlin | Six thousand personal letters written and received by Scott, housed at the McFarlin Library at the University of

Tulsa in Tulsa, Oklahoma. The Scott Collection includes the private letters of Clive and Ruth Sansom, Francine Weinbaum, and Sandy Dennison, which have been donated to the archives. Letters are catalogued as Series 1. Cited by box and folder numbers.

Private holdings Made available by their recipients: Steven Wood, Dr. Thomas Staley, and Carol and Sally Scott.

FREQUENT ABBREVIATIONS
IN THE LETTERS

BBC	British Broadcasting Company
BOP	*The Birds of Paradise*
CLP	*The Chinese Love Pavilion*
DHA	David Higham Associates, Scott's British agents
E & S	Eyre and Spottiswoode Ltd., Scott's publisher from 1950 to 1962
HOA	Harold Ober Associates, Scott's American agents
MS or mss	Manuscript, or the state of the novels before publication (could be in holograph or typescript form)
NAL	New American Library
PAN	Pan Books, specialized in publishing paperback editions
PP&H	Pearn, Pollinger and Higham—literary agents, later divided into Laurence Pollinger Ltd. and David Higham Associates

S & W	Secker and Warburg, Scott's publisher from 1962 to 1965
TLS	*Times Literary Supplement*
TS or ts	Typescript or typed drafts of the novels before the proof stage

CHRONOLOGY[4]

1920   Born Paul Mark Scott, March 25, in Palmer's Green, the second son of Tom and Frances Scott.

1929   Enrolls at Winchmore Hill Collegiate School.

1933   Tom Scott's business fails; the family moves in with aunts in Wyphurst.

1934   Leaves school because of family's financial difficulties.

1936   Trains in accounting with C. T. Payne. Tom and Frances Scott move from Wyphurst to a home of their own in the Cannon Hill area.

1939   Scott family moves to Bourne Hill. Paul writes the play "Young Woodley" and a novel entitled "Rachel."

1940   Paul is called up and assigned to the Eighth Battalion, the Buffs.

1941   Publishes a trilogy of poems entitled *I, Gerontius* in *Poets of This War*. Marries Nancy Edith Avery (Penny) on 23 October.

---

[4] Compiled from archival materials at the McFarlin Library, University of Tulsa, especially Scott's own synopsis of his publishing history in his letter to Hugh Corbett (McFarlin 2:36) and from Spurling's *Paul Scott*.

1942   Writes two plays, "Brilliant City" and *Pillars of Salt.*

1943   Deployed in March to India. Continues to write plays: "After Our Labours" (never published) and "The Pilgrim Michael" (unfinished).

1944   Joins an air supply unit (No. 1 Indian Supply Company) in Comilla as a cadet officer. Promoted to captain and placed in command of 10/10 section.

1945   August, Scott posted to Malaya, then Singapore for the "mopping up."

1946   Returns to England in May and settles into 8 Hampden Way. Works as an accountant for Falcon and Grey Walls Press.

1947   Birth of Carol Vivien (March 7).

1948   Scott's play *Pillars of Salt* published by Gollancz in *Four Jewish Plays.* Joyce Weiner acts as his agent.

1948   Birth of Sally Elisabeth (May 30). Family moves to 61 Brookland Rise.

1949   Circulates his novel "Dazzling Crystal," which is rejected by seventeen publishers.

1950   Places his new play *Lines of Communication* with Donald McWhinnie of the BBC.

1950   Joins Pearn, Pollinger and Higham as a literary agent.

1951   *Lines of Communication* produced by Ian Atkins for BBC radio and television.

1952   Publication of *Johnnie Sahib*, a novel enlarging upon the characters and themes of *Lines of Communication.* Wins Eyre and Spottiswoode literary award for *Johnnie Sahib.*

1953   Publication of *The Alien Sky* (American title: *Six Days in Mayapore*). Scott replaces Joyce Weiner with David Higham as his agent.

1954   Scott made junior director of Pearn, Pollinger and Higham. The family moves to 78 Addison Way in June. A radio version of *The Alien Sky* is performed in July on BBC radio.

1955   Scott's play *Sahibs and Memsahibs* is drafted for television but eventually produced for radio (not broadcast until 1958).

1956 A television version of *The Alien Sky* is aired in January. *A Male Child* is published in March.

1958 Publication of *The Mark of the Warrior*, which was published in the United States by William Morrow & Company. Tom Scott dies in August, and Paul's mother, Frances, moves in with Paul and Penny until November, when Paul asks her to leave. Pearn, Pollinger and Higham divides into Laurence Pollinger Ltd. and David Higham Associates.

1959 Lectures at the Swanwick Writers' Summer School.

1960 Leaves David Higham Associates in March to be a full-time writer. Publication of *The Chinese Love Pavilion* in September. Scott prepares radio script for adaption of *The Mark of the Warrior* for BBC. Returns to lecture at the Swanwick Writers' Summer School.

1961 Invited to cohost the Swanwick Writers' Summer School.

1962 Publication in April of *The Birds of Paradise*. Leaves publishers Eyre and Spottiswoode in June for Secker and Warburg. Presented at the London Writer Circle with Harold Pinter. Cohosts (with wife Penny) at the Swanwick Writers' Summer School.

1963 Elected a fellow of the Royal Society of Literature. Publication in October of *The Bender*. Travels to New York for a publicity tour.

1964 Publication of *The Corrida at San Feliu*. Travels to India 24 February–9 April. Adaptation of *The Bender* aired by BBC in July. Undergoes treatment with family for amoebiasis in Paris.

1965 Secker and Warburg signs over its publishing rights of Scott's work to William Heinemann Ltd. in February. Scott gives the opening lecture at the Swanwick Writers' Summer School.

1966 Publication in July of *The Jewel in the Crown*.

1967 Delivers the closing lecture at the Swanwick Writers' Summer School.

1968 Publication in September of *The Day of the Scorpion*.

1969   Returns to India (5 January–11 February). In May 1969, Frances
        Scott dies. Completes the play "The Situation." Receives Arts
        Council grant in November.

1972   Publication in October of *The Towers of Silence*, for which he
        wins the *Yorkshire Post* fiction award.

1972   Makes final visit to India under the sponsorship of the British
        Council (30 January–5 March).

1973   Gives the opening lecture at the Swanwick Writers' Sum-
        mer School. Invited to become president of the London Writer
        Circle.

1975   Publication in May of *A Division of the Spoils*. Lectures at Swan-
        wick Writers' Summer School. On U.S. tour 27 August–19 Sep-
        tember visits Urbana, Illinois; Washington, DC; Austin, Texas;
        and New York City. Delivers the keynote speech at the London
        Writer Circle in November.

1976   Penny leaves the Scott home on July 15. Scott teaches as a writ-
        er-in-residence at the Institute of Modern Letters, University of
        Tulsa (August to December).

1977   Publication of *Staying On* in March. Scott begins a new novel,
        entitled "Mango Rain" or (alternately) "Married with Two Chil-
        dren." Heinemann republishes the four books of the quartet in a
        single volume. Scott returns to Tulsa at the end of July to teach.
        Enters St. Francis Hospital in late September and undergoes
        cancer surgery. *Staying On* wins the Booker Prize in November.
        Returns to London in December, where Penny and his daughters
        welcome him home. *After the Funeral* is published in *The Times'*
        Christmas supplement, including an illustration by Sally Scott.

1978   Publication of an article in *The Times* on travel in India.
        Undergoes a second operation on February 14. Dies of cancer in
        London on March 1. *Staying On* is made into a film.

1979   Publication of *After the Funeral*, with illustrations by Sally
        Scott, by the Whittington Press.

1983   Granada Television airs the dramatic series *The Jewel in the
        Crown*.

BEHIND PAUL SCOTT'S
Raj Quartet
A Life in Letters

The War Years (1940–1949)

Paul Scott was born on 25 March 1920 to Thomas and Frances Scott of London, artists by trade (Tom) and by temperament (Frances). Tom's studio was at Wyphurst on Southgate High Street, where his sisters Florence and Laura lived and worked.[1] The Scotts educated their sons Peter and Paul at the Winchmore Hill Collegiate School, an exclusive public institution. But in 1933, their economic situation deteriorated; they moved into Wyphurst to live with Florence and Laura, who had never welcomed Frances into the family, feeling that Tom had married below his station.[2] In the fall of 1934 at the age of fourteen, Scott was forced to leave school to work as a junior audit clerk for C. T. Payne, an accountant on the West End of London (Spurling 54). Scott studied nights to pass accountancy exams and later took evening courses in bookkeeping.

In 1940, one year into World War II, Scott was called up and assigned to the Eighth Battalion (the Buffs), serving as an intelligence sergeant for the 209 Brigade, Home Defenses. In November of 1940, Wyphurst was destroyed in a German bombing raid that killed Florence and Laura—an event that Scott called his "baptism of fire" (McFarlin 17:5). In early 1941, he met Nancy Edith (Penny) Avery, a ward sister at the hospital in Torquay, where he was stationed. Paul and Penny married on 23 October 1941. Scott was deployed to India in March of 1943, where he trained as an officer in Belgaum, then served in air supply with stations in West Bengal, Imphal, and Malaya. He was demobilized at the rank of captain in 1946, returning to his wife, Penny, and a bookkeeping position at Falcon and Grey Walls Press.[3] Their daughter Carol Vivien was born in 1947, and their daughter Sally Elisabeth was born in 1948.

The letters from this period were preserved by their recipients: Peter Scott (Paul's older brother) and friends of the Scott family—Clive and Ruth Sansom. The Sansom letters are housed in the Paul Scott Collection at the McFarlin Library, University of Tulsa. The correspondence between 1940 and 1949 tells several compelling stories: of a young soldier who was homesick for his friends and family, of a young man discovering his sexuality, of a newly wedded husband (I will return to this event momentarily), and of a future novelist's initial exposure to India—the place Scott would later call his second home.[4]

It may be disappointing to readers that the subject of India evokes few comments in Scott's extent letters from this period. Still, these and subsequent letters provide information about Scott meeting his fellow officers Bob Mason, James Leasor, and James Corben. After forming a deep friendship with Corben, Scott was demobilized some months before his friend, and several of Corben's letters replying to Scott's can be found in the Tulsa archives.[5] Some of the news pertained to their shared military interests, such as that new jeeps had arrived: "How I wish you were here to enjoy them with me," Corben wrote. "They really are good vehicles with a lot of new things on them" (McFarlin 2:35). In a letter dated 16 August 1946, Corben described the violence that was erupting with the creation of the state of Pakistan.

> All hell's let loose! The Muslims are having a pitched battle with the Hindus in every open space in Calcutta. They—the Muslims—have so far succeeded in setting fire to the Hindustani Stand and buildings, have set over fifty shops in lower Circular road on fire, have

broken into a Hindu girls school and raped most of the inhabitants and are now charging forward into Chowrin Street where they are going to have a massed demonstration. Nice people.

The only consolation about all this is the fact that no military personnel have been touched and Europeans have been left entirely alone. This I take to be a good sign and one that bodes well for the future. […] I can't help feeling that people at home have become awfully belly conscious to the exclusion of everything else. Rationing I know must be terrible, or at least six years of it, but apparently nothing else matters.[…]

P. S. The civil situation is going from bad to worse. About 500 have been killed to date, and another two thousand seriously injured. The police are standing watching it and the military are going to be called on if it goes on. (McFarlin 2:35)

It is difficult from this one-sided conversation to guess how much Scott and his peers understood about the culture and history of India. But clearly they were neither indifferent to nor oblivious of the political events in the months before India gained its independence.

Scott's initial experience of India could be digested only years later, through reflection, study, and creative reshaping via his novels.[6] In hindsight, he reminisced,

So there I was, 23 years old, looking at India, knowing nothing about it, and not liking it one bit (I got jaundice, to start with). The first time I knew the place had worked its way into my system (even my heart) was 2 years later when I was in Malaya and threatened with a posting that would have kept me in Singapore until the time came for me to be repatriated. I wangled out of that, and without awaiting confirmation, flew back to India, and spent these last months blissfully happy under canvas in Bihar. […] After a few months back home I used to find myself thinking and dreaming India. (McFarlin 19:1)

His comment that India had "worked its way into my system" was true both literally (he carried home a parasite that caused an infection called amoebiasis) and figuratively (he would spend his literary life defining the importance of India in his life).

In 1972 Scott told a university audience that during his third and last professional tour of India, "I had not wanted to come out here," but

> I was sent; and [...] my ignorance was immense, as great as my disappointment at finding it, when I arrived, raining. In my ignorance of the place, the people, and the history, I was representative [...] of many of my countrymen who in the main had for years been under the misapprehension that the uttermost point attainable— ultimate truth—lay midway between Dover and Cal[a]is, and that everything beyond was bad news. (*My Appointment* 120)

Scott's ignorance would be self-correcting in the coming years, as he voraciously read histories, biographies, and memoirs about India and its colonial period. In the 1950s, Scott found that his fellow countrymen wanted to insulate themselves from their imperialistic past. India no longer aroused their curiosity or invoked their interest, as, Scott observed, "they feel no real commitment" to its future (*My Appointment* 92, 100). Although his subsequent return trips to India would reveal a side of Scott that haunted him—what he called his sahib's face (see the introduction to section 4 in this volume)—his experience of India would instill in him a kind of joy that "springs from the heightened perception of time and place and people and history" (109).

Scott as a Writer and a Soldier

One of the overarching narratives of Scott's war letters reveals a young writer who was being mentored by his fellow poet Clive Sansom. Scott was a fledgling poet and playwright seeking affirmation of his work, a writer wholly dedicated to learning his craft. Before he enlisted, Scott exchanged with Sansom commentaries on his works in progress. The artistic side of his life became even more important to him after he joined the army. He wrote and published three poems from this period, "The Cross," "The Dream," and "The Creation," published collectively as *I, Gerontius*. He also began exercising his dramatic skills in several plays (publishing only one, *Pillars of Salt*, after the war).

Scott's life as a soldier—separated as he was from his family and immersed in tests of physical endurance—fueled a sense of himself both as "the poet at war" and as a suffering artist "living a life which might have forever stopped his inspiration" (McFarlin 17:9, 17:11). Often-times Scott indicated to Sansom that his roles as a soldier and a poet were incompatible. Before being posted to India, he spoke of "the iron barrier of war," which made the minutes of each day "long and arduous" (McFarlin 17:6). "Writing seems impossible," he wrote from India in July of 1944. "I feel at the moment that no more achievement is possible until the war is over" (McFarlin 17:9).

His artistic and personal developments, of course, were intertwined. The early months of 1941 seem to have marked a turning point in Scott's personal life. On 18 January 1941, Scott was demoted from lance corporal to private. The cause of such disciplinary action is undocumented. According to Hilary Spurling in her biography of Scott, Corporal Scilloe, the company clerk of the Buffs, reported that Scott's kit "had failed to come up to scratch at a surprise inspection" (Spurling 92).[7] But Scott told his brother Peter that "he had been caught writing something he shouldn't have in a letter to his friend, the solicitor Howard Smith.... Peter assumed that Paul had accidentally given away dates or troop dispositions" (92). Scott never revealed the cause of his demotion.

By early February, Scott was tormented by sleepless nights and was in emotional crisis. It was at this point that his friend Ruth Sansom visited him unexpectedly, bringing with her a poem her husband, Clive, had written to Paul entitled "For One in Darkness," which describes the loneliness and isolation of humankind. There are some people who have no friends, the poem acknowledges, who can't rely on advice, who don't look to faith for guidance. There are other people, however, who also walked in "unchartered lands" but who "found the green oases and the light ... / Is it a comfort to the mind to know?" (Spurling 93). The Sansoms were able to bring some solace to Scott—whether simply by the unexpected balm of the presence of his dearest friends or through some spiritual support they may have offered him. His letter to the Sansoms after this visit allowed Scott to "unburden" his heart "at an unbearable stage" and so (he told them) begin the necessary healing process, hoping he would "live to see happiness again" (see his letter of February 1941; McFarlin 17:6). The early months of 1941 therefore marked a turning point for Scott. As the February 1941 letter makes clear, his former self had been broken down. The young man who met Penny Avery two months later was already very far removed from the narcissistic and self-consciously "artistic" poet of the past.

In her biography of Scott, Hilary Spurling constructed an interpretation of these events that hinges on Scott's homosexual experiences.[8] To build her argument, Spurling turned to what she called an incident of the "love and treachery of friends" (Spurling 92) that occurred in December of 1940. She quoted from a letter addressed to the Sansoms dated 22 December, wherein Scott wrote, "How strange it is that people are so double-faced. We go through Life & trust many of them—but soon we discover their defects" (92; see the full letter below). Spurling argued that these lines reveal Scott as a victim of an act of treachery, a situation that may (so the biographer reasoned) have had something to do with a homosexual relationship. She made the same assumption about Scott's demotion the next month, implying that there was a link between the "treachery" and the demotion: "It seems likely that he [Paul] had committed some more personal indiscretion" (92). Spurling concluded that Scott was caught writing something sexually inappropriate in a letter to Howard Smith, and as a result, he was demoted to a private and threatened with exposure and imprisonment. Her view is supported by Ruth Sansom's conjecture (many years later) that Scott was guilty of "some kind of sexual stumble" (92) and by Scott's friend Mollie Hamilton's sense that "someone he trusted & loved & admired ... let him down badly" (qtd. in Spurling 94). On 14 March 1941, Scott wrote to Ruth Sansom as his alter ego[9] "Ivan Kapinsky,"[10] revealing, according to Spurling, the consequences of his homosexual orientation:

> Have you heard that I am crazy, and going to be locked up in a dungeon for the rest of the war? Will you come and give me biscuit and cake through the bars of the cage, or dungeon, so that

I can remember my former life. It is all very difficult, and one cannot think what is going to happen from one day to another. (Spurling 97–98; see fuller excerpt below)

There are several problems with Spurling's interpretation of the evidence. Military policy dictated that "deviant" sexual behavior was punishable by expulsion from the armed forces (on the basis of mental illness), and military law opened the possibility for a court-martial and imprisonment.[11] Demotion in these circumstances was not a part of the policy or the process. Was Scott fearful of such prosecution? It seems unlikely on two grounds. First, during the first twelve months of the war, in 1939 and 1940, only forty-eight men in Great Britain had been court-martialed for "indecency between males."[12] Second, several months later, Scott seems to be entirely comfortable talking about, admitting, and displaying his homosexuality. In a letter dated 3 April 1941, Scott wrote to Ruth,

> Dot recognized Mr. 21 & when she saw me at the Epicure, celebrating Peter Lumley's 21st & in no fit state to converse—her suspicions as to my "leanings" were confirmed. Incidentally Peter & I were discussing my being queer & his not—but understands—as he is from Chelsea. (McFarlin 17:6)

This was not the attitude or behavior of a man who had been persecuted for his sexual orientation.

The second problem with Spurling's interpretation may involve lines from Scott's letters being used out of context. Of special importance is her use of the 22 December 1940 letter, which supposedly hints at abject treachery. Here are the first two paragraphs in full:

> Last night Kapinsky was very tired. He has been tired for a long time. He sits & watches the far-off hills when he goes out at dawn to the outside lavatory. And there he sits & contemplates on his life and sometimes forgets where is he & sits there all day like a Patrician when the Barbarians entered Rome.
>
> Otherwise he is quite well & has asked me to enclose a short note which he says explains the secret of life if one reads between

> the lines. Personally I think the letter means nothing but perhaps
> Anna will understand it. I should like to meet Anna. Kapinsky
> says she is very frank. I like people to be frank. How strange it is
> that people are so double-faced. We go through life & meet many
> of them—but soon we discover their defects. Let us always be
> frank. Just as we were that time in Maidenhead when we sat &
> discussed sex for so long over tea. I can see it all so clearly. It is
> like a page from a Book of Memories—that though the book has
> been destroyed the page has somehow been torn out & left lying
> about in the old boxroom. (McFarlin 17:6)

Scott was contrasting Anna's[13] frankness with the hypocrisy of others.
The purpose is (in effect) to thank Ruth Sansom for her frankness and
to urge her continued honesty and openness. Scott would proceed in this
same letter to describe a new club he had started, "The Ancient Order of
the Stooge," and invite Ruth and Clive to join:

> There will be a stiff exam to pass to prove whether or not you are
> a stooge. Please send me an application—& you will hear from
> me on the matter later. A copy of the rules & regulations will be
> forwarded before the exam paper. (McFarlin 17:6)

Rather than the tragic heartbreak that Spurling suggested was in her
selective quotes, the full letter reveals a comic, almost burlesque tone.

By way of conclusion, Spurling argues that Scott's writing from
December 1940 through March 1941 revealed a young man who was
realizing that the world in general and the military in particular would
not tolerate his homosexual nature. He felt "split in two," Spurling con-
tends, and consciously made the decision to bury one side of himself
(Spurling 99). Sally Scott, however, holds a different view:

> The cause of his demotion was clearly not his sexuality—any
> prosecution for such offences would have brought far greater
> penalties, demotion being essentially a disciplinary measure.
> But above all the fact remains that during World War II, the
> Armed Forces took a distinctly and noticeably relaxed attitude
> to homosexuality (manpower was far too short, for one thing).

This, together with his cheerful references to his sexuality in his correspondence—well aware that all letters were read by the censor before being sealed and posted—hardly suggests someone living in fear of exposure. So Paul Scott here is hardly the tormented soul, cowering under the shadow of prosecution.

As I see it, his descent into his dark night of the soul (when Ruth Sansom came to his aid) was the result of a combination of personal crises in an alien situation to which he could see no end, the humiliation of being demoted for all to see, the possible betrayal by a friend, intense inner anxiety about his art, the enforced absence from friends and everything he knew, the sheer bloody routine of army life through that first winter (which was gruelling)—and of course the shock and bereavement of losing his aunts so suddenly in the bombing in London—which brought the war right home to his door, along with the reality of death—all this was a "perfect storm" of everything coming to a head, everything going critical at the same time—bringing him to despair. (Personal correspondence, 13 August 2010)

Throughout this difficult time, Scott's obsession to write did not diminish. But his confidence was fragile, and he desperately needed support and admiration from his friends. In 1942 he was deeply hurt by criticism from his friend Gerald Armstrong about his play "Brilliant City." Disappointment spawned by negative reviews forms a motif in Scott's letters. Although his skills as a writer would improve with experience, his confidence would remain vulnerable to critical reception. He dreaded reviews of his work; criticism inevitably spawned moments of personal crisis. It is true that he felt personally affirmed when his novels were praised. But throughout his life, Scott sought an equilibrium between writing for himself, on the one hand, and on the other, needing the praise of his readers. Despite his insistence about writing the kind of novel that pleased him, the failure to launch a best seller would always weigh upon his mind.

Armstrong's criticism of "Brilliant City" is significant for yet another reason. It had, in Scott's own words, "shaken the very base of my belief in myself, something that my wife has fostered most beautifully for me during the past year" (McFarlin 17:8). The juxtaposition of these influences—his friend Armstrong and his wife Penny—had personal as well as professional implications for Scott. Whose voice would triumph: Armstrong's negative voice or Penny's supportive one?

The role of Penny in her husband's creative life is no less profound than her role in his personal life. The two, in fact, are intertwined—a point that previous scholarship has minimized. There is no doubt that his earlier homosexual relationships with worldly, older men (Geoffrey Armstrong among them) fed Scott's sense of himself as an artistic personality, a Noel Coward type (or as Spurling phrased it, "the lonely little poet," [88, 90]), seeking exotic experiences that would fuel his creative expression. He had written to Ruth Sansom in August of 1940, "For me sex is an all important—I should say the most important part of life—all emotions & creative instincts are (to me) based on the sensual impulse in man" (McFarlin 17:5).

Given the link that Scott believed to exist between the artistic and the sexual needs within an individual, how did he regard his life-changing decision to marry Penny Avery, and what did it mean for his future as a writer? The answer can be found most accurately, I believe, in Scott's letters—material that was made public only selectively in Spurling's treatment. Consider her use of Scott's letter to Ruth Sansom on 26 August 1941, which she introduced as evidence that Scott was "done with one side of himself":

> Winter is approaching again...I must find my new way of Life soon or I shall rapidly grow stale again as I did last winter. And it was not I who was recalled to Life in the Spring. Myself is glancing over my shoulder ever as I write this letter...In what way have I changed? In no way. In what way have I looked at myself of late. I have gazed in the same mirror but seen a different reflection—that is the only way I can explain the change in myself. You know to what I refer. It was a passing phase essential to my necessarily wide understanding of Life....
>
> I lay my new self—or my own self newly expressed—before you for your consideration. In the meantime, please write...In my

detachment I seem to grow even more dependent upon others. Loneliness has a great deal to do with it. Even though now I have someone who returns the affection I have thrown out to the winds, even though we are wildly happy, sensibly considerate in that mutual affection—we are still both lonely because we must walk unmasked among masks, which is far worse than wearing yourself a mask. (qtd. in Spurling 112)

Leaving these words to speak for themselves, Spurling proceeds to describe the surprise and dismay of his friend Geoffrey Ridehalgh upon learning of Scott's engagement; Frances Scott's resistance to attending the wedding; the warnings to Penny from her bridesmaid, best man, and father about her choice of a husband; and the less-than-successful meeting of Penny with Clive and Ruth Sansom. The section ends with Scott's reported words to his friend Mollie Hamilton (M. M. Kaye) some years later, that he had married Penny "for protection and safety," which Spurling takes to mean protection from "persecution in the army on homosexual grounds," but also protection "against unstable elements in his own temperament" (Spurling 113).

If readers consult the full text of Scott's 26 August 1941 letter (see below), the words quoted by Spurling take on a quite different meaning. Scott was taking a metacognitive view of his past ("Myself is glancing over my shoulder even as I write this letter"). He hadn't changed, he insisted, but he found a different reflection in the mirror, the reflection of a man who was ending a "passing phase" and giving himself fully to someone "who returns the affection I have thrown out to the winds" and with whom he was "wildly happy." Scott continued,

Don't you think friendships & lives stay static as from the moment of last memory? In other words, don't you feel that our friendship is static at Torquay Railway Station. No real advancement can be made through any sort except a physical communication. My friendship with Peter is static at the moment when I last saw him on Charing Cross Station. (McFarlin 17:6)

His memories of Ruth, of his brother Peter, and of Geoffrey Armstrong would be pigeonholed until their physical reunion. But separation (a condition that is necessary in war) assures a static condition; unless he physically wrote to his friends, Scott was "content in my static memory" (McFarlin 17:6).

Can a writer thrive in a static state? Scott did not believe so. "Reactions are the most essential things in life" (McFarlin 17:6), he told Sansom. More importantly, his relationship with Penny marked a major change from the past into the future, away from his "passing phase" with Armstrong and away (it seems) even from "our old ways" with Clive and Ruth Sansom, which Scott "did not feel competent to continue" because they had all "travelled far." He lay out his "new self"—an aspect that was previously unrecognized and untapped—or more accurately, his same self "newly expressed," for Ruth's consideration. True, he and Penny must walk "unmasked among masks"—a difficult prospect, which isolated them from others (certainly a prophetic remark, since Armstrong's tirade against "Brilliant City" would come as a retribution after Scott's wedding). Scott longed "for the hour of reclamation"—referring to his reunion with Penny, certainly, but also perhaps to himself as reclaimed from "this great barrier" of war (McFarlin 17:6).

One thing was clear to Scott: "That I mean & intend to become a great artist if I possibly can be" (McFarlin 17:6). His friends might have feared that his marriage to Penny would impair his creative nature. However, that hardly can be viewed as the true outcome of this life-changing decision.

Works Cited

"Increasing Oppression of Homosexuality at Mid-century: United Kingdom II: 1900 to the Present." *GLBTQ Social Sciences Encyclopedia*. 2007. Web. 1 August 2010.

Scott, Paul. *My Appointment with the Muse*. Ed. Shelley Reece. London: Heinemann, 1986. Print.

Spurling, Hilary. *Paul Scott: A Life of the Author of The Raj Quartet*. New York: W. W. Norton, 1990. Print.

Tatchell, Peter. "A Gay Soldier's Story." *WW2 People's War: An Archive of World War II Memories—Written by the Public, Gathered by the BBC*. June 2004. Web. <http://www.bbc.co.uk/ww2peopleswar/stories/36/a2688636.shtml>. 1 August 2010.

Box 17, Folder 5 (McFarlin)
63 Bourne Hill
From a letter to Clive Sansom[14]
4 May 1940

Dear Clive,

Thank you for putting "The Creation" through the door yesterday. The result is that, for your kindness in doing so, I now present you with a very pukkha copy of the poem, complete with the dedication, which is quite serious.

One day, when I find time in the office, I will do "The Gerontius" poem in the same style for you, so that you will be able to remember me when I am gone ... (theme music here ...).[15]

I did not reply to the naughty answer to the naughty play, because I did not quite know whether your naughtiness hid genuine disapproval of the content of the play. It is so difficult to deceive all the people all the time, isn't it?

Well, anyway, no other play can touch the "Atonement"[16] for downright lewdness, and that is in itself its reward! [...]

Box 17, Folder 5 (McFarlin)
63 Bourne Hill
From a letter to Clive Sansom
n.d., [1940]

Dear Clive,

Thanks for your note inviting me to the meeting.[17]

I have carefully considered the idea of my going, but must admit I felt unable to do so. The moon does not enter the sun—& if I went I should only wear a mask—& I prepare not to do so. I cannot find it in my heart to profess religious feeling amongst other men—the religion I hold is in something only I can see or feel at the moment of death.

If I admitted the existence of omnipotence in a form one can worship of as a Being with whom the worshipper can make contact by going to a given place & amongst others, my whole spiritual self would collapse.

I must not allow that. That a God is more approachable through connec-
tive prayer, I am unable to understand.

I admit there must be & is a Superior Force—& I admit the life of
Jesus Christ who was the Supreme Genius of the world & his life is a
perfect pattern in <u>itself</u>, but some of his teachings appear to me to have
been learnt rather than inspired.

You may think this confession strange coming from the perspective
of "The Cross"—but my poem was a veiled hint—("The Dream" was
my soul's inspiration—& "Credo"). My heart revolts at the thought that
man must rely on a God to bring justice to the world—even if the act is
through man with Christ as the sacred example.

An uneducated person—I mean one whose spirit & soul never play
upon the heart—looks blindly for help. A sensitive soul creates the need
for help & also the help itself. From these traits it appears to me, that
the less fine the degree of educated spiritualism in man—the less that
man wants a God, & if the soul is sensitive—through pain or worry or
supreme uplift of the mind—that some [soul-]searching for a yet more
supreme sensitivity.

[…] As for life after death I believe it not impossible. To my mind
man's spirit is no longer strung to emotional contact with life that a mere
deadening of the body might merely release the spiritual senses into
some boundless region of thought […].

Your sincere friend,

Private Correspondence, Carol Scott
Regent Arcade House, London
To Peter Scott
5 July 1940

My Dear Peter,

Yes, I will be down 4 p.m. on Sunday. Will have lots to tell you I expect.

I enclose a copy of my will in case I get popped off in an invasion or
by a bomb splinter, etc., which I want you to memorise more or less.[18]
Of course if I get blown to pieces the Devon part will not be any good.

If it is any good at some future time I should like you and Clive and Gerald[19] to do it, just like Byron and that other bloke did for Shelley ... only they swam out and looked back at the beach.

After the war of course for any attempted publication, and the manuscripts are to be yours and no one else's. I shall show a copy to Clive, too, so that you both know what to do, should I get called up to The Heavenly Concert Hall!

Wurl Churuir Brurndurn.[20]

THIS IS THE LAST WILL AND TESTAMENT of me PAUL MARK SCOTT of 63, Bourne Hill, Palmers Green in the County of Middlesex. I GIVE to my mother and father, Mr. and Mrs. Tom Scott of the same address, to be divided equally among them all such sums of money as I die possessed of or which have accrued to me at the date of my decease and I DIRECT that my account with the PHOENIX BOOK COMPANY LIMITED of 66 Chandos Place Charing Cross London be settled as soon as conveniently may be after the date of my decease. I GIVE to my brother PETER BEWICK SCOTT all the original manuscripts of mine which are left intact and I desire that he shall receive the remainder of my library after a book from my library is given as a token of my esteem and affection to my dear friends GEOFFREY RIDEHALGH[21] of 12, Arlow Road, Winchmore Hill and GERALD AND DORIS ARMSTRONG of 13, Woodcombe Crescent Forest Hill and RUTH AND CLIVE SANSOM of 61, Bourne Hill Palmers Green and I DESIRE that all other personal belongings of mine be given to my said brother and I leave it wholly to his discretion as to whom he gives there from some token and I DESIRE that my said brother and CLIVE SANSOM if meeting with their joint wishes shall in my memory make a collection of my poems and other writings and if possible attempt publication and in consideration of their so doing I do give the said works wholly and completely to my brother and desire that he shall pay to CLIVE SANSOM in the event of their being published 20% of all such sums as are wholly paid or become due as the proceeds of such publication and <u>I DESIRE</u> that in the event of such publication the following inscription be placed as a Dedication:

> "To My Mother and Father
> and all my dear friends"

FURTHERMORE if a publication of my poems is impossible I desire that several typed copies be made to distribute to the following persons viz GEOFFREY RIDEHALGH, FLORENCE AND LAURA SCOTT,[22] GERALD AND DORIS ARMSTRONG, who have during my life afforded me encouragement in such works and copies also for RUTH AND CLIVE SANSOM and my mother and father. <u>FINALLY I DESIRE</u> to be cremated and my ashes to be taken to the Devon coast and thrown into the sea. AS WITNESSED MY HAND THIS FIFTH DAY OF JULY IN THE YEAR NINETEEN HUNDRED AND FORTY.

Box 17, Folder 5 (McFarlin)
Dropmore Hall, Buckinghamshire
To Ruth Sansom
6 August 1940

My Dear Ruth,

I have written several letters this morning—leaving yours until the last because it is so difficult to answer. It's afternoon & I am sitting outside my tent watching the lime trees shuddering in the [unreadable] warm wind—& I hardly know what to say. There is one part of your letter, which puzzles me very much. You say you want me to let you know whether or not I hate you. This passes my understanding, as such a feeling toward you is impossible.

It is true that women fail to interest me generally. You will have already gathered that from the various conversations we have had concerning sex. Also you will have gathered with what man I have an affair[23]—& also that all my love poems are written to persons of my own sex. This may seem unnatural to you—it does to most people—but I think you will understand & appreciate that it is a popular failing with people of my type.

For me sex is an all important—I should say <u>the</u> most important part of life—all emotions & creative instincts are (to me) based on the sensual impulse in man. For me proof of this is shown in the fact that artistic people—who experience more complicated emotions than others—are on the whole very highly sexed in either one way or another. And yet an artistic person can live his sex life in his art—so that for long periods— sometimes indefinitely—the sexual act is unnecessary for him. At other times—mostly in periods of artistic inactivity—his actions will become of a highly emotional & physical character.

This is one reason I have against marriage between an artistic person & an unartistic one—& even in the case of marriage between 2 artistic persons—the periods of inactivity may not coincide with the mate's & thus producing a cause for mental distances.[24]

Life is certainly very complicated—but sex itself should not be the cause of complications but the simplifier. A perfect sex life is a perfect life.

Sex is the great Simplifier. It sets aside all loyalties—ties & bonds & restrictions. Accept the need for sex & the mental troubles of the moment will pass away.

I have a slim chance of getting home on Sunday for a few hours—but don't bank on it—because I doubt that it will come off.

We are not alone.

Adieu,

Box 17, Folder 5 (McFarlin)
Dropmore Hall, Buckinghamshire
From a letter to Clive Sansom
n.d., [August 1940]

My Dear Clive,

I am now again suffering from inoculation for anti-typhoid 50% injection—& am glad because it gives me plenty of time (+8 hours) to reply to your long & interesting letter. I am sorry the poems are dropping off a bit—what about sending some to the place you mentioned in Oxford or Cambridge? It might help the sales. I am unable to think of anything else—unless I walk soulfully around the camp reading a copy—forgetting to salute the officers as I pass!

Well—I am pleased to hear you were able to lunch with Gerald [Armstrong]. I expect he smoked endless cigarettes explaining his relations with me! It's funny—but I see nothing wrong in it you know—except certain pricks of conscience as regards Doris [Armstrong]. It is always the way—& makes life very hard. I don't know whether he told you his life history—but it is most interesting—& exceeds "Dorian Grey"— Oscar would have loved him for "copy". We have spent some wildly happy lush luxurious times together—& always I shall remember them as the greatest achievement in my life.

Gerald wrote me—but just said you & he had lunched together & talked about me.[25] I hope I have some character left! [...] Do you remember our long & interesting walk & talk re. Quakers—& the tea at the Cock Inn? Halcyon days—never to return in that form—as the atmosphere will be changed.[26]

I wish we could be inoculated all the time—then we would have "ensured duty" for the duration, which would suit me down to the ground.

By the bye—I have never thanked you & Ruth for the very acceptable parcel—& I have not been bitten by gnats all the week—I think it must be the cream you sent me!

I should like this letter to have been longer, but the noise is increasing & I cannot concentrate.

Adios Senor,

Box 17, Folder 5 (McFarlin)
Dropmore Hall, Buckinghamshire
To Clive and Ruth Sansom
n.d., [1940]

Dear Ruth & Clive,

Thanks for all communications. I have written to ask Mother & Father if they would meet me in Slough this Saturday about 5—& also if either or both of you could come, then you could travel down as a Sports Club & get reduced fares!

The army life is fine—less it rains as it is doing now. Have met a DECADENT person (in the way I mean) who likes Tchaikovsky, Keats & Shelley. He also looks well.[27]

Yours in haste,

Box 17, Folder 5 (McFarlin)
Torquay, Devon
To Clive Sansom
n.d., [1940]

My Dear Clive,

Just to wish you all the very best of luck, strength & courage for Saturday.[28] You are doing a far braver thing than I, because you are putting your soul before the eyes of the public. May it remain unstained—& as instilled with great ideal as it is today.

Put away, if possible, all material thoughts during the few days you have, and surrender yourself completely to the loveliness of freedom and you will be strengthened for the coming Crusade to rescue the Holy City of your spirit from the barbarity of civilization.

May you remain always young, free, and lively in your life—so that when the winter of life comes you can say "I lived and was loved dearly by my friends."

For he was a good man, and did good things.

Your dear friend,

Box 17, Folder 5 (McFarlin)
Torquay, Devon
From a letter to Clive Sansom
15 November 1940

My Dear Clive,

I managed to get my 7 days leave in order to attend the service today.[29] I travelled all Wednesday night & arrived in Paddington at 8:15 a.m.—& after various routes arrived home in time to say goodbye to Geoffrey, who was returning to Wales yesterday. I have to report back to Torquay by night on Thursday next—so I am afraid I should be unable to visit Oxford this time.

[…] Wyphurst looks terrible. There is nothing left at all—just a heap of bricks & stones. A Japanese vase—one of a pair—was found intact in the debris.[30]

It was a double funeral of course. I supposed you know Auntie Laura died on Tuesday? There were beautiful flowers—& several old friends in the church who followed us to the graveside. Peter came home this morning—but has to be back by 8.30 a.m. tomorrow so he went back tonight. He will, however, have the weekend off.

The Jerries are overhead & the guns going. My baptism of fire. I don't know how London stands it. It seems so hopeless just sitting down & waiting for the end to come—when one has had a soldier's training it becomes essential to be on the move when the guns are going. Even if it is only carrying a rifle in the sheets. It is most unnerving….

Yours ever,

Box 17, Folder 5 (McFarlin)
Corps HQ, D. Coy [Company], The Buffs, R.E.K.
To Ruth Sansom
22 December 1940

Dear Ruth,

Last night Kapinsky was very tired. He has been tired for a long time. He sits & watches the far-off hills when he goes out at dawn to the outside lavatory. And there he sits & contemplates on his life and sometimes forgets where is he & sits there all day like a Patrician when the Barbarians entered Rome.

Otherwise he is quite well & has asked me to enclose a short note which he says explains the secret of life if one reads between the lines. Personally I think the letter means nothing but perhaps Anna will understand it. I should like to meet Anna. Kapinsky says she is very frank. I like people to be frank. How strange it is that people are so double-faced. We go through life & meet many of them—but soon we discover their defects. Let us always be frank. Just as we were that time in Maidenhead when we sat & discussed sex for so long over tea. I can see it all so clearly. It is like a page from a Book of Memories—that though the book has been destroyed the page has somehow been torn out & left lying about in the old boxroom.

By the bye—who is holder of the Supremeship? I suppose I am as usual, unless our correspondence between Ivan & Anna can be counted as a literary achievement—which leaves Clive holding the Jetty Pail.

Another fellow & I have started a new club—the Ancient Order of the Stooge—which is very exclusive & hard to enter. The main object of the Club is to meet once a year at least when the war is over. I hoped that you & Clive would put up for membership.

There will be a stiff exam to pass to prove whether or not you are a stooge. Please send me an application—& you will hear from me on the matter later. A copy of the rules & regulations will be forwarded before the exam paper.

Have you heard anymore about the Quaker School? You said it was in Devonshire. I hope you manage to meet me one day. We can then adjourn to Addisons & get the Annual meeting of the Jetty Pail over. Otherwise it must be done by post which is most irregular.

Your Lawrence skirmish was most exhilarating. You say you returned to the hut in disorder. Surely you did not lose the fight. Supremeship is definitely indicated, I trow.

Please write me a long letter. A dissertation of anything. I will give you some subjects.

1.   Effects of music on the artistic temperament.
2.   The main object of reading.

3. Surrealism in thoughts & its application to art.
4. The sex instinct of the Spirit.

   Adieu, Adieu, Adieu.

Box 7, Folder 6 (McFarlin)
Torquay, Devon
To Ruth and Clive Sansom
n.d., [February 1941]

My Dearest Ruth and Clive,
   Great News!
   Peter Baker states 4 Broadsheets are now out. Lockwood Simpson is including four of your poems in the anthology.
   This has made me happy again. Already I feel it was meant that Saturday should have turned out as it did—& that it was not just a sudden break-down. It made me feel so much better just to be able to sit & tell someone all I had in my heart—I can see that I was suddenly physically overcome & unable to understand why you were with me so unexpectedly.
   You see—I had wanted you with me so much & had tried to put the possibility out of my mind and surrendered a chance of happiness by warning you what I felt was probable—that I should have no time to see you.
   But now I am myself quite suddenly again—though I am working hard—up until 11–12—it is gone eleven now & I have just proved that I still retain my mental alertness up to the time I go to bed—and last night I slept and did not toss in my sleep as I had been doing.
   You see, quite suddenly I understand why it is that I have been tortured so—that is that it has been necessary—& that I should unburden my heart at an unbearable stage was also intended for my "Brush with the Spirit" (as you say, Ruth)—& now the first milestone is reached—& I know that as the way continues at least I know [if] I shall be tortured again I shall live to see happiness again.
   Oh my heart goes out to you,
                              Love,

Box 17, Folder 16 (McFarlin)
Torquay
From a letter to Clive and Ruth Sansom
13 March 1941

My Dear Clive & Ruth,

[...] My Leave was a glorious beanfeast. But unfortunately I cannot remember anything really outstanding—except the bomb craters & Peter arriving home for ten hours leave on my last day. He had "scrounged" it at the final or 11th hour.

Geoffrey was also on leave from the Friday. So there was a happy reunion of the 3 Mustgetbeers.

I spent the weekend at Forest Hill.[31] They call their shelter Bauhautian Hall.[32]

Peter Baker has not asked about a title.[33] Any suggestions. Somehow I cannot get down to it. What about "I travel the Road, who Cares?" or "Three Little Maids from school are we. He-he-he-he-he-he-he".

Quite seriously I am sterile as far as a title goes. Isn't it awful. Usually I write down a title & then write the matter around it. Saves such a lot of trouble.

I celebrated my 21st birthday while on leave—at least I received my presents—I am not quite of age yet. Mother & Father gave me a Goldsmith watch—which is a beautiful thing. Peter gave a silver cigarette lighter & my best Aunt (one I cultivate) a silver cigarette case.

Actually I "pooled the dibs" & went out shopping—mentally allocating the gifts of diverse persons. The balance is keeping me in Decadence in Torquay. Savez-vous?

I also received from Miss Land apart from a donation a rather handy little attaché case & this stationery. Unfortunately it all smells of her bottom drawer—including the bar of chocolate—or was it soap? The parcel was wrapped in a way which would have made the Ministry of Supply weep & tear its hair. I did.

I hope you manage to get that place in the country. I might join you after my release. I paid a visit to the accountants who took over my old bosses' practice. Oh. No. I shan't be an accountant if I can help it. They are all so smug & self satisfied.

I am contemplating another attempt with Fabers for the Trilogy if it goes down well. How can I boost the Broadsheet in Palmers Green? Smiths I suppose.

Now when can you come to Torquay? I was thinking. Your 3 months is nearly up isn't it?[34] If you are going to leave to go to the cottage—if & when could you both have a rest cure in Torquay before taking up residence. There is a little place here where Stephen Badham's wife[35] stayed very very very reasonably. Bed & Breakfast. Not much of a place but a private room—telephone & a bathroom. The people are very nice—if you are interested I could get particulars for you. My day off is Wednesday—I supposed you couldn't—make—it?

I am feeling quite different after a week's rest.

Ah well. The months will pass. Where shall we all be at the end of the war. It is difficult to say, impossible even.

Could you send "The Dragon" to 63 [Bourne Hill] when you have finished—it does not interest me—it won't interest you. I just wanted you to see how "normally" I could write!!

We were all inspected for venereal disease this afternoon. I told Jacques[36] & he was promptly sick he laughed so much. I saw Kapinsky coming out of the M.O.'s room looking worried. Afterwards he met Anna (she is no longer little Anna) & they went away talking hurriedly in whispers.

Poor K! Is it the Beginning of the End?

As ever & Bon Adieux,

Box 17, Folder 16 (McFarlin)
Torquay
From a letter to Ruth Sansom
14 March 1941

My Dear Ruth,

[...] Have you heard that I am crazy, and going to be locked up in a dungeon for the rest of the war? Will you come and give me biscuit and cake through the bars of the cage, or dungeon, so that I can remember my former life. It is all very difficult, and one cannot think what is going to happen from one day to another. I have often tried to read my thoughts, but I am such an awful speller in my sub-conscious.

When I am sought by the crowds, let me remember that I always avoided the places with the thickest inhabitation. It is a good motto. We should all adopt staggered living, just as they used to stagger the holiday period. It is all getting too complicated.

[…] Kapinsky wants a word, but has been taken with the SALVAGE CAMPAIGN, and is saving paper, so writes on the end of mine.

Adios.

My Anna,

Yesterday I bought a bunch of snowdrops, and found that they were the only snowdrops that had ever been bought in March, but that was a flower-seller's lie, because I bought a bunch off his rival, Patrovtich Petrogad Petrefied last season at the same time. It is amazing how people cheat one another, and at times one is bewildered by the rapid change in appearance that a flower-seller adopts.

My Anna.

Ivan Kapinsky

Box 7, Folder 6 (McFarlin)
Torquay, Devon
To Ruth Sansom
3 April 1941

My Dear Ruth,

Your letter was waiting for me this morning when I came in at 5 a.m. I had slept the night in Room I at the Clydsdale with Peter. They have altered my day off now & it works like this. I am off from Friday at 7 p.m. & can sleep out—report back at 7 p. m. on Saturday & then go out again for the night (until 23.59 hours). I think I shall book a room at some small joint where I can write. Could you both come down on Saturday? Think I will ring you tonight in any case, in case you are contemplating coming down tomorrow (I mean Saturday not tomorrow) when I have a date with Barbara[37] who is rather beautiful & likes music, reading & dancing, etc. etc. I met her at our dance at the Marine Spa.

I have now an awful reputation in Torquay—& cannot go into my favourite haunts without meeting females of a notorious character. Mary of the Epicure, José of the Gibbons, "Dot", etc.etc., which all started by my getting drunk on my 21st birthday party at our weekly dance & being driven home in Mary of the Epicure's taxi. They had to put me to bed (I mean the boys of the Maycliffe).[38] On the next night—Reg Baker & I met in Addison's & so I asked the pianist to come over to the Gibbons & celebrate. Apparently she is Dot's landlady & told her all about it. By her description—Dot recognized Mr. 21 & when she saw me at the Epicure, celebrating Peter Lumley's 21st & in no fit state to converse— her suspicions as to my "leanings" were confirmed. Incidentally Peter & I were discussing my being queer & his not—but understands—as he is from Chelsea.

The next night was the Spa dance—& Dot insisted on treating me to a double for taking the Lady from Addison's out to the Gibbons. Mary of the Epicure was there. "Hello Ducks, what's yours?" etc. etc. Meanwhile I had to hold up a very fat Epicurean waitress.

I was selling raffle tickets (or supposed to be) & everyone was getting intoxicated.

Eventually I arrived back at the Maycliffe about 1.30—with half of the boys still out! That night when the mess steward had gone to bed, the officers raided the bar by knocking the door down.

When we came down in the morning there was a row of Gin & It[39] all lined up on the shelves.

That was yesterday—my day off—& in the evening Peter & I & Lumley and a W.A.A.F. celebrated in the Gibbons—of course there they all were all lined up at the bar—Mary—Dot—José behind it—thousands & thousands of faces all staring and saying "Ducks".

Then there is Pauline who looks like Margaret Sullavan—and Mary Bennett—there was Joyce Bachelor (only 17—& never been kissed)—Gladys of the Co-op who sat in the most expensive seats at the cinema—new one is Kay of the Burlington who gives one a free entrance ticket to the cinema for a free one at the dance.

Everyone thinks I am married—everyone knows I have been drunk 4 nights out of 10—& everyone sees I look awful—but nobody knows I have written a new work—only Peter Lumley who says it is marvellous. I'm having to do something to stop feeling crazy—so it's quite simple—one just becomes intoxicated—say once a week.

Fortunately I do not get a hangover!

You may think I'm doing wrong—but I'm not—here is the truth as I see it.

The woman at Addison's has a son in the navy—and is still having to work for a living—Dot is a kind-hearted woman who was so pleased that two young soldiers took her landlady out for a bit of fun. Mary is a girl who "loves us all" & spends her money on us to give us all a good time. She has squint eyes & glasses—probably has some secret sorrow she is hiding. José of the Gibbons is a prostitute who doesn't mind shouting it from the roof tops—she has a defiant look in her eyes, has once had a classical beauty which has been ruined by perpetual vice & hardship.

Pauline has her husband in the army. "I don't like leading this sort of life but its better than sitting at home & remembering—" Mary Bennett is the same. Kay of the Burlington is out for a good time. "Why bother to save up when one day you will be dead".

—But Barbara—whom I have known for an hour or less has a calm clear vision—& music & poetry in her eyes. She is a nurse—need more be said. She speaks beautifully—& Paul—what of him—shall he go on—or backward. Shall he know reality or dreams. He is 21—& is afraid he will never be 22—afraid he will never be able to give his mother that house in the country—& give those afternoon garden parties—or have those cool nights in old flannels on a river—reading Shelley by moonlight. Yet if these things all come again—& he is not there—he would be happy & every time a lime tree blossoms he will sing—and when there is sad music—he will weep—& he will go on remembering & remembering through all the tomorrows this Earth shall know—for he has walked in Beauty & has seen the Despair in beauty—& the kindliness in ugly things.

Dear Ruth—a Great Friend.

Adieu,

Box 17, Folder 6 (McFarlin)
Torquay, Devon
From a letter to Clive Sansom
6 April 1941

My Dear Clive,

Thank you for the letter, the post-card, and the two magazines, under separate cover. It has just struck me that I never thanked you for the Picture Posts, Listeners, and John O'London's, which you send me with such regularity. You must think I am very rude.

I am sorry our two conversations on the telephone were so short, but in any case, unless you have about half-an-hour a telephonic conversation is of little real value. I quite understand your position as regards coming down here, and perhaps it is as well, because with us, a "date" is always liable to be broken for any reason at any time, and one never feels completely safe until out of the place, and not even then, because we have already been recalled once, when we were all out for the night! I quite agree that the short verse "Spring, 1941" goes all to pieces, but I do not feel it is worth improving. I wish I could get the chance to copy out "Out of the Darkness" for you, but then again, it is hardly safe to type out verse here, without being found out, as people often look over your shoulder to see what you are typing, and I am rather shy of appearing as a budding poet, & until "I, Gerontius" appears in Smiths Bookstall down here (I can contact the manager through a certain connexion), I shall continue to hide my light beneath a bushel.

[…] The war seems to be taking very peculiar turns, and leaves one absolutely bewildered, especially when you are in the army, and never know just what is going on except that "Jerry must be up to his trick, By Gad, sir."

The whole point is, that it's so un-gentlemanly to be up to tricks, and so we can't possibly lose.

Ach, well. I get very tired, and bored at times, especially when things happen as they do. You have no idea of the utter hopelessness sometimes [...]. But it is, like Spring, a passing phase, which renews itself with regularity, each time making it seem as though the world has come to an end.

Private Correspondence, Carol Scott
Torquay, Devon
To Peter Scott
20 April 1941

My Dear Brandon,

Received your letter containing news about the air raid yesterday. I have been rather worried during the week since Thursday morning as I have had no news from home at all. However, I tried to ring yesterday, and apparently they were all out for the afternoon, as there was no reply to the bell.

It must have been a fatigue trying to catch a train with all that noise going on. I expect you shrieked with laughter the whole time. Your description of the "scared people" at Brigade HG when you arrived back amused me very much. I expect they were more frightened than the people in London. St. Paul's now seems to be on its last legs. The times I have walked round there during the lunch hour when I was on the Milford Manners audit. Happy days, all gone now. Selfridges seems to have been visited by the Architectural Justices, also. I suppose they will now hang banners all over the place again, and proclaim that they are still Carrying On despite ALL.

Clive and Ruth came down on Friday night. It was my day off, so I was able to stay with them at the Clydsdale overnight. Of course there was more gossip in the company, especially when I was seen out with Mrs. Sansom next day, Clive having got left a bit behind in the crowd! Still these things are definitely amusing. It is so nice to have a private life all to one's self. It was a lovely morning yesterday. We walked through the Torre Abbey Gardens, and into the Hothouse. Saw the ruins of Torre Abbey, which are just as disappointing as the Roman Theatre at St. Albans … and finished up at the Coffee Terrace of the Palm Court Hotel. They had to leave Torquay at Midday, so I saw them onto the train and then hiked my case back to the Maycliffe, had dinner, read your letter, and one from Gerald (in which he states he now has a GOLD identification bracelet) and then went off to the Odean to see The Mark of Zorro. It could have been Yus Yus but in the true style of modern pictures, events failed to materialise, and when they did, it was all off stage—or out of the action.

In the evening, Lumley and I went to the Marine Spa Dance, and Barbara [Phillips] turned up as promised with another Sister.[40] We had a most enjoyable evening, and I arrived home, when it had just gone twelve. Altogether it was a most successful twenty-four hour leave.

I see Virginia Woolf has committed suicide. I always thought she had a strange temperament. But you cannot wonder at people of her type doing a thing like that.

Next week we have Bette Davis and Charles Boyer in All This and Heaven Too. Barbara [Phillips] and I are going to see it together. Evidently she is an admirer of Bette Davis—or perhaps of Charles Boyer.

As Stand To is now at 4.30, Reveille at 3.45 a.m., we only do it on alternate mornings. On the off morning one stays in bed until 6 a.m.

Probably add to this letter after tea.…

I am contemplating s short play. Just about what I am not sure, but it will be full of strong situations. I wish I were going to dig the land with the Sansoms, and cycle home with them over the hills, and settle down by the cottage fire, with my old briar, and a book of Rupert Brooke.…

"I came back late the other night
to my little room
to the warmth and the firelight
and comfortable gloom."

Not good, but the feeling is correct. I wish everything would finish, and you and I could go on as before … and yet not as before, but differently, toward something much greater ... much finer (Bette Davis crops up again, damn the woman genius!).

As I look out of the window, the late sun is catching the bare gleaming branches of the plane trees outside. And I realise that things are no different. I realise that my life is only a pattern, a pattern which can be made and remade and undone by the will of the moment. I can smell lime trees.

Au revoir, et je jous donne mes adieux.

Box 17, Folder 6 (McFarlin)
Torquay, Devon
From a letter to Clive Sansom
24 April 1941

My Dear Clive,

Thank you so very much for the typed copy of the thing.[41] Also for the paper, and carbon, and the cover for the fair copy. I am sending a P.O. to cover after tomorrow (Pay Day!).

To get down to your remarks of criticism. I think if you re-read your letter now, you would feel rather as if you had overstepped the marks of politeness. Actually, I was rather disappointed—because reading your letter has given me the impression that, as a whole, you dislike the work quite intensely, and that it is only a line here or there, which you think worth anything at all. Knowing that you border upon being quite right about the whole thing from a theoretical angle, I am inclined to overlook some of the more devastating remarks. Looking through your letter again now, I cannot pick one out for exceptional stress, but looking upon your criticism from the bird's eye view, I feel inclined to state definitely that it is quite fair.

Since we are being very frank, we may as well continue to do so. First of all, you do not like the repetition. Before I defend this style of mine (which I shall continue to use until it bores me, too), I might state that the poem is in its absolutely raw form, and has not even been studied for spelling or grammatical errors. The other night was the first time I had read it through completely. You cannot quite realise the very difficult time I have in being able to settle down to it. There is never a moment which I spend reading poetry, which I do not fear will be shattered by the most ordinary person walking in and disturbing me. Again, the whole thing was written in two sessions. Once during an evening from about 9–10 p.m., when people were dashing about outside, and I was in mortal fear of putting pen to paper, without being discovered. The second session was during the hours when life is at its lowest ebb—from about 2 a.m. until 4.30 a.m., when I alone was awake, and could not help writing the rest of it, despite the snores of about 3 lusty soldiers around me. If I had written it in my little room, with the soft smell of the summer outside the window, and the gentle hush of the curtains blowing against my polished table, and the sound of the 6th. Symphony coming from the lounge, the occasional easy stride of someone walking up Bourne Hill, which rather assisted than hindered my natural rhythm, then I dare to suggest that it would have been a far finer, more complete work than the Trilogy.[42] The Trilogy came from a soul who looked upon torment, as Christ and the Devil observed the cities below, during the temptation. "Light out of Darkness" came from a soul who was in the city, and in Christ and in the Devil and was the Temptation. You cannot grant me that the first inspiration was better than the second. The first was abstract, the second was concrete, and pure. When I wrote the Trilogy, I was a scholar. When I wrote "Light out of Darkness" I had, unfortunately lost my scholarly instinct, but I was a soldier, and had suffered parting, sorrow, misery, hope, despair, had shed tears before my friends because I gazed upon the only token I had from my brother who was far from me, and who had shared all my boyish emotions with me, but could not share them with me anymore, except through the medium of music … a music we had listened to in happier days … and which suddenly failed hopelessly to bring him any nearer to me than my thoughts could. I have woken up, dog-tired in a train, and found myself 250 miles away from everything I had ever loved and known, 250 miles away from my books, from my lime-trees, and my dearest friends with whom I had sat and recited and been recited to, and eaten fat gooseberries and lime juice, and watched the hot night descend on the impersonal lamp posts outside. I have been on the edge of writing last letters to my mother, telling her that I am sick at heart because I cannot repay her for everything, because that night I would die, and all around me would be white faces with the red glow from London reflected in their eyes and their hearts which were speeding along some dingy street in Edmonton—or some country lane in Kent—or some once-lighted thoroughfare in Knightsbridge. I have despaired at the intelligence of man—I have exalted in his everlasting hope. I have wept with impotent fury at the pettiness of Life—and I have remembered that Life is Good. If I died tonight I could not have been more alive—more dead—more hopeless—more full of joy.

But I am carried away from my subject. I am always carried away from my subject. That is why my repetition resounds and resounds.

Yes, I grant you that as a finished product, the new work is inferior to the other. But surely it is only a question of a single adjustment to a line—not as you seem to suggest a wholesale lopping off of lines, phrases. After all, if people do not like it, why then it is their own fault. I cannot expect people to understand my subconscious mind, after all.

[…] I spent a very peculiar evening yesterday. Firstly I went on a 22-mile route march to Teignmouth, on which I need not enlarge. I made it anyway, and was the hero of company Headquarters. Anyway I proved that the much looked-down upon Office staff can "take it". When I arrived back, very footsore and weary, I found Pay parade would not be until about 6.30, at which time I was supposed to be meeting Barbara [Phillips] outside Addisons,[43] prior to what I thought would be a very quiet evening for me. However, I arrived at Addisons about 7.15, and about 8 p.m., she declared that she had promised to take me along to the dance at the Marine Spa, as the Sister wanted her to turn up. Funnily enough the Sister (whom I have met before, said "Bring Paul, even if he's been on a route march", which they both thought quite an impossibility! Well, we arrived at the Spa, and as you can guess the last thing I felt like was dancing, and Barbara was in rather a peculiar mood. Penny Avery,[44] the Sister, was feeling very jolly, and we all went round to the bar to have one to celebrate my mother and father's Silver Wedding. Barbara would not have more than one or two drinks, but Penny was playful, and had more than enough. Barbara became more and more religious looking, and very annoyed, though we were only a little merry, and it rather set me wondering. When we got into the hall, she refused to dance, saying she had not felt like it in the first place. As things went on, Penny and I danced together and escaped from the Iceberg into the bar, where over some peculiar cocktail, I suddenly found myself madly in love with her, and we were talking as if we had known each other for ages; I told her all about my poetry, a thing I had never even dared tell Barbara—and would not. And now I am sad, unsettled, and wanting only to see her again, but feel she will try and fade out to give place to Barbara. Was I right? She has warmth, an emotional outlook just like mine; she likes the same little things as myself. She is not nearly so attractive as Barbara to look at (Barbara gets excused all over the place when she is on the floor), but there is a tenderness with her, a subtlety of wisdom which makes me desire her terribly. She is engaged, but then I cannot worry about that.

I supposed this sounds rather like a Dorothy Dickson Open Letter in the Daily Mirror. What Shall I do Now?

Let me change the subject. But what other subject is there for me at the moment?

Did you receive my little Kapinsky, Ivan and Anna Playlet?[45]

I must close as I have tons of letters to write.

As always,

Box 17, Folder 6 (McFarlin)
209 Ind. Inf. Bde. [Independent Infantry Brigade]
To Ruth Sansom
26 August 1941

My Dear Ruth,

I am taking Clive at his word & hoping to stir you to activity & to write a long long letter full of Anna-isms and Stepanisms.[46] Actually I have spent the entire evening writing letters—as this is practically the first opportunity I have had of doing so. As you know I have been shoved from post to pillar during the last few weeks & eventually landing at the above rather vague address which is all I can supply. Anyway here goes for a really long letter (always providing I don't get interrupted).

There is really no news to impart—because all my doings are of little interest to anyone but myself—& 99% of them not to me either. I have woken up in the morning—worked—gone out most evenings & wandered around—returned to billet & gone to sleep. A year ago last Sunday was the anniversary of my first Sunday Day Leave from Slough & you will no doubt remember what mixed feelings we all had that day. I was unable to adjust my outlook upon the old things which even in such a short space of a month I had glossed over with an almost worshipping brush of glamour. And returning I found them no less beautiful, too unbelievably beautiful in fact for me to bear them as I was then. The 6th Symphony was too much like my memory of it. The entire day was in stereoscope. Well— since then we have all travelled far—though here is an interesting point. Don't you think friendships & lives stay static as from the moment of last memory? In other words, don't you feel that our friendship is static at Torquay Railway Station. No real advancement can be made through any sort except a physical communication. My friendship with Peter is static at the moment when I last saw him on Charing Cross Station.

The present is so much to the fore in our lives that we cannot let the past catch up & communicate dually [?].

In a way it is a good thing. Life has a habit of "too much continuing". There's no immediate place for the past except in the little pigeon hole in the memory, marked "Ruth", "Peter", "Geoffrey", etc. Then when the time of reunion comes, we can take down what is in the pigeon hole, carry on from there or travel back to that time & carry on from the present until once more we must replace these friendships back to their appointed place.

Winter is approaching again. This is interminable—this awaiting seasons & hoping they will bring with them a new way of life. I must find my new way of life soon, or I will rapidly grow stale again as I did last winter. And it was not I who was recalled to life in the Spring. "Myself" is glancing over my shoulder even as I write this letter. I am glad that

I have chosen <u>this</u> moment to write you after so long a period of silence. Any other time would have been meaningless. You see I have not forgotten our old ways, but did not feel competent to continue them—& any new way would have been more than useless. There are many things I remember & wonder about. The White Gate still stands indomitably still & white—there is no one who will open it for me again.

There is little else I can say of myself. Except this. That I mean & intend to become a great artist if I possibly can be. There is so much to purify both in my life & in others' lives. My own life calls my first attention. In what way have I changed? In no way. In what way have I looked at myself of late. I have gazed in the same mirror but seen a different reflection—that is the only way I can explain the change in myself. You know to what I refer. It was a passing phase essential to my necessarily wide understanding of life.

I once set out to understand all passions all beliefs & all persons. I have ceased the struggle—because the most important person to understand & believe in, myself, remains inscrutable. How then can I <u>understand</u> others. Yes I can learn to tolerate, to accept, to disregard unessentials & bother myself only about essentials in make-up. I shall never understand Peter or you, or Clive or myself—this is even more difficult because of the bond of friendship.

How goes it with you? How do you re-act to <u>your</u> new way of living. Are you at peace—or uneasy. Do you still remember limes—or the memory of limes?[47]

Yes. We can have All This & Heaven too.[48] We can have many melodies & many memories. We can enjoy peace & struggle, sincerity & hope. We can go on our Voyages of Discovery—& discover nothing or everything as it most pleases us. We can end up in a back street of sorrow & happiness—or a penthouse of despair & joy. Reactions are the most essential things in life. The present the most important phase—the past the happiest & the future the most glamorous or forlorn.

There is nothing beyond nothing, a peace beyond Hoping. Negation I have cast from me like the plague. Negative emotions, no, but a complete throwing away of positive reactions, yes.

I lay my new self—or my own self newly expressed—before you for your consideration. In the meantime, please write, as writing to you has made me want to hear from you. I <u>was</u> content in my static memory.

In my detachment I seem to grow even more dependent upon others. Loneliness has a great deal to do with this. Even though now I have someone who returns the affection I have thrown out to the winds, even though we are wildly happy & sensibly confident in that mutual affection—we are still both lonely because we must walk unmasked among masks, which is far worse than wearing yourself a mask. I long for the hour of reclamation. There are no minutes and no days I do not count long & arduous—since there is forever the iron barrier of war against which we can only thrust with unfeeling fingers, numbed by that very war against which we fight in our spirits.

If only I could cast off from my inner self this great barrier—then I could stand the positive thing itself. But it is not for me <u>alone</u> but for all of us to see that afterwards, the remnants of a soul are snatched from the debris of living.

Please still come to me in the wind and the rain as you used to.

Always,

Box 17, Folder 6 (McFarlin)
209 Ind. Inf. Bde. [Independent Infantry Brigade]
From a letter to Clive Sansom
24 September 1941

My Dear Clive,

[…] I have been having a frantic time, what with having teeth out, saying au revoir to Peter, who is now far across the ocean seas (I hope safely), and with the added distraction of working hard, and also (Trumpets and Hautboys) planning to get married on my next leave. Don't faint!

I will let you have more details when I write again, as everything is very hazy yet, as I do not even know the exact date of my leave, except that it will be late October or (I hope not) early November. I also hope you will be able to come up to town and see that I am safely churched! The young lady in question is Miss Avery, S.R.N., so you see I shall now be Mr. Paul Scott, J.P.B.F., H.O.A. J.P.S., S.R.N., as she will I suppose with all her worldly goods me endow (or do I do that?). You will have to increase the length of your envelopes to get me all on![49]

[…] I hope tonight I can finish off typing my latest work, MYLOR CREEK, so that I can enclose you a copy. It was really a sort of public Apologia (as if it were necessary!). Actually that place did a lot for me. I stayed there one week with the platoon, and found myself completely up-ending myself, and having a brain spring-clean. It was a place of complete negation, except for the continual presence of a spiritual vacuum. I stretched one day, it being my day off, on the beach, and I remember the other time, the last but one day of peace, when Warsaw had been bombed, and Peter and I sat on the deserted beach at Felixstowe, throwing interminable pebbles into the sea. "Before my pain had stretched my limbs, enabling me to reach from shore to shore, and not see beauty anywhere" (quote—MYLOR CREEK). I hope you will like it, as I think I have found my first personal phase—as you always said I would after a lot of "lifting". I want both of these poems, that and C. Cross, to be treated as important works to me, as I have completely changed again. Gone is the lyric, and gone is the church incantation. I am left with a spherical object called a poem.

Box 17, Folder 7 (McFarlin)
209 Ind. Inf. Bde. [Independent Infantry Brigade]
To Clive Sansom
[n.d., marked in pencil "Summer 1942"]

My Dear Clive,

[…] I cannot resist writing to you and telling what Mr. Armstrong thought of the "Brilliant City".[50] He said that he was very disappointed, and that he thought that my experience in life was insufficient to meet the needs of such a large attempt at a life portrayal. Not the exact words, but the implication.

Other remarks. Vague, indefinite, no plot, not sufficient interest to hold the attention. Obviously of no appeal at all to the "masses", and not well enough written to appeal to the would-be intellectual. (Who wants to appeal to any would-be anythings, anyway?) He said also that some of the lines were quite brilliant but that the characters were not the type to say them. Also that some of the cynical remarks (are there any?) were badly placed. Finally he ended up with this remark, I haven't the letter before me but I will try to remember it as I want to know who said it. "It is not for the artist to dramatise or simplify life, but to portray as well as he may the…complexities of what we call the experiences in life" […].

As a result of this criticism I begin to wonder whether or not I am leading myself into an abyss of absurdities from which I shall never rise again. I shall think that all these complex thoughts and actions I have been endeavouring to portray are incomplete, unnecessary and totally untrue and ridiculous, and that I should write something quite different.

I want your frank, honest and complete opinion. It has stopped me short in the middle of my new play, my beautiful new play "Pillars of Salt", which has been living with me for over a year—the basic theme, anyway. I was going ahead, triumphantly ahead and had brought down the curtain on what I considered one of the best acts I have ever written when along comes this most unkind slating of my "idealism". And I thought at first, Absurd…the eternal poseur, with the plagiarist's pen, writing biting remarks because they roll smoothly onto the paper, and sound brilliant and well-considered. Then I analysed my new play, and discovered that it was again based on "your idealism, which flames in all your works"…that is good…but then I also find that my idealism is false, it is untrue, it is bad for me and those who read it because I am NOT SPEAKING FROM EXPERIENCE. GOD'S ABOVE! I have been in the army for two years, and I cannot write anything but brilliant satire, because one does not have to have EXPERIENCED anything to write satire, except perhaps a little perversity and paltry pleasure. The eternal satirist […] seated in his plush chair casting barbs at the simple people of the world because he is afraid of them deep inside him, and would make them laughing stocks. It makes me bloody sick.

I am not trying to talk about someone in a nasty way. I have said all this to Armstrong himself. It does not in any way affect our relations, but I don't think he realises how this bit of theatrical criticism can affect a man who tries to be an artist amid all the pain he undergoes every day and every hour of every day, living a life which might have forever stopped his inspiration. I am so deeply hurt right deep down inside, because, you see, Clive, he has not just criticised my writing of various scenes, or my development or an action here and there, or a speech, which might strike a false note. I could thrive on that sort of criticism. But this is so damnably destructive. It has shaken the very base of my belief in myself, something that my wife has fostered most beautifully for me during the past year. And at the moment she is not here to make me believe again. I forgot to tell you she has had to go to Ashby[51] because her father is ill, and I dare not tell her that I cannot write another single word of the play. I tried yesterday. I sat down and waited for two hours for my muddled thoughts to disentangle themselves. I would think of something and then somebody would say SENSELESS, CAN'T BE DONE, ABSURD, WHERE'S THE POINT, WHERE'S THE PLOT, WHERE IN HELL IS THE PLOT, and all my ambitions for "Pillars of Salt" as a play, as an appeal, as a portrayal of the difficulties of a handful of people who are so real to me that they hurt me when they are hurt, all these things have become satirical and masked. They say, "GO AHEAD, WRITE ME LIKE THAT. YOU DON'T BELIEVE IT THOUGH SO WHY WRITE IT". The damned part is I did believe it once. I don't agree with what some of them did, but I knew it was right for them to do it … and now I have lost them all in this dreadful fog that has clouded my brain.

Glancing through this letter, it strikes me as hysterical and theatrical … even the words I have just written are now unreal, so what am I to do, Clive? What on earth am I to do. IS "THE BRILLIANT CITY" A PIECE OF TRITE RUBBISH, A COMPLETE AND ABSURD FAILURE AS AN ARTISTIC WRITING? I SOLEMNLY BELIEVE IT IS AND ALSO "PILLARS OF SALT". THAT IS WHY I AM DESPERATE TO KNOW. If it is, HONESTLY, then I might as well pack up, because I have put all myself, for two years, into the writing of the two of them. I believed that they were a true outcome of my physical and emotional experiences. God knows I've had a few. And I said to myself, you hate what you are doing now, but it has been good for you, it has given you a balance, and a perception which you lacked in "Gerontius", which you glimpsed in "Mylor Creek"[52] and which you triumphantly portrayed in the "City" and which has culminated in "Pillars of Salt". I was going to rest for three or six months after the new one, because I am almost played out as far as creation is concerned. I had enough moral strength to end the "Pillars", I had that final spurt of power which is so alive and thrilling to a writer, the energy that, spent, leaves one breathless and happy and contented to rest for awhile until taken up again with all that is around one.

If I crack before the "Pillars" is finished, as I believe I shall, then I shall be the most miserable being on the face of God's earth.

But if you can show me that perhaps it is only a phase, and that even if the "City" is no good, I shall go on (like Mark, and Nellie and Preston[53]—it serves a man well, because he can always go forward to it), then I shall resign myself with a good face to temporary sterility.

Box 17, Folder 8
Home Forces
To Clive Sansom
23 January 1943

Dear Clive,

Just a short note—I have not previously had time to write you. I think Penny has told you the news—it's pretty cold around here, though. The rain we have had recently has warmed things up a bit.

I am at least applying for a commission & go before the board next Thursday. The interviews last 2 days. I expect you have read all about them. One even goes before a psychologist nowadays!

Peter Baker asked me at dinner to prepare a selection of prose & verse (for the next editors). If you are writing him, please explain my very busy situation—

Love to Ruth & hoping to see you both soon,

Box 17, Folder **8** (McFarlin)
63, Bourne Hill
To Clive and Ruth Sansom
9 March 1943

My Dear Clive and Ruth,

I think this is about the right time to say au revoir, at least I am seeing that I make sense of saying it properly & do not worry if you don't hear for some time. And do not worry about Ivan—because he so hates the cold—having experienced Siberian winters!

Bless both of you—to see you again is a joyous hope—but just suppose—but thanks for everything—& I would have been a great writer!!

Don't answer this—you'll be hearing from me.

Always,

Box 17, Folder 7
Indian Command
From a letter to Clive and Ruth Sansom
n.d., [March 1943]

My dear Ruth & Clive,

This is written en voyage. There is very little that I can tell you except that I have a comfortable cabin & have not (so far) been seasick. One gets very tired (& hungry) with the sea air, though. Don't know how or when you will get this. We merely write letters & hand them to the prescribed authorities.

The weather is gradually getting hotter though nothing to speak of, really. We have been told to put the above address on our letters so presumably you can write me straight away [....]

As always,

Box 17, Folder 9 (McFarlin)
Bombay
To Clive Sansom
7 May 1944

My dear Clive,

Many thanks for a) airgraph 15 April, b) letter 26 February, c) "Land of Prester John", d) Poet's Corner".

My last airgraph to you went to Blackburn road or whatever the name was. Since then you seem to have been available at two addresses but am selecting Belmont Road as being the latest. Afraid I'm extremely warm at the moment—tho' I am a bit further north since my last airgraph. It's not quite so hot & stuffy as there, but it's quite enough. Have been writing some verse during the past 4 or 5 months & have suddenly realized I might group it all together & send it to you to see if you think I can still write poetry! Have been tying desperately to blot out the memory of the mistakes in "After Our Labours"[54]—but put it down to a) 10 months preliminary thoughts during which time I changed its spots to shapes, & b) 8 days concentrated pen-pushing in a hot climate as far as the new one is concerned—tentative title "The Pilgrim Michael"—have very completed drawings of the set & as things are it looks as if I shall now get the chance to put pen to paper.

In a couple of months I should have been with the army for 4 solid years—so you can well imagine that *anything* will be welcome, Clive. There is only one possible way of living in India unless you are to become hopelessly homesick—anyway, one take steps, hopes for events to materialise. Afraid I must talk about it to someone, Clive—& certainly I don't wish to worry anyone at home. I've been doing a spot of flying lately—(of course I don't mean piloting an aeroplane!)—but going up in one. It's a strangely exhilarating feeling—I feel as if I am starting my life in the army all over again.

There's still only one thing I want in the world & that is to get home & be with everybody again—but in the meantime I hate to be static. Space & distance no longer mean anything & to be shut in some plane is an agony. I am terrified of stagnating in an Indian station—be it on the plains or in the hills. I've seen the results a year or two in one place has on people & I must avoid it at all costs. I have decided that one of the most fruitful periods in my life was the 6 months in which we knew each other before I came away. After the war I should like both of us to go away for a fortnight & plan things about life in absolute peace & quietness. Then I think I shall be ready to settle down to a spot of sensible achievement.

Keep writing often,

Box 17, Folder 9 (McFarlin)
1010 India Air Supply Section, India Command
From a letter to Clive Sansom
5 July 1944[55]

My Dear Clive,

The few bits & pieces of mail which have caught up with me during the past two or three weeks have hardly encouraged me to gales of hearty laughter. [...] I feel at the moment that no more achievement is possible until the war is over—the years are at last telling on the mind—& the many & varied illusions of great things to be born are now disappeared. There is only one thing now, Clive—I need another personal talk with you. Do you remember Torquay? It is full circle again.

The one bright spot in life is that Penny tells me you like "After Our Labours" better than the previous plays. I thought you would hate it. I don't think Penny likes it at all—& yet this was my Big Effort—the one collection of thoughts born in 1940 & fostered up to the end of 1943.

Please excuse my always talking about the plays—but it is one method of keeping in touch. Criticisms from home are tardy—by the time I receive them I have given the play up for lost & consigned it to the mounting pile of things, which didn't quite "get there".

If only I could shut myself up for months—preferably in England—I could write the new Pilgrim's play so beautifully that I should fall completely in love with it. God alone knows how long I shall be out here—& writing seems impossible. Perhaps at the age of 30, I shall be able to sit down in England with a clear mind & a full pen—& fulfil your kind & early promises for my future.

Sometimes I wish my nerves weren't so strong—because my inside has suffered so often from a breakdown—but the old nerves keep on going. I supposed on the whole I magnify every time I feel ready to scream until that is all I can remember. But I seem to have that strange capacity for remaining cheerful in the eyes of casual observers with whom I come in contact—though I am becoming on the morose side gradually—& can do nothing about it.

The trouble is I can offer no reasonable grounds for complaint & would be as happy as a sand boy if I were completely normal. But it's the old question of living two lives at once—& *it is* becoming rather a strain.

Dear Clive, write to me … I wish I could believe wholly in God for I have often found temporary relief inside a church—but that is always spoiled by the place resembling too much the known places of child-hood. I cannot, either, let myself be unfaithful to my wife, for there can be only one woman in the world for me—I strongly believe this—tho' I could I suppose draw a curtain over impatient & patience & forget myself. "Last night, ah! yesternight—"

Write, Clive,

As always,

P. S. Kapinsky is dead.[56]

Speech from THE BRILLIANT CITY, by Paul Scott
Mark speaks:
"If we fight on they can never truly have victory. For we shall meet them at night—in dark streets, and stab in the dark! We shall meet them at dawn in the squares and they shall be no more. We shall meet them at midday in the houses, and they shall be dust. We shall meet them when the sun is hot, and they shall fall beneath our swords. We shall watch their bodies stiffen in the winter; we shall never truly be vanquished. We shall go on fighting though the months and years pass. We shall build our city—our Brilliant City—and it shall be our courage, our will to live, our undying anger. Its light shall shine through all the world. It shall be your city; you shall build it through your sufferings; and from its gran-deur you shall have grandeur; from its heroism you shall have heroism; from its faith and holiness you shall become shriven. Let them kill and

burn, destroy and ruin; let them torture our bodies; let them starve and murder us; let them fill our hearts with anguish; let them take our loved ones from us. We shall rise through all the earth; we shall rise from the ruins of our homes; we shall rebuild; we shall find; shall make a new way of living. <u>This</u> is your Brilliant City! <u>This</u> is our City!"

Box 17, Folder 9 (McFarlin)
Bombay
From a letter to Clive Sansom
14 September 1944

My dear Clive,

[…] Your letter of criticism of "Labours" & your later general letter re discipline, level & understanding—arrived within a day or two, one from the other.[57]

This is rather an absorbing problem—I mean the question as to whether a play <u>should</u> present a philosophy of life[58] […]. I think I might claim to present a "love of wisdom"—in other words, I present "philosophy"—but not a philosophy of life.

[…] To get back to the main point. Should the playwright attempt a message—(here we overlap into yr. second letter)—I refer to my "any message will have more chance of being understood by all."

I'm afraid that possibly my choice of the word "message" was bad. But it can remain. It depends upon what <u>level</u> (!) the word is interpreted. I'm afraid the artist will translate it to a <u>low</u> level without thinking—& the man in the street will upgrade it either to a plane remote from himself (i.e., he will hear the message & believe it good but impractical) or to a pedestal he would attain—in both cases stripping the message of its real purpose.

That's why the artist should <u>discipline</u> himself to give the message in such a way that it may be <u>understood</u> by as many as possible. There are two ways of doing this […]: 1) He may become the Daily Express of the theatre (!), 2) He may write <u>of</u> the people, <u>for</u> the people (but never <u>to</u> the people!!!) in such way that he retains his integrity.

No. 2 is a stage. I am at it. I may grow out of it. I may find I'm on the wrong track. I may make a success of it & become the arch playwright of Charing Cross Road [...].

Box 17, Folder 11 (McFarlin)
1010 India Air Supply Section, India Command[59]
To Clive Sansom
28 March 1945

My Dear Clive,

As I have just passed the first quarter century of my life, I thought a short note in memory of the occasion would be fitting. Of course, I cannot say that I feel particularly thrilled about the whole business, this growing old. Twenty-five—it seems a far cry from the old days as a khaki-clad civilian at DROPMORE—or have you almost forgotten those days? Perhaps you remember them, though, more clearly than I do. I have quite a vivid recollection of Ruth eating, or rather cutting for me to eat, a bacon and egg pie, which was the first decent food I had tasted for several weeks, I believe. In the afternoon you disgraced yourself by falling to sleep. Those were peculiar days, as the whole point of life seemed to be suspended (if you can suspend a point, even metaphorically) in mid-air, and hovered between South and Maidenhead, which is another way of saying Despond and a mental preoccupation with sex.

After this period, came the TORQUAY expressive period, which called forth a rather dreadful poem, which I cannot even remember, except that it seemed to have some sort of affinity with the Virgin Mary. I remember crouching upon the floor of the Clydsdale Hotel (later to become the scene of the opening act of married life, if my memory does not do me wrong), and reading this rather absurd verse to you and Ruth, perfectly aware of the blank look of amazement on both your faces. Why you should have been amazed I have not the slightest notion, but the fact remains, I realised that the whole thing was not an overwhelming literary milestone.

TORQUAY seems to become dreadfully mixed up with all kinds of relationships, as no doubt I had visions of becoming a PUB POET, seeking the aeolian strains of life in sawdust and bitter—with a faint worship of somebody whose name I have forgotten but who wrote poetry about "poor humpbacked Anne". The only real thing about the TORQUAY literary scene was the seagull. One cannot say seagulls, as life was rather centred upon a single thing at one time, including the dull red lights, which were something to do with the barbed wire and motorists. This was a drizzling episode, in which a shelter bench played a large part, and the sound of unspoken words vied with a whistle of the trains. Thinking of these things brings back the old style of writing.

After a while, we had the CORNISH interlude, which succeeded in breaking away the chains and producing MYLOR, with Howard Spring's house as a background, and a rosy vision as a future. Somehow I cannot help feeling that my New Day has taken a long time to break through, and that my High Sun tends to sink on occasion, and give way to a bleak moon. This no doubt being the policy of war.

Then of course something quite different happened, and the single man was joined much to the astonishment of many and varied people, myself expressing more singular astonishment than any one else. For a while the aspirations of the soul were diminished, and one may say the wind might be more clearly felt, more keenly, about the tips of the ears—and the vague imaginings became absorbed in objectivity, which once again evolved itself into a complexity of the Subjective I. Which is the way the poet might have expressed it in those days.

CURTAIN UP—and the plays had started. Life was not worthy merely of informal verse, but the blood had to be warmed with the arc lamp and the windrush of curtain down. Act upon act upon act upon action. Speech was coarsened to approach life's level—not its real level, but its dramatic level—the adoration of Steinbeck and the European prophets. The pistol replaced the harp—distinctly the sabre rattled. The handling of arms had had its effect upon a startled being—startled into the realities of the internal combustion engine and the bullet's trajectory. Life became an open page with ACT ONE writ large like an interrogation.

AMBITION. This awakes clothed in purple. The advancement of man in an imposed sphere of life. Tear down the stripes of office and superimpose the stars of officialdom. The sea made its inroad upon the blood channels, and everything was split up into flotsam and jetsam, until Cape Town hove into sight, or rather came down one morning painted upon a backcloth. South Africa was a period of applause. This young man from England—such manners—such verse—such a shame khaki should spoil the being. Write from India, <u>please</u>. Life here is so devoid of the artistic young.

BOMBAY. The curtain comes down finally for six months, and rises desperately, knowing either days insufficient but necessary. The idea, the hopes, the self-imposed discipline was cramped as the hand of the writer. This was an abortive sortie. The play was ended. Copied hurriedly in manuscript since no typewriter graced the country. It was consigned to the post rather as I imagine an appeal to the Home Secretary for leniency.

And the purpose bloomed richly—the skin became tanned and yellow in turn—finally seeking the cold mountains to return to its former pallid self. The monthly liquor ration provided the necessary conversation for three weeks—and the final week was spent in drinking it. Will it be Scotch do you think this month, or that awful American stuff. Of course American is better than rude word. I wish the rain wouldn't <u>look</u> so much like a short story by Maugham. Nobody else has a chance to do anything literary with that man's shadow haunting the scene. They will merely say, "Oh a cross between Sherwood and Maugham"—the army and the monsoon.

We seek solid relief in work, and the synthetic desires and interests of the poet at war. The curtain cannot go up again, and fall successfully until the bug is out of the blood, and the mind clear of the sun.

Think well for MICHAEL,[60] should he be premature through lack of self-discipline, or too late through too much self-discipline. Perhaps his finest jewels will be born and will die only within the mind.

Always,

ENDNOTES

1. For more details on Tom Scott's work and the other artists in the family, see the following letters: to B. M. Scott (20 April 1967), to David Pease (3 April 1970), to Peter Scott (31 August 1974), to Alan Jenkins (4 October 1974), to Francine Weinbaum (19 July 1975), and to Sally Scott (7 November 1976).

2. Scott later remembered, "For weeks at a time, half the household wasn't speaking to the other half" (McFarlin 9:5). Spurling argued that because of these turbulent years, Scott developed a horror of emotional scenes, tense encounters, and raised voices that would remain with him the rest of his life. See Spurling 19, 46. But Scott saw things differently: "I suppose this taught me something. Taught me to see both sides of a question. My loyalties were divided. I loved my parents. I loved my aunts" (McFarlin 9:5). Tom and Frances moved to Cannon Road, then to 63 Bourne Hill in 1939.

3. A merger of Falcon Press, run by Peter Baker (who would publish Scott's poetry in a volume called *Poets of War*), and Grey Walls Press, run by Charles Wrey Gardiner, who also published the journal *Poetry Quarterly* (Spurling 100, 158).

4. "A place grows into your bloodstream," Scott would write many years later. "He responds to a place—the place where he was born—the place where he was born a second time.... After just three years—this country was in my bones" (McFarlin 9:5).

5. Much of the correspondence concerns his family. Corben had sent to Penny three pairs of shoes and a sari he bought in Calcutta. "I am also sending you a booklet telling you by photographs how to put the damn thing on," Corben wrote. "She should look gorgeous in it." But the prospect of meeting Penny frightened Corben: "You come and meet me in London somewhere first," he told Scott before he left India, "because I am absolutely terrified of Penny, probably due to the fact that I am so—shy." Scott had written several times to Corben's mother and planned to see her. But Corben counseled, "On thinking things over I feel it would be better if you did not go and see mother until I get home. Not only worried it be pretty bloody for you but I think it would upset mother pretty badly as well to meet someone who is as closely connected with me as you are" (McFarlin 2:35).

6. In fact, Spurling's biography interpolates Scott's first encounter with India primarily through material from his subsequent novels: *Johnnie Sahib*, *A Male Child*, *The Mark of the Warrior*, and *A Division of the Spoils*.

7. This might sound like a minor infraction, but men were put "on jankers" for such lapses in military discipline. Jankers could involve confinement to the barracks or being assigned to a demoralizing activity, such as weeding the parade ground by hand, cleaning out the latrines, picking up rubbish, or painting rocks white, then brown, then white again. More importantly, infractions could block a soldier's promotion; it is known that Scott was passed over for officer training during this period (Spurling 91). In Scott's case, giving in to the military routine was mind-numbing; it seemed to jeopardize his artistic nature and creative energy. But, he learned that submitting to that routine was the only way he could prove himself to be reliable.

8. In preparing this project for publication, I have depended on Spurling's biography as an important resource, noting on numerous occasions the facts as she documented them. In this and other instances, however, she advanced her interpretation for the facts. I believe that the letters require another interpretation.

9. As Sansom introduced him to Russian, Scott created characters that worked as alter egos to the three friends: Scott was the boisterous "Ivan Kapinsky," Clive was the appreciative "Stepan Ilyaitch," and Ruth was the deflamatory "Anna Gavrialich" (Spurling 72).

10. Scott was not always consistent with the spelling of this name, Hilary Spurling uses "Kapinski" but I am retaining "Kapinsky," the form that Scott used most often.

11. See Allan Bérubé, *Coming Out Under Fire: The History of Gay Men and Women in World War Two* (New York: Macmillan, 1990) and Paul Jackson, *One of the Boys: Homosexuality in the Military During World War II* (Montreal: McGill-Queen's University Press, 2004), two of many recent studies of gay men in the military during World War II.

12. See "Increasing Oppression" in the *GLBTQ Social Sciences Encyclopedia*. Historical evidence suggests that because of the desperate need for willing and able-bodied men, whatever their sexual orientation, homosexuality did not, as Spurling asserted, carry "graver penalties in the army than in civilian life" (Spurling 98), although military policy called for homosexuals' dismissal from the forces and imprisonment. Interviewed by the BBC, Private Dudley Cave (a self-identified gay soldier) remarked about his induction into the military during World War II, "There was none of the later homophobic uproar about gays undermining military discipline and effectiveness. With Britain seriously threatened by the Nazis, the forces weren't fussy about who they accepted." The BBC documentary concludes, "Cave's experience was typical of the sudden relaxed attitude towards lesbians and

gays in the services. Faced with the danger of German invasion and the need to maximize combat strength, military chiefs unofficially waived their objections to homosexuals in uniform. Even soldiers caught having gay sex rarely suffered severe punishment. A few got off with a reprimand and warning from their commanding officer. Some were hastily transferred to a new unit. Others were assigned to hard labor for a few weeks to 'knock the queerness out of them' and turn them into 'real men'" (Tatchell).

13. Anna is a persona for Ruth Sansom as Ivan is a persona for Scott.

14. Clive (1910–1981) and Ruth (1906–1994) Sansom lived next door to Scott's parents on Bourne Hill. A teacher, Clive Sansom was also attempting to carve out a living as a poet. The Sansoms were lifelong correspondents with the entire Scott family (Tom, Frances, Peter, and, of course, Paul). After the war, Paul worked as Clive and Ruth's literary agent, first with Grey Walls, then with Pearn, Pollinger and Higham/David Higham Associates.

15. "The Cross," along with two other poems, "The Dream" and "The Creation," were published collectively in 1941 under the name *I, Gerontius*. Scott would later refer to them as "the Trilogy" (see his letter to Sansom dated 24 April 1941). The Sansoms (not Scott) carefully preserved these typescripts, which are available in the University of Tulsa archives.

16. In a subsequent letter dated "Monday," Scott described "Atonement" as an outrageous morality play "which somehow developed into an Opera—with Peter singing tenor, & I baritone. One evening I _must_ read you 'The Atonement' though hardly in mixed company" (McFarlin 17:5).

17. The Sansoms were Quakers.

18. Paul Scott was called up in July of 1940, and he wrote to his older brother, Peter, who was also in the military. Although Paul was not sent overseas until 1943, he obviously wanted to arrange his affairs well beforehand.

19. Gerald Armstrong, a client of Scott's employer, accountant C. T. Payne. Armstrong, ten years Scott's senior, was married and a patron of the arts.

20. A transliteration of "Well, cheerio, Brandon" (Brandon was Paul's name for Peter). The brothers had several "voices" they used to communicate with each other. There is this "slurred" voice; another was an imitation of their deaf and lisping cousin. Note courtesy of Sally Scott.

21. A friend of Scott's from the collegiate school.

22. Scott's aunts on his father's side, who lived together in Wyphurst on Southgate Street. See the introduction for further details.

23. Gerald Armstrong, mentioned in Scott's will. Armstrong was Scott's lover for several years.

24. The topic of appropriate partners continued with Clive Sansom's reply: "I know that I have a lot of the feminine in me. Ruth has a lot of the masculine in her. That's why we're so happy together, I suppose. We're far happier than a very manly man and a very womanly woman could be, that's certain. The balance is closer. There's less natural antagonism, more understanding, because we're not separated by that huge gulf of sex. And each is free in mind and imagination to love the other—which is probably the most important thing about it—that neither of us 'possesses' the other. One doesn't need the other in order to gratify their sense of <u>power</u>" (dated 14 August 1940; McFarlin 17:5).

25. Armstrong also wrote to Sansom on 14 August 1940, "I appreciate very much your letter received this morning conveying your good wishes and although I usually reply by return to letters of invitation, it may not be the custom of others to do so. However, being rather unconventional myself I was not duly perturbed and quite understood on receipt of your reply. May I express to you my gratitude for the lesson that one is never too old to learn and for your explanation that confidences, sometimes given in all sincerity, might be misplaced. Thanking you, Gerald R. Armstrong" (McFarlin 17:5).

26. Sansom replied on 14 August 1940, "Your reference to halcyon days sounded very final. I don't think the difference [between homosexuality and heterosexuality] need be as great as you imagine. Ruth and I have enough imagination—and enough in common with you—to understand your position even if we haven't experienced it in quite the same way. After all, there's nothing very unusual in it—except in degree. It happens in teachers' training colleges, for instance, to the extent of about 40% of the population, I believe. And it is even more frequent among artistic people. It's not merely that they have more of the other sex in their make-up (and through imagination and sympathy) but artistic creation, like animal creation, needs both sexes present" (McFarlin 17:5).

27. This "decadent" person may be Howard Smith, a solicitor and, like Gerald Armstrong, a client of C. T. Payne (Spurling 87).

28. Sansom's hearing as a conscientious objector.

29. The double funeral of his aunts Florence and Laura, who were killed when their home at Wyphurst was bombed.

30. In a letter to the Sansoms dated 9 November 1940, Scott's mother, Frances, wrote, "Some very dreadful news. Wyphurst is completely demolished on Thursday night. All the windows were blown out by blast from a bomb in

the roadway outside the Church Hall & on Friday 10.30 a.m. the whole place was wrecked by a time bomb which had gone right under the house & had not been seen. Florrie was killed instantly, but was not recovered from the debris until 4 p.m. A neighbour who had gone in to see how they were, was killed. Overnight Laura was taken to the hospital with broken hip, badly injured back & head [...]" (McFarlin 17:13).

31. The home of Geoffrey and Doris Armstrong.

32. The word should be "Bauhausian," after the German expressionist Bauhaus movement in architecture. Scott was referring to an Anderson bomb shelter, a type of air-raid shelter of corrugated iron huts that were erected in people's gardens. Note courtesy of Sally Scott.

33. For the trilogy of poems eventually entitled *I, Gerontius*.

34. The Sansoms were completing three months of agricultural training in Kent for conscientious objectors (Spurling 93).

35. Scott worked under Corporal Stephen Badham, who ran the office staff in D Company (Spurling 83–84).

36. The fictional personality Scott created called Jacques de Matelot, a "saucy French sailor" (Spurling 71).

37. Nurse Barbara Phillips.

38. D Company headquarters were at the Maycliffe Hotel (Spurling 85).

39. A gin with Italian vermouth, which was therefore sweet (as opposed to French, or dry, vermouth). Note courtesy of Sally Scott.

40. Barbara Phillips brought with her Penny Avery. Penny was the ward sister, and so Barbara's superior, at the hospital in Torquay.

41. Scott had sent Sansom his latest poem, "Light Out of Darkness."

42. Refers to "The Cross," "The Dream," and "The Creation."

43. A café in Torquay.

44. Within a few weeks, Scott was no longer seeing Barbara. In a letter dated June 1941, he wrote to Sansom, "By the way, Barbara was discarded long ago. She was discharged by sister Avery of the same hospital—named Penny. She was far more satisfactory. She is engaged to a Lt. Commander" (McFarlin 17:6).

45. Scott's play was called "The Blue Waltz" and depicted a three-sided friend-ship (Spurling 71–72).

46. A reference to Ruth's alter ego, "Anna Gavrialich," and Clive's, "Stepan Ilyaitch."

47. Lime trees lined Bourne Hill, where Scott's parents had lived since 1939. See his letter to Clive Sansom dated 24 April 1941, describing the trauma

of military life: "I found myself 250 miles away from everything I had ever loved and known, 250 miles away from my books, from my lime-trees, and my dearest friends" (McFarlin 17:6).

48. The title of the Bette Davis film, one of Scott's favorites. He referenced a second film title in the next line.

49. Paul and Penny were married on 23 October 1941.

50. What Scott thought of as a "modern" play. He had sent copies to both Sansom and Armstrong for comments. At the time of this letter, Scott was already hard at work on yet another play, *Pillars of Salt*, which was published in 1948 by Gollancz as an inclusion in *Four Jewish Plays*.

51. Ashby de la Zouch, in Leicestershire, the home of Penny's father, Percival Francis Avery. Note courtesy of Sally Scott.

52. Spurling described the poem "Mylor Creek" as a break from the past, expressing hope for renewal because of Scott's newfound love for Penny (108–109).

53. Characters in Scott's play, "Brilliant City."

54. A play he was writing while on the troopship.

55. Scott was stationed in Belgaum, near Goa.

56. See the previous note. Spurling believed that Kapinsky signified Scott's homosexual self (112).

57. Scott had written the previous May that his choices about "Pilgrim Michael" were either to proceed "free and undisciplined" or meet his audience "on mankind's self-imposed level" in order to be understood. In his letter of 16 July 1944, Sansom quoted T. S. Eliot about working on many levels at once: "No play you write will satisfy you or, in the long run, an audience, which isn't what you wanted to write yourself. If your main aim is to give the public what it wants, you will be prostituting your gifts." But, he continued, writing for one's self didn't mean being "undisciplined." It meant bending "one's individual talent to make it capable of expressing exactly one's individual vision" (McFarlin 17:9).

58. Sansom believed that "to write a play to express a philosophical idea is propaganda of a sort, a kind of sermonizing." If writers served a cause, he told Scott, "they have allowed themselves to be persuaded that their master is 'society' or some political or religious body." The better alternative was to write a play "which doesn't start with a fixed idea, but one which will develop out of a love and understanding of human character and emotion, and an intense dramatic sense of situation, and which will, in a sense, be beyond good and evil, politics, and material or philosophical conceptions" (McFarlin 17:9).

59. After completing his apprenticeship, Scott was posted in the summer of 1944 to an Indian air supply unit in Bengal until the closing days of the war, when his unit was sent to Penang Island in Malaya. See his letters dated 26 November 1972, 8 May 1974, 16 May 1975, and 17 July 1975 for Scott's summary of his military experience.
60. A persona Scott adopted when he wrote to his close friends and to his brother, Peter.

SECTION 2

THE AGENCY YEARS (1950–1959)

In 1950 Paul Scott left the financially precarious Falcon and Grey Walls Press to work first as an accountant, then as a junior director for Pearn, Pollinger and Higham Literary Agents (PP&H), later David Higham Associates (DHA).

Scott's professional correspondence from 1950 through 1960 can be found in the David Higham Collection at the Harry Ransom Humanities Resource Center, University of Texas–Austin. From the letters in this collection emerge several distinct features of Scott's experience as a literary agent who sold manuscripts and sometimes authors. In his autobiography, David Higham described Scott as "patient, sympathetic, creative, and with an enormous nose for talent" (144).[1] The letters included in the following section bear witness to such attributes, certainly, but even more important was Scott's insistence on presenting the author with various views (his own, a Higham reader's, a publisher's) and then allowing the writer—and no one else—to make the ultimate decision, whether artistic or financial. He was, in his client E. M. (Chris) Almedingen's words, "a prince among agents."[2]

I have included his letters to his various clients, among them Muriel Spark, Gabriel Fielding, Morris West, Kay Dick, E. M. Almedingen, Gerald Hanley, John Braine, Mary Patchett, Hank McCoy, M. M. Kaye, Jean Plaidy, and Arthur Clarke, as well as his friends/clients Clive and Ruth Sansom and Peter and Lal (Lalage Pulvertaft) Green. I have also included his correspondence with John Fowles, Dorothy Sayers, Graham Greene, and Dame Edith Sitwell, all of whom were represented by Pearn, Pollinger and Higham, which in 1958 split into Laurence Pollinger Ltd. and David Higham Associates (DHA).

Scott's colleagues at Pearn, Pollinger and Higham/David Higham Associates are frequently mentioned in the letters: David Higham, of course, Scott's agent since 1953; Higham's assistant Jacqueline Korn, later the director; Jean Leroy, the first secretary to Gerald Pollinger and later the serial editor; Sheila Watson, the foreign language sales agent; and Monica Preston, the secretary to the firm. After Scott's resignation in 1960, David Bolt, Hilton Ambler, and Bruce Hunter joined DHA. Hunter acted as Scott's agent in Higham's later years.

As an agent, Scott was above all a reader who was particularly skilled in recognizing a publishable book and also in diagnosing what would be required, in terms of revision, in order for a particular manuscript to become publishable. In some cases, Scott would work with a writer on an undeveloped plot or a weak characterization, using other readers' observations but more often his own developing instincts as a writer. He coached aspiring authors on the pace of their concluding chapters, on the efficacy of first-person narratives, and on bringing a reader along on a writer's journey of discovery. In other cases, with professionals who were not writers but who had unique stories to tell, he would broker a ghosting relationship with people who were willing to "author" under the professional's name.

Scott was also a committed advocate of authors whose talents he believed in. There is the case, for example, of Gabriel Fielding, a genius in Scott's mind, whose fiction had limited sales potential. But there were also relative unknowns such as Maurice Carpenter, a poet who worked as a farm laborer; the war veteran A. R. Milbourne, who had lost both of his hands at Arnhem and sought to publish his memoirs; and Diana Graves, the niece of Robert Graves, who was struggling with an illness that brought her life as an actress to an untimely end. Perhaps Scott can be seen at his most passionate in representing a manuscript he believed to be of extraordinary value: Elizabeth Nicholas's *Death Be Not Proud*, which he sent to half a dozen publishers before placing it. In writing to the publisher Hamish Hamilton on 4 July 1957, Scott admitted that

> it is a long book, and probably over-long. It is also a complex book, and obscurities should certainly be ironed out, but it is an interestingly personal book, and if any revisions proposed were to have the effect of pouring the author's work into a mould just not hers, then my guess is it would become just another SOE[3] book, for which, frankly, I should have said there isn't much need. (DHA-HRC 251:4)

He worked for many months, encouraging Nicholas not to despair, until the book was published.

Scott was a reader, an advocate, and a business manager. He worked tirelessly for writers in finding them a publisher and negotiating their advances, royalties, and options on future manuscripts. He sold novels, poetry, plays, works of nonfiction, and children's books. He begged on behalf of starving writers but was quick to disillusion his clients who expected his agency to advertise a new publication or arrange for friendly reviews. He schooled Gabriel Fielding and Morris West in what an agent should do and could not do. To Fielding, he wrote on 8 November 1954, "I think you will readily appreciate that I, no more than the next man, can react kindly to a charge of ineptitude." Scott continued,

> What I refuse to take responsibility for is the reception in the press and if you expect that of any first rate agent who knows his business—where it begins and where it ends—then you'll obviously want to look elsewhere. If you do it will be the greatest disappointment I've had as an agent, because I think we have done and can continue to do a job for you—and yours is the sort of work it gives me the great personal pleasure to be connected with. (DHA-HRC 100A:7)

He wrote to West on 7 June 1956,

> What you are really asking us to do is act as a sort of form of
> public relation officers—whereas our job is to negotiate the rights
> in the work which our authors produce. [...] We should like to act
> for you, but we can only work in our way and if that way is not
> yours, then we had better mutually decide to call it a day here and
> now. (DHA-HRC 217:2)

And finally, he was a mediator. Scott worked tirelessly to negotiate
between the publisher and the writer to ensure amicable outcomes in
terms of both the creative and the business aspects of publishing. He
helped writers understand that a publisher who believes in a book—its
value as well as its marketability—is essential in an effective partnership. Many writers were too invested in their own words (for example,
their original titles), which would make it impossible for a publisher to
sell a book. In other instances, writers would consider an advance to be
too meager. If Scott agreed, he would meet with the publisher. If he knew
the offer to be fair, he would give the writer the necessary reality check.

In what he called the "author/publisher alliance" (DHA-HRC 44:12),
Scott's influence grew in the 1950s. Scott himself was schooled by experienced hands, who early in on his agency career admonished him to
be more patient with publishers who were having to read mountains of
manuscripts that were submitted to them. Later, Scott would school publishers in turn. "I should be grateful," he wrote to an editor at the Thames
Bank Publishing Company on 18 June 1959, "if in future you would
refrain from using such expressions as 'infantile foolishness', 'unethical' and 'discreditable', when writing to me" (DHA-HRC 304:1).

Scott's decision to leave his position at David Higham Associates to
work as a full-time novelist was a difficult one for him to make. As he
wrote to Gerald Hanley on 15 October 1959,

> I need hardly say I shall miss the work, not only because I have
> felt it useful work to be doing, but also because I shall miss the
> personal associations arising from it. These, though, I hope may
> continue beyond it. (DHA-HRC 408:25)

As is clear in the letters Scott wrote after 1960, when he left David Higham Associates (see section 3), his clients remained his mentees and often became his lifelong friends—colleagues in the war against the blank page, fellow pilgrims maddened by the muse.

Through this period at the agency, Scott continued to write. With Joyce Weiner as his first agent, he published his play *Pillars of Salt* (1948), set in Europe during the war—a drama about a family that jeopardizes its own safety to rescue Jews who are fleeing from German persecution. For the next several years, Scott worked primarily as a playwright, and then revised his plays into novels. His first novel, *Johnnie Sahib*, released in 1952 and the winner of the Eyre & Spottiswoode Literary Fellowship Award,[4] was based on his play *Lines of Communication*, which was performed on BBC radio and later adapted for television. In *Johnnie Sahib*, Scott dramatized much of his own experience with the Indian Air Supply Unit during the World War II. He would later call it a "frightful little novel" of autobiographical origins (see his letter to John Mellors dated 16 May 1975). His next play, "The Return of the Dove," was the basis for his second published novel, *The Alien Sky* (1953), a study of prejudice against people who were of mixed Anglo-Indian blood. In these, Scott addressed his "personal theme":

> that men & women, in these years which concern us, are increasingly aware of the absence of roots, increasingly aware that whatever "place" they've made for themselves is artificial [...]. And the tragedy (to me) is that they are at once associated by their common need, disassociated by their individual interpretation (& consequently action) of it (letter to Morchard Bishop dated 3 October 1953). (McFarlin 19:2)

For the next three years, Scott worked to adapt *The Alien Sky* for television, and he also wrote *The Colonel's Lady* for television.[5]

A Male Child (1956), a semiautobiographical novel based on two sides of a family sharing a house (much like the Scotts had done at Wyphurst), grappled with "the nature of a man's concern with his world & eventually to an attempt to express what it is that makes nonsense of atom bombs & the whole mummery of 'Civilization's ended'" (McFarlin 19:2). Scott later denounced it as being somewhat of a mess (19:2). He and editor Frank Morley of Eyre and Spottiswoode strongly disagreed about the ending of the novel (see the letter dated 15 May 1955). Still, *A Male Child* marked a turning point for Scott. Although he would keep radio and television in mind as outlets for his work, his primary focus shifted to writing novels first and foremost, crafting books that might be adapted into plays rather than plays that could be adapted into novels.

The Mark of the Warrior (1958)—a study of the warrior's psyche— was the first novel Scott had simultaneously published in the United Kingdom and United States. The novel

> sprang from an exciting realisation that the truly great soldier is, when fully extended, emotionally involved with the terrain over which he fights. I say, "realisation", meaning, of course— interpretation—of signs, clues, evidence and personal intimations based on personal limitations. Such a man, <u>in embryo,</u> is Ramsay, and it is in the end a condition of such a man that his emotional involvement with landscape—<u>heightened by the coincidence of physical conflict within it</u>—should lead him to reject the society of other men. (McFarlin 12:16)

Scott confessed to Adèle Dogan of William Morrow that he had had grave difficulties with the book, but observations by Dogan and others had helped him come to understand "what the damn book's about" (McFarlin 12:16). Unlike his first three novels, Scott would later recommend *The Mark of the Warrior* to readers of his later novels.

In terms of his personal life, in June of 1954 Scott moved his family from 61 Brookland Rise to 78 Addison Way, which would remain the Scotts' home until after his death. In August of 1958, Scott's father, Tom, died. The family welcomed the widowed Frances into their home. But Frances' disapproval of Penny, her attempts to manage the lives of Carol and Sally, and her jealousy of Paul's affections made life unbearable. A heated scene between the mother and the son ended with Frances leaving in November of 1958 and Paul being unwilling to have contact with her for many years.

Box 20, Folder 14 (McFarlin)
61 Brookland Rise
To Joyce Weiner[6]
28 November 1950

My Dear Joyce,

Frank Morley lunched me today. I think he's a delightful person, and, from my point of view, we get on fine.

He'd already read DAZZLING CRYSTAL.[7] I think it's the first time a publisher's really been honest about this mss. He said its sale would be about 1000 copies, and they couldn't afford that; even if he could make his partners take on the risk of publishing me. He'd read it and he talked effectively about it. There was no hedging, no hints that it didn't "quite come off". He accepted the fact that it was a legitimate piece of writing and I accept the fact that no one is going to publish it—yet. We'll shelve it. If you like I'll have the mss back here to relieve your files, etc. In about 5 years the time might be ripe to do something with it. I'll be frank and say that only now, after talking to Morley, am I really <u>happy</u> about shelving it.

I asked him to listen to my radio play, and told him I was preparing a novel from it. He said he'd prefer to read the play script rather than listen, and also said he'd like to see what so far is written of the novel.

After we last met I began to think seriously about the novel, and after that I couldn't not start writing it. I'm sending you the first 17,000 words, for two reasons: A) because Morley asked me to send him the material through you, and B) so that before you do so, if you have time, you can look at it and see if I'm learning any technical lessons. The novel will stem from the play; in other words, the play script is really the dialogue/synopsis of the novel, although, as you'll see, the tangents and undercurrents will be the novel's strength. I've taken very much to heart what you said about it not being just a war novel; I'm trying my utmost to put everything I've got into it and as you can guess my problem is to know what to leave out, rather than what to put in. I have a work programme on it. Mondays, Wednesdays, and Fridays; two hours in the evening. Saturday mornings, 9.30 to lunch time. Sundays, either morning or afternoon; or both if the mood's right. I see no reason why I should get stuck, and if I keep on saying, "One day I'll get down to the novel", it's going to go stale on me. If I really get down to it I think I'm going to be quite pleased with the result (as pleased as I'm ever going to be with what [rest of sentence is off the carbon.]

Between you and me (Morley outside this), I have half an eye on that Eyre and Spottiswoode Literary Fellowship that runs from February 15th–March 31st, next year (that is the period for the entries). It's conceivable that this novel could make the grade during March, as far as a complete script goes. This <u>is</u> only a half-eye affair; and rather amusing, because I'm trying to think up PP&H[8] authors for the same things. You know about it, I suppose?

<u>Domestic Episode.</u>

Father's daily trip to London to the office is now known at home as Poppa going to Wuk. (Work)

Last Monday:

Time 8.30.

Poppa: Bye bye, Carol.

Carol: Where Poppa going?

Poppa: Poppa going wuk.

Pause:

Carol: Poppa not go wuk. Poppa stay home with Carol, Ba, and Sa.

Poppa: I'd like that, but poppa has to go wuk to earn pennies. (Light of interest in Carol's eyes.) You see—unless poppa earns pennies Ba can't buy things in shops.

Carol: Poppa gets pennies going wuk?

Poppa: Yes.

Pause:

Carol: Poppa not go wuk. Poppa get pennies from bank.

All our love to you both,

Box 27, Folder 27 (DHA-HRC)

Pearn, Pollinger & Higham, Ltd. 39–40 Bedford Street

From a letter to John Blofeld, Chulalongkom University, Bangkok
2 January 1951

Dear Mr. Blofeld,

I have your two letters of 18th and 20th December and I'll deal, first of all, with your point about the monies due under the agreement […].[9]

With regard to the second half of your more recent letter—I wish I could paint a brighter picture of the economics of writing for a living! Any figures about income would clearly be hypothetical—even supposing one wrote and published a novel every year. It would be reasonable to say, though, that establishing a reputation—and having an income (although the two do not necessarily go hand in hand!)—is a slow job; and it would be more reasonable still to say that few writers can afford to be "professional" in the full sense of the word. I really do hesitate even to hazard a guess at what you could reasonably expect to make yearly, assuming you published a novel a year. Authors' incomes fluctuate widely—the lean years supported by the fat years: if one says that a first novel sells, say, 200 copies—more or less, and that the author's average earnings per copy sold at 1/-, you have a basis for a sum!

On the other hand a first novel can sell 10,000 and more copies, or even, as you say, "hit the jackpot". And of course there are the American, foreign and film markets among others to be explored.

I'm sorry that it is impossible for me to be more helpful. Let me end by sending my best wishes for 1951; may it be prosperous too!

Yours sincerely,

Box 29, Folder 33 (DHA-HRC)
Pearn, Pollinger & Higham, Ltd. 39–40 Bedford Street
To Gerald Hanley,[10] NE Punjab, India
20 February 1951

Dear Mr. Hanley:

Mr. Higham was very glad to have your letter of February 5th, and thank you very much. He has asked me to answer in detail.

Yes, the enquiry from Kenneth T. Dutfield[11] is the sort of thing that we deal with for you. Actually our associate in Switzerland, Dr. Mohrenwitz, is readily seeing what he can do to get an offer for the German language rights of <u>The Consul at Sunset</u> from a publisher over there. Please do, however, forward any enquiries along these lines that you may get. Collins have, and quite rightly, been passing such enquiries to us but this one has apparently slipped through.

Your remarks about the cold nights and snow-covered Himalayas reminds me of the two best holidays I have ever had in my life, when I went on leave once to Gulmarg and once to Srinagar. I believe, though, that Gulmarg is no longer as I remember it. I heard that it had been burned down by tribesmen.

With kind regards from both Mr. Higham and myself,

Yours sincerely,

Box 31, Folder 33 (DHA-HRC)
Pearn, Pollinger & Higham, Ltd. 39–40 Bedford Street
To William Luscombe, Museum Press Ltd.
20 April 1951

Dear Bill,

<u>Was Arnhem the End?</u>

I spoke to you about A. R. Milbourne and his book <u>Was Arnhem the End</u>. You may remember that he is the young man who lost both his hands at Arnhem, and after the war worked for a month underground in a coal pit. He is now settled in a job at the Ministry of Pensions.

In my opinion he tells the story simply and movingly and I feel, perhaps wrongly, you may tell me later, that here is a book Museum could make a very successful job of publishing. Tom Driberg, incidentally, would write an introduction, I understand; he took Milbourne back to Arnhem after the war for a Reynolds News story.

Will you let me know as soon as possible? I hope favourably.[12]

Yours,

Box 16, Folder 2 (McFarlin)
61 Brookland Rise
To N. K. D. Purkayastha[13]
29 April 1951

My Dear Nimu,

This is by way of a request. Some time ago I mentioned that I had written a play about Air Supply and that I had used your "nickname" as a real name for one of my characters, also a Havildar Clerk. I enclose a cutting from our Radio Times that shows the programme when it was broadcast last February. After the broadcast I heard from Colonel Newman and Major King, and they had both enjoyed it and were glad to know that the Indian Army Service Corps air supply units had got some publicity at last. The point is, dear Nimu, that my first novel, which is on the same theme as the play, and will be called Johnnie Sahib,[14] also includes the character called Havildar Clerk Nimu. This character is, of course, imaginary and is not intended as a reference to you. It is, need I say, a sympathetic character, and I used your nickname for the sake of old times. Johnnie Sahib is going to be published here by Eyre & Spottiswoode, who are big publishers in England. They used to publish your very fine Madrassi novelist, R. K. Narayan, when Graham Greene was on the board of directors. Well, the character Nimu will appear in print. If you have any objection please let me know immediately, and I will alter it when I am correcting proofs. In any case I shall be very delighted to send you a copy of the novel when it is published as a token of affection and esteem from an old comrade to one who still works in air supply.

There is of course no use of any name but NIMU—by that I mean that Nimu is taken as a surname, a proper name, which of course it is not, in your case.

I am making this letter short so that you can reply very briefly. Please let me know soon.

I'll write you at length a little later on. A friend of mine, James Leasor[15] (who was at Belgaum with me), is in India for The Daily

Press for a month. How I wish I were he. But if my novel is a very big success (that rarely happens with a first novel), perhaps I shall be able to afford the money and time to come out myself one day. How I would love that!

Yours very sincerely,

Box 17, Folder 12 (McFarlin)
Pearn, Pollinger & Higham, Ltd. 39–40 Bedford Street
To Clive Sansom, Tasmania[16]
24 May 1951

Dear Clive,

This is to give you all my family's sincerest congratulations on your success in the Festival of Britain Poetry competition. It was nice to see that among the three top winners you were the only professional author.

I think this means that the famous old insignia we used to pass between us finds its permanent home with you, together with a brand new laurel wreath.[17]

What news of your first novel with Methuen? I haven't seen it announced yet. And what news for me about the possibility of our acting for you? You remember I made a tentative suggestion when last I wrote. I really should like to be doing that.

Please give our love to Ruth. I hope you are both now very much better and enjoying Tasmania.

Yours,

Box 31, Folder 33 (DHA-HRC)
Pearn, Pollinger & Higham, Ltd. 39–40 Bedford Street
To William Luscombe, Museum Press Ltd.
27 June 1951

Dear Bill,

You will remember that I had a word with you on the telephone the other day about Hank McCoy, the Western Writer. I promised to let you see an example of his work in that field and so here is a proof,

Savage City, which is the most recent under the Werner Laurie imprint, for whom he also writes as Brett Cameron.

As I explained to you, McCoy, whose real name is R. A. Martin,[18] is an unusual sort of chap. He is a publisher's representative and so has the distinction of being able to subscribe his own books, which must give him a great deal of satisfaction. Apart from that, I really think he is a very fine writer in the Western tradition and since he has purchased a dictaphone he has just about doubled his output, more in fact than Werner Laurie can absorb. He is anxious, and they are quite willing, of course, for him to find another publisher to help him absorb it.

I really would like to get him fixed up with you. You will find that he turns out these Westerns in a really professional way. If Savage City doesn't decide you then I will show you more. You would like McCoy. He has had the sort of adventurous life that I think one day will make a very fine book in itself, rather up your street. Apart from an early boyhood and manhood in the Argentine, he was in Africa with Martin Johnson, and got out of Africa [on a] "dead man's passport"! In other words, colourful in every way.

I would be particularly glad to hear from you about him.

Yours sincerely,

Box 29, Folder 28 (DHA-HRC)
Pearn, Pollinger & Higham, Ltd. 39–40 Bedford Street
To Mrs. G. J. Hamilton [M. M. Kaye][19]
29 June 1951

Dear Mrs. Hamilton:

I enjoyed our talk yesterday very much and Mr. Higham and I are delighted that we are to act for you.

I am afraid our long talk on India made me forget to ask you if you have a second copy of There's a Moon Tonight. We shall not necessarily wish to have one but Miss Jean Leroy, who looks after the serial side of things, is considering the book for serial possibilities. If we feel that it could be offered serially with a reasonable chance of success then, of course, we should like a duplicate in order not to hold up on offer of the book rights.

Perhaps you would let me know when you send the agreements and text of the Fairy Story.[20]

Yours sincerely,

Box 30, Folder 1 (DHA-HRC)
Pearn, Pollinger & Higham, Ltd. 39–40 Bedford Street
To Ralph Hodder-Williams, Hodder & Stoughton Ltd.
12 July 1951

Dear Mr. Hodder-Williams,

I feel that you should have our first offer of <u>There's a Moon Tonight</u> by Mollie Kaye, on which we have had an encouraging report.

She has been published before, by Hutchinson in 1939 and Tackers in India in 1944, but we have only just taken her on ourselves. She has lived quite a number of years in various countries in the far and Middle East and I know that she will continue to write. I do hope that you will want to take her on.[21]

Yours sincerely,

Box 20, Folder 14 (McFarlin)
61 Brookland Rise
To Joyce Weiner
13 July 1951

My Dear Joyce,

Here, initialed and signed, is the agreement with Eyre & Spottis-woode, for <u>Johnnie Sahib</u>. Whoever thought I should sign an agreement with a publisher on Friday the 13th? Anyways, a suitable date on which to end all the shouting; twilight falls quietly on the battleground....

As a matter of policy I'm just going to drop a friendly line to McWhinnie[22] to say that I hope one day to think up another idea for him (mentioning nothing about TV) as I think it'll do no harm to reestablish that particular relationship. It's true, anyway.

I now feel completely relaxed (or perhaps I should wait until I know Morley isn't going to ask me to change the ending again!)—there's a short, true story I want to work on—purely for pleasure; but I'll write it for broadcasting, in case it has sales appeal. Then there's that ANAT-OMY OF CULTURE. If you think it's worth working on, may I have the text back? I've no copy. And of course already I'm working mentally on Novel Number Two; and when autumn comes I'll start putting it on paper. How nice to think I can approach it with an air…! By that I mean with a definite goal; and semi-professionally. It becomes—thinking ahead to it—an enjoyable job of work, rather than something that has to be done in the hope of breaking in somewhere. Thank goodness you made me write novels instead of plays!

Penny took the children, against my best advice, to the Festival Pleasure gardens; but they had a wonderful time. Apparently they were supposed to meet another mother and two children of similar age. They never met up, but afterwards Penny's friend told her that Maxine had met Sally in the play land (where children are left alone with toys), and played for about half an hour. Sally, on being asked about this said, oh yes. I played with Maxine! One's children are strangely independent!

Lots of love to both from all, P.S. Raspberry jam spread all over sun-bathing mattress; "It's like a big sandwich."

Box 27, Folder 32 (DHA-HRC)
Pearn, Pollinger & Higham, Ltd. 39–40 Bedford Street
To John G. Braine, Northumberland[23]
30 August 1951

Dear Mr. Braine,

I was very interested in your "Irish Quarter" in the New Statesman and think it possible that our organisation might be of service to you in connexion with your work in general. You may perhaps know something of us but I enclose a pamphlet, which tells you the terms and conditions on which we act for authors.

We represent a good many authors of distinction including such as Graham Greene, Sir Osbert, Dr. Edith and Sacheverell Sitwell, P. H. Newby, Kate O'Brien, F. L. Green, Geoffrey Gorer, Norman Nicholson and Walter Allen.

If you have no agent already I shall look forward to hearing from you and would welcome the opportunity of a talk with you.

Yours sincerely,

Box 4, Folder 6 (McFarlin)
61 Brookland Rise
To Ruby Millar, Eyre & Spottiswoode Ltd.[24]
3 October 1951

Dear Ruby Millar,

Johnnie Sahib—Blurb

Writing one's own blurb is rather embarrassing; the attached is my attempt at one for Johnnie—and it incorporates the things I should be flattered by in someone else's criticism. In other words that part of the blurb is to give your publicity people an idea of what I aim at. Perhaps they can put it in some other way.

As far as the descriptive part goes I'll have another attempt if you feel there should be stronger indications of the storyline. I prefer myself to leave it at a statement of the problem facing the characters in the hope that people will want to find out what happened and so buy the book.

Would you tell Frank Morley that Television has been in touch with me; I'm to see Michael Barry[25] and a scriptwriter next week to discuss, I'm given to understand, how the radio play (the same as the novel) might be turned into a television play. I'll be interested to hear their proposals and certainly a showing on television could be good publicity for the book, though (as I've told Frank before) I don't want to write this subject to sterility. It's all going to depend on what TV is suggesting—and it's going to depend too on how I can fit in further work on this with work on the new novel, which is in the planning stage and will soon start on paper.

One final point; I wonder if communications from E & S[26] to me as an author, as distinct from an agent, could be sent to the above address rather than to PP&H? I'd appreciate that.

Yours sincerely,

Box 4, Folder 6 (McFarlin)
61 Brookland Rise
To Ruby Millar, Eyre & Spottiswoode Ltd.
12 October 1951

Dear Mrs. Millar,

<u>Johnnie Sahib</u>

Yours of 10th October.

The play was originally broadcast in February of this year. It was specially written for radio and the title was <u>Lines of Communication</u>. It was a Monday Night play and I was told in confidence by the producer (Donald McWhinnie)—I say in confidence for he gave me to understand the information was private to the BBC—that it had a Listener Research Index six points above the average for Monday Night plays. He read me some letters they received—one person was kind enough to say it was "Better than <u>Journey's End</u>"—someone else said with, I feel some justification—for the actors pounded away for all they were worth—that if that's what went on in the Far Eastern Theatre it's a miracle we ever won the war.

But to the point; the play was written first—but before it was in production or finally accepted I was away on the novel, and <u>Johnnie Sahib</u> is a development and extension of the theme of the play. There's quite a lot of difference, even in the bare bones. But "development and extension of the theme" is a good line, I believe.

I must just tell you that my meeting with Michael Barry the other evening went well. The problems of putting the play in front of a TV camera are enormous—for the play had plenty of movement. But they seem to think it very worthwhile going right ahead and finding solutions to the problems. If it goes ahead, though—they are keeping firmly in mind linking up on the novel's appearance. It couldn't in any case be ready until the first quarter of next year—if ever. When I find they <u>are</u> going ahead I'm going to talk over with [George] Kerr[27] how the TV play can come more into line with the book—be in fact retitled <u>Johnnie Sahib</u>.

Yours sincerely,

Box 17, Folder 3 (McFarlin)
61 Brookland Rise
To R. F. Rubinstein, Rubinstein Nash
12 October 1951

Dear Mr. Rubinstein,

I wonder if I may ask you to advise and help me personally in my capacity as an author?

As an author I am not quite sure what, if anything, I should do about obtaining war office clearance for my novel which, as you may know, has a war background and stems from my own particular experiences in an air supply unit of the R.I.A.S.C.[28] (now no longer in existence!). I know that in the case of nonfiction books, etc., dealing with particular aspects of the war and making use of material in which the War Office might be said to have a parental interest, one has to have a manuscript cleared. But does the same apply to fiction? Novels, plays?

This all comes to a head for me because Television are actively investigating how to put the play in front of the camera—and this promises to be really exciting and just what I want. I am pretty well convinced that I make use of no material which comes under a blanket of security. Some years ago when I was getting hold of some notes on air supply for Compton Mackenzie for his book on the Indian Army, I managed to get my ex-colonel to draft out the full details for him. These notes were I know submitted to the War office and passed—and my memory of them is that they stated facts far more roundly than my own fiction works.

The book is due for publication in the spring—(Eyre and Spottiswoode have never raised this point)—and if the Television thing comes off I believe production will coincide—so there is plenty of time to submit if that is the correct course.

If in your opinion clearance is needed—is that something you would be willing to negotiate for me? I have a horror of official channels of this nature!

I am taking the liberty of enclosing a stereotype of the radio play script, which was cut for transmission. If clearance is needed could we obtain it on this script, or must we get separate clearance for play and novel? I don't know how necessary it is to explain that a transmission has actually been made.

So sorry to bother you with this, but it has begun to worry me a little. I should hate to find myself at the wrong end of a court martial! Or worse—indemnifying publishers and BBC for all sorts of unpleasant costs!

When you have had time to consider this I should be very grateful indeed were you to give me a ring at the office (Pearn, Pollinger and Higham—EM 8631).

With kind regards,

Yours sincerely,

Box 34, Folder 4 (DHA-HRC)
Pearn, Pollinger & Higham, Ltd. 39–40 Bedford Street
To George Greenfield, Werner Laurie Ltd.[29]
18 October 1951

Dear George,

<u>Royalties at special rates</u>

I have been in touch with Eleanor Hibbert[30] about the copies of <u>Poison in Pimlico</u> and <u>The Flesh and the Devil</u>, which were sold at 5/- net, and I am glad to say that in this particular instance she will accept a royalty of 10% on that price rather than the full published price. I have also written to Michael Leigh, but as he is abroad I haven't yet had a reply.

The point I wish to make generally is that what we are being asked to do, or rather what the authors are being asked to do, is to give Werner Laurie <u>carte blanche</u> in the matter of terms and subsequently royalties, a thing which no other publisher has ever suggested to us. There are as I see it two provisions: a provision for a specific royalty on the published price, and the provision for any specific royalty on the net proceeds where the books are sold above a certain discount. Those are two clear-cut principles, but anything else moving vaguely between the two seems to me, as I said before, to cut at the roots of any agreement.

I have given this quite a lot of thought and quite honestly I do not see any reasonable clause coming into view. If, though, you yourself can suggest something which imposes limits on price, on time, and on rate, we might be a step nearer—but I cannot help feeling that all we should then be doing is creating an arbitrary precedent as a solution to the occasional deal.

I am not convinced, you see, that these special deals cannot be dealt with as and when they arise and in a more leisurely manner. I cannot criticise your giving your travellers[31] powers of discretion—but working it logically back it means our authors are giving your travellers powers of discretion, and that I think is just not right. Since other publishers have never brought such a problem to us, I feel that either their travellers have to make such deals subject to the firm's confirmation, or that if their travellers have powers of discretion such as yours, then it is the publisher who takes the risk of a smaller return, or in other words, has the courage of his convictions.

I must just repeat that I realise in the fullest extent the importance of getting the highest returns from slow moving stocks but I do not like substituting strategy for tactics.[32]

Yours,

Box 2, Folder 3 (McFarlin)
61 Brookland Rise
To Donald McWhinnie, Drama Script Unit, BBC
21 November 1951

Dear Donald McWhinnie,

Many thanks for your letter. It is pleasant to know that I am among those with whom Val Gielgud[33] asked you to get in touch. I shall very much hope to let you see—in the not far distant future—a synopsis and outline treatment for a new radio play. I am at work on the idea at the moment (and eventually it will become my second novel). The setting is India towards the end of 1948 and briefly it is the story of an Anglo-Indian woman who is faced with the problem of returning to England, the home she has always pretended to, but has never actually seen. But there's a lot more to it than that and I hope it's going to work up into something I can show you.

Thank you, by the way, for sending the previous script to Television. Michael Barry has recently been in touch with me and it seems there is a fairly good chance of adapting <u>Lines of Communication</u> for TV. That could be quite exciting, especially if it coincides with the publication of the novel next spring.

With kind regards,

Yours sincerely,

Box 2, Folder 3 (McFarlin)
61 Brookland Rise
To Ian Atkins, BBC Television[34]
15 March 1952

Dear Ian,

<u>Lines of Communication</u>

Thank you for your letter of March 14th, detailing points Michael Barry has made. We'll certainly have to discuss these together, and by the time you get this letter I hope to have been in touch to arrange when we could meet. Before we do meet and talk, though, I want to put down my reactions on paper so that these can form the basis of our discussion.

Let's take the points in the order you set them down in your letter.

1) <u>"The impression of strain and furious work, which was the impact of the radio script, has gone"</u>. In your comments on this point you say, "This is true for three reasons". But, you know, we all agreed, after hearing the recording, that whatever impression

of strain and furious work the <u>script</u> gave, actual performance
didn't. George Kerr summed up our combined reaction when he
said, "it's all a lot of fuss over nothing", or words to that effect.
You made a point of the need to show the section at work, and
I showed it at work by introducing the bits of business over the
demand for five planeloads and the consequent night loading of
these. I think if you analyze the radio script it becomes quite clear
that the "strain and furious work" impression is falsely created by
the quarrelsome tone of the dialogue—and here again we agreed
it was necessary to cut the quarrels and show, in the first phase,
the section and indeed the company as a "happy family". The
play always <u>did</u> begin with a lull in actual operations and Johnnie
always <u>did</u> go on leave because of the lull and Jim's arrival.
Whatever the present effect in the TV script is, I can't agree with
MB [Michael Barry] that the impression of high-pressure work
has <u>gone</u>. I can't think it was ever really there—or only falsely
so; and I think there's a much stronger, realistic feeling of a unit
doing its job and putting a good face on it, which is one of the
effects we agree to emphasise along with our soft pedalling of the
bolshie quality of the radio-play dialogue. (I take it, by the way,
that in the main we are discussing the first third of the play in this
context, for you outline means of strengthening the impression of
hard work by reference to that part of the play only.) Let's take
those suggested means:

a) <u>Re-introduction of "ticking-off".</u> This would cut in slightly
   upon our happy family basis—and of course it was left out
   deliberately because I was trying to show that at this stage
   the Major's attitude to Baxter is that Baxter is hardly worth
   bothering about—a chair-borne perfectionist who is critical of
   anything going on "in the field". If we do introduce the ticking
   off it would fall into place on page 15 where the Major and
   Johnnie have their brief "Try and make a go of it" with Jim
   Taylor's scene. But I'm rather afraid of throwing the mood off

key, and emphasising minor points. The ticking off would have to be extremely good natured—both in giving and taking—and it might tend to give undue prominence to Johnnie in a play which now seeks to soft pedal him—as I think, again, we agreed. Personally I like the understatement, "Try and make a go of it with Jim Taylor"—not for the statement alone but for its place in the dialogue; it seems more in keeping than any ticking off would be.

b) Emphasise the Jemadar's speech on page three. Here again we're on the "hard work" theme. References to "hard work" without action to back [it] up seems to me to create the wrong impression if we overdo them. I knew we <u>had</u> to indicate that everyone had had a pretty rough time, but it would be completely out of character for anyone to make a song and dance about it—and apart from that I've been anxious to keep any references to such things in their proper perspective—keep them, that is, always subordinate to the general sense of confidence—the feeling that "when we work we work—we don't call this work—we can do it standing on our heads"—a feeling which Johnnie plays up 100%. In this first phase I've made a real effort to create this atmosphere. In these scenes there isn't any STRAIN; but we end strongly, I hope, on a note—a counterpoint—where the Major says, "We stick out our chests and think we know it all because we've been here a year. What's a year", etc. etc.

c) Further action as "interruptions". I tried to avoid clutter and repetition—but we could have Scottie called from the mess— just prior to the binge at the club to prepare an emergency drop.

2) "By any standards one must get the impression of a 'pretty scruffy unit'". Does this mean Three Section or the company? In either case I'd oppose this strongly. True, the standard in Delhi, where Baxter hies from, is different from the standard in the field. And

Johnnie's standard is different from the Major's. But there just can't be any question of a scruffy unit in my sense of the word scruffy. I can think of nothing more calculated to enlist viewers' sympathies and cheers for Ramo than the feeling that the company, or one of the sections in the company, is "scruffy by any standards". You can laugh kindly at scruffiness, but at bottom I'm sure you censure it. This business of the lines in Three Section calling forth Baxter's criticism is to show Baxter once again as the chairborne perfectionist. The Major is never intended to appear as a lax nincompoop who would allow "scruffiness by any standards" to go unchecked. If you look carefully at page seven—fourth speech you'll see the development—the logical one I'm sure—of Baxter's plant about the "untidiness" of the lines; and it's all mixed up with the word picture of the hard work the company's done. The Major, staring out of the window says—"Ankle deep in mud; store bashas on the verge of collapse—" and then for a fleeting moment he sees it with Baxter's eyes; and he hesitates, "well—it looks a bit of a mess I suppose"—then his own work-a-day vision takes over and although he's talking to Jim, he's answering Baxter or any odd type who pokes his nose in unwanted; "but it's no worse than when we came here a year ago and since then we've had some pretty hectic times". Then he turns to Taylor and says what he'd've liked to have said to Baxter instead of the formal "It's difficult to make a place like this look spick and span". I'm sure that with the visual duplication of scene this point will come over; not that it matters a great deal if it doesn't.

When we first met and talked about the play you said that one of the things you liked was that first of all [we've] shown the company doing a good job by itself, and then the Staff types coming in, and a good job still being done. Because, of course, that is what usually happened in the army. The whole point is that there was nothing wrong with the old way, and that there's nothing wrong with the new way; the drama is in the human expendability which—for this very reason—seems senseless. It would definitely be wrong to show the company at a disadvantage by reason of its scruffiness or the scruffiness of any one of its sections. And any unit that was scruffy just couldn't cope with this sort of work.

3)   a) Officers don't express their resentment of Ramo as effectively; b) the sudden news of Ramo was the starting point of Johnnie's resentment and final crack up. Now the effect on Johnnie is not so clearly marked and his drunken scene seems to come very suddenly and without preparation. Both of these criticism are reasonable, I think; but I've been careful of course to tone down the quarrelsomeness and of course it's not intended that Johnnie should "crack up". He is sacked because he suddenly decides to back the old firm as it were actively against the new. In the present script I felt it was more typical of Johnnie that he'd treat the Ramo as a bit of a joke—(until he sees its effect on his section)—as something which really cannot interfere with him.

Still, there's some clarification to be done here, and I think it can all be done, (with the exception of the dog-tired business which can be introduced into the Johnnie/Jemadar scene with a line or two of the dialogue). Quite briefly in the scene immediately after Baxter has left HQ tent after his speech. The existing backchat can develop into a "backing up the Major against Baxter's campaign", which the Major cuts short with the remark, "Right, before you go", thereby proving to Johnnie that the Major has, as he thinks, sold himself to Ramo. In the present script there is a brief scene—page 38—in which Johnnie says practically nothing. We can make him accuse the Major, semi-seriously, semi-banteringly, of "toadying up" to Ramo because he hasn't had promotion, and saying that Ramo's not going to make any difference to Three Section. This, of course, is all implied at the moment, and I'm not convinced it isn't really enough as it stands. What d'you think?

4)   Johnnie's voice over the letter. I had doubts myself. Shall we try it before taking another way? Certainly Johnnie's lines are not supposed to be spoken sentimentally, but openly and friendly—to

point the difference, audibly, between him and Jim, who arrives immediately afterwards for the Jan Mohammed scene.

5) Last scene too sentimental. Doesn't it depend on the way it's played?

Sorry to have written at such length and, at first glance, rather uncooperatively, you may feel. I do think, though, that MB's reaction is conditioned by his reaction to the radio script—he did not hear the run through, whereas we did! You didn't by the way pass on any of the uncritical remarks he may have made, so I'm left with the impression he doesn't much care for it.

Yours,

Box 20, Folder 14 (McFarlin)
61 Brookland Rise
To Joyce Weiner
15 June 1952

Dear Joyce,

I have decided to change my agency arrangements, as I am no longer convinced that we can work together to our mutual advantage. I have thought deeply about this for some time, and more particularly in the last month or two. I am going to David Higham.

There are two reasons for my decision. First and foremost I believe we are too similar in temperament. In my private life I am always torn in two by the parallel demands of earning a living and creative writing and I am consequently inconsistent; optimistic and pessimistic; at once full and devoid of understanding. For no good reason I can thrive on criticism and in another instance break under its weight. We are all entitled to our own temperaments but I am convinced that I must now put my agency arrangements on a less personal, indeed impersonal, basis.

I can well see that a charge of ingratitude can too easily find its home. One is helped over a hill and it is one of the perplexities of life that having been helped one grows suspicious of the need for help in the future. You know my work well enough, I think, to see that this problem is a very real one to me. Its solution does nothing but take me one step further towards the eventual disillusionment I have, in the past, seen awaits me finally.

The second reason is one that is no concern of mine; your own administrative arrangements; they were certainly no concern of mine while the first reason was not apparent to me and now that I am changing they are less so. But the two reasons are there, and I owe you the explanation.

It is useless to end on a "no hard feelings" note. There are I am sure. And I hope you will not ring me at least until we have both readjusted.

If Little Brown decline Johnnie Sahib I will want the list of USA pubrs who have seen and declined it. If Litt. Brown had a copy of the book (not a proof), would you then tell them to pass it on to Wm Morris in New York? They could destroy a proof or mss. Ad interim was applied for? I shall want, too, a list of the Continental Pubrs who have seen and declined.

Yours,

Box 43, Folder 22 (DHA-HRC)
Pearn, Pollinger & Higham, Ltd. 39–40 Bedford Street
To Arthur Clarke, New York[35]
17 July 1952

Dear Arthur,

Holborn Public Library rang me yesterday to ask whether you would consider giving an hour's talk—or thereabouts—to a group of boys in their Children's Book Week on November 10th, either in the morning or the afternoon (they are not quite sure which yet). Naturally they want you to talk about space travel.

The fee they pay is very small, being only five guineas. Would you let me know what I am to tell them?

Another point has cropped up. Gerald Pollinger[36] has received from Otis Klein Associates the book The Year's Best Science Fiction Novels published by Dell, and we have noticed that in it is a short novel of yours called <u>The Seekers of the Sphinx</u>. Vague bells rang in our heads, and we realised—of course—having checked up on the manuscript—that this is the same as <u>The Road to the Sea</u> which is under option with <u>Against the Fall of Night</u> to Sidgwick & Jackson. The information we had about it was that it had been published in magazine form in the states and had also been sold to an American anthology. The point I want to clear up is whether by any chance Scott Meredith[37] disposed of world English language rights in it—or whether the British Empire volume rights are still free for you to negotiate yourself. May I have word from you about this?

Yours,

Box 45A, Folder 14 (DHA-HRC)
Pearn, Pollinger & Higham, Ltd. 39–40 Bedford Street
To Ruth Sansom, Tasmania
5 November 1952

Dear Ruth,

We have thought very carefully about "Tasmanian Sketches" and much as I regret to have to say it, I do feel that we should not be successful in finding a publisher for this work as it stands at present. The most difficult obstacle is that of length, for at 35,000 words it isn't really in the book category.

The reader who reported on the manuscript felt that there was good material for a nostalgic novel of childhood, and I feel she is probably right.

I am so sorry we cannot be more helpful, particularly as I remember these sketches so well; but you are up against publishers' economic difficulties.

I'll hold the manuscript here until I hear from you what you would like us to do with it. Meanwhile my best love to you and Clive. I hope you are both flourishing. Did Peschmann[38] arrive in Hobart? I met him at a party over here during the summer and he told me he had been in touch with Clive about a teaching job.

Yours,

Box 156, Folder 6 A–2 (DHA-HRC)
61 Brookland Rise
To Mrs. Ruby Millar, Eyre & Spottiswoode Ltd.
14 January 1953

Dear Ruby,

Many thanks for your letter of the 13th. I am so glad the revisions were all in order from your point of view.[39]

I'll look forward very much to hearing what the editorial committee think about the titles. My own preference is, from the list I left with Frank, in this order:

The Goat Song
The Caged Beast
The Dark Root
The Root of Violence

Another possibility is The Kingdom of Jackals. Otherwise we can always more or less give up the ghost and called it The Anglo-Indians. That term at first being used for any British person who made his or her career over there. It is only over the past 20 years or so that it has been used to describe a Eurasian. That being so nearly all the English characters in the book could rightly be described thus.

When you say that you want to get the book out as quickly as possible, does that mean early autumn? Or even earlier? I would be in favour of the end of the year, actually, as there won't be another novel for quite some time and we don't want too large a gap between them.

I'll produce materials for a blurb and catalogue as soon as I can.

Love,

Box 53, Folder 20 (DHA-HRC)
Pearn, Pollinger & Higham, Ltd. 39–40 Bedford Street
To J. S. Knapp-Fisher, Sidgwick & Jackson Ltd.
16 September 1953

Dear Knapp-Fisher,

Many thanks for yours of the 11th telling me that Pan are not prepared to increase the advance on <u>Prelude to Space</u> by Arthur Clarke from £100 to £150. We are therefore making the necessary note to our records here, and just confirming to Arthur.

I saw Arthur the other day, incidentally, and we had a word about his short stories. There are, at the moment, enough stories to make more than one volume, but the principle volume and the first with which we will want to deal, is one originally called <u>Tales from Space</u> but now called <u>Expedition to Earth</u>. Ballantine are doing it on the other side.

As you know, there is no actual commitment about the future of Arthur's fiction but we are hoping that when <u>Childhood's End</u> is published Arthur will definitely want to go on with you. As the first book to come along after <u>Childhood's End</u> will be the volume of short stories (he would like to see the latter out in the autumn of next year), he wondered whether, with a view to saving time at a later date, you would care to have a look at this at this stage and then give us an indication of whether you would want to publish. Shall I send the manuscript therefore?

Yours,

Box 19, Folder 2 (McFarlin)
61 Brookland Rise
To Morchard Bishop, <u>John O'London's Weekly</u>[40]
3 October 1953

Dear Morchard Bishop,

I have delayed replying to your long & interesting letter until the weekend in order to give some time and thought to it, & to my reply. Please forgive this rather peculiar paper.

I take it as a great compliment that you should show so much interest in my work—& while I hope you will read & review many more novels of mine, I should like to say that this very pleasant correspondence with you will not in any way lead me to expect to be let off lightly in the future. My first letter to you about your review of <u>Johnnie Sahib</u>

was written after some slight hesitation, for writing to a critic after a favourable review might suggest a hope that foundations are going to be laid for further favourable reviews of later books. It is my last wish that this correspondence should make you feel any more kindly disposed to my work than you are to books by people completely unknown to you. When my next novel comes along (I begin work on it this month)—that is, if it is published!—I shall certainly send you a copy & I hope you will have the opportunity of reviewing it; but I can't expect to be treated otherwise than according to its merits.

This fertile imagination of mine is—if I'm honest with myself— probably more undisciplined than fertile. And this question of form is one that I grapple with considerably. For the moment I realise I'm nowhere near solving it in relation to my own problems. I suppose every writer is concerned with a particular problem & its interpretation—& he probably sees life & interprets it (rightly or wrongly) in terms of the problem. It's also true, I think, if a writer deals with events which took place several years before the writing of them, that he has carried his problem one step further along the road to final (?) solution than the step of interpretation he deals with in the book.

The theme, or problem, underlying both Johnnie Sahib & The Alien Sky, is my personal theme (personal as a writer I mean)— and can possibly be simply stated—even although the simple state-ment immediately becomes grandiose. It is that men & women, in these years which concern us, are increasingly aware of the absence of roots, increasingly aware that whatever "place" they've made for themselves is artificial. It is my concern with this, which led me to the Anglo-Indian aspect of the problem, for there it becomes physi-cal: and what I had to do in The Alien Sky was to state the theme in a series of variations. There is nothing artificial about this (I think and hope), for it isn't a question of moving people around & making them do this thing or that thing in order to prove a point: it so happens that—for me—whatever people do they automatically play a variation on the theme—for me—because of what is, I suppose, a state of mind in myself. And the tragedy (to me) is that they are at once associated by their common need, dissociated by their individual interpretation (& consequently action) of it.

And it is, of course, with the individual, the man or woman, that a writer has to be concerned; had my powers as a writer been greater then I could probably have dealt with the things I wanted to deal with on a far smaller canvas. I have plans toward that end in novel number 3, & perhaps some sort of form will emerge (emerge is the wrong word: one imposes form upon a subject: to say "emerge" is like saying, "Oh, by then, the characters begin to take over & I just write what they tell me!")

However, I feel I am right to say the things I want to say, & go on saying them until I've disciplined the technical act of writing & produce a novel that can stand on its own feet. I believe you would agree with me there.

I'm so sorry this letter is so long, so hard to read (I suspect) & perhaps so muddled. And I do hope I haven't given you the idea that I've only got one thing to write about. What I've tried to do is to excuse myself for the failing in The Alien Sky by seeking to show that the failings arise out of a general, as yet unmastered problem. Novel number 3 can, I hope, take me a little further along the road towards solutions.

And once again, many thanks for all your kindness and encouragement: & please do not feel I look for a reply to this long rigmarole.

With kind regards,

Yours sincerely,

Box 111, Folder 21 (DHA-HRC)
Pearn, Pollinger & Higham, Ltd. 39–40 Bedford Street
To Clive Sansom, Tasmania
5 March 1954

My dear Clive,

It's quite awful to think how long ago it must be since I last wrote to you, and worse to think I generally begin my letters like this, and even worse to think this is prompted by business! But how are you? And how is Ruth?

A publisher rang me the other day to ask me whether I could think of an author likely to be interested in writing a book for the ordinary man on accent and pronunciation. I said at once that an old friend of mine called Clive Sansom might be interested and your name rang his bell at once. He promised to set his ideas out in a letter and I attach a copy. The published is John Baker of Phoenix House—who, as I expect you know, are a Dent firm. John Baker is the man in charge.

As you know I've always hoped you'd one day think an agent might be some help to you, yourself so far away at the other end of the world. If you _are_ interested in John Baker's idea, and it doesn't cut across your Methuen arrangements, I'm sure we could arrange a satisfactory commission for you. Perhaps this could be the beginning of an association between C. S. and PP&H whereby we look after your fiction, but not the specialised stuff you do for Methuen? That would be nice. In case you want us to go further ahead with Baker, I'll be formal and enclose a pamphlet setting out the terms and conditions on which we act for authors!

Penny sends her love to you both, and I do too. Carol and Sally are now seven and nearly six respectively and fight like demons.

Let me hear from you soon? All best wishes,

Yours,

Box 105, Folder 15 (DHA-HRC)
Pearn, Pollinger & Higham, Ltd. 39–40 Bedford Street
To Mr. John Fowles, Ashridge, Herkhamsted[41]
10 March 1954

Dear Mr. Fowles,

We have now had our report on A Journey to Athens and have been able to consider the prospects. We are most interested in your work and only wish we could be more optimistic about the chances of marking arrangements for this short piece. The difficulty is the length, and our reader seems to feel that, in its present form, it doesn't quite stand up as a publishing proposition.

If the longer book on Greece had not, so to speak, just been around the corner, I think the answer would be for us to show A Journey to Athens to two or three good publishers and see where we could go from there. But as I understand the longer book is nearly ready I do feel it would be a much better plan to put off approaching publishers until we can do so with the travel book, coupled perhaps with this <u>nouvelle</u>.

Our reader has made a point: he says—

> "His extended and battling game of canasta is the same tension category as Hemingway's <u>Old Man and the Sea</u>: a battle of skills and wills dominated by non-human factors like luck. I was so pleased with this that I at once saw the book entirely continued in the canasta game, not in the vague conventional voyage (which is useful only for a cosmopolitan detachment in the eye of the writer). Mr. Fowles could have made the same points more briefly, pungently, and wholly by means of character."

I'm wondering therefore whether you might not like to consider recasting the canasta-game sequence as an introduction to the longer book? It's only an idea and at this stage I wouldn't suggest your working on it even if it appealed to you. Once we have considered the travel book we could perhaps offer the two, and put the canasta-game proposition up to publishers at the same time.

What do you think? Is there any chance of your being in town in the near future, when we could meet and talk? And what is the present situation about the longer book?

I'll much look forward to hearing from you.

Yours sincerely,

Box 104, Folder 24 (DHA-HRC)
Pearn, Pollinger & Higham, Ltd. 39–40 Bedford Street
To Charles Monteith, Faber & Faber Ltd.[42]
17 March 1954

Dear Charles,

Can I ring your bell with "Tingaling"? This is the sort of children's book we do not ourselves do a great deal with, but this one is by one of our most promising young authors who wrote an enchanting travel book for Longmans. Irish Myddylton isn't his real name, of course, and I have not shown the book to Longmans—merely enquired whether they would be interested in seeing it. They aren't taking on new juveniles, though, so I thought I would come to you first.

It is the sort of book that obviously has to have the right sort of illustrations. I hope you like it and want to do it.

Yours,

Box 100A, Folder 7 (DHA-HRC)
Pearn, Pollinger & Higham, Ltd. 39–40 Bedford Street
To Dr. Alan Barnsley [Gabriel Fielding][43]
18 May 1954

Dear Alan,

I am afraid there is no good news yet from America but I thought you might like to see what Cass Canfield of Harper said when he declined <u>Brotherly Love</u>:

> This novel is quite good in a quiet introspective way; but the characters are seen clearly and with depth. At the same time I am afraid that in spite of some fine writing we don't feel that the novel has enough dramatic impact to warrant the hope of successful publication. So I am afraid we must decline with regret.

William Morris are now sending the manuscript to Alfred Knopf. Previously it has been seen by Viking (twice), William Morrow and Little Brown.

Please don't bother to reply to this.

Yours,

Box 105, Folder 23 (DHA-HRC)
Pearn, Pollinger & Higham, Ltd. 39–40 Bedford Street
To Mrs. Peter Green [Lalage Pulvertaft], Chelsea
19 July 1954

My dear Lal,[44]

Many thanks for yours of the 17th. I'm glad you aren't too disappointed by Michael Joseph's rejection. I'm making a careful note of your hunch about Rupert Hart-Davis—who certainly shouldn't be ruled out of the list of probables, although they haven't been particularly strong over fiction in the past year or so.

Thank you for confirming the dates you and Peter will be away, 24th July to 24th August. We're also making a note that Peter's bank is Westminster Bank, King's Road, Chelsea, and take that unless we hear to the contrary all cheques we find ourselves paying to him may go to his account there.

Yes, The Alien Sky is tonight.[45] I hope you and Peter enjoy it, although I'm not sure anyone will know what it's about if they haven't read the book, for I spent most of the weekend slashing page after page in order to keep to time. However, my fingers are crossed.

Yours,

Box 105, Folder 39 (DHA-HRC)
Pearn, Pollinger & Higham, Ltd. 39–40 Bedford Street
To Mrs. Peter Green [Lalage Pulvertaft], Chelsea
21 July 1954

My dear Lal,

Many thanks for your very kind letter of the 20th. I am glad you and Peter enjoyed the play. I know exactly what you mean about Gower and the way Colin Gordon[46] played it. He was so much better on the night than he had been during rehearsals that I felt reasonably pleased with him. But there is no getting away from the fact that he was badly miscast but something also went wrong in the adaptation as far as he was concerned.

Ever yours,

P. S. Michael Joseph have phoned through to say they think there has been a mistake about No Great Magic and that they'd like to have the book back to reconsider if Collins return it. We haven't committed ourselves but I thought you'd like to know this. I had a feeling something had gone wrong.

Box 2, Folder 4 (McFarlin)
78 Addison Way
To Ian Atkins, BBC Television
10 August 1954

My Dear Ian,

The Alien Sky

Here it is, the draft treatment for a Television play based on the novel and radio dramatization, which I sat down to do immediately after having Hugh Stewart[47] send you the radio script.

You'll appreciate that it isn't written with, in mind, your own feeling that what we need is a central character so much as written in an attempt to provide a simpler framework for a complicated plot. In the course of doing it I have, naturally, tried to reduce as much of the development to visual action. My own view is that the honours are now shared between Dorothy Gower, Tom Gower and Harriet Haig, in the sense that they are the people who provide the conflict—with MacKendrick and Steele on the sidelines. Whether it would be possible to dispense with characters or not I cannot at the moment say—but on the basis that all things are nearly always possible I should say that it is.

It has always been, and still is, something of a Noah's Ark of a play (without Noah, you'll tell me!)—or rather tale, for the novel was designed similarly, and I am rather of the opinion that its being so doesn't automatically lessen the dramatic qualities. It would be difficult to say everything one wants to say about the end of the British-Indian epoch in terms of a central, towering figure—they all tended to be pygmies, if you see what I mean. And it isn't just a question of trying to be politically fair (it's not a political play) and seeing all sides of the question in a sort of dreary ABCA way (if you remember what ABCA stood for!),[48] and trotting out one's puppets to say their pieces. However, that's all by the way.

I'm going away for a fortnight at the end of August. It would be jolly nice if before then I could be given some sort of go-ahead, although I realise the difficulties. I am <u>keen</u> to write a good TV play on this theme and if Wood Lane[49] is also keen to have a way round through the difficulties, then it would be a pity if we did have to drop the whole thing simply because in the early stages the whole thing wasn't quite in focus. You may recall that rather a similar set of circumstances existed over <u>Lines of Communication</u> and I think you were always a bit worried about how it would develop; but when you had my finished script you rang me and said it was first rate. I mention that simply because I believe I have enough powers of self-criticism to enable me to produce a workable answer, even if I can't produce an exciting outline. As you know, these things grow, and as they grow you see where they're becoming misshapen or top heavy, or what have you.[50]

I'm sorry. Authors write frightfully long letters, as I know to my cost in my other professional capacity![51]

All best wishes,

Yours,

Box 100A, Folder 7 (DHA-HRC)
Pearn, Pollinger & Higham, Ltd. 39–40 Bedford Street
To Dr. Alan Barnsley [Gabriel Fielding]
8 November 1954

My dear Alan,

Thank you for your letter of 3rd November. I think you will readily appreciate that I, no more than the next man, can react kindly to a charge of ineptitude. I have reread your letter at intervals and am writing this, my reply, in the uninterrupted quiet of my own study, so that it can be typed in the office tomorrow.

You make it clear that you believe both your publisher and your agent have let you down. Let us consider these complaints separately.

You may recall that in the interval between your very first visit to my office and the appearance upon the scene (I say appearance advisedly, for I did not invite them) of Hutchinson as a ready, able and willing purchaser, we had at least one talk on the telephone: that was after I had read the first chapter of Brotherly Love. I seem to remember that, aware of [Richard] Church's interest,[52] and Heinemann's presumed interest via Erica Marx,[53] I told you we should not commit ourselves in any direction whatsoever, you then showed me two more chapters and at the same time sent them to Church.

At this stage Hutchinson decided they wanted to offer on the basis of the three chapters. Before we could put the offer to you we had to negotiate it with Mrs. Webb.[54] I consider we negotiated excellent terms for a first novel (unfinished at that)—£150 advance against first-rate royalties. We then met for lunch and I put the situation to you fairly and squarely—weighing up with you the pros and cons of Hutchinson as publishers for your sort of work. You will remember the details of our talk.

At that time neither of us could anticipate Church's disappearance from Hutchinson. He was a friend of yours: you had given him your chapters. So far as we were concerned his joining Hutchinson had indicated that at least there would be someone there who could instill a bit of literary vigour into their list.

Church's Hutchinson demise was unfortunate. It was not disastrous. He had your Book Society Recommendation and your puffs[55] from eminent authors to whom you wrote as a matter of course as people you had met and whose opinions could be useful. You also had a publisher whose organisation could get into the bookshop over 2,000 copies of a book, so that when reviews came along and your friends and correspondents went in to buy it or borrow it, there were more likely to be copies available than not.

There was the obscenity scare and the libel scare. The first, in the present state of the publishing world, had to be reacted to with understanding. The second was annoying and would probably not have arisen if Church had still been there, for possibly he was much more in the picture than Dorothy Tomlinson.[56] Even the libel scare need not have caused delay had you been on hand, and not abroad.

I think therefore, within their limitations, Hutchinson have not let you down. That they are, without Church, the wrong publishers for you, I do not—need not—dispute: but only wrong in the sense that there is now no one there you can meet on your terms, no one who can understand that you are an unusual person with a high degree of literary talent and—I suspect, a spark of genius. I'm not flattering you.

Now, for your agents, P.P. & H., on whose behalf I face a charge of ineptitude.

I think the cause of your dissatisfaction may be that you entirely misunderstand the scope of an agent's work. We are not public relations officers. We are not publicists. We do not keep in tow a row of tame reviewers to write reviews of books by authors we present. We control no papers nor literary editors. We do not even control the publicity departments of publishing houses. Very well, you'll say, what the hell do we do? We act, in the first place, for the author, over matters of business. Money. We seek to make the best possible financial arrangements for the rights in works he writes and publishers publish. We try to ensure that the arrangements work, that the author gives away as little as possible and gets as much as we can persuade the publisher it is fair he should have. The agreements we draw up are the pointer to our degree of success or otherwise.

I have already said what I think about your Hutchinson agreement. What else have we done? We have tried to sell the book rights to a U.S. publisher—both by personal representation over here when the right sort of publishers came on a trip—and through our associates in New York. We have recently changed our associate from the William Morris Agency to Harold Ober Associates, an arrangement with which we are most pleased. When David Higham went to New York in October to effect the change I asked him to have a special word with the Ober people about Brotherly Love. He did. I wrote myself the other day as well. I have also made a point of writing over especially to our foreign language associates asking them to give Brotherly Love a very special push. "Pushing"—here—meaning a push in the matter of selling rights, not getting publicity.

It is also our job to try to get the author-publisher relationship working harmoniously. Many is the phone call I've had with Hutchinson about Gabriel. Had I not done so your charm and easy-going manner would have allowed Dorothy Tomlinson to continue under the mistaken impression that you were entirely—but entirely—happy with the way they were handling your book. I'm sure you will see the benefit of having someone to say the right thing at the right time. The author can continue to show his best face to a publisher. That is, I think, helping the relationship to harmony.

When Church left, I took Katherine Webb to lunch with really no other purpose but to talk to her about Alan Barnsley. I was even able to tell her that Dannie Abse[57] was to you like a red flag to a bull—something you could not have done yourself without appearing the opposite of altruistic.

On these counts, therefore, I think there's nothing we have left undone which we ought to have done. You cannot in all fairness blame us for your lack of reviews. If you do, you would, by the same token, have to pat us on the back for the reviews you got. What, for goodness sake, would our responsibility be for the one in this week's TLS? Surely you see that there comes inevitably a time when the author, the agent and the publishers, having done their job, can only await the verdict? Of <u>course</u>, you've "spoken" to people. I have spoken to people too. Of <u>course</u> your friends tell you what a good book it is.

Advertising? I should say Hutchinson gave it the essential preliminary show. There isn't, though, a publisher in London who wouldn't tell you that having done that it's better to postpone further advertising until it can carry quotable extracts from reviews. As you can see from this week's TLS, hope of national reviews should by no means be quenched. Advertising won't get reviewers to review, by the way. Advertising is for the public, not the profession. If it became clear that reviews had failed then it would be my responsibility to discuss with Hutchinson some practical step to push the book in spite of—as it were—the critics having ignored it: a special form of advertising, say. But that time is not yet, and I could not <u>make</u> Hutchinson carry out any suggestion I had.

Quite apart from my duties as your agent I have followed up a particular reviewer who is actually a client. That is something I would only do if the circumstances seemed to warrant it, as they do here. He is Peter Green of <u>The Telegraph</u>.[58] I originally asked him to look out for the book. [John] Betjeman[59] had it and Betjeman would react to it anyway. So I gave Green my copy. He is enthusiastic. His wife is enthusiastic. They are telling all their friends and Green is trying to persuade his literary editor to get the book back from Betjeman so that he, Green, may review it. If that happens I think this one review could turn the scales entirely. But can't you see, from this example, how circumscribed we are in this matter of promotion? Who can make reviewers review? And if you could, what influence could you have on what they say? And, in any case, promotion is the publisher's job.

You mention three books which have been reviewed. Why these three out of the many hundreds in the past twelve months? Can you believe Hutchinson have "pushed" [Dannie] Abse more than they've pushed you? The fact that Abse has been reviewed is good proof that Hutchinson books aren't automatically ignored in literary quarters. And why mention <u>The Alien Sky</u> or Jean [Leroy]'s[60] book? You can't surely mean that we push our own wares at the expense of other authors? And yet at the end of your letter you talk about it being bad enough to have to write books without personally spurring on agent and publisher to see that the books get "fair play".

So where do we go from here? I have written you at length because you say the next three novels must have a different publisher and you "imagine" a different agent. So I have hopes that you haven't irrevocably decided to throw us over. Are you in the back of your mind blaming us for fixing [you] up with Hutchinson? That wouldn't really be fair, would it? Do you remember ringing me some months ago and saying that so far P.P. & H. had done nothing for you—that it was you who found the publisher. I didn't wholly agree with you—(although, if it had been left entirely to us, if no one but we had seen the book I should not have gone to Hutchinson)—but you can't have it both ways, Alan. In my opinion we are jointly responsible for the fact the Hutchinson is your publisher and that we've come just a bit of a cropper through a wholly fortuitous event—Church's going.

What I refuse to take responsibility for is the reception in the press and if you expect that of any first rate agent who knows his business— where it begins and where it ends—then you'll obviously want to look elsewhere. If you do it will be the greatest disappointment I've had as an agent, because I think we have done and can continue to do a job for you—and yours is the sort of work it gives me the greatest personal pleasure to be connected with.

May I ask you in any case to come in and see me before you make a final decision?

Yours,

Box 113, Folder 19 (DHA-HRC)
Pearn, Pollinger & Higham, Ltd. 39–40 Bedford Street
From a letter to Geoffrey Wagner, New York[61]
16 December 1954

Dear Geoffrey,

Many thanks for your letter. Yes, the Peter Baker business must have been a shock to many people, especially to those who knew him in the old days. No, I'm not worried about having been Secretary (to the company, not to Baker personally by the way).[62] I don't believe there's anything which happened in my day which need cause me unrest […].

Yours sincerely,

Box 148, Folder 14 (DHA-HRC)
Pearn, Pollinger & Higham, Ltd. 39–40 Bedford Street
To Mrs. Blanche Knopf, Alfred A. Knopf, USA[63]
20 January 1955

Dear Blanche,

Welcome to London. Mrs. Dodd fixed for me to come along and see you next Wednesday at 3.30, and I'm looking forward to that.

Meanwhile, I'm sending you two books to look at over the weekend. The first, Brotherly Love by Gabriel Fielding, you've already seen and declined in New York and you may think it odd that I should bother you with it again. It is, however, a book by an author I really believe that someone like yourselves should take on and since it was published at the end of last year a number of critics have shown that they feel the same about Fielding as I do. Several of your colleagues in New York have seen the book, and bluntly I think you are being short sighted about Fielding's quality and potential weight. C. P. Snow, Graham Greene, John Raymond, John Davenport and Peter Green although all varying in their opinions nevertheless feel he obviously has very definite quality. He's working on a trilogy of novels all about the same family to whom <u>Brotherly Love</u> is an introduction and a number of publishers here would only be too glad to get him away from Hutchinson (to whom he went when his friend Richard Church was advising them). Naturally I'll understand if you throw the book back at me with a rude remark, but I'm going to take that risk.

The other book I'm sending you, a first novel by D. J. Enright, <u>Academic Year</u>, which Secker & Warburg publish this year. Also worthy of your distinguished list, I believe.

Yours,

Box 156, Folder 6 A–1 (DHA-HRC)
Pearn, Pollinger & Higham, Ltd. 39–40 Bedford Street
To A. J. Kidwai, India House
30 March 1955

Dear Mr. Kidwai,

Please forgive me for troubling you on a personal matter. Actually I do not believe it is a matter on which you yourself could advise, but I would be grateful if you would pass it on to the right department at India House—if indeed there is anyone there who deals with this sort of thing.

I have just had a letter from a Havildar Sadhu Singh—whom I knew during the war. He served in the same unit of the Indian Army as I did myself.

I gather from his letter that his father, a Niranjan Singh, c/o S. Lal Singh, Patera, Jullundur, India, received a "permit" from his son-in-law, Jaswant Singh, 20 Red Lane, Coventry, England, to enable him to apply for a passport to the Government of India to come to England. Sadhu Singh says, "unfortunately it is rejected due to something wrong in the permit which, I think, is that my brother-in-law is only in England since four years". What Sadhu Singh has asked me to do is send his father a permit myself. I have no idea what all this means and know nothing of the father—but if there is some quite straightforward thing to be done which doesn't involve me as a sponsor of Mr. Niranjan Singh, I should be glad to know what it is—for Sadhu is an old friend.

With kind regards,

Yours sincerely,

Box 2, Folder 20 (McFarlin)
78 Addison Way
To Hugh Champion[64]
8 April 1955

Dear Mr. Champion,

Thank you for your note of the 4th, addressed to me, c/o my publisher (Eyre & Spottiswoode Ltd.).

I quite understand your decision not to read a book in which there occur passages you find painful. I have reread the book up to the point at which the first blasphemy against Jesus Christ appears within the dialogue and must confess I find it offensive to my sense of religious values that you should find the blasphemy painful but not, apparently, the fornication which takes place in the previous section.

Yours sincerely,

Box 4, Folder 6 (McFarlin)
78 Addison Way
To Frank Morley, Eyre & Spottiswoode Ltd.[65]
15 May 1955

My Dear Frank,

Many thanks for yours of the 10th May, telling me of John Raymond's[66] reactions to A Male Child.[67]

I've been thinking very carefully about the various problems, both while awaiting Raymond's views, and since, because I do appreciate your and Ruby [Millar]'s reasons for pointing them out, as you see them.

In the past, when suggestions for alterations have been made, I have—as you'll recall over <u>Johnnie Sahib</u> and <u>The Alien Sky</u>—agreed with them in the main, and carried them out; but in those two cases I saw almost at once how the changes could be made and how, when made, the book would be better.

What has exercised me most during the past four weeks is this set of questions: if the Helena[68] scene goes, what takes its place? If nothing takes its place, how does the book stand without it, or where else may emphasis be altered to adjust the balance?

In short, I've tried to get the feel of the book—minus Helena at the end—and rather disturbingly I've so far found myself facing a blank wall, as it were. I say "disturbingly" because I've usually taken the view that a book never really suffers from revision; indeed, that you could go on almost indefinitely rewriting and revising and still, at what seemed the end, follow a further suggestion with advantage.

From a practical point of view—the balance of pro and con—I get nowhere, because FVM [Frank V. Morley] plus Raymond are counter-balanced by Peter Green and Ivan von Auw[69] (who read a copy of the mss when he was here. And each of these protagonists—if the irate gentlemen who write to <u>The Times</u> will forgive me—is a worthy man)—and I suppose one could go on weighing John Smith against George Brown until Kingdom Come. Obviously I must, in the end, depend on my own feelings and judgment, and take the consequences.

The other and very important consideration is the effect upon the poor chap who finds himself publishing a book he sees so clearly could be better, were it not for the boneheaded author. I'm acutely aware that where enthusiasm is tempered at the top a book starts on its way to publication with certain disadvantages, however well the man at the top goes through the necessary motions, and in the last resort I've wrestled with the problem in an attempt to break it down so that, in doing so, I could also adjust the psychological scheme of things. I want to write good books, but I also want to make good money. One makes good money better when one's publisher is pleased because I'm sure pleasure or displeasure have their effect on sales. Also, I dislike the attitude of mind, which says, What I have done, I have done; and let no dog bark.

But—A Male Child. I begin to think it's a sort of monster, a two-headed baby to which there are three attitudes. a) Drown it at birth, b) Perform a surgical operation and give it a chance of a normal life, or c) Treat it as a judgment upon us. Love and cherish it, poor bastard and let it find its own level in life.

I'm afraid I can only feel at one with (c). I hope, in spite of your present adoption of (b) you won't—in the face of my obstinacy—want to adopt it!

Publishers and writer in books: I agree that a novel set in the publishing world can be an enormous bore, but I don't think A Male Child is a "publishing novel" in the sense we understand it. Selby is quite a minor character, but I can't agree with Raymond that his affair with Helena is "unlikely". We plant the seeds of it on page 26 where Selby is shown as distinctly sympathetic towards her as a woman and not merely as one of his authors. (Please remember Selby publishes Helena. In fact it's fairly obvious that Ian Canning only met her because she was either published or being groomed by Selby in pre-war days). Helena is probably a better mistress than she is a novelist. She has racketed about for a number of years. Her liaison with Selby, with all its commercial implications, is a defeat for both of them; and that of course is the whole point. Their liaison does as much as anything to point the escape of Canning into a wider, saner world because it joins the two unsatisfactory aspects of Canning's old life and seals off the loose ends of his points of contact with it. And that, in itself, in my view, is an additional reason for his seeing Helena once again, before the end. Probably my real failure, if there is a failure in this aspect of the book, is in not having Helena close enough to the surface of the reader's imagination through the book. I intended that she should be. And how frequently is she mentioned—and not just as a name, but mentioned in the descriptive, communicative sense? I thought I used Helena in two ways, a) to communicate Ian's past failures and inhibitions and b) to communicate Stella's problems.[70] What about the last scene with Stella and Ian, in the tea shop, when he sees Helena in Stella, but sees also the "point at which she was bound to Alan and he to her in a way which transcended everything else". Doesn't, at that point, Ian—vicariously in love with—if not Stella, the idea of Stella—begin to wonder whether he and Helena are not bound to each other in the same way? Wouldn't he decide then to offer "a chance to her, but not that, a chance to me, to both of us, and yet not. Perhaps it was an attempt to discover again, like something long buried, the love which once we bore, and for the other".

I thought Helena grew throughout the book as a character, and I'm inclined to believe I haven't really failed in this. That is why I can't see how I can remove her at the end without destroying in my own eyes part of the end to which the means are directed. If Helena's scene went, Canning would go out into the world still connected by an umbilical cord. It is, in the final count you know, Canning—as much as Alan's son—who is delivered.

You say I mustn't be angry with you, but all I can say in reply is that I'm not and couldn't be, but hope you won't be angry with me for not being able to do anything about Helena. The same goes for the repetition, I'm afraid, in fact to any alteration in construction. I would have no heart to tackle it as I tackled such things over Johnnie Sahib and to a lesser extent over The Alien Sky—and the result would be disastrous from every point of view, I think.

But you have some minor comments, I believe. Perhaps we could go into those?

Finally, let me say how delighted I was to hear from David [Higham] that you're willing to do a three novel agreement. (Coals of fire!) I'm afraid that at the moment it looks as if the next novel will be rather a long one about Warren Hastings.[71] It's probably a good thing to tackle the sort of novel you don't think you have the stamina for. There were two other subjects jostling for pride of place, but I think it will be Hastings.

Love to you and Ruby,

Yours ever,

Box 147, Folder 22 (DHA-HRC)
Pearn, Pollinger & Higham, Ltd. 39–40 Bedford Street
To A. Dwye Evans, William Heinemann Ltd.[72]
12 August 1955

Dear Dwye,

Graham Greene

I think you will have had my message of the other day when I explained to your secretary that after my bustling you over signing the agreement (for which, forgive me!) I now find that the signing and exchanging can't take place until after Greene has completed the formalities of the assignment of the rights to his mother.[73] The latter operation involves stamping and dating, and the agreement between his mother and yourselves will have to be exchanged and dated accordingly. Actually this involves a delay of several seeks but I take it this need make no difference to your publication plans.

The agreement signed by you is back in my hands and I promised Greene I'd be redrafting it to take care of one or two technical points so that he would have a new draft awaiting his return.

The question of warranty is taken care of in the document assigning the rights, which is what I thought, so there's no difficulty about the proprietor giving her warranty about libel, etc. Actually anything requiring the author's liability should go into a separate letter for we can't really interpose a third party in the publishing agreement. Greene says two copies of the novel for his mother should be adequate.

Ever yours,

Box 156, Folder 4 (DHA-HRC)
Pearn, Pollinger & Higham, Ltd. 39–40 Bedford Street
To Miss Dorothy L. Sayers, Essex[74]
31 August 1955

Dear Miss Sayers,

We have received a request for permission to use "The Man Who Knew How" in an anthology to be published by Messrs. Harrap, edited by J. G. Bullocks, Professor of English at the Royal Naval College, Greenwich.

They are asking for the right to include the story on the understanding that the book could be sold in the British Empire, India and Eire. Would you have any objection to this, subject, of course, to our being able to arrange for the payment of a suitable fee?

Yours sincerely,

Box 150, Folder 4 (DHA-HRC)
Pearn, Pollinger & Higham, Ltd. 39–40 Bedford Street
To John Guest, Longmans Green Ltd.[75]
2 September 1955

Dear John,

M. M. Kaye—Shadow of the Moon

Here as arranged back for consideration are the three volumes of this novel. I have written to the author to tell her of the situation which arose at Staples and, as this is going to be in some ways upsetting news to receive out in Kenya, I am also telling her of our previous dealings with you and of their continuation. I am telling her that I am hoping very much that in due course we shall receive a firm proposal, and I warned her that this would almost certainly be subject to cuts, possibly substantial. I still hold the view that for sheer readability it isn't too long but I may well be talking through my hat and of course my view isn't one which takes into account publishing economics.

You wanted me just to fill you in a bit more about the author and her book. She is a great niece of Sir John Kaye, the very eminent Victorian biographer and author of the standard history of the Mutiny, The Sepoy War in three volumes. I think she once told me that there have been Kayes in India for 150 years and she herself has spent a considerable amount of time over there both as a child and as an army wife. She is the wife of a Colonel Hamilton, commanding the first Battalion Royal Irish Fusiliers, and recently joined him in Kenya. I see from the Times today that this Battalion is expected to come back to England and she has already told me it is possible she will be back here in November or December. There was a very early novel, which Hutchinson published at the beginning of the war. Then Thacker in India published a book of hers. After the war she turned to the thriller and wrote <u>Death Walked in Kashmir</u> (Staples), <u>Death Walked in Berlin</u> (serial John Bull and Staples) and one to come, <u>Death Walked in Cyprus</u> (Staples and serialized in <u>Woman and Beauty</u>).

<u>Shadow of the Moon</u> is the result of years of thought and planning and recently she told me that with the exception of one incident (which I can't recall) every event in the novel is authentic—in other words, such things happened to somebody during the period of the Mutiny.

I enclose a Staples publicity leaflet, which shows you what she looks like.

As I told you, I have just heard from our associates in New York,[76] from Ivan von Auw, who says that his partner Dorothy Olding has read it and agrees with my verdict (I suggested it was a potential best seller). He says that from her description it sounds as though the book might have a first-rate chance with the Book of the Month Club or Literary Guild. They are going to get moving right away.

It is too early to say yet but it is just on the cards that John Bull may want to serialize. They have got as far as drafting six specimen instalments to see how it looks.

My own feelings are, frankly, of relief about the Staples situation and I am of course only too glad to be able to come back to you after having had to treat Longmans just a little cavalierly! But I am sure that you did understand about that.

I'll look forward very much to hearing from you in due course.

Yours,

Box 210, Folder 8 (DHA-HRC)
Pearn, Pollinger & Higham, Ltd. 39–40 Bedford Street
To Robert Lusty, Michael Joseph Ltd.[77]
14 March 1956

Dear Bob,

Diana Graves

She is the actress, and a niece of Robert Graves. Some while ago she was struck down by an unusual lung complaint which meant her giving up the stage and going to live in a warmer climate. At that time she was introduced to me by one of our authors and came in to see me to discuss writing possibilities. I found her a delightful person and soon after that we began to sell articles for her (two to Harpers Bazaar and one to Woman's Own), each of which has had to do with her experiences in Italy. The BBC have also recorded talks of hers.

I think she has a charming and natural writing gift and I send you with this letter the first 20,000 words of her Rome Journal, which will extend to 60,000 words and which she hopes to finish in a month or so. Her most recent letter says, "I believe, to my surprise, that it'll have a happy ending as I'm much better and walking about and so on, and the doctors are very cheerful".

You have first offer of this material—which I'll now leave to speak for itself. But I hope you'll want to make an agreement in advance.[78]

Yours,

Box 2, Folder 4 (McFarlin)
78 Addison Way
To Donald Wilson, BBC Television[79]
19 March 1956

Dear Donald,

The Colonel's Lady[80]

At our recent talk you'll recall it was arranged that I should go away and re-think this idea in television terms, and then produce another outline which would help you to see it coming out as a play, from a constructional point of view. Although we began by disagreeing on certain fundamentals you made your points so well, in principle, that I went away fairly certain that I could do what you asked with little trouble.

But The Colonel's Lady obstinately refuses to be re-thought in what you would call television terms; she remains firmly entrenched in Smith's

Hotel, as does the action. This does not mean that I'm <u>not</u> visualising the play taking place on my television screen; I am, and always have, from the beginning, but it does mean that we're back to where we were before we met at the Café Royal.

I think we had better agree to disagree! Up until last night I wondered whether I was wrong, but having seen Mackie's comedy[81] my views have hardened. Now Mackie is a first-class playwright, as we all know (some of us enviously) from <u>The Whole Truth</u>. But there, I think, he was first and foremost writing a play. In <u>Drink Doggie Drink</u>, he was, I'm sure, writing a television script—which is my own name for a particular category of writing which, from my point of view, is neither fish nor fowl. I will go so far as to say that if Mackie had accepted the discipline of trying to concentrate his action within the poet's cottage he would have had to work twice as hard for his dramatic effects. The mobility of television and the cinema is often a snare for the writer. It tempts him to take the line of least resistance (however unconsciously). After all, if you can communicate something to the audience by the simple expedient of taking the audience to the spot it might appear that to do so is better than not to do so. But I think you often lose dramatic shape by doing so.

This may seem terribly reactionary to you. I see it to be the contrary. I have become more and more convinced that what television almost physically is is an extension of the room in which you view. The dimensions are too small for you to lose yourself physically in a constantly changing panorama. Its true value, for my money, is in the close and intimate and emotional use of the camera (e.g. <u>The Confidential Clerk</u>,[82] for one, Ian Dallas' fine play <u>The Face of Love for Another</u>[83]). The small moment is magnified, or should be, rather than the big moment diminished. Intelligent use of the camera can add a dimension to the most static of stage plays—and if it's a good play I'm convinced that a good producer can make it good television.

So you see I'm far from sure there's such a thing as "writing for television" in what I think has come to be the accepted sense—only such a thing as "writing a play". I think there is such a thing as "writing a film script" (I'm not <u>that</u> far gone), but until the television service can compete technically with a film unit, I think the writer should avoid cinematic thinking: and when TV can compete with a film unit they'll just be producing films for broadcasting and the whole sense of immediacy and sustained performance will have gone for good.

Having said so much, and at the risk of a charge of self-contradiction, I'll grant you there are some moments in the most static play which will communicate better through a change of scene; and there are plays whose nature demands scenic expansion. The Colonel's Lady isn't one of them. It is only funny in Smith's Hotel. Once you start to consider the situation outside you have to deal with reality, and then it is drab or sombre or plain tragic, or farcical—like a sort of dreary Ealing Comedy. And, from my point of view, we're dealing with a character rather than with a situation. The other people only exist in relation to their present, potential, or past relationship with her. I visualize it as a sort of up-to-date Edwardian comedy, very formal, nonexistent in analysis, one which does not dissipate its humour by trying to extend it beyond its true limits.

I expect you've given me up by now, but if not, then the question you're going to ask is whether I can give you a synopsis of The Colonel's Lady, as I see it, but in such a way that you can see its dramatic shape; situations, development, climaxes etc.

The answer to this is that I could, but only after I've written the play. I don't think I could offer you a satisfactory outline of a play any more than I could outline my new novel for my publisher. Dramatic shape is something I have to sweat over. Half a dozen ideas might look reasonable on paper, but they could only be slick ideas. In any sort of writing I know where I'm to begin, where I'm to end and, in broad outline, what I'll seek to communicate in between. You have all that in the rough notes and you have the 30 odd pages which give some hint of the mood but of which perhaps no more than 10 minutes is salvageable. I don't at all want to give you the idea I'm being difficult about this. It's a natural inability of mine. I wrote a dreadful outline of The Alien Sky, which was promptly sat on by Ian Atkins and Basil Bartlett.[84] Eventually, as I told you, I was just sent away to write a play about Tom Gower. I know you have your own views about its failings, but I think it was a success.

This is all a matter of economics for a writer—or for me. I'd like to write the play, and one day I will, but I can't roll up my sleeves any further and begin the 2 or 3 months sweat unless I'm selling my time. The alternative is so simple. I just get on with the next novel and collect my advance on delivery! On the other hand, the last thing I want is for the BBC to commit themselves to anything they have reservations about and I think what had better happen, if you and Michael Barry agree, is for me to put <u>The Colonel's Lady</u> on the pending shelf and take her down again one day when the economics impinge less so that I can work her out for the stage, and then sell you the TV rights!

I do apologise for the length of this letter, and for the rather odd typing.

All Best wishes,
Yours,

Box 202, Folder 30 (DHA-HRC)
Pearn, Pollinger & Higham, Ltd. 39–40 Bedford Street
From a letter to John Braine, Northumberland
25 April 1956

Dear John,

I have not answered your two previous letters of the 4th and the 13th because I more or less knew I should be having good news for you. After Hart-Davis, Gollancz, Hamilton and Longmans had declined <u>Joe For King</u>,[85] I went to Eyre & Spottiswoode where a young man, Maurice Temple Smith, has just taken over Frank Morley's editorial job.

I am delighted to tell you that he and his colleagues are extremely keen on the book although there are certain things they want altering, which I will tell you about. We can, however, enter into an agreement right away, subject to your agreeing to the revisions, and the following are the terms we can obtain, subject to your approval. [specifies royalties, number of books printed, etc.]

Now see what Temple Smith writes about the revisions:

> "This is as I mentioned earlier conditional upon the author removing from the book all objectionable words, phrases and passages. Of course, we are not going to be silly about this and you can't describe a violent love affair without mentioning sex, but I am sure that John Braine is a good enough novelist to get this effect without having to use words that a lot of readers would find objectionable.
>
> By far the best way to settle this would, I am sure, be for him to come up to London and talk about it. Can you arrange this? If so, I shall very much look forward to meeting him because as I told you I think his novel is extremely promising and shows that he has an essential gift of vitality which can be welcomed but cannot be learned."

When Eyre & Spottiswoode are enthusiastic about a book I believe they can sell it as well as the next man, if not better, and their advertising is always pretty useful. I am much in favour of going ahead with them and shall look forward to hearing from you.

Yours sincerely,

Box 217, Folder 2 (DHA-HRC)
Pearn, Pollinger & Higham, Ltd. 39–40 Bedford Street
To Morris L. West, Cookham[86]
7 June 1956

Dear Morris,

When we spoke on the 'phone yesterday, I had not then seen your letter of the 4th to Jean [Leroy], but have now done so and I have discussed this with her.

I think at this stage of our association we ought to be quite clear about this sort of thing. What you are really asking us to do is act as a sort of form of public relation officers—whereas our job is to negotiate the rights in the work which our authors produce. I don't think either that you can accuse us of being "slow but sure"—at least so far as the "slow" part of it is concerned. I think within about 24 hours of your arrival we had arranged for you to see Grafton Green—in connexion, of course, with a specific subject—but I gather that in the event we had to withdraw the material we had submitted to him so that you could do something else with it. I think, too, that not everyone could have arranged for you to see Donald Wilson [of BBC Television] just for a general talk.

We should like to act for you, but we can only work in our way and if that way is not yours, then we had better mutually decide to call it a day here and now.

Perhaps you would like to come in and see Jean and myself to discuss this? But I thought at least I would outline my thoughts on paper first.

Yours,

Box 215, Folder 36 (DHA-HRC)
Pearn, Pollinger & Higham, Ltd. 76 Dean St.
To Dame Edith Sitwell, Sheffield[87]
18 September 1956

Dear Dame Edith,

I have been in touch with Peter du Sautoy of Faber about <u>Alexander Pope</u> and the Michigan enquiry and find that he is already in touch directly with them. According to the records which I looked up this is a book in which Faber still hold the English Language rights throughout the world.

Mr. du Sautoy promised to let me know as soon as he heard from Michigan with any definite proposal for publication over there and so as soon as we hear from him we will let you know what the proposal is.

With kind regards,

Yours sincerely,

Box 19, Folder 2 (McFarlin)
78 Addison Way
To Morchard Bishop, <u>John O'London's Weekly</u>
5 October 1956

Dear Morchard Bishop,

Thank you very much indeed for your long letter about the new novel. I value your criticism a great deal because you pay me the compliment of appraising it on the level at which I aim it—how few reviewers do that: indeed how few are capable of it. What you say about A Male Child reminds me of what you said about The Alien Sky and I'm not sure that there isn't a lesson here for me to learn. You may recall that you found the last novel over full—perhaps more with regard to action than to theme: but it seems to me that whatever faults there are must stem from a single fault. Pamela Hansford Johnson[88] in The Bookman remarks on my allusiveness, my blurring of edges: these may be symptoms of the malady you are diagnosing. But what is it? Obviously I must become aware of it in some inner way before I can do anything about it. I'm not sure I should get rid of the illness—supposing it to be an illness—merely by telling myself that the book is to be about such and such.

At an early stage it <u>was</u> to be a book about Alan Hurst. In fact I had to set myself what later appeared to be the impossible task of telling the story in the first person (Alan)—for I have always been interested in the "inarticulate man". Johnnie Sahib was one such. I am interested in the <u>range</u> of such a man's emotions; which, being unexpressed, sometimes appear lacking. I discarded the plan of first person narration (Alan) as it seemed too limiting: absurd, too, because such a man could not have narrated. Frankly, I compromised—as one always does—& then it seemed I had to come to an understanding of Alan through someone like Canning. At that point, I suppose, the thing caught fire because the differences between Canning & Hurst—& the similarities—were exciting. This, I think, led me to consider—pompous thought—the nature of a man's concern with his world & eventually to an attempt to express what it is that makes nonsense of atom bombs & the whole mummery of "Civilization's ended". So, in the end, when asked what the book was to be, or is, about—I would have said, "About why I dislike to think I shan't be alive in AD 2056!" Hole-in-the-ground and all.

But of course this takes me rather beyond the point. A Male Child, technically, was conceived almost in over-formal patterns—& it has been faulted (by the publisher!) for its coincidences & repetitions. I know I bit off more than I could chew, but I'm not at all sure that isn't going to be an ineradicable fault—or I <u>know</u> it is a fault. Even now, the book I had planned as a fairly simple story is leading towards complications & the answer seems to be with the fact that I don't get really <u>interested</u> until I've wound something up into a <u>mess</u>! I'm sure that one day I shall achieve the right sort of balance, discover a technique which creates an illusion of simplicity. At least I hope so. I hope I haven't bored you with all this—but I feel I have a sympathetic listener.

The thing I found honestly surprising is what you say about compulsive readability. Is this really so? Can you analyse it? You see, part of my trouble may be that in a desperate attempt to <u>make</u> a reader want to turn a page, I cram in too much. If you could break down what it is that actually compels the reader on I might be able to divert part of the effort into more useful channels.

I look forward so much to seeing you in the not too distant future. Please don't feel you have to reply to this until we meet, unless you feel compelled to do so!

And forgive my horrible handwriting.

With kind regards,

      Yours sincerely,

Box 266, Folder 5 (DHA-HRC)
Pearn, Pollinger & Higham, Ltd. 76 Dean St.
To Mrs. Elizabeth Nicholas
12 February 1957

My dear Elizabeth,

I have not been able to read all of <u>Death Be Not Proud</u> but what I did read excited me so much that I wanted to get it off to [Robert] Lusty right away and not hold on to it during the week when my reading time is severely limited.

I told him that I think you have a winner, and indeed I think you have. I think I shall reserve the full pleasure of reading until this is in the form a book can only properly be read—that is nicely printed on nice paper and between cloth boards.

Sincere congratulations.

Yours,

Box 291, Folder 41 (DHA-HRC)
Pearn, Pollinger & Higham, Ltd. 76 Dean St.
To Robert Lusty, Hutchinson & Co. Ltd.
12 February 1957

Dear Bob,

Elizabeth Nicholas

I have a very great deal of pleasure in sending you the carbon of her SOE[89] book, tentatively entitled <u>Death Be Not Proud</u> (taken from the quotation from Donne, which she asks me to give to you: "Death, be not proud, though some have called thee / Mighty and dreadful, for, thou art not so, / For those, whom thou think'st, though dost overthrow, / Die not, poor death".

This carbon is complete except for the final two or three chapters and as there is already about 105,000 words, the whole thing will probably be at least 110,000 words.

She did ask me to read this myself before sending it to you. I have not read it all but what I have read, both now and in the past, makes me confident she has a winner which is going to knock every other special operations book into a cocked hat.

I do hope you will agree, and that you will be putting up to me a truly magnificent offer.

Best wishes,

Yours,

Box 256, Folder 21 (DHA-HRC)
Pearn, Pollinger & Higham, Ltd. 76 Dean St.
To John Braine, Yorkshire
16 April 1957

Dear John,

Room at the Top—Foyles Book Club

As I told you in my last letter, I had to discuss the division of proceeds between yourself and Eyre & Spottiswoode over this book club deal.

During the last twelve months or so publishers have hardened in their view that the proceeds from such deals should be divided in equal proportions between themselves and the authors and more recently the Publishers' Association [P.A.] has urged members to arrange such a division, believing as they do that it is a fair and reasonable one.

I should explain that we, in common with most agents, have always done what we can to resist such a division in the view, for our part, that the author should get rather more than the publisher.

I have had the friendliest discussion with Maurice Temple Smith[90] about this and he does, of necessity, take the official P.A. view about the division. I told him, though, that in the next few weeks David Higham and another agent will be seeing the P.A. on behalf of a number of agents to put the agents' view and see whether they cannot persuade the P.A. to agree with it. We hope to get the P.A. to agree that a division of 60/40 in the author's favour should be considered as normal.

The way I have left it with Maurice is this—that we would agree to what they are asking for over Room at the Top, i.e., 50/50 subject to your approval and also subject to the possibility of re-negotiating the division in the light of any arrangement made with the P.A. in the next few weeks, which would give us grounds for a better division.

Would you let me know whether I may confirm to Eyre & Spottiswoode on these lines?

I should perhaps just add that publishers take the line—and Eyre & Spottiswoode strongly do so here—that they earn their 50% division through their publishing and promotional activities generally. Book Club rights are of course part of the exclusive volume rights and there is no question whatsoever but that they are entitled to a substantial share in any proceeds. As I say, though, we feel and always have felt, that it is the author's work, which is the more important contribution to the combined operation.

Best wishes.

Yours,

Box 251, Folder 4 (DHA-HRC)
Pearn, Pollinger & Higham, Ltd. 76 Dean St.
To Hamish Hamilton, Hamish Hamilton, Ltd.[91]
4 July 1957

My dear Hamish,

Elizabeth Nicholas

Many thanks for yours of 2nd July, enclosing copies of the long readers' reports, which I have read through, but not thoroughly digested.

In recent months I have a feeling I've stuck my neck out with you on several occasions about how much I or one of my readers have liked a particular book, only to find you thought it was a stinker, and this is why, when sending you Death Be Not Proud, I made no comment at all.

It is a book I've read in its entirety with the greatest possible admiration, and I can't pretend otherwise, now that you've come up with a rather different reaction.

I have a feeling that except for the question of style—which is a matter of personal taste and over which, in this case, I expect I'm odd man out—the general feeling is that this is an important book and one which should be published.

Let me refer to page 3 of the longer report, and take the reader's comments one by one.

Points 1 and 2: Prologue and Epilogue. There shouldn't be any difficulty here. At one time, the matter contained in these sections all appeared at the end, and the division into Prologue and Epilogue was rather my idea than the author's.

3. Style. The question of drastic blue-pencilling—qualifying classes, etc. Dealt with tactfully, I can't imagine the author objecting to criticisms, so long as these don't stem from a reader's own personal prejudices about style.

4. The seven different tracks and the confusion of the reader is an important point. What I don't think could be done is to do away with the present construction in favour of the sort of construction which would lead to a book containing, in essence, seven more-or-less unconnected narratives. I see the book as the story of a journey taken for a particular purpose, and the journey, and what prompted the journey is, for my money, the backbone of the book. Therefore, I see the present structure as essential to the overall design, but obviously something needs to be done if even one reader finds it difficult to understand, whether the information followed up is about Diana Rowden or Andree Borrell or about one of the others—or, of course, the following up of a clue in the general picture.

5. Verbosity. This particular reader is obviously the sort who likes the stripped phrase. Knowing my Elizabeth, she wouldn't see any reason why she shouldn't be allowed to say she rang up Gollancz to find out the whereabouts of Jean Overton Fuller, but say instead that she got in touch with Miss Fuller through her publishers.

6. Gush. Something of the personality of the author ought to come through a book like this. Whether that is a personality that would appeal to the majority is not easy to say. It is in Elizabeth's nature to say, "I had been delighted to get" instead of "I got", but there again, tact could overcome anything that was thought to be a blemish, I'm certain. Similarly, it is in her nature to say, "If a digression may be permitted", even if there has been no point but only digression. A solution—tactful suggestion of eliminating for the express purpose of reducing length!

7. Infuriating Phrases. Personal taste, I think.

General. It is a long book, and probably over-long. It is also a complex book, and obscurities should certainly be ironed out, but it is an interestingly personal book, and if any revisions proposed were to have the effect of pouring the author's work into a mould just not hers, then my guess is it would become just another SOE book, for which, frankly, I should have said there isn't much need. This very long letter, Hamish, is written on the, perhaps mistaken, assumption that you would very much like to publish the book, to publish it in the spirit in which it is written, and with the idea, therefore, of tipping you off—in the same confidence in which you wrote me—what I think would be the successful line to take in any discussions with Elizabeth.

If, after ploughing through this rigmarole (!) you'd like me to come along and have a chat, I'd be glad to do that. She'll be back in London any day now—and may be already, and will no doubt ring me presently to ask if I've heard from you.[92]

Best wishes,

Yours,

Box 12, Folder 16 (McFarlin)
78 Addison Way
From a letter to Miss Adèle Dogan,[93]
William Morrow & Company, USA
21 July 1957

Dear Adèle,

The Mark of the Warrior

The enclosed are NOT my solutions to the editorial queries. They are comments, which I send you for consideration, with the idea that the actual nature of your queries or suggestions may change. I think you'll see what I mean when you've waded through them!

The literals[94] I've dealt with, and the queries about the manoeuvres I'll deal with later, perhaps after you've helped me a little further with specific points.

With regard to the others, all I can say, for the moment, is that this is a very difficult novel to write and I think it important that you should now see exactly what I was trying to do. As you'll gather, this novel is really not at all about command or military matters, or the influence of one military mind upon another. It's simply saturated with nasty things like symbolism and is balanced upon the most delicate mechanism. I don't suggest that the symbolism must be apparent—save us from that!—and I fell over backwards to tell a story that a fairly average reader could enjoy for its own sake—but an amendment that, in the round, will give a wrong emphasis, will send the mechanism haywire (nearly spelt that with an Oxford accent), and make the whole thing a nonsense, from my point of view.

If you think I'm being difficult, please bear in mind that <u>never</u> has any publisher on either side of the Atlantic ever made the sort of comments that have sent me with large spade and bucket right back to the root source. You and your editors have done that, and I'm indebted, because now even I know what the damn book's about! And every day I learn a bit more about it.

The irksome point is the one about bringing Esther back. I struggled with that problem for weeks when I was coming to the end of the book, and now feel rather light headed about it. 9/10ths of me feels that the book <u>has</u> to end before they get to the far bank of the river, because the conclusion that the book reaches is a metaphysical one, indeed the reason for the book is all bound up with unpleasant things like God and what-have-you, and to go back to the bungalow-with-hunched-shoulders, and Esther, and Craig, is like ending the book in the basement of a tall tenement. The other tenth of me says you're right, in the name of Form, and Shape. But that tenth doesn't tell me the two parts of me are both talking about the same form and shape, and it even suggests that the form and shape of this novel would be put out of joint by Esther.

I'll stop now, and leave you to read the confession.

As ever,

...GENERAL EDITORIAL QUERIES[95]

Before I deal with these it's necessary for me to clarify what I'm up to in this book, and such a clarification is always difficult when one is cursed with a complex attitude to everything.

The book sprang from an exciting realisation that the truly great soldier is, when fully extended, emotionally involved with the terrain over which he fights. I say, "realisation", meaning, of course—interpretation—of signs, clues, evidence and personal intimations based on personal limitations.

Such a man, <u>in embryo</u>, is Ramsay, and it is in the end a condition of such a man that his emotional involvement with landscape—<u>heightened</u>

by the coincidence of physical conflict within it—should lead him to reject the society of other men.

But of course these are only symptoms—a particular variation of what might be called the general theme of the Search, whatever that may be—for proof of identity, of existence, of God, what you will—and this is what Ramsay is looking for, as unconsciously as Craig—only Craig looks for it in a corporate existence, his fellow men, Life, Esther, where Ramsay looks for it in himself. The Garden destruction. For the subconscious Ramsay, the act of destruction is a creative act, a stripping away of one more onion skin.

And so, ironically enough, Ramsay and Craig have aims in common. It is their separate ways of looking which produce the conflict, their ignorance of the fact that they are looking which produces the tragedy, their misinterpretation of each other's acts and motives which produces the book.

Since the book deals, from a narrative point of view, with misinterpretations, I found the only effective technique to adopt was that of alternating narratives each seen strictly as at the time through the eyes of one man only. The problem was of course how to provide the reader with the sort of view that would give a general focus. I suspect that many of your general editorial queries can be traced to a failure on that score.

Now let's take the queries:

page 113: "Craig watches the thing you haven't found yet". You say this gives an aura of mystery and wish there were another way of expressing "the thing". Also, you say, hasn't their estimate of each other changed at this point?

The section in which this query arises is a Ramsay section. He only communicates to us what he thinks and feels. He knows that Craig is watching him and he tells us here that he believes Craig must have a special reason for doing so. Not just because he is "a clever boy". Ramsay has passed that point. "Craig is watching the thing you haven't found yet, but will find because it is near to you and Craig sees that it is near to you ... this is what he is waiting for. You are both waiting for it".

Ramsay is telling us everything that he knows or feels at this point. In doing so he communicates to us something about Craig and himself.

What he communicates about himself is that he feels himself on the verge of a discovery, something that (should tie) ties up with: "He looked at this loneliness closely and found that it was one of the things he wanted" (page 112)—that ties up with his wish to go into the jungle (page 111) and the fact that there is a secret feeling about this wish. (Quote: He had locked these things away from Lawson: page 111.)

What does he communicate about Craig's motives for watching him? It's necessary that the reader here should be a step ahead of Ramsay. We ought to know what Craig is waiting for, or watching for, in Ramsay. My intention was that the reader would know Craig was watching him for the mark on him, signs that Ramsay was becoming aware of his killer instinct. We are supposed to know, without any real doubt, that this is the secret into which Ramsay is about to let himself, the instinct just around the corner.

Your second point: Hasn't their estimate of each other changed at this point. Craig's estimate of Ramsay has certainly changed in that it has developed. Ramsay is not much interested in Craig, mainly in himself. Already he is sloughing off an interest in his fellows. His interest in Craig is an interest in Craig's interest in him.

Do you mean that page 113 gives an impression of some reversal of relationship? The relationship at this point is simply that for Craig, Ramsay has developed from the young (possibly dangerous?) brother of John (feelings of guilt, fear, inferiority) to the killer-in-the-making (best kind of soldier, what a soldier should be). Ramsay, on the other hand, sees Craig not as the C.O. and ex-co of elder brother (awkward relationship) but as a too-kind commander, with certain failings but an odd, concentrated interest in him, which is both companion to, and stimulator of his own intimations of—power? immortality? The jungle has the answer?

Page 137. Here because he is in the forest and unaware of having found anything, he asks himself, "What was that thing. Had he found it?" But we, the reader, have seen him find something akin to the thing we expected him to find because Craig expected it—an almost supernatural understanding of the forest—(a first-hand account of what we only saw Craig and Esther watch at work in Thompson). We've also seen what Craig would call the killer instinct, at work—the sudden need of a weapon. If we're not satisfied that this is, after all, a killer instinct, then that is actually as it should be. Ramsay doesn't feel like Craig would imagine [what] a killer felt. Craig's imagination has dramatised the warrior's instinct. In Ramsay we see a sense of creativeness about it, a "one with nature" awareness, in spite of the reprehensible (?) need to be armed—and, most important, we see: "There was" (as Craig is seen down on the road) "an inescapable burden of heat" (the physical world of men again) "of heat and, unexpectedly, <u>contempt</u>".

Ramsay, one step further in his kind of search, already feels superior, as a man, to Craig. In this section our own contempt for the "killer" instinct is mingled with a certain sympathy for it, as it works in Ramsay.

Should Ramsay be shown as more aware of having "found" something? What I was afraid of doing was vitiating the picture of a born instinct at last released. I didn't think Ramsay would be "aware" of the release of the instinct, only observe it at work in himself and feel— what, stronger? Happier? Released? He would I think observe the effect without questioning the cause. If he doesn't question the cause and only observes the effect, as a natural effect, he wouldn't be aware of <u>finding</u> anything. Right? Wrong?

Page 148, line 2. The crisis

We're seeing it through Craig's eyes now. "You did finish him off, didn't you?" Ramsay says. The answer should have been "No". If at this point, Craig was honest with Bob Ramsay and with himself, if he had told the truth, wasn't there a chance that Ramsay would have been moved to an understanding of Craig's sort of person? He's very young still, he is capable of reacting to warmth and love, of the process of fear.

But at this moment Craig is determined that Ramsay shall <u>be</u> a killer. He doesn't appreciate at this stage <u>why</u> he wants Ramsay to be a killer—that comes later on pages 202/203/204. I doubt if he really appreciates that he <u>is</u> determined young Ramsay shall be a killer and take the place of John, who died and left him alone in the forest to cope by himself. If Craig really saw what he was up to—creating a destructive, indestructible force, which would provide safety for those the force directed—creating an inhuman (in Craig's terms) man, then Craig, being Craig, would surely draw back and tell the truth: No, I didn't finish him off.

As it is, he is aware of crisis without quite knowing what that crisis is, and so he passes the ball back to Ramsay. He is sufficiently (in himself) aware that to say "Yes, I killed John" would be untruthfully unkind, and similarly aware that to say No, truthfully, would join himself and Ramsay into a human understanding. In passing the ball back to Ramsay he shirks responsibility and, within the terms of his scheme is un...

Page 149 ...rewarded, as he thinks, by Ramsay's "dangerous anger" which he misinterprets because, here, Ramsay is angry on behalf of his brother. Craig has missed the opportunity of exploring, with Ramsay, the ramifications of Ramsay's belief that he, Ramsay, would have finished John off, to put him out of pain. This younger Ramsay is not a killer, but a man who thinks he would have ended another man's suffering (the killer instinct, all the same, just glimmers through in the subsidiary thought: because he was going to die anyway). And, on the next page, Ramsay has become angry and determined to know what happened—to another man. He is involved, like Craig, in humanity. But Craig misses it. Does the reader?

Page 151. In Ramsay (6)[96] which follows we see almost the last of Ramsay the man, the human being. It is a kind of Threnody. "He would leave something behind him forever. He did not know what it was. In a way it was connected with John, with all of the past".

Meaning, childhood, happiness, human grace. But Ramsay wouldn't consciously know what he was leaving behind (just as, I think, he wouldn't consciously know or recognize the reverse instinct which had manifested itself in the forest). Craig's treatment of him, a negative treatment and one which springs from the un-Craig like savagery which is in Craig, has the effect of hastening the process of Ramsay turned killer and ousting the childlike Ramsay. Ramsay feels something draining from him. I hoped intimations of what it was would reach the reader, even although we can only see it through Ramsay's mind.

So the whole point about Ramsay in this section is that even at the moment he finds himself one with the forest and on the first rung of the ladder by which he'll opt out of humanity and continue the common search in an uncommon way, he is still young enough to have been what Craig and the reader and (part of) the author would call "saved". Here it is [that we] should first turn and find Ramsay waiting for us. Later we can, like Craig, only look up and find that we are waiting for Ramsay, that he has cut himself off from us and will never come back.

That's what's in store for Craig, but for the moment, Craig has crossed the river and we only hear his voice, "Come on, Ramsay"....

Page 224. Should Ramsay <u>ask</u> for help? Perhaps. He does in a way. "Do you disapprove?" This is the <u>second</u>, and the <u>last</u> time Ramsay "waits for us" and he does so because at last he contemplates active inhumanity towards a particular person, Baksh. I think (thought, that is) that if page 149–151 is clear, page 244 is clear enough, and that any clarification now must be in the early pages, so that page 224 is a hard echo. You see Ramsay just isn't going to ask for help. He knows, militarily, that he's justified in doing what he proposes to Baksh. Humanly, aware of Craig as a different sort of person, the more usual type of person, he understands also that Baksh is a person. What would Craig's sort of person think of the plan to make Baksh suffer. Do you disapprove? And again Craig who now, page 202/4, understands the nature of what he's doing to Ramsay, reacts negatively, allowing the stronger instinct of Ramsay to continue in power.

CRAIG IS A SELF-APPOINTED CATALYST IN THE DEVELOP-MENT (OR DEGENERATION) OF RAMSAY, MAN, TO RAMSAY, SAFETY MACHINE....

Queries, Pages 229, 241–2, 264, 265, 268, 319–20.
These queries all relate to the Craig-Ramsay relationship and their solution rests almost wholly on earlier clarification, I expect. I'd prefer

to concentrate, for the moment, on arriving at a satisfactory clarification of the foundations of the relationship. The conflict between Craig and Ramsay—and perhaps in view of all the foregoing it will be seen that I'm right—is NOT over by page 229. The catalyst has worked, but Craig isn't sure it has. He won't know until he's seen Ramsay at work in the jungle, actually watching Baksh suffer, which is why, on the morning he goes off in the rain, into the forest, to start the march he says, "He is the quarry and I the hunter". When it comes to it, on page 283, he, after all, is not a hunter. He delivers himself, along with the others, into the hands of the man who had become, in his eyes, "the sum of their separate longing to survive in the dark, green, drowned world". Thereafter we see Craig but twice more—in the ravine where the dream reaches its conclusion. Where we see that even within the machine of safety he has helped to create his fear and uncertainly remain, along with his human desire to have Ramsay as a companion in the forest, a desire sharpened because it is too late now, where once it might have been possible. Here, at last, he sees the nature of the past crises, which are crises no longer, simply because they are gone. And the last Craig section shows him misinterpreting Ramsay's death which for him, Craig, is a tragedy of life. He cannot understand that Ramsay has found the thing they have both been looking for and Craig, still not having found it, is sorry for him. The "end" for Ramsay we saw through Ramsay's eyes. "He entered peacefully into the world which was himself, the world he had looked for and which, at the end, he knew no man could enter until the end".

But poor Craig! He is still committed to his compromise. "It is only given us to live and we cannot live except in each other". All that Craig has learned is, given the premise of living only in each other, it is not permitted to destroy others in order to survive oneself.

But Ramsay learned something, too, just before he died. He learned, in effect, that, living, it was not possible to be alone. Once in the jungle Ramsay wanted to be alone, until he conceived the image of himself as a powerful centre to a complex pattern, which would move where his heart and instinct dictated. The river destroyed that image. The reason why Ramsay finds the image distorted is simply the sight of the men, who composed the image, at the mercy of something inhuman, the river, the river-god if you like, and struggling against it with their individual human weaknesses. "It was not men he went to save" we are told when he jumps to his death, but the separate components of the whole image of himself. Ramsay is made at this point.

- - - - - - - - -

I thought, originally, long and hard about a reappearance of Esther and finally rejected it because so long as we know that Craig thinks he has reached an understanding with himself, we should also know that things will be all right for Esther. Their love for each other is deep, and, on her side, telepathically understanding.

I wonder whether the felt need for Esther at the end is because the whole nature of the Craig-Ramsay relationship is not—apparently—wholly and successfully communicated?[97]

Box 268, Folder 32 (DHA-HRC)
Pearn, Pollinger & Higham, Ltd. 76 Dean St.
To Mrs. Muriel Spark,[98] Camberwell
11 October 1957

My dear Muriel,

Just to acknowledge the safe receipt of <u>Memento Mori</u>. I'll read these chapters as soon as I can and then talk to Alan MacLean.[99] Actually, I'm due to lunch with him on October 19th.

I've had a word with Jean [Leroy] about your previous letter in which you said you thought it would be better if you continued to handle stories and radio pieces yourself.

Both Jean and I hope very much that you will let us continue, because although, as you say yourself, the market for works of literary criticism is limited, it is not at all an embarrassment to us to deal in that market.

I think you must have misunderstood Jean about the radio play, which Ober has indeed been asked to offer for radio performance, but not for publication.

I'll look forward to hearing from you, and hope it will be to say please carry on.

Yours,

Box 4, Folder 7 (McFarlin)
78 Addison Way
To John Bright-Holmes, Eyre & Spottiswoode Ltd.[100]
3 February 1958

PRIVATE AND CONFIDENTIAL

Dear John,

This bit is separate and marked confidential so that it needn't go on the file or pass through office trays, etc.

The burden of it is that I'm pretty depressed in general and have an awful defeatist attitude towards <u>Mark of the Warrior,</u> which the sensible side of me insists is quite unwarranted. I feel so much that I want a stroke of luck at this stage, to get me over the hump and save me from becoming yet another author who gets patted on the head by leading reviewers.

How have the travellers[101] reacted to it? Have they forgotten <u>A Male Child</u>? The unreasonable side of me has never quite forgiven poor, sweet Frank [Morley] for giving that book the kiss of death at the top, right from the start while, all the time, it was my best book and the first that really made the important critics take a bit of notice.

Forgive me if I'm making you a shoulder to weep on; I don't think I've ever done it before, if only because I've never had time to take off from being a permanent wailing wall for other authors.

I forgot to say on the phone this afternoon how pleased I was about the full page in <u>The Bookseller</u>: very gratifying to vanity and very effective. The trouble is of course that my gratification at this sort of thing is always soured by sly remarks that, as an agent, I get favoured treatment. Even as well-meant jokes (and sometimes not so well meant) this sort of remark palls. It all adds to my depression.

For instance, with perhaps two exceptions, the list in the other letter is full of names of people about whom I'm in two minds because I believe they might be in two minds about me.[102] If I were merely PS, author, I'd have no hesitation about writing to Pamela H. J. personally, or Walter Allen (whom I can't approach because he's a PP&H author). I'm uncertain particularly about John Davenport, because David [Higham] more or less is to act or has acted for him. Peter G[reen] is the one name (other than R[osaleen] Whately) about which I have no qualms. It's mainly, I supposed, that I imagine these people are slightly on the defensive, professionally because I'm an agent, and therefore not a thoroughly seriously intending novelist. Oh well, what the hell!

I started a new book on January the first, and I think it is going to be IT.[103] I have never felt more seriously intentioned in my life about novel writing and of course you and I know that if the Warrior is the flop of the decade it won't in the end make any difference to my confidence in what I'm doing now. The new one is going to be long—long because it can be supported in the narrative at length, and only at length wholly effectively.

Now I am going to take you into my confidence, John. Please show this letter to Maurice [Temple Smith], but I shouldn't want either of you to say a word to anyone either inside or outside the firm, nor to anyone in PP&H. I have mentioned this only to a couple of very close personal friends. (Incidentally, Maurice, I'm addressing this letter to John because I'm already writing to him about official matters, but it concerns you, as editor, even more than it concerns John.)

The confidential matter is this—that I realise quite clearly that in the not too distant future I shall have to withdraw, perhaps only gradually at first, from agency. The two jobs become increasingly difficult to combine. I think I know in my bones that I'm going to make it as a writer, and I must have time to be one. I can't at the moment afford to be one, as you well know, and in any case I have fairly acute responsibilities to my colleagues and to the authors whom I personally represent. But be one I must be and be one I shall, full time, professional. If I've not had a biggish success by the time I give up agency it will make no difference. I shall try to arrange some guaranteed income plan (such as I'm doing from time to time for other young authors) either with my British or American end, or failing that I should freelance as reader-cum-lit adviser. Tough no doubt, but—quite essential. It seems to me now that there's no use in playing at it, trying to get the best of both worlds. I'm not an academic chap, I can't even do a simple translation, there are no plums or sinecures for me to latch on to that are complementary to my "original creative" work. I simply know about novels, and mean to know more. I shan't mind reading other people's to earn money because if people pay me to read and report on novels they'll be doing so because I know about them. If agency were simply reading and knowing about novels I'd be as happy as a sand boy, perhaps, but of course it isn't.

I'm sorry to write so long a letter, John and Maurice, and in the end it comes to very little. One gets so pent up with these things, though, and there are so few people one can talk to about them. It seemed both sensible and fair for me to tell my publishers what is going on in my mind, and I know you'll keep my confidence.

The new novel has a long working title: <u>Portraits from a Chinese Love Pavilion</u>, which will probably be shortened for publication to <u>The Chinese Love Pavilion</u>. It is set in Malaya, a background I know personally but have kept from using until I knew exactly what I wanted to use it for; time, just post war, 1945, autumn. There'll be quite a lot of characters, including Madame Chin, Madame Cha, and Madame Ho (Chin Cha Ho is Chinese for Very very good) who are the inhabitants of the Love Pavilion. Main male character is Tom Freshwater, an army observer (public relations in close liaison with intelligence) attached to the HQ of an Infantry company in the garden of whose mess is the Love Pavilion where the ladies are installed. Freshwater's job is to "observe" their job of trying to track down the bands of Chinese guerrillas who are gradually turning bandit (intimidating and slaying Chinese who collaborated)—but he is also there to find out what's happened to a man called Saxby who was left behind in Malaya to indulge in the sort of cloak and dagger operations people like Spencer Chapman were mixed up in. Saxby, of course, has decided to disappear and join the guerrillas-cum-bandits. The other central male character is a young man of 19 who has missed the shooting war, deems it eventually, because of merciless ragging, a bitter loss. He began as a man of joy, the luckiest chap alive to get out to Malaya. In general the idea is to show in opposition the two worlds, the Malaya of the young man (who was really born too late, for he's a potential empire builder in a crumbling empire) and the shagged out eccentric round the bend Malaya of men who'd been in uniform for 6 years. Freshwater is typical of shagged out Malaya. He (like me as an agent!) has come to believe he doesn't really exist spiritually, but is a sort of sympathetic receiving apparatus through which men who still believe they exist explore the mystery of their souls. Freshwater has always rather hoped to be explored by a man of joy because he experiences vicariously the emotions of men who "explore" him. The young man and Madame Ho jointly heal Freshwater; but the young man, thrown into this particular shagged out world, can only react by running amok in true Malayan fashion.

That's it, roughly!

                                             Ever yours,

Box 315, Folder 17 (DHA-HRC)
Pearn, Pollinger & Higham, Ltd. 76 Dean St.
To Miss Kay Collier [Kay Dick][104]
6 February 1958

My dear Kay,

                            Solitaire
As you know, I told Dwye Evans of Heinemann what my personal reaction to this book was and how excited I was about it. He replied saying that he indeed agreed with me, but that it all depended on what the critics said and that what they must do is "hope" for a succes d'estime.

This is all excellent so far as it goes, but I do worry about the possibility of it not going far enough. Sometimes, you know, it is just that much too late in the day if things are left on the basis of "hoping" for a succes d'estime. One has seen it happen before. The critics over a period, after publication, acclaim the book, but if it is not also a book that the trade have become excited about, sales do not necessarily measure up.

What I feel pretty strongly is that at the very early stage something should happen to make the people at Heinemann stop saying, "we must hope for a succes d'estime" and say instead, "we are going to have one, let's try and make the sales measure up".

You see, if at the top—starting from Dwye—the word goes round that it is a brilliant book but terribly difficult to sell, and that of course the travellers will not understand it, a defeatist attitude to the sales situation is already established. Although I know you told me that Dwye said he thought my judgment was sound, the right sort of effect is certainly not created by Dwye being able to say that the author's agent thinks it is a brilliant book!

I am, in general, mostly in favour of letting a book find its own level, but every so often there comes the sort of book which, the trade being what it is, is often denied an opportunity of finding that level. The trade continues to underestimate the public intelligence and there seems to me to be far too much of this attitude amongst publishers—"of course, we understand it, but very few readers will".

What I want to suggest to you, Kay, although I quite understand and appreciate your reluctance to do this sort of thing, is to ask someone recognised as a critic of standing, who also commands the attention of the public at large, to read the book in manuscript and, if he or she reacts to it in the way I would expect, to say something explosive about it that could be used on publication as what we all call a "puff".[105] But—and far more importantly—something that could be used to make the people at the top at Heinemann start treating the book within the house as something pretty special. I am sure you can imagine the difference between a sales conference which travellers attend, at which Dwye says, "This is a brilliant book but is going to be difficult to sell" and such a conference at which Dwye is able to say, "This is a brilliant book and so-and-so says so". Do you see what I mean?

I do hope so. If so, put your thinking cap on and consider whom you might approach.

Best wishes,

Yours,

Box 312, Folder 31A (DHA-HRC)
Pearn, Pollinger & Higham, Ltd. 76 Dean St.
To Ivan von Auw, Harold Ober Associates, USA
26 February 1958

My dear Ivan,

Morrow are publishing The Mark of the Warrior on March 5th, I know, and I wonder whether you would do something for me? I would like to send a bottle of Scotch to Thayer [Hobson][106] so that he and all his colleagues can drink and bless our enterprise. In addition to that, I would also like to send two small posies of flowers to Adèle and Frances just as a token of my personal esteem. Do you think you could possibly arrange for that and charge the cost to me? The cost could be deducted from the next part of the advance that Morrow will be paying when I "demand" it.

I hope this is not a bother for you but I do feel very indebted to all the Morrow people who have been so kind and helpful.

Yours,

Box 19, Folder 20 (McFarlin)
78 Addison Way
To The Editor, The Times Literary Supplement
15 March 1958

Sir,

A slight error made by your reviewer in his review of my novel, The Mark of the Warrior, gives me the opportunity of begging space in your columns to bring to your readers' notice the volume of staff work in which the novelist must now engage by virtue of a recent judgment in an action for libel.

According to that judgment we are apparently under an obligation to check the names of our characters with the names in professional directories and similar sources. At the time of the judgment I went on record as saying that I should resolutely refuse to become involved in such a (to me) absurd chore: indeed, I deprecated the increasingly bad habit real people have of using the same names and following the same occupations as characters in books. Libel, it seemed to me, was libel and coincidence was coincidence.

Unfortunately, the matter does not rest with the author and his conscience: publishers and printers have to be considered. When my publishers severely but justly explained the financial consequences of my resolution, it had of necessity to fade.

The Mark of the Warrior is set in an imaginary OTS (the Indian name for OCTU)[107] somewhere in India. The characters are officers on the staff and cadets under training. The professional directories relevant to this case were the Army List, the Indian Army List and the confidential files of the officers concerned. One had not only to check the name but to check in what period of what year an office trained as cadet or was appointed to the training staff of a school. There were several near misses and one amusing coincidence, which mean changing the name of the imaginary commandant. I was not, of course, allowed myself to look at the confidential files. Instead, a somewhat puzzled but never less than cooperative official of the CRO spent musty hours with me in a sad, dark room crammed with nostalgically coloured papers. Eventually we felt that all that could be done had been done and he walked a little way home with me, past the statue of Clive.

And now your reviewer says my novel is set in "of all places, Poona". Further down he refers to "the OCTU". To my recollection there was indeed an OTS (or OCTU) at Poona, but Poona was a place at which my draft of cadets only changed trains, to continue their journey by narrow gauge railway "to the east and then to the northeast, for a day, a night and part of the next day". And this was a journey calculated to take them deep into the heart of my imagination, far, far from the scorching land of unintentional libel.

If there was (and I'm sure there was but don't propose to "check" this too) an OTS at Poona, will officers who taught or trained there please note?

Yours,

Box 258, Folder 17 (DHA-HRC)
Pearn, Pollinger & Higham, Ltd. 76 Dean St.
To Ivan von Auw, Harold Ober Associates, USA
25 April 1958

[Memo]

<u>Solitaire</u>

You haven't heard of Kay Dick before from us and, although she's published several novels with Heinemann, she's never sold in America.

She's a very old personal friend of mine and she came to us recently with this new novel, which I think very highly of indeed.

Paul Brooks of Houghton Mifflin declined it and then I showed the manuscript to Harry Brague.[108] At first, Harry returned it to me, though very reluctantly, saying he felt he was probably doing the wrong thing. Then a few days later he met Kay with Pamela Hansford Johnson and, without realising who she was, seemed to take a great shine to her. So much so that when he realised she was the author of <u>Solitaire,</u> he asked to have another look at it.

He's bringing back with him the spare corrected carbon typescript and fixed with me yesterday on the phone that he would buy an option for $200 and during this next six weeks will come to a decision in New York. No other terms were discussed so could you link up with him right away and make the formal arrangements for the option?

Dear Kay is always desperately short of money and actually this option money comes as something of a godsend at the moment, so do you think you could rush it through?

I think presently I shall be sending you an outline of the next book she's working on which should, from both Heinemann's and Scribner's point of view, be a much more marketable proposition. I thought it would not be a bad thing for all the people of Scribner's to see more exactly what is going to happen in the future. I do hope that they take their option up.

If you would just drop me a line as soon as the option thing is fixed, then we shall probably advance Kay some of the money.

Box 17, Folder 12 (McFarlin)
78 Addison Way
To Clive Sansom, Tasmania
22 June 1958

My Dear Clive,

I was delighted to get your letter of the 12th about <u>The Mark of the Warrior</u>, and to know that you liked the book; in particular to know that you liked Esther and the relationship between her and Craig. In many ways Esther is based on Penny—and that is not to suppose that Craig is based on myself—but the relationship between them is, as you say, concerned with the less spectacular but continuing aspects of marriage, and my understanding of these is gathered from knowledge and appreciation of Penny. I'm not sure she's seen this yet, probably not. I shan't tell her!

No one has quite seen yet (I think) that I personally do not believe in the myth of the warrior, or at least in the myth Craig builds for himself. I think there are such men as the older Ramsay, and such men as the younger Ramsay was becoming, but I don't think, as Craig thought, that they are in the forest to kill. The reason for the alternating sequences seen individually and entirely through the particular eyes of Ramsay or Craig was to avoid author-identification—and of course the argument, if looked at again when the book has been finished, is another clue. In the broadest, simplest terms, Craig and Ramsay were both looking for God, but in different ways. Ramsay, without knowing it, looked for God in himself. In himself he only wanted to be alone in the Garden (the forest) and subconsciously the appearance there of another man was almost a challenge because there was only room for himself and God, or for God in himself. Another man therefore became an enemy of the relationship. Ramsay never <u>knows</u> any of this. He's too young. The divine spark prompts him to aggression. But at the end, the author allows the reader a peep through the natural curtain into the supernatural—and this is the final clue—"But my image is not destroyed after all, I've won, I've beaten Blake". Ramsay-alive never knew this. Craig will never know it.

Poor Craig looks for proof of existence or of God in the general human condition. Other people, living, are proof of God's hand. The Ramsay image is the devil image, almost; certainly a potential sacrifice. Ramsay and Craig both look for God in the garden, and Craig kills Ramsay and Ramsay comes near to killing Craig (spiritually) because neither can see that their search is a common search.

Anyway, that is the urge behind the book, but I do try hard to tell these things against the simplest possible background—in the form of a story that can be enjoyed for itself. I was pleased that the "my right arm is a platoon of men" imagery made its impact. Whatever I do or don't believe about Craig-type warriors, I do feel strongly that great soldiers are moved poetically by their physical situation, and that the truly great soldier only comes to the full extent of his power when he is emotionally concerned with the terrain over which he fights. This is an emotionalism even the lower rank soldier can share in; it explains the desert and jungle myth. No soldier was ever emotionally concerned, in the military sense I mean, with the French or German countryside; the alien ground was necessary. The simplest soldier was moved by dawn over the western desert; and in the jungle, God, I think, was always nearer than the enemy. Or Satan.

I'm now engaged on a very long novel under the title The Chinese Love Pavilion, and this is set in Malaya after the close of the last war. Somehow I'm getting known as a war-novelist, which is hardly fair! Out of four novels only two have been about soldiers. This fifth will also be about soldiers and will attempt to say everything I now want to say about soldiers—not because they are soldiers but because all the things that happened [in] 1939–45 are my keys to what is happening now. And I don't mean in the obvious political sense. After The Love Pavilion, which in the main treats of the degeneration of a youthful, untried Man of Joy, who missed the shooting war, in the company of long-service soldiers who are all round the bend (which we all were in Malaya in 1945–46), then I shall embark on all the novels I want to write about present day society. I expect the title of the first will be "An Able Young Man" and will fall into two parts, a) The Swan, b) The Ugly Duckling—because all able young men move downwards in the scale and reverse the fable. Another possible title is "The Careerists". Self-explanatory!

May I live so long.

Many thanks again, Clive. I am most grateful to you. The Paignton Days[109] are not so long ago. They are always with us.

My love and Penny's love (and yes she says she is proud of the book) to you and Ruth.

Box 319, Folder 12 (DHA-HRC)
David Higham Associates, 76 Dean St.[110]
To George Weidenfeld, Weidenfeld & Nicolson Ltd.[111]
19 September 1958

Dear George,

Would you be interested in a project that Herbert van Thal[112] and I more or less thought up together?

The idea is to collect together, say, up to a dozen of the younger novelists to retell in their own way up to a dozen of the traditional fairy stories. By in their own way, I mean bringing to bear on a particular story all their own novelist equipment, using either the original historical background or even dressing them up modern, although the latter would not be my personal choice of method.

The title of the book would be <u>The Sugar Plum Book</u> with Bertie [Herbert van Thal] acting as Editor.

The following people have already agreed in principle to contribute and I think two other very likely contributors would be Kathleen Farrell and Kay Dick:[113]

Gabriel Fielding	Roland Gant
Peter Green	Gerald Hanley
Nadia Legrand	Wolf Mankowitz
Lalage Pulvertaft	Muriel Spark
Paul Scott	

The idea would be I think for a British publisher to control volume rights throughout the world, paying in advance on a scale of royalties for his own edition, which would be divided amongst the contributors and the Editor and retaining something like 10% to 15% of the proceeds from the sale of the book to America or abroad.

I look forward to hearing from you.[114]

Yours,

Box 317, Folder 3 (DHA-HRC)
David Higham Associates, 76 Dean St.
To P. H. Hebdon, Michael Joseph Ltd.[115]
14 October 1958

Dear Peter,

<u>One Can Play</u>—Elizabeth Avery[116]

Many thanks for your letter of the 9th. My wife has decided after very careful thought—and also after receiving another opinion—not to make any of the small amendments that D. M.[117] suggested in her report.

As you may know, Roland [Gant] sent us a copy of that report. Actually the outside opinion is that of Peter Green, who, hearing that she had written the book, particularly asked to see it, and has said some very flattering things.

So I now enclose a list of what really amount to literal corrections together with a dedication page—and of course a note of the new title.[118]

I think Roland liked the new title, but you might like to check with him.

I am also returning to you the draft blurb Roland sent us. You already have the draft blurb that we prepared. Actually we do rather prefer the first part of our own, but the sentences in Roland's which we have underlined could, I think, with advantage be worked into the other, that is if you agree.

Do let me know if you have any further queries, or anything further you want Penny to do.

Yours,

Box 318, Folder 7 (DHA-HRC)
David Higham Associates, 76 Dean St.
To Elizabeth Nicholas
21 October 1958

My dear Elizabeth,

I am sure our telephone conversation left you with the impression that I had failed to support you at exactly the wrong moment. I can't revise, at distance as it were, my original reaction to Collier's piece, but I had no idea you would be so angry.

I suppose, myself, dismissing it, I had thought you would do so, too. But you hadn't, and since you are still angry forty-eight hours afterwards, I am sure the answer is to write the letter you have in mind and see what happens.

I told you long ago, that in my opinion it was just about the best book I had read dealing with the last War. I still think so, but obviously the Establishment never will. It might, however, be both interesting and amusing to invite them to explain themselves.

Yours ever,

Box 311, Folder 12 (DHA-HRC)
David Higham Associates, Ltd. 76 Dean St.
To Miss Adèle Dogan, William Morrow, USA
6 December 1958

My dear Adèle,

Thanks you so much for your letter of December 1st. I heard yesterday from Ivan [von Auw] about <u>One Can Play,</u> and at once wrote to John.

Penny was most interested in what you all say about the book and indeed thinks she couldn't have been rejected more kindly. Naturally we hope we will be able to find an American home for her, but we do more than appreciate the difficulties for this sort of book on your side. But Penny, who still doesn't really think of herself as a novelist, believes on the whole that it has all happened to somebody else, is continually grateful for the nice things that people—and in particular yourselves—are saying.

I do hope you have a tremendous success with <u>Eight Days</u>. I am sad that so far it hasn't had a truly stunning review. It is a fine book that goes on pressing on you months after you have first read it—at least that is what I have found.

As for myself, I have been badly held up this year, what with one thing and another, but I don't think it is going to be too long before you see a new manuscript [*The Chinese Love Pavilion*]—late spring or early summer, I sincerely hope.

All best wishes,

Ever yours,

Box 403, Folder 6 (DHA-HRC)
David Higham Associates, Ltd. 76 Dean St.
To A. Dwye Evans, William Heinemann Ltd.
5 February 1959

Dear Dwye,

Neither Kay [Dick] nor I have heard how <u>Solitaire</u> has gone since publication, but we hope the news is encouraging. It seemed to be one of the most noticed books over Christmas, and I hope this had some effect in the bookshops.

I am enclosing a somewhat revised version of the very impressive outline Kay did—and a copy of which you saw a little while ago—about the series of novels she has now embarked on, and I am doing this because we are very anxious to make practical arrangements about Kay's future.

I don't know whether you have heard—probably you have—that after all this time Kay and Kathleen [Farrell][119] are parting company. This will take place as soon as Kay has been able to find a suitable flat in Hampstead. This new domestic arrangement, as I am sure you will appreciate, makes Kay's position even less secure than it has been in the past. We are doing as much as we can in the various directions open to us—for instance, we have managed to get her a commission to do one of the books in Hamish Hamilton's series—in Kay's case, <u>Six Great Diarists</u>—and, as she told you a little while ago, she is also at work on an extended version of the piece she did about <u>Pierrot</u> for Hutchinson's "Saturday Book".

There has been progress on the novel <u>Sunday</u>—for which some while ago you made a general payment of £75, and as you will have gathered from the outline the whole book has been planned in some detail—as indeed have some of the subsequent books.

She has not, naturally, been able to do much in the last month, for the private reasons mentioned above, but she desperately wants to get back to work as soon as she is settled, and this series of novels is her major concern. I know that when you paid the £75, you made it pretty clear that nothing else could be done, unless <u>Solitaire</u> did very well, and that indeed it was partly the realisation that there seemed little hope of getting any further finance from Heinemann that finally persuaded us to fix the <u>Pierrot</u> thing with Hutchinson, although of course it was already in their house, so to speak, and they made all the running.

However, I do hope very much that we can now make some long-term arrangement.... I mainly have in mind the possibility of monthly payments over a year....

I do hope, very much indeed, Dwye, that everybody at Heinemann will feel ready to take a long-term view of it. When you have thought about it and had the necessary discussions, perhaps we can meet for lunch?[120]

Ever yours,

Box 405, Folder 5 (DHA-HRC)
David Higham Associates, Ltd. 76 Dean St.
To Mrs. Mary Patchett
3 June 1959

Dear Mary,

Under separate cover I'm returning to you the two copies of <u>The Singing String</u>. And first of all I must apologise for the long time I have kept you waiting.

I must admit, though, that I found the going extremely difficult because of the tremendous number of pencil corrections. They do not look bad at first glance but they certainly held me up considerably.

The total impression I have, therefore, isn't an entirely satisfactory one because I feel as though I have read the book wearing dark glasses, if you see what I mean. On the other hand, what penetrated the dark glasses was rather appealing and on the whole I think you have probably pulled it off. If I have one complaint, as it were, it's that the building of the overland telegraphy really seems to play no real part in the story at all, but to be simply vague background to a romantic story set in the Australia of that time. Why don't we have a chat about it? When you are ready give me a ring and come and have a cup of tea.

Love,

Box 403, Folder 20 (DHA-HRC)
David Higham Associates, Ltd. 76 Dean St.
To P. H. Hebdon, Michael Joseph Ltd.
11 June 1959

Dear Peter,

Here signed by Penny is the agreement for <u>The Marigold Summer</u>—which she was delighted to have. We'll look forward to receiving the amount due on signature (you bet!)

Incidentally, Penny is going with me to this Writers' Summer School in Derby where I've got to give a talk. They have a Book Room where the books written by lecturers are on sale and this would apparently be the first time the wife of a lecturer has also been an author. So they would like the opportunity to have <u>The Margaret Days</u> on sale. And who ever it is in your firm who writes to W. J. Milne at The Hayes, Swanwick, Derbyshire asking how many copies he anticipates being able to get rid of, should just make it clear who Elizabeth Avery is, as she won't be known by him as a lecturer, obviously. Many thanks in anticipation.

Yours,

Box 304, Folder 1 (DHA-HRC)
David Higham Associates, Ltd. 76 Dean St.
From a letter to F. N. Ball, The Thames Bank Publishing Co. Ltd.
18 June 1959

Dear Mr. Ball,

<u>Muriel Spark—Child of Light</u>

Thank you for your letter of the 15th June. I should be grateful if in future you would refrain from using such expressions as "infantile foolishness", "unethical" and "discreditable", when writing to me.

If you had taken trouble—which in your letter of 5th June you implied was not necessary—to look up our previous correspondence, you would find the whole situation to be perfectly clearly set out—in particular in my letter of the 27th September 1957. As you must have that letter on your files I will not trouble to deal with the points you raise in your letter to us except to repeat that Mrs. Spark would not be uninterested in purchasing the remaining copies and so relieving you of the remaining stock of a book which plainly has not been financially satisfactory to you […].

Yours sincerely,

Box 6, Folder 3 (McFarlin)
78 Addison Way
To Peter Green, Hodder and Stoughton, Ltd.
18 July 1959

My Dear Peter,

Coming under separate registered cover is a carbon copy of <u>The Chinese Love Pavilion</u> (tentatively renamed <u>Saxby</u>, but I think will revert to the old title.) I'm enclosing an addressed label and stamps to cover return postage.

Once again I have qualms about bothering you, but you were kind enough to say the other day you'd read it, and I do—more than ever in this case, if that's possible—value your advice.[121]

Having typed the whole 130,000 words in top and 5 carbons, and corrected the draft over and over I came out at the end convinced it was punk stuff from start to finish. I even rang M. Temple Smith (silly, hysterical me) and asked him what his reaction would be if I said I was going to withdraw it entirely. He said he would think I was mad, which was gratifying. He's not seen the final typed version yet, but the top is going to him this weekend. I talked to David Higham about the whole problem, and he took a carbon away with him on Thursday evening, and had finished it by 11.30 p.m. I saw him yesterday and he said he's enjoyed it enormously. He also put his finger on a spot that's worried me subconsciously. He said, "Is the first chapter justified?" And the answer, I believe, is that it is NOT. But you will be able to tell me.

Bless you for all your help so far over this fucking book. If it reads well, and "works", then everything's fine. I have come to the brute realisation that I can't write at all, but that I can write novels, if you see what I mean. Bonjour, tristesse, and up you round the garden. Tolstoy's in his grace and Nevil Shute is in Australia. Nearer my Shute to thee, is me.

As you'll see, I can't even type straight any more.

The most I can hope you'll say is that it has a certain narrative drive and skill and that it's about something that's worthwhile.

And of course, any time, any time. I've got lots of copies. You can't actually cut this copy up and hang it in the loo, but you could read a page each day in that place. Might be appropriate.

Ever yours,

Box 12, Folder 18 (McFarlin)
78 Addison Way
From a letter to John Willey, William Morrow & Company, USA[122]
7 August 1959

Dear John,

Many thanks indeed for your most welcome letter carrying the splendid news of your tentative reactions to Saxby.[123] I'm sorry to have seemed impatient. I'll try to hold myself in now until you're able to collate various other opinions. I hope I'm right in assuming from your own reaction that quite apart from another issue altogether this is a book you will want to publish. If the other issue is not "on" then you know you have only to say so. I think part of my impatience was due to the fact that I suddenly realised nobody might want to write to me about the book until something could be said one way or the other about the other thing and the other thing is clearly not a thing to be decided quickly.

You certainly don't cut the ground from under my feet in suggesting Saxby is the wrong title. You're quite right. It is wrong. Over here people are veering towards my old firm working title of The Chinese Love Pavilion (for which months ago, I got—through a friend in Bangkok—a lovely bit of calligraphy, that is to say "Love Pavilion' in Chinese, in Chinese characters which I had thought would look nice on the jacket at least, if not worked into the title page).

Putan Singh. I know just what you mean. I did try to avoid manipulation. The passage is, perhaps, finally unclear. It is Brent's instinct[124] (heightened by fever and a subconscious revolt from what has happened at the pavilion) that leads him to the place where Saxby had gathered his plants, and it is only when he begins to recognise the road itself that he remembered the name of the village. It isn't manipulation for Saxby to have chosen the name; perhaps Brent should only discover the name Singaputan when he actually arrives and questions the children. Or, at least, only remember it then. Or perhaps he should see the connexion even earlier and deliberately set out to find the village. This is one of the several points we shall have to go into.

The last chapter is, perhaps, the least of my present worries. It has been suggested that the first chapter is finally not justified. I am inclined to agree, although not, I think, that it is a bit pretentious (which David Higham hinted). My main worry is to what extent Saxby's problems are integrated into the main structure; is it enough that his conversion was as abrupt as Saul's on the road to Damascus, enough that his anger was stirred by the invasion of the yellow men (what actually happened was that during the invasion the Japanese set fire to a village and it was the sight of trees and leaves and flowers burning that set Saxby off on his revenge drive. I kept getting cold feet about too much Saxby).

Peter Green (a leading younger critic, classical scholar, novelist published your side by Donald Friede) has read Saxby and is most complimentary. He is one of the new Book Society Committee members and thinks the book stands a strong chance. He's showing a typescript privately to Godwin who bought the Book Society recently. But that is far into the future at the moment. He particularly admires the hidden depths, the kind that even the author is hard put to clarify. I'm a bit nervous that there are depths capable of clarification which haven't been. I guess I need the help of the kind of penetrating questions which you all asked me on the previous book. That kind of question sends you scuttling to look into the dark corners with a flash lamp.

Mostly though, John, I am thrilled by your choice of two words, sensuous and magical. It's what I was aiming at. We want a title and revisions to match. They are two words that I'd like to see becoming permanently attached to the book. I'm also thrilled that you love Teena. She is rather a honey, isn't she? [...]

Finally, many thanks for putting me out of my misery. I hope other opinions consolidate your own estimate. In spite of the again military background I fancy it has a chance of selling, I hope, I hope, I hope.

Ever yours,

Box 12, Folder 18 (McFarlin)
78 Addison Way
From a letter to John Willey, William Morrow & Company, USA
28 August 1959

Dear John,

Your stimulating letter of the 25th has arrived this first morning of my 3-week break from the office and needless to say it is the best of all possible beginnings. I shan't comment in detail about The Love Pavilion beyond saying as follows:

a)   The first chapter remains as it is. E & S have already convinced me that it is right after all.

b)   All that you say about Brent and Saxby makes its mark with me and goes a long way towards clarifying my own confused state of mind about just what has gone wrong. It becomes clear to me that some rewriting is definitely on the cards.

c)   I am as anxious as you to make this book <u>clear</u>, so that it <u>will</u> sell. I can see that once again it will be my American editors who pave the way for the right sort of revisions.

d)   Even if E & S stick to Chinese, I am quite happy for you to call it simply "The Love Pavilion" over there, plus calligraphy. (Editor of <u>Books and Bookmen</u> over here, the monthly magazine, who wants to do a feature article on my work next year, suggested "The Pavilion of Love". Yes? No?) Is "The Images of Heaven" right, wrong? Just a thought. Too near <u>The Roots of Heaven</u> and <u>The Winds of Heaven</u> [...].

I await Adèle [Dogan]'s reactions with great interest. I'm dropping her a separate line as I know you're not back in the office until next Thursday.

But this letter is mainly about the financial situation. I don't need to say how grateful I am for the understanding that is being shown. I'll get down to brass tacks so that you can all consider my end of the picture and then see how it could fit into yours.[125]

First of all, <u>The Love Pavilion</u> is the third novel under my three-book agreement with E & S. I'm not negotiating a new one yet (on David Higham's advice) until I see how they do with this one. Michael Joseph and Bob Lusty both want me (so does Longman). I suppose that over the past few years most of the leading publishers have hinted that if I move I'd be welcome. Not that I really want to move. I like Maurice Temple Smith and he seems to like me. And on this book they promise a decent promotion campaign. My inner reservation, as it were, is that since they tied in with Methuen they have lost that certain something that gives a publisher "drive". You'll be smiling at the glimpse of the author under the agent!

<u>The Love Pavilion</u> ranks at £400 advance and I have had £200 (to finance my Spanish holiday). The other £200 I don't want to touch until publication, so all things being financially equal £200 would be a credit for the kitty. It is always possible that I could get Maurice to guarantee a larger advance, because it is only £400 by virtue of a clause in the

3-book agreement which stipulated a £250 advance on each book <u>or</u> a sum equal to the earnings of the previous book in the first six months. I've never had an unearned advance in Britain in my life, by the way— the figures on this three-book contract show Book 1 £250, book 2 £320, Book 3 £400 (odd, a little plus). These figures on the basis of hardcover editions. Three of my novels have gone into paperbacks. PAN publish <u>The Mark of the Warrior</u> in November. I get 60% of the advance, which is only £200 (I get £120); paperback advances over here are small-beer normally in comparison with your own paperbacks. I guess I'll need the £120 from PAN to pay my freelance income tax next January, otherwise that could gladly have been suspended for appearance in the kitty; and perhaps still can be.

Let me explain other figures. Tax year ended 5 April last. I found to my horror tax-wise that I had earned from writing £1000. This included $500 (£161 net) from Morrow, the second half of the advance from your edition. This <u>was</u> the best year: average until then was nearer £500 than £1000. The point is that I do earn money from radio and TV. Three of my novels have been done on both sound and television (my own adaptations), and I have done an original radio play as well. At the moment I'm working on the sound radio adaptation of <u>The Mark of the Warrior</u>. Translations have been confined to Sweden where Norstedt and Söner publish me. They publish <u>The Mark</u> next month. The point I'm trying to make is that if and when I freelance entirely, television and sound radio are two fields I intend to exploit if I can, because I have got a bit of a reputation there (in spite of what I think of as a <u>bad</u> TV version of <u>The Mark</u>).

I shan't attempt to do sound or TV on <u>The Love Pavilion</u> because the material isn't really suitable and our film man, Richard Gregson, thinks there <u>are</u> film possibilities. When the text is complete a copy will go over to Swanson in Hollywood.

Summing up on one side of the account, life as a freelance writer would involve novels (I can't see myself doing more than one a year), original sound and television scripts, try my hand at short stories (which I've never had time to do) and reading, advising. I can normally expect paperbacks over here (PAN have already asked about <u>The Love Pavilion</u>), and I should think Norstedt and Söner will keep going).

Summing up on the other side: i.e., failure to extend writing activities beyond novels and what can normally be got out of them, it leaves reading and advising. As I mentioned in my first letter, reading and advising fees would from my point of view be chargeable to the "kitty". Confidentially I already do a bit of reading privately for Maurice Temple Smith. I imagine that when it's announced that I'm leaving agency and freelancing I could exploit this further. It might be slow because I wouldn't want to go cap in hand to publishers <u>asking</u> for reading: in any case I'd only want highly paid "decision" reading.

The following is in real confidence. I mentioned in my first letter that I'd been offered a publishing "plum". This was the job of <u>chief editor at Collins</u>. Later private talks with Billy[126] gave me a clear impression that my freelance services might well be welcome there if I ever broke away. I tell you all this so that you can get some idea of the feeling I have that eventually I can make a go of freelancing with my own writing as the backbone, assisted by what you might call "finger in the publishing pie" revenue.

It is the building of such an arrangement that presents the difficulties. On the one hand there are the overheads of being a family man; on the other the need <u>not</u> to spend nervous energy and time scraping odd jobs together, because the whole aim is to make <u>writing</u> pay. I have been unable to save money; frankly, the rewards from agency haven't been high enough—and Penny and I would start freelance life on a joint capital of no more than £300. Against that I have a mortgage of £3000 on the house! I've done some approximate figuring of my yearly expenditure, and show it over leaf […].[127]

So, as you'll see, this produces that familiar figure of £1800 approximately; it's the minimum, unfortunately, not allowing for oddities like holidays, repairs, etc., but savings can be made here and there, I expect, and it's always in our minds to move out of London itself eventually. What it comes to is that £1800 sterling net guarantee would provide freedom but <u>into</u> the kitty would go <u>all</u> earnings, not just from writing.

Five years would be ideal, less would do. A lower guarantee would make it difficult to put <u>all</u> reading and editorial fees into the kitty.

I have to give six months notice to the partnership that holds the shares in David Higham Associates. Ideally I would like to start free next April 1st, so there would be no question of starting a guarantee arrangement <u>before</u> then. But by then I expect I'd have had my PAN money, and my sound radio <u>Mark of the Warrior</u> money. So the only <u>definite</u> credit would be the balance of the <u>Love Pavilion</u> advance from E & S.

<u>Thinking aloud corner</u>. Can my services be used any way by Morrow? Scouting, reading for your visiting firemen over here? Is there something to be thought of on the basis of a <u>reducing</u> guarantee, that is to say, the maximum for the first (and most difficult year), less the next and so on?[128]

I apologize for the length of this letter but—unless I've forgotten something—it puts all the cards on the table. As you may have guessed from the above my writing has always subsidised my job. I want the job now to subsidise the writing and to be the kind of job that melts automatically away when the writing subsidises itself. Given a few years I'm sure, indeed determined that it shall.

In all this I haven't mentioned Penny. [Michael] Joseph have taken her new novel,[129] which takes the story of the first one several steps further. Ivan [von Auw] has a copy of the mss, but I've asked him not to do anything further until proof stage. If Morrow were to take her up on this one then of course we could probably do a joint guarantee business. Her earnings are small so far but she too is determined to go on. Or even, if she approved, her earnings whether or not you published, could go into the kitty.

One final thing! I've been feeling very despondent about having to keep Ivan [von Auw] in the dark. He has always been a good friend to me and genuinely interested in my work, I think, but in view of all this business I've not even sent him a copy of <u>The Love Pavilion</u>; otherwise, being a good agent, he might have been hammering on your door about terms! One day I'll be able to explain to him, I hope, and I hope he'll understand. I felt from one of his recent memos that he was a bit puzzled about not getting a copy of the book immediately. But it would be wrong to take him into my confidence when I still have to break the news finally to David [Higham] and my other colleagues, that is, if it comes to breaking the news.

Enough now! Don't worry about "harassing me in Spain". I'll be only too anxious to hear as much as possible while I'm there. Ideally I'd like to be able to tell David by September 30, and <u>if</u> the answer's yes from you, to tell him directly I return from holiday on Sep. 22 would be best.

Yours ever, and grateful whatever the outcome,[130]

Box 4, Folder 8 (McFarlin)
78 Addison Way
From a letter to Maurice Temple Smith, Eyre & Spottiswoode Ltd.
25 September 1959

My Dear Maurice,

Back from Spain which was wonderful [….] am now sending you a copy of Adèle [Dogan]'s suggestions[131] because a lot of these make great sense to me and are I think complementary to the sort of thing you and I discussed on the telephone one day.

I'm now starting work on some very careful revision and rewriting, and my guess is that the final text will be ready by the end of October, a fortnight later than I suggested when on the phone to you before I went away. I hope that doesn't matter. I'm so determined to make Saxby as watertight as possible so that it stands every possible chance of selling big—for all our sakes. But let me know if there's anything in Adèle's suggestions with which <u>you</u> violently or even slightly disagree. I've not fully digested them yet, and as I work with them by my side <u>I</u> may find points of disagreement.

The USA problem is the title at the moment. They are veering to <u>The Pavilion of Love</u>, which is actually the title proposed by Bill Smith and <u>Books and Bookmen</u> who didn't like <u>The Chinese Love Pavilion</u> when I mentioned it to him at the Michael Joseph party last year. What do you think? Bill Smith, by the way, wants a few months warning of pubn because he said he wanted to do a feature article on my books in general. Things are looking up!

My love to Jean. Has son and heir a name yet?

Yours ever,

Box 12, Folder 18 (McFarlin)
78 Addison Way
John Willey, William Morrow & Company, USA
25 September 1959

Dear John,

Well, here I am at the end of my first short week back at the office. Costa Brava is a fond memory and both feet are back on the ground. David Higham and my two other colleagues on the board, Jean Leroy and Monica Preston, have now been told.[132] I was greatly moved by their understanding and friendly cooperation because it was something of a blow to them, particularly to Jean and Monica who, unlike David, had no knowledge of my thinking. For the moment it is to be a board secret, but only for a short time. The first step will be for me to tell all my authors and after that of course it will be generally known in the publishing world. I told David that by this weekend you might have had a private word with Ivan [von Auw] and David is dropping him a personal note from home this weekend in any case. David, Jean and Monica's spontaneous reaction was that I was doing the right thing in the wide, long-term sense, and this was encouraging to me as a writer. I'll drop you a line as soon as the matter comes out of the confidential file. When I tell authors I shall discuss with them the question of which of us at DHA should represent them. Apart from David himself there is my younger colleague David Bolt and also the excellent Sheila Watson who has been in charge of foreign language sales but who has been groomed recently for book rights negotiation in England.

Three-year term. No, I was not at all disappointed and feel as you do that this shorter term ought to do the trick. I'm feeling tremendously stimulated and am now longing to plunge into my new life.

Scouting. I've tried to think further about fees, etc., but am still a bit at a loss. Perhaps the best thing would [be] to write into the agreement that for the first year a small retainer should be credited to the kitty plus payment of out-of-pocket expenses. Then at the end of the year each side could consider whether this needed adjustment, either way. Directly I start freelance life I should ask all leading publishers to keep me posted about their lists (and some of the agents), and on top of that I'd keep my hand in by periodic visits; this apart from general ear-to-ground interests.

Mark of the Warrior. I'm glad you agree about this because it's a way of clearing up the past. Just how best it should be recovered probably time will tell. Perhaps if the agreement stipulates that it ranks for recovery during the term of the agreement, that will be enough for contractual purposes?

Banker and freelance. I covered this point in my last aerogramme. The alternative would be for me to pay cheques over to DHA, or have them paid over, DHA making note that they don't earn commission on them!

I think that's all the technical side for the moment. When you get round to drafting the agreement could I (apart from your letting Ivan [von Auw] have a personal copy for information) have the draft sent direct to me at home? The only reason for this is that at the moment of writing I'm not sure at what time the office staff will be informed about my future.

I'm writing Adèle [Dogan] separately about the editorial points, and am beginning work this weekend on The Pavilion. All that remains for the moment, John, is for me to say once again how very very grateful I am to you all. It's been like Christmas in September. In my letters I've not mentioned Thayer [Hobson] because Adèle told me that his wife was so unwell and I've not wanted to intrude even with the briefest message to him. But if the right moment comes do give him messages from me for them both.

Ever yours,

Box 7, Folder 13 (McFarlin)
78 Addison Way
To Messrs. Higham & Co., 76 Dean St.
30 September 1959

My Dear David, Nell, Jean and Monica,

This is just to put officially on paper what has been discussed and agreed, that is to say my resignation from the partnership holding the share capital in David Higham Associates, Ltd. to take effect six months from now—in other words effective from 31st March 1960.

Ever yours,

Box 17, Folder 12 (McFarlin)
David Higham Associates, Ltd. 76 Dean St.
To Clive Sansom, Tasmania
13 October 1959

My Dear Clive,

For some time now I have had to consider whether to go on in business and write part time or take some chance on the future and write full time. I have now decided—correctly, I hope—that I must give all my time to writing. I have discussed this with my colleagues on the board, who have been most understanding, and it has been agreed that I shall retire from DHA Ltd. on March 31st, next year.

We shan't be making any formal announcement at this early stage; on the other hand there won't be any secret about it. But clearly the people to be told first are those with whom I have been dealing on the book side.

This is work which I shall miss, just as I shall miss working with the team which, as DHA Ltd., we have now built up, but when I do go I shall do so feeling that I'm leaving in good hands that side of your affairs with which I've dealt. The transfer of actual responsibility is some way off yet, of course, and is something I feel sure we can arrange without difficulty when the time comes.[133]

Yours,

Box 408, Folder 33 (DHA-HRC)
David Higham Associates, Ltd. 76 Dean St.
To Ivan von Auw, Harold Ober Associates, USA
24 November 1959

David Higham—<u>A Trip to Parnassus</u>

My Dear Ivan,

I am delighted to tell you that David has just finished a novel which I have read and enjoyed enormously. In fact we sold the Swedish rights straight away to Ragnar Svanström of Norstedt & Söner who has been over here.

I don't know whether you know that apart from plays David did publish a novel years ago with both Heinemann and Doubleday, albeit under the name of David Stewart. And this actually leads to what, from David's point of view, is rather an awkward situation. Both Heinemann and Doubleday have an option on his next novel, on terms to be agreed (the Doubleday agreement was dated 28 August 1930 and was made through the agency of Curtis Brown with Doubleday Doram, as it then was). The novel was called <u>The Several Caskets</u>. For various reasons David is not at all keen on being published by Heinemann or Doubleday and we are at the moment trying to deal with the Heinemann situation. Presently, though, it will be question of dealing with the Doubleday situation too and I thought at this stage I'd write and ask you for your advice about the best way to go about it. David imagines there will be nobody at Doubleday who will even remember the old novel but although in Blanche Knopf's famous phrase, "What's an option between friends," the option does certainly exist. What do you think Doubleday's attitude is likely to be? Both David and I are rather keen on the idea of Mike Bessie[134] and I'm actually talking to him tomorrow and will show him a copy of the manuscript, on the side, as it were. If he comes up and says he wants to publish it this would probably be the ideal basis on which to go to Doubleday, because one can probably take the line that Mike being in London and hearing about the book asked to see it and wants to publish and that the only thing outstanding in this very old option with Doubleday, which, looking at the contract, David sees they have.

Over here, if we can get out of the Heinemann option, we have decided to go to Maurice Temple Smith at Eyre & Spottiswoode. Having read the book I feel that from the point of view of British publication it's almost a question of our choosing a publisher rather than being chosen, if you see what I mean.

I look forward to hearing from you.

P. S. David tells me that over here the novel was published under the title <u>Treasures Upon Earth</u> and he's pretty sure that was finally the title in America.

ENDNOTES

1. David Higham, *Literary Gent: Autobiography* (London: Jonathan Cape, Ltd., 1978).
2. In a letter from Almedingen to Scott dated 4 October 1954 (McFarlin 1:5).
3. Stands for "Special Operations Executive." The SOE was formed during World War II to carry out acts of espionage and sabotage behind enemy lines.
4. The staff at Eyre and Spottiswoode included Ruby Millar, John Bright-Holmes, James Wright, Charles Friend, and Frank Worley, the editor-in-chief, who was replaced by Maurice Temple Smith.
5. It was eventually produced for radio under the title *Sahibs and Memsahibs*.
6. Scott's first literary agent. Weiner was beginning her career as a literary agent at the end of the war and was actively seeking clients. Solicitor Harold Rubenstein (a judge for an Anglo-Palestinian International Play Competition, in which Scott's *Pillars of Salt* placed fourth) introduced them (Spurling 156–157).
7. Scott's first attempt at novel writing. It was rejected by seventeen publishers. See the letter to Sally Scott dated 18 February 1968.
8. The abbreviation for Pearn, Pollinger and Higham throughout Scott's correspondence.
9. Scott acted as Blofeld's agent to place *Red China in Perspective* with Allan Wingate Ltd.
10. Gerald Hanley (1916–1992) was first a client, then a friend of Scott's. Hanley published *The Consul at Sunset* (1951) and *The Year of the Lion* (1953), among other titles. He also published short stories and wrote radio plays and film scripts, including *The Blue Max*.
11. Dutfield represented several publishers in Germany, Austria, and Switzerland.
12. Luscombe did publish the book under the title *Lease of Life*. In early 1952, British doctors had to amputate more of Milbourne's arm because German surgeons had left nerves exposed (DHA-HRC 45:12).
13. Purkayastha served under Scott as a havildar during the war.
14. Alternately spelled *Johnny Sahib*.
15. Scott and Leasor (1923–2007) had met on the troopship bound for India in 1943. Scott acted as Leasor's agent in the 1950s. Leasor was a journalist and prolific novelist, specializing in thrillers. His novel *Boarding Party* (1978) was made into the movie *Sea Wolves*, starring Gregory Peck and David Niven. He also published under the name Andrew MacAllan.

16. Scott's neighbor before the war (see their extensive correspondence in section 1). Scott would act as an agent for Clive and his wife Ruth, but their friendship would wane after the Sansoms moved to Ruth's native Tasmania because of Clive's health.

17. As fellow poets in the early 1940s, Sansom and Scott created the order of the Jetty Pail, with the chain of office awarded for the completion of a new poem (Spurling 71).

18. In addition to the name Hank McCoy, Martin (who lived in Sussex) also published under the pseudonyms Scott Martin, Brett Cameron, Tex Bancroft, Clint Callaghan, Buck Savage, Russ Brannigan, Rex Dixon, and Burt Merrill (DHA-HRC 31:19, 45:3, 45:4).

19. Mary Margaret (Mollie) Hamilton (1908–2004), who wrote under the name M. M. Kaye, was (according to Scott) a great-niece of Sir John Kaye, "the very eminent Victorian biographer and author of the standard history of the Mutiny, *The Sepoy War* in three volumes." Hamilton had told Scott that there "have been Kayes in India for 150 years and she herself has spent a considerable amount of time over there both as a child and as an army wife. She is the wife of a Colonel Hamilton commanding the first Battalion Royal Irish Fusiliers and recently joined him in Kenya" (from Scott's letter to John Guest of Longmans Green Ltd., 2 September 1955; in DHA-HRC 150:4).

20. Refers to *The Ordinary Princess*.

21. Hodder-Williams rejected the book on the basis that although it had a "nostalgic interest," there was not a "good market" for the subject of British India (DHA-HRC 30:1).

22. Donald McWhinnie (1920–1987) was the drama script editor and then the assistant head of sound drama for the BBC. McWhinnie later directed films in Hollywood and received a Tony Award for best director in 1962. Scott eventually acted on McWhinnie's behalf to place a nonfiction book on the aesthetics of writing radio plays (DHA-HRC 265:20).

23. John Braine (1922–1986) published twelve novels, most notably *Room at the Top* (1957), which was turned into a film in 1959.

24. An editor with Eyre and Spottiswoode.

25. Barry (1910–1988) was the producer of BBC Sunday Night Theatre from 1950 through 1959. In 1952 he became the head of drama at BBC Television.

26. The abbreviation for Eyre and Spottiswoode throughout Scott's correspondence.

27. A writer for BBC Sunday Night Theatre.

28. Stands for "Royal Indian Army Service Corps."
29. Greenfield would eventually work on the other side of publishing as a literary agent. See his memoir, *A Smattering of Monsters* (Rochester, NY: Camden House, 1995).
30. Hibbert (1906–1993) published under the names Jean Plaidy, Elbur Ford, Eleanor Hessenford, Ellalice Tate, Anna Percival, Phillippa Carr, Victoria Holt, and Kathleen Kellow.
31. Meaning publishers' representatives. Scott referred to them not only in his dealings for his clients but also in terms of the sales of his own novels.
32. In a note written on 15 November, Scott offered the following clause to Greenfield, "On copies sold to Commercial libraries at a discount of over 40% a royalty of 10% of the price received provided the number of copies sold in this way shall not exceed a total of 100 and provided that no copies shall be sold in this way within three months of the day of first publication." Greenfield accepted the wording (DHA-HRC 34:4).
33. The head of drama at BBC Television. He would be replaced by Michael Barry in 1952.
34. Atkins produced nine shows for BBC Sunday Night Theatre between 1950 and 1956.
35. Sir Arthur Clarke (1917–2008) was known as one of the big three writers (with Robert A. Heinline and Isaac Asimov) in science fiction. He published ten collections of short stories and more than fifteen novels. His *2001: A Space Odyssey* (1968) was made into a movie, directed by Stanley Kubrick.
36. The son of Laurence Pollinger, one of the founders of Pearn, Pollinger and Higham along with Nancy Pearn and David Higham (Spurling 187).
37. Clarke's American agent.
38. Hermann Peschmann, the editor of several poetry anthologies.
39. Of the novel *The Alien Sky* (1953), which was published in the United States as *Six Days in Mayapore*.
40. Morchard Bishop was the penname for the critic Oliver Stoner. He had just reviewed *The Alien Sky*.
41. Fowles (1926–2005), a novelist and poet, had taught school in Greece. He would later publish (among other titles) *The Collector* (1963), *The Magus* (1965), *The French Lieutenant's Woman* (1969), *The Ebony Tower* (1974), and *Daniel Martin* (1977).
42. Monteith (1921–1995) was the director at Faber & Faber. He published authors such as William Golding, Samuel Beckett, and Ted Hughes. He also published Seamus Heaney's first book of poetry.

43. Barnsley (1916–1986) published under the name Gabriel Fielding. He was related to Henry Fielding on his mother's side of the family; Gabriel was Barnsley's middle name (from notes in a letter dated November 1954; DHA-HRC 100A:4). His publications included *Brotherly Love* (1954), *In the Time of Greenbloom* (1956), *Eight Days* (1958), *Through Streets Broad and Narrow* (1960), *The Birthday King* (1962), *Gentlemen in Their Season* (1966), *New Queens for Old—A Novella and Nine Stories* (1972), *Pretty Doll Houses* (1979), and *The Women of Guinea Lane* (1986).
44. Pulvertaft (b. 1925) was a client of Scott's until 1956. She was the author of *No Great Magic* (1956), *The Thing Desired* (1957), and *Golden October* (1965). At this time, she was married to Scott's friend Peter Green.
45. The BBC airing of the radio play based on Scott's second novel. The play was directed by Julian Amyes.
46. Gordon (1911–1972) was a producer-turned-actor who later would have roles in the *Doctor Who* television series.
47. An actor who had roles in various television plays, some of which were produced by the BBC.
48. The referent isn't clear from the context. ABCA stands for "Army Bureau of Current Affairs" but also "American, British, Canadian and Australian."
49. Home of the BBC Television center.
50. *The Alien Sky* was performed for television in January of 1956.
51. As literary agent for Pearn, Pollinger and Higham.
52. Richard Church (1893–1972) was a poet, novelist, and critic. Both he and Scott wrote book reviews for *Country Life*.
53. Marx (1926–1963) was a poet, publisher, and promoter of the arts. Her Hand and Flower Press published young poets from 1940 through 1963.
54. Katherine Webb of Hutchinson.
55. Puffs were short promotional statements which were often included on book covers or in newspaper ads.
56. An editor at Hutchinson.
57. Hutchinson published Abse (b. 1923), a medical doctor, poet, and musician.
58. Scott had first met Green in Calcutta during the war. Green was in RAF Intelligence and had studied classical literature at Cambridge. He later worked as a consultant editor for Hodder and Stoughton and wrote reviews for *The Daily Telegraph* and the *Times Literary Supplement*. Scott acted as Green's literary agent in the 1950s, and they traded reviews of each other's publications for many years. At this time, Green was married to Lalage Pulvertaft.
59. Sir John Betjeman (1906–1984), a poet, journalist, and critic, was poet laureate in 1972.

60. Scott's colleague at Pearn, Pollinger and Higham.
61. An American writer and translator.
62. Immediately after the war, Scott had started working as a bookkeeper for the newly combined firm of Falcon Press and Gray Walls Press, and in 1950 he served as the company secretary, a position he resigned because of Baker's financial practices. Baker was charged with fraud and forgery and sent to prison for seven years (Spurling 176; see Scott's letter to Geoffrey Wagner dated 16 December 1954). However, Scott's experiences at the press were formative. There he met Roland Gant (who had worked his way up to publicity manager), Charles Wrey Gardiner (an editor), and Gardiner's assistant, Muriel Spark.
63. Blanche Knopf (1894–1966) was at this time the vice president of the publishing firm. In 1957 she would be named the president when her husband and cofounder Alfred was named the chairman. She worked with authors such as John Updike, Willa Cather, H. L. Mencken, and Langston Hughes.
64. A reader who had written to Scott about *The Alien Sky*.
65. Then the head of Eyre and Spottiswoode.
66. Raymond was a reader for Eyre and Spottiswoode. He also edited a collection of essays called *The Baldwin Age*, published by Eyre and Spottiswoode in 1960.
67. This is Scott's third novel, published in 1956.
68. In *A Male Child*, Helena is the estranged wife of Ian Canning, one of the main characters of the novel.
69. Of Harold Ober Associates, the American literary agency that represented Scott in the United States.
70. Stella was pregnant and married to Alan Hurst, Canning's good friend.
71. Hastings (1732–1818) went to India with the British East India Company in 1750. Eventually, he became the first governor-general of Bengal in 1772, then the governor-general of India in 1773. He was impeached in 1787 on charges of corruption but was later acquitted in 1785. Scott never wrote this novel.
72. The director at Heinemann.
73. This reference involves the publication of *The Quiet American*. Greene (1904–1991) was a longtime client of Pearn, Pollinger and Higham, with thirteen previously published novels and one book of short stories by 1955. He would go on to publish eleven more novels, three volumes of short stories, and an autobiography.
74. Sayers (1893–1957), known for her series of detective novels featuring Lord Peter Wimsey, was also a poet, playwright, essayist, and the translator of Dante's *Divine Comedy*.

75. Guest (1911–1997) was a literary advisor to Longmans, Green and after 1972, an advisor to Penguin.
76. Harold Ober Associates.
77. Sir Robert Lusty (1909–1991) began his career in publishing with Hutchinson, then moved to Michael Joseph, where he later became the deputy chairman.
78. Lusty suggested a third-person narrative rather than the "rather scrappy journal form." Graves complied, but the publisher thought the second draft was "a little dull in comparison with the first 20,000 words" (DHA-HRC 206:31). Scott took the manuscript to Secker and Warburg, Longman, Jonathan Cape, and William Collins. Finally, in late 1957, Arthur Barker Ltd. accepted the manuscript, to be published under the title *To My Astonishment* (DHA-HRC 260:10).
79. Wilson (1910–2002) was an assistant director for MGM Studios when Michael Barry recruited him to the BBC, where he was put in charge of the script department.
80. A play written by Scott set in World War II India about a beautiful divorcée who flirts with British cadets. The television script would be rejected because it was "out of date." Donald McWhinnie accepted the play for radio under the title *Sahibs and Memsahibs*, airing it in the summer of 1958 (Spurling 206–207).
81. Philip Mackie, playwright (1918–1985). His teleplay *The Whole Truth* (1955) was one of several of his broadcasts in the BBC's Saturday Night Theatre slot.
82. The play by T. S. Eliot.
83. *The Face of Love* was published in 1953. Dallas also published an earlier play, *A Masque of Summer*, then *Oedipus and Dionysus*. Dallas' published *Collected Works* includes his three plays and four prose pieces: *The Ten Symphonies of Gorka Konig*, *The New Wagnerian*, *The Book of Strangers*, and *The Gestalt of Freedom*. After his conversion to Islam in 1967, he changed his name to Abdalqadir as-Sufi.
84. Bartlett (1905–1985) wrote television scripts for the BBC.
85. Published by Eyre and Spottiswoode as *Room at the Top*.
86. West (1916–1999), an Australian dramatist and novelist, published (among other titles) *The Devil's Advocate* (1959), *The Shoes of the Fisherman* (1963), and *Vanishing Point* (1996). He wrote the film adaptations for five of his novels.
87. Dame Edith Sitwell (1887–1964), an English poet and critic, published eight books of poetry and six works of nonfiction.

88. A critic married to the author C. P. Snow (later Lord Snow).

89. Stands for "Special Operations Executive." The SOE was formed during World War II to carry out acts of espionage and sabotage behind enemy lines. As a woman, Elizabeth Nicholas was less conspicuous in her work with the Resistance. Many of her fellow agents were imprisoned or executed by the Germans.

90. Maurice Temple Smith had replaced Frank Morley at Eyre and Spottiswoode.

91. Hamilton (1900–1988) published Lillian Hellman, R. J. Narayan, Raymond Chandler, James Thurber, Jean-Paul Sartre, Albert Camus, and J. D. Salinger.

92. Hamilton solicited the help of an editor (Alan Wykes) to reshape the first portion of the novel to illustrate to the author the kind of reorganization he wanted. Nicholas did not accept the cutting and rearrangement (DHA-HRC 266:5). In August of that year, Scott submitted the manuscript to Cassell & Co., and in December, he submitted it to Longman. The book was eventually published by Cresset in 1958.

93. Scott's fourth novel, *The Mark of the Warrior*, was the first to be published by William Morrow in the United States. Dogan became Scott's editor. On July 12, Dogan sent a marked manuscript copy to Scott with Morrow's collective questions and corrections, to which Scott responded in this letter.

94. Referring to typescript errors (either the author's or the printer's) versus more substantive issues.

95. This section is preceded by a discussion of literals, or specific word changes in the manuscript.

96. The novel was structured with alternating centers of consciousness in Craig and Ramsey. The "turns" of each mininarrative were numbered. In the published version, Ramsey's narratives go up only to five.

97. There were several more exchanges between the two as the novel was revised. It is clear in the correspondence that Dogan argued forcefully (and successfully) that Craig's wife Esther should reappear at the end of the book. She also encouraged Scott to be less oblique in some cases ("You can still be metaphysical without losing the reader in mystery") and less detailed in others ("the maneuvers ... I don't think they are ever unintelligible; they are simply too taxing)" (McFarlin 12:16).

98. Muriel Spark (1918–2006) had hired another literary agency before returning to Pearn, Pollinger and Higham in 1957. She published more than twenty novels, short-story collections, children's books, pieces of literary criticism, essays on philosophy, biographies, and plays, but she is perhaps best known for *The Prime of Miss Jean Brodie*.

99. MacLean (1924–2006) was the director at Macmillan and Pan for some twenty years.
100. Then the publicity manager at Eyre and Spottiswoode.
101. See note 31 in section 2.
102. Scott and the staff at Eyre and Spottiswoode were identifying possible reviewers for *The Mark of the Warrior*. Scott mentioned Pamela Hansford Johnson from *The Bookman*, Walter Allen from the *New Statesman*, John Davenport from *The Observer*, Peter Green from *The Daily Telegraph*, and Rosaleen Whately from *The Liverpool Daily Post*.
103. Refers to his work on *The Chinese Love Pavilion*, which was published in 1960.
104. Kay Collier (1915–2001) published as Kay Dick and later, as Jeremy Scott. She moved from A. D. Peters as a literary agent to Pearn, Pollinger and Higham in November of 1957. Scott was her agent.
105. See note 58 in section 2.
106. Hobson (1897–1967) was the president and chairman of the board at William Morrow.
107. Stands for "Office Cadet Training Unit."
108. Of Scribner's.
109. Paignton is in Devon, near Torquay, where Scott was stationed before being deployed to India.
110. Pearn, Pollinger and Higham had divided into Laurence Pollinger Ltd. and David Higham Associates.
111. Weidenfeld (b. 1919) partnered with Nigel Nicolson to form their publishing house, attracting authors such as Vladimir Nabokov, Mary McCarthy, and Saul Bellow.
112. Van Thal (1904–1983) was a publisher and agent.
113. All of the authors listed were clients (or former clients) of Scott's in his capacity at David Higham Associates. Nadia Legrand was the wife of Roland Gant, Scott's associate from Falcon Gray Walls Press who moved to Michael Joseph as the editorial director, then to Stodder and Houghton, and finally to Heinemann. Peter Green was then married to Lalage Pulvertaft. Wolf Mankowitz (1924–1998) was a Jewish playwright and screenwriter. See the additional notes in section 2 on Gerald Hanley (note 10) and Kathleen Farrell (note 119).
114. By 27 January 1959, Scott and the publisher couldn't resolve the issue of paying a contributor for a "dud story," and so Scott wrote to Barley Allison at Weidenfeld and Nicolson, "All in all he and I both rather feel now that perhaps it would be better if we dropped the whole idea"

(DHA-HRC 405:29). Scott's retelling of the Cinderella story, which was published posthumously as *After the Funeral* (1979), illustrated by Sally Scott, marked the fulfillment of a lifelong ambition.

115. A codirector at Michael Joseph.

116. Under the pen name Elizabeth Avery, Penny Scott published *The Margaret Days* (1959), *The Marigold Summer* (1960), *Nurse Has Four Cases* (1961), and *Sister Bollard* (1963). Later, she wrote were several unpublished works: one that was untitled about a young girl named Nellie (completed in 1963), "Eliza Rowen" (circulated in 1966), "The Probationer" (completed in 1971), "Back to Nursing" (circulated in 1972), and "The Foster Child."

117. Doreen Marston, a manuscript reader for several publishers, including Michael Joseph and Collins.

118. The original title, *One, Two, Buckle My Shoe*, was already in use in an Agatha Christie novel that was still in print (DHA-HRC 317.3). The final, published title was *The Margaret Days*.

119. Scott had been Farrell's agent when he worked at David Higham Associates. Farrell (1912–1999) published six novels in her lifetime: *Home From The Fair* (1942), *Mistletoe Malice* (1951), *Take It to Heart* (1953), *The Cost Of Living* (1956), *The Common Touch* (1959), and *Limitations of Love* (1962). She lived with her fellow novelist Kay Collier (Kay Dick) for two decades.

120. Collier left Heinemann for Hutchinson later in the year.

121. Two days earlier, Green had responded to an earlier draft of *Pavilion*. He found it beautifully written but the structure too complicated for the ordinary reader, as if the novel consisted of discrete short stories that were only remotely connected: "I'm not honestly sure that the reader's grasp of extended and discrete form can extend quite as far as you would like it to. By the time I reached Sutton I'd frankly given up trying to hold the total pattern [... as] the book seems to be several books in one. The tone switches about in a rather disconcerting way [...]. You should stress one particular facet to provide a clear and consequent narrative; make the rest subsidiary [... because] the purpose of the whole novel at a deeper, symbolic level [...] is to explore the truth of man's sexual integration in all its aspects, simple and complicated alike [...]" (McFarlin 6:3).

122. John Willey (1914–1990) was the managing editor at Morrow. As will be clear in their subsequent correspondence, Willey proved to be a close friend, an attentive reader, and an ardent supporter of Scott's.

123. At this point, a possible title for *The Chinese Love Pavilion*.

124. Tom Brent had replaced the Freshwater character mentioned earlier.
125. I include most of this very long letter about finances because it became the vehicle whereby Scott would resign his agency position in order to write full-time.
126. Publisher William Collins.
127. What follows is a half of page of figures showing his yearly expenses.
128. A penciled note was written in the margin: "My unearned balance on The Mark of the W (year earlier) could always be suspended to bank for eventual recovery, too. I hate unearned advances. They make me feel guilty!"
129. Scott referred to *The Marigold Summer* (1960).
130. On 17 September, Willey cabled to Scott's hotel on the Costa Brava: "Happily commit ourselves to eighteen hundred pound annual guarantee for three years beginning next April first with provision for review and possible extension at end of period. Mailing air letter London Friday. Hope this dear Paul a proper fillip for your and Penny's vacation" (McFarlin 12:18).
131. On 1 September, Dogan sent some ten single-spaced pages of questions and suggestions to Scott. Scott marked one of the points having to do with the triangle relationship of Brian Saxby, Tom Brent, and Teena as "most important." Dogan suggested that "Teena might have been the embodiment of everything Saxby was denying on this earth and he yet loved her—lost his heart-soul again to her but it conflicted with his other souls because she was tainted [...]. Teena would understand the love-hate of Saxby. Tom, having more Faith, believes only in love and again feels anger against Saxby" (McFarlin 12:18).
132. This refers to Scott's decision to resign from David Higham Associates effective 31 March 1960, a step that was made possible by Morrow's guarantee.
133. Scott sent this letter to all of his clients, who were dismayed (in some cases) but on the whole supportive of his decision. His client and friend E. M. Almedingen wrote, "This is just to assure you that the news did not come as a shock. I knew it would happen. I have known since last summer—nobody telling me—just a few things put together. I do so want to send you a blessing & heartfelt wishes for the future. You have both faith & courage & I am quite certain you are right in your choice. There is nothing for me to forgive—I feel grateful for all you have done for us. I called you a prince among agents, & I feel sure the same rank will be reached by you in the other field. This is a most inadequate letter—but you don't

need a laboured composition from me. My love & gratitude always—"
(McFarlin 1:5).

134. Then with Harper and Brothers. He later established Atheneum Publishers, where he worked with John Cheever, Daniel J. Boorstin, Aleksandr Solzhenitsyn, and Elie Wiesel.

LIFE AS A FULL-TIME WRITER (1960–1963)

With a financial commitment for the coming three years from his U.S. publisher, William Morrow, Paul Scott left his agency position with David Higham Associates in 1960 to write full-time. He published three novels in this period—*The Chinese Love Pavilion*, *The Birds of Paradise*, and *The Bender*—and completed a fourth, *The Corrida at San Feliu*.

The Chinese Love Pavilion (1960) "was a bit of a hybrid," Scott later explained, "but the job motif recurs in a theme of madness brought on by obsession with occupations for their own sake—occupations disrupted or invented by war" (*My Appointment* 116). The letters in section 2 between Scott and his editors at William Morrow[1] reveal how difficult this novel was to conceive in terms of its theme and structure. After John Willey's initial response to *Pavilion*, Scott confessed,

> I'm a bit nervous that there are depths capable of clarification which haven't been. I guess I need the help of the kind of penetrating

> questions, which you all asked me on the previous book [*The Mark of the Warrior*]. That kind of question sends you scuttling to look into the dark corners with a flash lamp. (McFarlin 12:18)

But his friends understood what a milestone *Pavilion* was in Scott's development as a novelist (see, for example, Scott's letter to E. M. Almedingen on 7 October 1960).

In 1962 Scott published *The Birds of Paradise*, which was honored as a Book Society Choice in the United Kingdom. *Birds* is "about a man who spent his childhood in India and returned there, taking a sabbatical year from his London office because he hated the feeling that he had become no more than a consumer of things made by other people" (*My Appointment* 116). As Scott explained to a reader, the novel

> is an attempt to give a picture, an impression, a sense, a feeling of that curious and restless little worm in men and women which reminds them of the mystery that remains behind when everything else seems to have been explained and pigeon-holed. When what is romantic has been seen through, what is real has been accepted; when the genes have played their part and environment has played its part. (McFarlin 20:19)

Birds was the last novel that Eyre and Spottiswoode would handle for him. That same year, he moved to Secker and Warburg, following his friend Roland Gant, with whom he had worked since the days of Falcon and Grey Walls Press.[2]

After the publication of *Birds*, Scott shifted his attention from India with *The Bender*, which was released in 1963 and later adapted for BBC television. Scott described the story as "a comedy of London life in the 1960s, its middle-aged hero a man ruined by a small inheritance which had been just big enough to make doing a job seem like something he could do tomorrow" (*My Appointment* 116). The novel, he observed, was

> a lyric, a poem, a sad little pavane for a middle-aged man who (like William Conway in <u>The Birds of Paradise</u>) did not feel that

> there was a real place for him in the modern world. However, he
> lacked William's stoical upbringing, and never had a chance to
> see the birds of paradise. (McFarlin 10:17)

Scott included in the novel a description of a bender of his own months
before, while he waited for his editors to respond to his completed draft
of *Birds*.

Family holidays to Spain from 1960 through 1963 provided the back-
drop to Scott's eighth novel, *The Corrida at San Feliu* (1964), which
he described as "narrated by an elderly writer who lived in Spain with
a beautiful wife and an unfinished manuscript—both of which were
unfaithful to him" (*My Appointment* 116). This novel, the most complex in structure he had yet written, centers on an aging writer (Edward
Thornhill) who drafts several stories about married couples "turning
up in disgrace" (McFarlin 9:12). "Disgrace" describes Thornhill's own
marriage, since he is morose, neglectful, and drinks too much. Yet he is
tormented when his wife takes up with a young, muscular "godling."
The *corrida* (or bullfight) itself symbolizes the contest between men and
women and the inevitable ruin that follows.

Although his novels were becoming deeper and more complex, they
were never the financial successes Scott was hoping for and needing.
With *Corrida*, Secker and Warburg released Scott of their claim to a
third novel, and he moved to William Heinemann, again following
Roland Gant.

Despite having disappointing sales, Scott's decision to support the
family solely on his writing skills seemed validated at this point in his
career. With the foreign language sales of his novels (which were translated into Dutch, German, Swedish, Spanish, Polish, and French) and
a paperback contract with PAN for his previous publications, Scott felt
financially secure enough to buy a car. He had supplemented his publishing income by writing regular reviews for *Country Life*, but in 1962
he resigned the role, arranging to take on that responsibility only when
the staff reviewers were on vacation.

THE LETTERS, 1960–1963

The letters from this period provide a variety of perspectives of Scott as novelist.

The writer at work: "Work" (as a concept and a necessity) was very important to Scott; he believed it was the "main road by which men and women come to terms with themselves and whatever god they believe in" (McFarlin 8:21).[3] He needed to do what he loved (writing), but he also needed to pour himself into a task, as he told his American publisher, John Willey: "I must <u>work</u> at something, otherwise I'm only half alive" (McFarlin 14:1; see also 13:21).

Relationships with publishers and agents: While he was employed as an accountant at Falcon and Grey Walls Press, then as an agent at David Higham Associates, Scott learned to bargain with publishers on behalf of authors. That experience made him a savvy writer who knew what was possible and what was not possible in the world of publishing. He could be fiercely loyal (to editors and publishing houses), but he changed houses when his own best interests, financial or artistic, were at stake. I've included only a few of the many letters that count to the pence what his income would be. But he spent a great deal of time not only acting as his own accountant but supplementing his income by selling scripts to radio and television. Financially, he worked all the angles.

Even though his publishers (Roland Gant at Secker and Warburg, then Heinemann, and John Willey at William Morrow) were his close friends, he understood that publishers first worked for their stockholders, then for themselves. The author came in a distant third. As he negotiated various schemes of advances and royalties on both sides of the Atlantic, Scott felt like a beggar raising his begging bowl for a charitable handout. "People like you and me," he explained to Gerald Hanley,

> are plain bloody navvies without a trade union. It always killed me when I saw money being paid about by a big mandarin to a small mandarin (because it's mandarin psychology to keep man-darism alive), and then a man bent with the need to <u>write</u> having to cap in hand it and getting a cold sniff and a handout like a soup

kitchen. It's all an act—what happens outside the study—and you
have to get into it. (McFarlin 6:13)

Engagement between Scott and readers of his work: Readers (beyond
his editors, agents, and personal friends) wrote to Scott praising his novels. He shared his thoughts about readership with a young author who
was trying to get published:

> To publish a book is to offer it to everyone who cares to read it, and
> the relationship set up then between reader and writer is a relation-
> ship between free-thinking and feeling people, each entitled to his
> and her view, and entitled to express it. (McFarlin 20:19)

Unsolicited interest and praise always touched Scott deeply; he would
write detailed letters in response to people such as Valerie Meidlinger
from Johannesburg, who told him that reading *The Corrida at San Feliu*
was like listening to Bach. He advised a reader from Albuquerque not
to read any of his books before *The Mark of the Warrior* because he
couldn't look the other books "in the face" (McFarlin 12:12).

Mastering the craft: For Scott, writing was a vocation—more than an
occupation, more than an act of economic production. After the end of his
first year as a full-time novelist, he wrote to his friend Gerald Hanley, "I feel,
in the past few months, to have grown several inches, and now that the end
of my first year's freedom is nearly here do, do admit that this is what I am
in the bloody world to do" (McFarlin 6:13). "Vocation" entailed purpose,
a direction for Scott's energy and talents, a life's work that proved worthy
and fulfilling. The agon of a writer trying to write great novels is one of
the most powerful motifs in Scott's correspondence during this period. In
November of 1961, he wrote to Willey, his publisher at William Morrow,

> There's something a bit wrong with my work. I talked to M[aurice
> Temple Smith] about this and asked him to be honest. He put
> it rather well. He said he always expected me to do something
> really terrific and that what I did do was streets ahead of most
> of the things that got real acclaim but that there was a kind of
> membrane in the books, the final membrane I might never break
> through but he thought I would, and if I did, well there we were,

perhaps part of lit. hist. and read fifty years from now, or maybe
he said a hundred. (McFarlin 13:2)

It wasn't until he completed *The Corrida at San Feliu* that Scott believed
he had achieved the immediacy he had lacked: "I felt I'd broken through
that little barrier that up to then had stood between me and my material"
(McFarlin 13:7).

In August of 1961, when he was completing *The Birds of Paradise*, he
wrote about his published novels to agent David Higham, "I don't believe
passionately in them. I think I'm learning to feel strongly (if not passionately) that I've done my best with them, but that's all" (McFarlin 7:19). To
Violet Wilkinson, who attended the Swanwick Summer Writers' School
and wrote to him about *The Birds*, Scott admitted in May of 1962,

> Once a book is finished it is, for me, finished in practically every
> sense. I can never read a book through once I've passed the proofs.
> A book is a kind of total vision, I suppose, and having had it and
> mapped it, the life goes out of it. You drain its substance away in
> words and leave scarcely a shadow for yourself. Who is Conway?
> Who is Cranston? I no longer know. I knew at the time. I knew
> very well. (McFarlin 20:19)

Despite his love/hate relationship with his past novels, Scott believed in
his capabilities as a writer. In April of 1963, he wrote to his friend Peter
Green, "I don't lack confidence in what I can do, only in what is going to
happen to it" (McFarlin 6:4).

PERSONAL LIFE

An indication of Scott's growing reputation was his 1959 invitation to
lecture at the Swanwick Writers' Summer School in Derbyshire, the first
creative writing workshop in England, founded in 1948. He returned to
lecture in 1960 (accompanied by his wife, Penny, and their two girls)
and then cohosted the school in 1961 with Jean Plaidy. In 1962 Scott
cohosted with Penny, herself a gifted writer who published four novels
under the pen name Elizabeth Avery.[4]

Scott flew to New York in 1963 for a book tour marking the publication of *The Bender*, his first and (from his perspective) least salutary of several visits to the states. That same year, he was elected a fellow of the Royal Society of Literature and was approached by Boston University with an invitation to donate his papers to their archives. Scott declined, choosing instead to sell his papers to the Harry Ransom Humanities Research Center at the University of Texas–Austin.

What isn't made explicit in Scott's letters to his correspondents is the increasing cost—to himself, to Penny, and to their daughters Carol and Sally—of the arduous labor that often kept him isolated from his family and friends over the long course of creating a story, its characters, its structure, and its plot. Writing full-time and depending on his income to support his family meant that for long periods of time, Scott felt forced into the role of a recluse as he crafted novels every eighteen to twenty-four months—a grueling pace. Such isolation was both a torment and a necessity, as he understood: "[I]n the end I suppose I have to sweat it out in solitary confinement!" (McFarlin 13:14). As he labored with *The Birds of Paradise* (in the closing months of 1960), he wrote to Willey,

> I think I know where I am as a writer, but have no idea where I am as a person with rights and obligations in society. It is all very curious, and no doubt simply the effect of sitting for the past two months on the high wall which divides glamorous progress from plodding. (McFarlin 12:20)

In what is perhaps the most revealing exchange of letters—between E. M. (Chris) Almedingen and Scott in the early 1960s—one sees Scott confessing to a "wretchedness" on the occasion of negative reviews of *The Chinese Love Pavilion*. Such wretchedness wasn't simply a response to cruel and catty critics, but an inner vulnerability he had felt even when he worked as an agent: "[U]nderneath that rather bland agency face I was a mess of wretchedness, far more tender than perhaps I looked" (McFarlin 1:5). Almedingen told him she had seen or perhaps intuited this aspect of his character, an aspect that "should never be pried into" (McFarlin 1:5). But she encouraged Scott not to lose faith in himself, for in that wretchedness, she told him, is "where your integrity comes alive in your work. Don't dismiss it as a paradox" (McFarlin 1:5). Almedingen continually reminded him of this true source of support: "You'll go on giving your friends as much as ever & more & more as the years go on. Such is your nature, and you'll be comfortable (in the good Elizabethan sense of the word) by Penny" (McFarlin 1:5). However, their friendship waned when Almedingen refused Scott's request to dedicate *The Bender* to her.

In Scott's own letters, there are few hints of tension or estrangement. Rather, what is made explicit is his devotion and connection to his wife. To his lifelong friend Clive Sansom, who had written to him about his enjoyment of *The Mark of the Warrior*, Scott confessed his pleasure:

> In particular to know that you liked Esther and the relationship between her and Craig. In many ways Esther is based on Penny—and that is not to suppose that Craig is based on myself—but the relationship between them is, as you say, concerned with the less spectacular but continuing aspect of marriage, and my understanding of these is gathered from knowledge and appreciation of Penny. I'm not sure she's seen this yet, probably not. I shan't tell her! (McFarlin 17:12)

Yet, there emerge the tips of hidden icebergs, such as Scott's apology to his friend Kay Dick in 1960: "Please forgive me for my silence and disappearance, but when I'm in this sort of state I'm not fit for human consumption" (McFarlin 3:20). There is also his confession to his friend the author Mary Patchett in March of 1962:

> Penny and I are looking forward so much to seeing you again, at the party. I'm sorry I've been so silent, but have rather been lost to the land of the living (other than agent and publisher and postman) for the last whole year; now I hope to be just about finishing the new novel by the time <u>Birds of P</u> comes out. (McFarlin 15:24)

Once he was out of his study in "the land of the living," Scott had difficulty coping. Note, for instance, his account of a bender to Gerald Hanley in July of 1961, when he was nearly arrested for attempting to steal a car: "The awful thing is that at a certain stage my mind seems to go blank (I mean during one of these alcoholic sessions)" (McFarlin 6:13). There is also his story of drunken misery in response to his treatment at Eyre & Spottiswoode, told humorously to Muriel Spark (9 November 1961) but ending with Scott sitting in the garage with the door closed and his car engine running until "there's a wind on a still night and the garage door swings wide open, so that I nearly jump out of my skin, and get away from that awful place very quickly" (McFarlin 18:19). His confession to Hanley—"sometimes [I] fear I'll become an alcoholic" (McFarlin 6:13)—would prove to be prophetic.

WORKS CITED

Scott, Paul. *My Appointment with the Muse*. Ed. Shelly C. Reece. London: Heinemann, 1986. Print.

Box 9, Folder 26 (McFarlin)
78 Addison Way
To Peter Hebdon, Michael Joseph Ltd.
1 January 1960

Dear Peter,

<u>Elizabeth Avery</u>[5]

Olive Shapley (BBC TV) wants to use some of my own and Penny's mss, typescripts, and finished copies to illustrate to viewers what a book looks like during the various stages of writing.

We are sending some stuff to her direct, but she would like a finished copy of both <u>The Marigold Summer</u> and <u>The Margaret Days</u>, and as we have nothing here except the file copies (and those wonderful leather-bound editions) we wondered whether you'd be so kind as to send them to her from Bloomsbury Street. I've told her that's what we'll arrange, so only the books and a compliment slip would be necessary, if the parcel is addressed to her personally:

Olive Shapley,
BBC
<u>MANCHESTER</u>

I think the programme is recorded on 13 Jan.

Meanwhile, still thinking of titles for <u>Private Nurse</u>, we thought yesterday (after Penny had written) of: <u>The Prodigal Nurse</u>. Reference to this could be worked into the text. I know that the narrator isn't prodigal, except in the sense that, like the son, she returned (to nursing), but from the nursing profession point of view her defection would have been like that of the famous son. Penny says she could also work in a joke about not having the fatted calf—(remember the meagre meals beautifully served up at her first case?).

Both of us rather like it.[6] What do you think?

Yours ever,

Box 12, Folder 19 (McFarlin)
78 Addison Way
From a letter to John Willey, William Morrow & Company, USA
16 January 1960

Dear John,

[...] Main reason for this letter is a) to say how thrilled I am at Ivan [von Auw]'s reaction[7] (I eagerly await a promised letter from him) and b) to tell you E & S react similarly. I had a session with them yesterday about their remaining editorial points and thought I'd give you the gist of them so that when you and Adèle [Dogan] come to the point of setting out your own you can take them into consideration. I don't want to work on them until I know your and Adèle's views—but when I get down to them I must be quick because E & S's deadline now, for September publication over here, is the middle of February for final typescript ready for press. In the main their remaining points are the ones I expected, since I had similar slight personal misgivings. They are:

a)   That terribly long scene between Brent and Turner at the beginning of Part Two. They want this cut down to about 6 pages.
b)   They want the old ending, with Brent's walk across the garden and the dialogue with Sutton, and Brent going into the room and finding Teena.
c)   They want the old time schedule, i.e., of Brent going to Singaputan <u>after</u> the masque in the pavilion, so that he feels Teena has rejected him and <u>then</u> finds Saxby dead, and <u>then</u> feels perhaps Teena hasn't rejected him, and so returns to find all hell let loose.

These are the major points. There are minor ones. They want a few pages put back into the scene of Tom's and Teena's first night in the pavilion, so that there is a more immediate feeling of Tom falling in love and being jealous of Hakinawa. They also want the fact that she slept with guerrillas put back in this scene. I'm not sure about that one. They'd like something of the old Reid-binocular-heatstroke stuff put back in.[8] Something I discovered was left out in the typing was the tremendously important para[graph] about Brent's reaction to Sutton as a man so "tight wound and unresilient"—and Maurice [Temple Smith] has made a good point. After the shooting in the clearing when Sutton thinks "he has had his beating", Reid's behaviour should suggest to him that he has, but that's not quite the end of it. This is good. It reaches forward to the motif of the <u>reward</u> (which Sutton can't cope with, i.e., physical relations with Teena).

They've had a complete cold reading on it from a new editorial boy they've taken in there called James Wright. Wright thinks it's a winner, but agrees re long Brent-Turner scene. Amusing about Wright. I turned him down as a reader for DHA about two years ago! I've bought myself a statuette of Ganesh, the Elephant god, and burn joss sticks in order that we might have a bestseller on our hands. Hope, hope, hope. And work of course.

As ever, to you and Adèle,

Box 12, Folder 19 (McFarlin)
78 Addison Way
To Adèle Dogan, William Morrow & Company, USA
22 January 1960

Dear Adèle,

You can imagine the joy with which I've read your letter of the 20th—and thank you for your thoughtfulness in getting a letter off to me so quickly. As you'll see it arrived in record time. I've copied it and sent it to Maurice Temple Smith. Unless he comes up with some pretty strongly reasoned arguments (and I don't think I adequately conveyed his feelings about the Turner-Brent scene, which were based more on the belief that it represented a constructional fault than a dull passage) I think author's vanity alone will persuade me to agree with you and John [Willey] about leaving things more or less as they are. Quite apart from author's vanity, however, is the sense of your deep understanding for what I've been up to—this sense is conveyed to me in every line of your letter. I'm more than usually grateful for this at the present time because frankly I wrote myself into the ground in the three months to the end of the year. At the end of it I wasn't sure whether I had cancer of the right lung, a tubercular infection of the left, or an incipient coronary thrombosis. But it was only indigestion! But I'm still pretty fogged about the broad lines of the book, fogged, I mean, when I try to look <u>back</u> at them. At the time they were all clear and exciting and felt right. But now I would be hard put to it to say why I wrote the Turner-Brent scene in that way and in that place. I feel it must be right, and now you say it is right (and give good reasons why). The same goes for the time schedule and for the last scene in the garden. You don't comment on the odd use of apparent quotations from the record of a summary of evidence (the opening of the final section entitled "The door by which men go"). I hope this means you either liked it or didn't dislike it. Maurice didn't like it, but that dislike was, I think, bound up in his sadness at not having the walking-towards-Sutton-with-his-sten-gun scene. It seemed to me that Brent, telling this whole story, would, when he came to it, find it less painful to tell us of Teena's death by letting news of it emerge in the quotation. And then there's the whole question of the trend towards ambiguity. Did Teena love him? Or not? Actuality has to take second place from the emotional point of view and yet actual happenings have to be recorded. Hence—the quotation from the summary of evidence. But perhaps John will decide he doesn't like this. I'll await your further letter and meanwhile be thinking about the Saxby notebook. (I can cope with that sort of thing because it is all specific.)

Re: the business of eight days for Saxby to do damage to Teena. True, the threat has been imminent for much longer. What I meant, though, was this: It was only on the day Turner rang Brent calling him to join the safari that Brent had decided there was really something in Turner's fears about Saxby's intentions. Within an hour or two of Brent becoming aware of the threat to Teena he is off into the jungle expecting to find Saxby. But it's not Saxby. 4 days wasted coming. 4 days more to get back. God! Eight days and nothing he can do about it. Anything can happen in eight days! It was eight days for <u>Brent</u>. Even if it had been eight months in reality, Teena was safe when he left. It is these eight days that count. He <u>must</u> get back. (But I'll clarify further if you feel this is a break in the flow.) Bless you all. I am happy, too. As a sand boy.

Ever yours,

Box 2, Folder 5 (McFarlin)
78 Addison Way
To Donald McWhinnie, BBC Broadcasting House
29 February 1960

Dear Donald,

The Mark of the Warrior

I'd be very grateful if you'd take a look at this section of the script.[9] I've got to the stage of not being able to get into it from underneath—or, at least, of thinking myself as unable to do that. I wanted very much not to make this a sort of straight forward surface adaptation but, instead, to do something exciting with it in terms of sound, and I'm sure I <u>could</u> do that if there wasn't this suspicion nagging away at the back of my mind that I've "lost touch" with the people and the events. I try to tell myself that the "lost touch" feeling is only due to the fact that since we last met, when I thought the new novel [*Love Pavilion*] would be off my plate well before Christmas, not a weekend has gone by when I haven't had to deal with a chapter, a paragraph or even a sentence as the result of a query either from the publishers here or the publishers in New York.

So if you could tell me frankly whether the enclosed "works" or is just plain dull, that would be the first step. You've no idea how guilty I feel about all this, but if—in view of the time that has elapsed since I finished the novel on which this play is based—I really have lost touch, no grinding away at the desk is going to produce the answer....

I'm very sorry indeed to find myself writing such a letter as this. It has meant pocketing my pride to a certain extent, but far better to do that than plug away half-heartedly and produce something that will just get by contractually but please neither of us in the final reckoning....

Ever yours,

Box 12, Folder 19 (McFarlin)
78 Addison Way
From a letter to John Willey, William Morrow & Company, USA
9 May 1960

Dear John,

[…] I'm delighted you like the title <u>The Birds of Paradise</u>.[10] I was telling Adèle [Dogan] a bit about how things are going when I wrote her last Friday. I have indeed begun to write and have set myself a kind of mental deadline for the completion of the first draft: September 30. This may not work out of course, but I'm in business to write novels, so some strict business planning is in order! I've started the book for the sixth time. Altogether I reckon I've put something like 16,000 words down on paper, including about 4000 words of start number 6. But the shape is still a bit obscure. The great thing about my newfound freedom is the time available for thinking on paper, instead of just thinking in the air. Of course I find myself having to adjust to the idea that a day of having done <u>nothing</u>, in the sense of nothing achieved, is not a day wasted. And having to adjust, too, to the realisation that an awful lot of time goes by very quickly. You will laugh, I know, but a while ago I absolutely panicked. This was round about start number four. Then I looked at the calendar and saw I'd only been freelancing for 3 weeks, and some words of yours came back to me, something about the object of the exercise being to produce novels, so I stopped myself ringing up Tom, Dick and Harry and saying, "Pile more reading on to me, I've got to earn some money!" No doubt from time to time I shall panic again; which is why I'm keeping those things above my desk, to remind myself I'm a "fiction headliner" on the Morrow list. Agency seems far away. I'm doing a bit of reading for E & S and Michael Joseph. I've also put down on paper outlines for three television plays. But if the latter, or one of them, isn't commissioned I shan't mind and I shan't bother. I have Bill and Dora,[11] and I'm sure they're firm people because through all the sweat of finding a way into the story and background and situation I've had the feeling of them waiting patiently in a certain spot, and saying, "We'll be here when you get round to us".

Please don't bother to reply to this rigmarole. It's nice for me to throw thoughts on paper to you and Adèle, but that's all they are, and only authors have time to waste other people's!!

Best regards from Penny & myself,

Box 4, Folder 8 (McFarlin)
78 Addison Way
From a letter to John Bright-Holmes, Eyre & Spottiswoode, Ltd.
7 June 1960

Dear John,

The advance copy of <u>The Love Pavilion</u> arrived today safe and sound. I'm thrilled with it. It really is remarkably handsome.

We're getting a recommend from the Book Society (Peter Green) but not, alas, a Choice. I've held up typing this note until evening, guessing Peter would ring me when he came out of the meeting. My blood is boiling a bit because one member, according to Peter, dismissed it as "perverted"! It was a close thing but the bastards played safe in the end and pushed a majority vote through for some crapulous novel. Apologies. I'm letting off steam. It won't make any difference in the end. Am longing to hear some of the reactions on your side, trade and elsewhere.

[…] Perhaps I'd better rewrite <u>The Pavilion</u> quickly, and turn Teena into a boy, introduce some good, wholesome sodomy and get a proper pass mark.

Sorry! But it still rankles. Reid was right: "They won't let you lose yourself in a woman any more". The important thing of course is that it's obviously made somebody <u>angry</u>. Good. Better than a shrug.

Now I'll calm myself down by holding your edition in my hands and <u>glowing</u>.

As ever,

Box 16, Folder 6 (McFarlin)
78 Addison Way
To M. E. Rolton[12]
9 July 1960

Dear Sir,

<u>Three things are to be considered: a man's estimate of himself, the face he presents to the world, the estimate of that man made by other men. Combined, they form an aspect of truth.</u>

Thank you very much indeed for your kind and interesting letter which was forwarded by the BBC and reached me this morning. Let me say at once that I am always glad to hear from people. Direct links between readers and writers (or listeners and writers) are rarer, I think, these days, than they should be.

The quotation which was spoken at the beginning and at the end of the radio adaptation actually appears in the novel[13] as "The Argument". It isn't actually a quotation but an attempt of my own to put into words, into a few words, what I felt (still feel) about people in relation to events, and in relation to each other.

If you decide to read the novel—and I should say here that because it is about soldiers it is, in some of its dialogue, outspoken in the fashion normally accepted today; only occasionally, but still outspoken—you will find that it is presented more or less alternately from two viewpoints; that of the older man, Craig, and that of the younger man, Ramsay. Each has an estimate of himself, each presents himself to the world in a particular way, and finally each has thoughts and feelings about the other. Every so often you could say, for example, No, Craig is wrong, that's not how it is. And yet, in one way, Craig is not wrong, and that is how it is.

Both Craig and Ramsay make errors of judgment, you could say. But the total picture, the combination of their "rightness" and their "wrongness", must be a valid picture. It must have a truth of its own. I have put that very badly but then something that can be explained really clearly is, in my opinion, suspect. And when you have expended some 70,000 words writing a novel it is difficult to describe its meaning in a few hundred. I may of course be wrong about that; my inability to discuss the "argument" more lucidly may simply be due to intellectual failure. But then I subscribe more to the argument "I feel, therefore I am" than I do to "I think, therefore I am".

I hope that the "argument", now that you can see it in black and white, doesn't disappoint you or fall short of your earlier conception of it.

Thank you again for writing.

Yours truly,

Box 18, Folder 19 (McFarlin)
78 Addison Way
To Muriel Spark
13 July 1960

My Dear Muriel,

Alan MacLean's secretary writes to me this morning to say that "we are now planning to publish <u>The Bachelors</u> on October 13th" and that they will keep me informed of any "pleasant developments". Whether the latter still means the Book Society or not I don't know, but I feel rather that the Book Soc must have had their meeting, and said no. Perhaps you've already heard from Alan. Anyway, I'm now writing to Bill Smith[14] to fix the date for the article on the basis of the book coming out on October 13, which I see is a Thursday. A good day. You could start off with a fine <u>Times</u> review on the very day of pubn. and the Sundays follow quickly, cutting down the awful waiting period which has to elapse if a book is published on a Monday or Tuesday. I see I am also a Thursday, Sept. 29 [*The Chinese Love Pavilion*]. We are coming out more or less together. Ours will be the best books of the month. Ours will be the best books of the autumn. We shall drip with mink, diamonds (you), Italian silk suits and sharkskin bathing trunks (me). I picture me somewhere in the sun, which is why I choose silk suits and sharkskin trunks. I find after 20 years of not caring a damn about how I look or what I dress in (between 17 and 20, I was a bit of a peacock) I am looking with an upsurge of interest at the shops in Regent Street, Shaftesbury Avenue, etc. I think I'm probably a teddy boy at heart. I lust after Italiante short jackets and tapering trousers. The only trouble is the waistband. I carry at least an extra stone of weight there. But I shall be able to afford expensive massage and steam baths.

Dear Muriel, I am a stinker. I failed to hear your talk about the House of MacNiece. By the way, don't all those chaps look old? Did you see that shaking picture of Auden and Day Louis? Those angry young men of the Thirties. The Dog Beneath the Skin now has rheumy eyes and an uncontrollable tremour in the hind legs.

Blessings,

Box 15, Folder 15 (McFarlin)
78 Addison Way
To Ivan von Auw, Harold Ober Associates, USA
12 August 1960

Dear Ivan,

David [Higham] is on holiday at the moment and several things have developed and been confirmed which you may therefore not know of but be interested in. First and foremost E & S are getting such a good subscription already on The Chinese Love Pavilion that they are reprinting 5000 copies making 15000 as a total first impression. Secondly, after some briskish bidding from Penguin, Pan and Ace, we have settled with Pan at an advance of £1000 plus reprint of The Mark of the Warrior plus promise of star billing when they publish. I was sorry not to be able to go to Penguin, but finally felt it better to stay with Pan while they want me. They may not want me when they see The Birds of Paradise, which is more Penguinish than Pannish. On the other hand, to have gone to Penguin now might have produced an awkward situation if Penguin don't like The Birds of P (which won't be finished until the end of the year as I see it at the moment).

The other event is sale of Swedish rights to Norstedt for £250 advance, which is good money there.

All the signs at this end are more than promising. I think Smith's will be backing it quite heavily. The advance publicity has been first rate, and we may get a television spot. Gradually all one's old friends move up in the world and if certain things happen two of them will be running the Commercial TV book programme. Even without that we'll probably get a spot. I'm also getting the front cover of our one and only lit. monthly, Books and Bookmen.

So this is fine. What I believe is not so fine is what is happening in New York. Reading between John [Willey]'s and Adèle [Dogan]'s cautious lines I see nothing but puzzlement on the part of people who have read advance copies. Maintaining a deliberately cheerful front I mentioned to Adèle in passing about 2 weeks ago that if things didn't look so promising on their side, I wouldn't be at all put out if they decided to postpone publication in the hope of getting some advantage from an English autumn success. So far I've not had any reaction from them, to that. But I get the feeling they are thinking about it none the less.

I mention this to you wholly to put you in the picture as I see it, and am not asking you to do anything, as it were. If there's anything you know which I don't know, or guess which I don't guess, or feel, or think, or have heard, as it were, do drop me a line though.

On the financial side the first Morrow year isn't going to look bad to them. I've had £750 approx so far, the equiv. of a $2000 advance on The Pavilion; and because of moneys accruing due here, it doesn't look as if I'll be asking for any more until April 1st next, which I think not bad going. They know this, because I've pointed it out in passing to Adèle.

I may be quite wrong in thinking they're all pretty downhearted; and please don't think (or let them think) that I am in any way. I just feel philosophical about it on the one hand and practical minded on the other, i.e., postponed publication might be better all round, because once the book is out on your side nothing that happens to it over here is going to make a scrap of difference. On the other hand, of course, the two markets are quite different anyway, and even a rave success (which I don't expect; I'm sure half the critics will try to shoot me down on the Suzie Wong angle) at this end need have no effect on US pubn, postponed or otherwise.

And it is wonderful being free. The Birds of Paradise moves slowly at its own pace, as novels tend to do, but at least I'm never frustrated by being kept away from it, only frustrated by not being able to put it down right, more often than not. With nice moneys coming in on advances, etc. I've cut down my extraneous reading, etc., to nil, almost, to give me a clear run until the autumn, when part of its back may be broken.

Lunched with Fred Warburg the other day and asked what news of Stanley Baron.[15] He said there wasn't any, which saddens me. Do give him my best regards when next you write or see him. And meanwhile my best regards, as well, to you and Dorothy.[16] I hope we'll meet next year.

Ever,

Box 1, Folder 5 (McFarlin)
78 Addison Way
From a letter to E. M. Almedingen, Shrewsbury[17]
27 August 1960

My Dear Chris,

[…] Things look fairly promising for The Chinese Love Pavilion, which comes out at the end of September. Meanwhile Walter Allen, who is now literary editor of the New Statesman, has asked me to try my hand at the once-a-month fiction review column, and I begin with the issue of September 10th. This is, in some ways, a nuisance because it means reading a lot of stuff you don't want to read; on the other hand it is good for prestige, since there are some who would never take me seriously, having been an agent (an ungentlemanly occupation which automatically disqualifies you from membership of the Garrick; not that I should want to be a member of the Garrick, being pretty unclubbable). I wonder when your next novel is coming? Perhaps I'll have the opportunity of saying in public the kind of things I've always wanted to say about one of my best friends and most generous client […].

Box 6, Folder 13 (McFarlin)
78 Addison Way
To Gerald Hanley
n.d., [September 1960]

My Dear Gerry,

Oh, Lord, just earned £3,000 in America, my share of a paperback deal. But when, how and why I get it, God knows. Anyway I've committed myself to buying a car on the HP[18] so that sometimes I can get out of town and smell fresh air.

You're in that awful proof stage, then. God, yes, how I loathe it. I hate the book violently when it comes to that. All that mass of words, and none of them seeming to say a single damn thing. Blank, flat, useless, and so damned expensive.

It was nice to hear again from you, Gerry. I am in a state of mild disorder: bad cold, a TV interview last Tuesday night for this Sunday's Bookmen, people telling me the pagoda will "run away" but a lot of debts hanging around with leers on their faces. And already I worked it out that any unlooked for money I get like that paperback dollop—half of it goes to the Inland Revenue or the National Society for the Prevention of something. Prevention of work I suppose. Anyway, half to the CIR or not, we rate a Dog and Duck on it. So when, how, how soon?

Films. Oh, Lord, yes. I used to tell myself I'd give my right arm to do some film scripting. Now I'd almost give my right arm just to be left in peace to get on with The Birds of Paradise. A hut, a lot of sun, sea, wife, children, no money troubles, a luxury flat I could descend upon occasionally if absolutely necessary, and piles of paper and a good workable typewriter, and time, and heaven smiling. And health, no sickness. And love all around me and inside me; not this coming and going and signing on the dotted line and being wooed by some crap publisher you don't want to go to. And this, I tell myself, all this that is now a bit nasty, this is what I used to have ambitions for; and worked myself up into a tizzy just to meet this great man or that useful woman.

The bloody trouble is we are only alive when we're half dead trying to get a paragraph right. The rest (except the love of a good woman) is high fever.

Do let me know about a trip to London soon. I'd like to knock back a sensible pint….

Ever,

Box 12, Folder 20 (McFarlin)
78 Addison Way
To John Willey, William Morrow & Company, USA
28 September 1960

Dear John,

Many thanks for your letter of the 23rd. I'm glad the scotch arrived in time. Don't worry about reviews. The book [*The Chinese Love Pavilion*] will make its way, I think, and even if the final result doesn't match all our early expectations we shall have the satisfaction of knowing we all did our damndest. And the paperback sale was a triumph.[19] The Bookseller didn't use the gossip piece; not that I imagine it would have mattered.

Tomorrow is D-day over here. The subscription will be just under 10,000 Maurice thinks, which takes care of their first printing. Their second printing of 5000 will be in a day or two so they don't expect to be out of stock even for 24 hours. Now we wait upon public reactions. The TV interview was liked by a number of people who rang me.

We shall now be exchanging news and views, I expect. I have first night nerves. Peter Green has got me for The Daily Telegraph, and I know Maurice Richardson is doing me in The New Statesmen (though what he will think I can't say). I'm keeping my fingers crossed either to be ignored by the Times tomorrow (pubn day falling upon the Times' once weekly book page) or to get a lead review from them. After that the main hurdle is the two Sundays. But, once again, I don't want to worry about reviews. Again, the book, I think, will find its way with or without them. This is rather stiff upper lip, I suppose, but I have a sort of conviction in the bones about the whole thing.

Blessings on you all,

Ever yours,

Box 3, Folder 16 (McFarlin)
78 Addison Way
To John Davenport, The Observer
2 October 1960

Dear John Davenport,

I apologize again for invading your weekend privacy—but, as I said, I was too unsure of your address just to send a telegram of thanks.

Ever since A Male Child you have been kind and generous and encouraging to me in The Observer, judging me by high standards, getting the books right, making me feel that I'm not wasting my time. What you say this morning in The Observer about The Chinese Love Pavilion is naturally what I hoped somebody might one day say (and, yes, hoped someone would say about this particular book), but when it comes one feels the deepest gratitude. I laughed the Grigson off on Friday morning, but by last night the words "parasitical" and "thirty years out of date" had made me feel dirty and useless, close to that special contemplative suicide writers mock themselves in.[20]

So you will see you have done me more than ordinary service. I'll try not to embarrass you with too much thanks on Wednesday, but look forward very much to meeting you between 12.00 and 12.15 at The York Minster. I have dark hair and a very large looking nose and shall probably be wearing a blue and silver horizontally striped tie which was described at a party the other day as very vulgar. Come to think of it, it probably is.

With warmest thanks, and kindest regards,

Yours sincerely,

Box 12, Folder 20 (McFarlin)
78 Addison Way
From a letter to John Willey, William Morrow & Company, USA
3 October 1960

Dear John,

In case this reaches you first I should tell you there is a separate letter in the airmail enclosing the first batch of reviews, together with comments of my own. And, just in case it is held up I should tell you that John Davenport in The Observer (the top lit. paper) puts it at the head of his column and calls it not only my best book but "one of the best English novels of the last decade".

[…] Now, what I was going to look into over here, and still intend to look into, is an arrangement with a British Publisher (and I shall ask David [Higham] to talk to E & S first) which would bring the British publisher into the guarantee system, reduce your guarantee, but increase my total guarantee. The way I see it as working is that the British publisher, having a similar undertaking from me to write one novel a year for a specified period, would pay, say, equal sums with you quarterly into the kitty. It always struck me as a bit grasping of E & S merely to say "how nice for you" when I told them about Morrow's gesture (gesture is an understatement). I had hoped they would say, "Well, come on, let's join in this". I know H & S [Hodder and Stoughton] are willing to. On the other hand I'm not absolutely sure about H & S. To put all modesty aside I should be their first "literary novelist" brought into the fold for their five-year plan. (They admitted as much; and I'm not sure Peter G[reen] as their Lit. Adv. hasn't staked his reputation on getting me. They have an idea. I think that once I joined them they would get other similar novelists who got jolly good reviews. H & S are fine on sales, but the lit. editors have until fairly recently rather written them off as purely commercial publishers). E & S have once or twice hinted that I could always have, within reason, what money I wanted, when I wanted it, but an author doesn't like to go "cap in hand". He likes a business-like arrangement involving obligations on both sides.

It won't be for a week or so (perhaps a month) that I start talking to David in these terms, and first and foremost I would like to know Morrow's views. There was a time when I wondered how you could have two guarantors, since there was only one source of income (the author), but now that my brain seems to be clearer, and I'm more single-minded, I can't for the life of me think what is against two publishers sharing the guarantee undertaking. Please tell me if I'm talking out of the back of my head. In a way the British publisher ought perhaps to pay more than the U.S. publisher, but with the present dollar exchange rate (operating in our favour) and the higher price of books on your side, and the much more glamorous perks from paperbacks, it looks, on paper, as if one earns as much, or more, from a book in the States which in terms of hard cover sales is more successful over here.

Box 4, Folder 2 (McFarlin)
78 Addison Way
To Dorothy Eden[21]
4 October 1960

My Dear Dorothy,

How nice of you to write to me about <u>The Pavilion</u>; and how nice to hear from you again. I'd not realised until talking to Mary only the other day that of course you were back from your trip. How quickly the time went. At least it did here. You sailed just about the time I sailed out of Dean St. and scarcely any time seems to have gone, and yet it is six months. I have at least done 140 pages of the new novel in that time, but otherwise the days have sped by.

I was fascinated by what you told me of your reactions to Malaya. Do you know that when I was there (about 4 months, Sept '45 to Jan '46) I hated it. I was very homesick for India, and hitched a ride on a plane to Rangoon to escape a posting that would have kept me in Singapore until my release from the army. I never really acquired any love for the country and thought I should never use it as background for a novel. But then, 11 years after, it all began to work, and like you I should love to go back, but only for a look. In a sense it was almost too civilised a country for me, all those metalled roads stretching for miles, and traffic lights mixed up with the jungle. I was a month in Penang, which was rather like a Hollywood location; then about 6 weeks on the mainland, in a village called Sungei Patani (or was it Bukit Mertagam?); then down to Singapore at the beginning of December. Singapore was full of ex-mems, who were rather pathetic. Looking for husbands, looking for their old homes, their furniture. I gave one a lift once. She didn't speak all the way from one end of the island to another but when she got off she said, "It is hard for people like me to thank people, but I do even though I am bitterly ashamed to be seen <u>walking</u> and so obviously in need of a lift".

In spite of all the nonsense there was always a solid streak of guts in the Empire sundowners. The other similar experience was the morning I flew out without permission. Waiting on Kalland aerodrome for my Rangoon plane I fell in conversation with a woman just back from Java (prison camp). She was going up to KL[22] to see if anything was left of their house. She didn't know where her husband was. Her plane and mine were announced at the same time. When we stood up I reached for her bag to carry it for her. She pushed it out of my hand quite viciously (before then she had seemed perfectly normal and gentle), and shouted, "No, no. It's because people like me always had our bags carried for us that what happened to us happened". And off she strode lugging her heavy suitcase.

I hope we'll meet up again presently. Are you going to the Romantic Novelists' dinner? Penny and I are.

With love from us both,

Yours ever,

Box 1, Folder 5 (McFarlin)
78 Addison Way
From a letter to Miss E. M. Almedingen, Shrewsbury
7 October 1960

Chris, my dear,

What more <u>could</u> you say if you sat down for a week? You have saved my bacon this weekend. This may seem odd to you; but when I work it out, apart from the pre-publication "puffs" my publisher got from people like Sitwell, Storm Jameson,[23] etc., of the reviewers only John Davenport and Peter Green (and a chap called Peter Forster in <u>The Daily Press</u>, which is nothing) have liked the book. Davenport was marvellous, and the quotation at the top of the advertisements goes a long way to cancel out any idea the public may have that it is an artificial and contrived book. BUT Lord, how these critics make you smart.

When your letter came[24] I was tearing my hair about Maurice Richardson in <u>The New Statesman</u>. Quoth he, "I enjoyed the CLP enormously, but I refuse to take it seriously". There followed a cunning and subtle attack on my integrity as a writer. Unfortunately I can read between the lines. He means that I was acting like a confidence trickster—"Full of ingenious tricks and chances and equivocations that make for <u>an effect of depth</u>". An effect. Only an effect. All done by mirrors. I am thinking hard this weekend whether to write to Walter Allen and say, "The question is, now, whether I can be taken seriously by your readers as a novel reviewer". I shall have to think hard. It may have been his way of getting rid of me quickly because I haven't a <u>New Statesman</u> coloured rosette, after all, he may think he has discovered.

Chris, dear, in the end one realises one's friends <u>are</u> one's friends because it is only with them that you can speak the language you're born with. Finding you speak it you become friends. Your letter has meant so much to me. Perhaps you did not know that, underneath that rather bland agency face I was a mess of wretchedness, far more tender than perhaps I looked. I always bleed when what you call the little men prick me. And when there are enough of them with their needles out I bleed a lot, and there's no denying it. No wonder so many writers disappear into the blue and have nothing to do with the so-called literary world.

You are right about Conrad and Kipling. They are not my people. The Conrad thing in The CLP is a private joke. Saxby has been influenced by Conrad, I think; but that is all!

The trouble is about bad reviews they make you feel dirty. There is always half-a-grain of truth in the worst of them. Every novel is, in a sense, a confidence trick; but this isn't the point. I'm not sure what the point is any longer, and have not much heart to tackle the new one; I can hear what everyone will say about it in advance! Except the few who really understand and see things your way.

I mustn't bleat any more. But I did want to let you know at once how much your letter has meant. Thank you many many times […].

Bless you for everything.[25]

Love,

Box 12, Folder 20 (McFarlin)
78 Addison Way
From a letter to John Willey, William Morrow & Company, USA
23 October 1960

Dear John,

[…] Today is Penny's and my 19th wedding anniversary.[26] 19 years ago just at this hour, midday, we were in a little church in Torquay, Devonshire, and presently going off to the Queen's Hotel for wartime lunch. We left the lunch because it was our only way of "going away"— seeing how the various families had come down to where P and I were both stationed. Left the lunch, had coffee in "our" restaurant, then went to the pictures to see Larry and Viv in <u>Emma Hamilton</u>. Blackout, hard drinks under the counter at pubs, shortage of cigarettes, air raid warnings. How long ago it all seems, and yet no time at all. Makes that reviewer's remark about "still young author" very encouraging!!!

Best from us both to you all,

Box 16, Folder 2 (McFarlin)
78 Addison Way
To R. G. G. Price, <u>Punch</u>
23 October 1960

Dear Mr. Price,

I was puzzled by your review of my book <u>The Chinese Love Pavilion</u>—or rather not by your review but by my reaction to it. Perhaps even puzzled is the wrong word. When you reviewed my last book <u>The Mark of the Warrior</u> I wrote to you. You may have forgotten. It was not the most favourable review I had but I liked it best. The same situation, more or less, applies again. After some hard thinking I solved the puzzle and once more invade your privacy.

Your reviews of both these novels have left me feeling like a human being still, and not like a performing monkey (clever or inept, depending upon the critic's attitude). And reading through the rest of the column I can see how possible it is that Mr. Duggan, Miss Brooke-Rose and Mr. Waugh[27] feel the same. You seem subtly to distinguish between a man and his work and at the same time to bring them together by treating both with humane seriousness. At the risk of appearing foolish, importunate, or ingratiating I thought I should write and say so.

Yours sincerely,

Box 1, Folder 30 (McFarlin)
78 Addison Way
To William G. Smith, Chairman, Swanwick Writers' Summer School
9 November 1960

Dear Bill,

Personal

Both Penny and I are absolutely delighted—and honoured—to be invited to next year's Summer School,[28] and we accept enthusiastically. Our movements next year are, possibly, a little uncertain but I think we can say that wherever we are or whatever we are doing we should want to come to Swanwick. I don't know whether any prior help is needed but if you wanted both or one of us to sit in on any committee meetings then we'd be glad to do that, too. For instance, any help I can give about lecturers, suggestions, approaches, you only have to let me know.

And of course at Swanwick I'll be glad to work on discussion groups.

We should, of course, very much like to bring Carol and Sally as paying students, but if this is an embarrassment to the Committee and an infringement of written or unwritten law we'll quite understand and try to farm them out somewhere. They'll be 14½ and 13½ respectively by then. If the committee does decide that they may come perhaps they can help out in some way.

Incidentally, I should have been writing to you presently to say that I'd like to help out with a "scholarship" again this year, but this is as good a time as any. I'll leave its details firmly in the hands of the committee.

Meanwhile all thanks and best wishes from us both to you all.

Yours ever,

Box 12, Folder 20 (McFarlin)
78 Addison Way
To John Willey, William Morrow & Company, USA
21 November 1960

Dear John,

Film. Still no definite news [regarding *The Chinese Love Pavilion*]: temperature even, though. Producer now looking for director who will share his enthusiasm and nothing to do meanwhile. Our meeting went well. Producer said he'd like me to have a go at the screenplay if he committed himself to the property, so I said yes. I liked his approach.

Meeting with Maurice [Temple Smith]. Very friendly, etc., but we didn't discuss finance. I didn't bring it up because the day before, dined with Maurice uncertain whether I was still going to be a struggling writer or the owner of (to me) vast sums of money. I did ask him whether he realised the 3 novel contract was finished, and he said he hadn't realised that but that he would want to tie me up backwards forwards and sideways "when the time came". I wasn't sure what time he had in mind, but left it at that and concentrated on telling him what I could about The Birds of Paradise, which seemed to excite him no end.

Foreign affairs. You know of the Swedish sale and Italian sale. This morning DHA have rung me to say that German Language rights have gone to a firm whose name I can't spell or pronounce[29] (they publish John Masters) for an advance of $1500. Uncertain about my whole financial structure, I asked them to make it payable on demand after signature.

The Birds of Paradise: Have spent the past fortnight reconstructing. Came a moment (still not quite over) when I thought my 40,000 words would have to be scrapped. 40,000 seems to be my danger level. It happened to The Pavilion, you may remember.

The Chinese Love Pav. Achieved place in Books of the Month bestseller list. Last word from Maurice (ten days ago) was that sale showed no signs of dropping off.

Money. DHA's told me on Friday that the $2800 is now on its way over.

$64,000 question. Is there any movement in New York? A friend returned from there said he had seen splendid displays in the bookshops. Is it, though, a bookshop flopperoo? Am I going to earn in royalties the money you have paid me by way of "guarantee" (leaving the paperback money intact—minus the agreed repayment for the u/adv on Mk of Warrior?) How tough are you going to be about April 1st as deliv. date for the Birds of P (I bet you saw that one coming!). Should we suspend the guarantee arrangement and leave me breast-stroking? David Higham told me a book a year was too much for me. I try not to admit he's right.[30] I have to have deadlines. But it won't go faster than it will in spite of my almost total absorption in it. When you have a moment your thoughts on paper could help me to think. I think I know where I am as a writer, but have no idea where I am as a person with rights and obligations in society. It is all very curious, and no doubt simply the effect of sitting for the past two months on the high wall which divides glamorous progress from plodding.

My very best to you all,

Ever,

Box 19, Folder 5 (McFarlin)
78 Addison Way
To Donald McLachlan, Editor, Sunday Telegraph
3 December 1960

Dear Mr. McLachlan,

As I promised when I saw you on Thursday morning I'm sending on to you, today, under separate cover, a copy of The Alien Sky—the novel of mine which dealt, amongst other things, with Eurasians in India. I should be most grateful if you'd let me have this copy back when you've finished with it, as it is the only copy I have of the hard-cover cheap edition. Many thanks in anticipation.

I enjoyed our talk a lot and if you decide I'm the right man I'd be more than delighted to go out to India. I'm a fairly free agent and a trip of this kind would involve no personal difficulties. I think the ideal time to go would be in late February, into March. Later, the heat is a deciding factor and after that the wet monsoon. From April to October is therefore, in my opinion, out. I don't mean only because of my own physical comfort but because of the difficulty of getting people to talk sensibly.

A possible itinerary which would cover both Western and Eastern Pakistan, and India, would be to make first for Rawalpindi and travel by rail from there to Calcutta, stopping perhaps at Lahore. From Calcutta one is within each reach of Ranchi (one of the smaller cantonments—whose Grant Hotel provided me with blueprint for Smith's Hotel in The Alien Sky) and—in the other direction—of Comilla and Chittagongo (East Pakistan). If I go I should want to get down in the Madras direction to see this Indian friend of mine (whom I mentioned in connexion with a South Indian Village), but I have a similar contact in Calcutta.

The Eurasians have always interested me as a writer (they popped up again in the Bombay section of <u>The Chinese Love Pavilion</u>) and it would be fascinating to judge at first how well or badly they are being absorbed into the social structure. Just off the cuff one wonders, for instance, with what dismay they view the proposal to make Hindi the language of the administration. In my day many of them affected to know nothing of Indian languages—I suspect that their life is still clannish, exclusive, but that now their exclusion tends to be self-imposed. Perhaps they see themselves as the inheritors of the British social tradition.

Again just off the cuff, my terms of reference might be observation of middle-class social life generally. What kind of top is therefore there to be room at? In spite of official Indianisation policies the social tradition is western.

On a different level entirely it might be interesting to have a look at the refugee camps, which I understand still flourish as a relic of the two-way exchange of populations. Could write up almost from the imagination: other writers, students, and ministers of the republic all busy with ideas. The daily bread and evening leisure of a Eurasian or educated Indian (clerk) and his wife would be much more rewarding subjects of inquiry.

I look forward to hearing what you decide.

Yours sincerely,

Box 7, Folder 19 (McFarlin)
78 Addison Way
From a letter to David Higham, David Higham Associates[31]
2 February 1961

My Dear David,

March 31st, the end of the first year's working of the Morrow guarantee arrangement is not far ahead. Neither for that matter is the due delivery date for the new novel. John Willey has already told me not to worry much about it; nevertheless the book is making a lot of progress, even on the 4 paces forward 3 paces back basis. I am much set on having the draft at the typist just before I go, as I hope, to Spain in April, when we are taking what amounts to our summer holiday. A lot depends on the next six weeks. The end is curiously in sight in a so near yet so far way. You know how it is. What I am more confident about this time than ever before is the draft turning out to be more or less final. It will be about 80,000 words, something like 150,000 will have been written. What I am also quite sure about is that devastating though this business of "concentrating all his time of writing" can be, particularly when it comes to a kind of puritan panic at the way time goes by and you can't for the life of you seem to justify it in terms of visible results, it is working in the way it was meant to work. A new novel <u>will</u> be ready soon. And whatever is thought of that novel by the people who read it, <u>I</u> can at least be sure it is my considered best, far closer than ever before to what I've set out to do. Whether what I've set out to do is worth a brass farthing doesn't make any difference. The reward of having time to concentrate is being able to control the instinct to take the easy way. As we know every word is a compromise but now I feel it is only first stage compromise; in other words, as close as I can get.

What I'm writing to you about really is finance. For a long time now, ever since September, I've been in a kind of muddle. There seemed at times to be a lot of pie in the sky, but the sky's cleared up now. No pie but no clouds. The film thing won't, I think, ever come off. The India trip is off. It's easier to sort out hard facts from soft ones, and with the novel running downhill the time has become ripe from my point of view to plan the immediate future.

[At this point, Scott detailed in three pages his proposal for renewing his guaranteed quarterly payments from William Morrow and in another page a second proposal—a new guarantee of income with Eyre and Spottiswoode.]

[…] From my own point of view this re-arrangement has the following effect. I can get my hands on the monies piled up and about to pile up in the kitty from leftovers and current foreign sales; I am assured of an income of £3000 gross for the year to March 31st, 1962. I am not taking from either Morrow or E & S any monies they can't get back. I shan't end up in debt to either (unless E & S sell 3 copies only of The Birds of Paradise—even then there are further monies to come from Pan, not only for CLP but also for a new edition of Mark of the Warrior). I shan't have shot my bolt financially by airily waving the guarantee system away and finding myself in queer street in 1962–63. I was about to say that, in fact, only Morrow are faced with 1962–63 as a year for putting hand in pocket but they will have The Birds of Paradise, and— God Grant Us—the third and last novel under the agreement. This will help w/my earnings elsewhere.

I'm sorry to burden you with all this, David. It may take some reading to see the hang of it. Once you've got the hang, it illuminates even more the slight cloud I've been under about feeling perhaps I was quite well off, but not seeing much sign of it. As I told John some time ago, when I worked out what I would want and said £1800, I overlooked a writer's expenses. I didn't overlook a holiday because I simply thought we shouldn't be able to afford one. Well, we didn't have one this year, only motored around a bit. If 1962–63, technically my last year of freedom (!) sees me having to make do with £1800, well at least I'll have had the more opulent air of 1961–62 to make up for it. 1961–62 represents, in my thoughts, gross receipts of £3000, plus the German moneys, £500, plus any freelance reading, etc.

[…] It would be nice to hear fairly soon that this is the agreed financial pattern of 1961–62. The novel will be on its last legs (I hope), the sun in Spain will be waiting, and I shall count my blessings.

Ever,

Box 13, Folder 1 (McFarlin)
78 Addison Way
To John Willey, William Morrow & Company, USA
1 March 1961

Dear John,

Thank you very much indeed for your letter of the 24th, telling me that my plan for the coming year finds favour with you all. Naturally I'm delighted and in spite of what you say about Morrow only acquiescing, there is, so far as I'm concerned, your usual generosity all bound up in it.

John, I've delayed replying to your letter—that is to say it came in two days ago, Monday morning. I delayed because I wanted my next letter to be one telling you something really definite about The Birds of Paradise.

I wrote "End" at the bottom of the mss at 4 o'clock this morning, having had one of those wonderful ten-hour stints when you don't even feel physically tired. I had one really difficult short scene to do, and round at 11.30 it began to come right. What it looks like today, in the light of late afternoon (having just got up), I don't know, but it still feels right in the bones.[32] I shall type these last few pages slowly this evening, and then I shall have a complete, chaotic and illegible typescript which represents IT, a more considered, hacked, returned and polished IT than I've ever had before, at this pre-fair-typing stage. I have wondered about just leaving it lie until I get back from Spain, but you have to be Graham Greene to have that kind of surface indifference! So I shall spend the next ten days or fortnight typing (as best I can, which when I try isn't bad—I did the CLP myself) one top and two carbons only. After Spain I can have more final copies typed if and when necessary. But round about the middle of March, therefore, I shall take these fair copies in to David [Higham], one for him to keep safe against my return, one for Maurice [Temple Smith], and one for airmail delivery to Ivan [von Auw] for you. So round about the time I'm setting off for the sun you and Maurice should both have your copies and, Heaven be Praised, without having to strain at it as a deadline, I'll have met it! Not that I shall consider the ts final until all opinions are in. My little ego bird tells me, of course (I seem to have heard his voice before) that this time there won't be so many queries! We'll see....

Penny, by the way, has been wonderful as always in this last two months since Christmas (and before!), but she's been conducting a kind of Operation BOP, and we've hardly been out of the house together since Jan. 1; so presently we'll be having a bit of a binge; and all our Spain bookings are made. Pity one can't press a button and be sure of sun.

Well, so here we are at the end, nearly the end, of the first business year. You know without my saying it again, what it has meant to me. Naturally I hope that what lies between the covers shows it, in the way of being best ever (fingers crossed): but in any case I do want to say in this letter what has always been my intention. I want to dedicate the book to you all, and thought that something to the effect of "To Wil Morrow etc...". Might be an unclumsy way of saying what is really meant: "To John, Adèle, Sam, Janet, Frances and all my friends at Park Avenue South". The dedication goes on to say "In gratitude for my own sabbatical year", a phrase that will be further illuminated by a reading of the text.

Blessings and cheers, and my best to all of you.

Box 6, Folder 13 (McFarlin)
78 Addison Way
From a letter to Gerald Hanley
17 March 1961

My Dear Gerry,

[…] Am feeling a bit depressed tonight. My <u>Birds of Paradise</u> aren't finished. I ended them with one of those wonderful small hours stints, finishing at 4 a.m. and staggering to bed drunk with success, horny with creative fulfilment. But it was all wrong. I knew it was wrong when I typed it. I knew it was wrong again when I thought about it. I knew it was wrong when I got to it in the fair copies I was typing in the hope of getting the bloody thing out of the house before we go to Spain. Yesterday Penny read the whole book for the first time, and agreed it went wrong just before the end. If she hadn't been so damned enthusiastic about all the rest of it I'd have thrown it at the publishers and left them to tell me what was wrong when I came back, but there's this farcical pride, like an old carpenter turning a chair nobody's going to sit in but has to look right and be all right from the point of view of his own arse. So now I go to Spain with the book still hanging over me. Why won't books come to a halt? Actually the part of me that's not bent with worry and desperation, the part of me that's not all over sackcloth and ashes, is glad, because it means I can go back and see <u>The Birds</u> and all those people I've lived with and got used to. I think authors should be paid by the man hour: man hour (work unit) and man hour (thought unit)—and that it shouldn't bother anyone whether he finished a book in 1, 2, 3 or 100 years.

I'm terribly worried to hear about your American plan and the idea of a job. It ought not to be for someone like yourself. I'm worried because I can always see that looming again on my own horizon. The bloody time goes and you get older and the work gets slower and slower and only disproportionately better and better, and the cost of living index goes up and Mr. Jones buys a new drip dry frig and somebody goes on strike and there's no paper anywhere for us poor buggers to write on, and our kids sit gawping with open mouths like new hatched birds and our wives mend a patch in the pajamas; then there's the sudden bit of money and you splash around like a kid in a mud pool until someone rings a bell and says income tax is being trebled, so you dash back and write another 1000 words of crap, tear it up because you know it's crap although someone else writes the same and earns six million pounds a year and hires hacks to put his grammar right. Not that grammar's worth a damn, but you know what I mean.

Do you think you can work too long on a book? You say you did three drafts of JH.[33] That's what I did on The Pagoda [*Chinese Love Pavilion*], which also took me three years. This one has taken just over a year. The divan of my study is piled with old throw outs but more work has gone on inside the head this time because there's <u>been</u> time. But of course time was fixed on a sort of contract, and April 1st should have seen the new novel delivered. Everyone says, Oh don't worry, but the puritan in me worries like hell. If you're not worried about money you're worried about time. There must come a stage when you're not worried about anything except senile decay? [...]

Ever,

Box 11, Folder 6 (McFarlin)
78 Addison Way
From a letter to Ruth Mark[34]
31 March 1961

My Dear Ruth,

So many thanks for your letter. You sound in fine form and Penny and I are delighted! Hope the scones that looked more like scones than scones tasted more like scones than scones taste too, if that isn't too involved a sentence. There seems to be a lot of food featuring in your programme, and that means a lot of cooking and catering. Still, I suppose it is fun, in a way, so long as there's not too much fun and it doesn't go on too long!

It has taken us nearly a month to get ready for a 3-week holiday and on Wednesday Little Bentley[35] had her first accident. We'd had a burglar alarm fitted because the Spaniards are supposed to be light fingered. It's one of those alarms that if you don't know the secret when you switch the engine on the hooter sounds. This is supposed to scare thieves off, and send them in search of a car they can start up without it sounding like an air-raid alarm. It worked fine, but then when I immobilised it (which I wanted to do because we were going up early to London and leaving it in one of those parks where the attendants move the cars about all day to fit in late arrivals) the alarm went up in smoke. We all piled out in double quick time. Fortunately only one wire was burnt out, but we had to go to town by bus, and this meant we didn't get back until 6:30 that evening. The garage had obviously wired the alarm up wrongly—but they pretend to be mystified. Anyway it works all right now, on or off, so I hope that is the first and last trouble we'll have on this trip.

We're off at the crack of dawn on Tuesday. First night we'll be on the train. Second night we'll hope to spend at Nimes and the third night in Perpignan. The next day we cross the border, over the Pyrenees, and down to the coast where we'll eat octopus and rice! They say it can be very cold so we're packing all our woollies and taking a minimum of stuff for the beach. The hotel is right on the sand, literally; you just step off the terrace and that's sand, and the next thing is the sea, very blue and buoyant—so buoyant you can almost stand up in it with your feet touching nothing but water. The girls had their first professional hair-do yesterday, and I don't recognise them. Sally hasn't had her pig-tails off, but in front she looks very grown up. They are hoping that their Spanish boy friends are still in Tamariu, Pepi and Franccico, who worked in the kitchens of the hotel next to ours. But (and I may have told you all this before) I tell Sally that Pepi will be married now and have children. Still she seemed to think he would wait for her. […]

Lots of love from all of us, and see you when we get back.

Ever,

Box 1, Folder 6 (McFarlin)
78 Addison Way
From a letter to Miss E. M. Almedingen, Shrewsbury
29 April 1961

My Dear Chris,

[…] Thanks so much for your welcome home letter. We got back late on Thursday evening and yesterday were too tired and depressed to do anything much except shop for provisions. But we had a marvellous time; 14 days of sun out of 17 actually spent in Tamariu. We toasted ourselves brown on the beach. It was a bit too cold to swim comfortably but one went in as a kind of duty to health. The journey in the car was easy and comfortable and I hope we can always go abroad that way; no humping of bags on and off ships, just drive straight in and out, up the ramps on to the train and down the ramps off the train and presto! One is in France, as far south as Lyon.

We are full of tristesse at leaving Spain. The three girls of the party all cried as we drove out of the village waving to the Spaniards, and I wasn't far off it myself. The Pyrenees were snow capped and shining in the sun, the grape vines were in leaf and the sky was that special blue. Aie! How cold and grey England looks; how full of trivialities the newspapers. But to work on Monday to finish the book [...].

All the cats were relieved to see us. Our neighbour who looked after them so well said that after two weeks (the most we've ever been away from them before) they all began to look lost and sad. They used to wander into the next garden and cry. Baron, the Russian blue tom, has a black eye (so the vet says) from a fight, and he looks pretty sorry for himself—as though his dignity is hurt forever.

Ever,

Box 6, Folder 13 (McFarlin)
78 Addison Way
From a letter to Gerald Hanley
29 April 1961

My Dear Gerry,

We got home only on Thursday evening, and your letter of the 11th April was waiting for me. It is difficult to get back into the swing of England, because Spain—as you know—was wonderful again. I'm afraid it went right out of my head about the books you asked me to look out for you—went out of my head before I went so that I didn't even have a note of the author's name. We went one day into Barcelona, which would have given me an opportunity, perhaps, but the trip was a disaster—the whole family feeling unwell, and having to turn back as soon as we'd had a meal; and the meal was a disaster for me, because it gave me Spanish Tummy, which seemed to be the same thing exactly as Belgaum tummy—that awful stale egg taste coming into the mouth. But Barcelona apart we had a marvellous time; almost no tourists, just the tender Spaniards working like stink for half a peseta a year or something, and not being paid for two months—there was a gang of workmen building a pathway through rocks to ease the passage of the tourists this coming summer and the Barcelona firm they worked for hadn't paid them for two months. Eventually they went on a sit-down strike—lazing on the rocks and sharing a litre of wine and playing a bit of football, and laughing. Think what would happen here if a gang of English workmen weren't paid for a week.

We became great friends with one Miguel and his Maria, who run the one and only sympathetic bar in Tamariu—that is to say the Spaniards go there too. Miguel, after a week, confessed that he'd been an officer in the old army, and was then in prison for four years. Now, he says, he "makes great welcome" of the Civil guard and says "Franco, three cheers", to make life easy; but he is a sombre, lost man, still. You can see that; his one remaining eye broods over the lost cause, and under the earth in Spain you still feel this thing, don't you; feel it churning away and waiting, and meanwhile feeding the grapes. The Pyrenees were capped with snow and we wept when we left. This time I felt Spain even more strongly; think I could live there—but work? I don't know. The sun might be my undoing too. April was a lovely month, although the sea was just too cold for comfort—like Margate in July; and the little nightclubs where they do the flamenco were all shut and being renovated for the coming season. Miguel took us up the "mountain" to see his farming friends the Domenechs—(whose daughter turned out to be working for someone called Jackson in Hampstead, as if you couldn't have guessed). At first the Domenech farm struck one as typical of Spanish hard work and poverty, but then one saw that it was hard work and riches—the sort of south of Pyrenees equivalent of homesteaders in Essex and Kent (such as Mr. Bates has lost his nut over). And as Miguel wisely said when we came away—"There, much pesetas. Work night, work morning. But all land is theirs". We sampled their rosada with the grape skins still swimming dimly in the bottle. I whispered to Miguel, "Should I pay something?" He said, "Here is not France", and he paid himself!

France! God, what meanness and pettiness. The smile disappears if you don't tip over and above the servicio—all those hard faced concierges counting out the nouvelle francs; like Devonshire, adding up the cost of Devonshire Teas, and being scanty with the cream. Ah, but Spain, there is <u>love</u>. One begins to wonder whether love only works in adversity, only works when there is nothing else to be received or given [...].

Ever,

Box 6, Folder 13 (McFarlin)
78 Addison Way
From a letter to Gerald Hanley
6 May 1961

My Dear Gerry,

[...] <u>Birds of P</u> may be a flop—I may dry up—you know all the fears we're subjected to daily—so I can't say I'm enjoying what amounts to the most money I've ever had my hands on in my whole life. I've bought a Ford Anglia, and we're going to do a bit to the house, but life hasn't changed otherwise (except Penny's been able to have a few extra clothes, etc.). But we have freedom, we don't owe, the children are growing; we like our two bottles of gin a week, and being able to have a decent holiday. It kills me when I see people round here in the lit. world living like Lords, and you know they're doing the whole thing with help from well-breeched parents, etc. Did you have any help like that? I suspect not. The last few years at DHA I was having to contribute to my aged parents' upkeep, and for all my directorship I was earning never more than £1000 or £1500, working like shit day and evening. My writing supported my work, so I thought the time had come when it had just better support me [...].

All these creeps, these lit. mandarins—they owe money all over the bloody place—advances for books never even begun let alone finished. In comparison people like you and me are plain bloody navvies without a trade union. It always killed me when I saw money being paid about by a big mandarin to a small mandarin (because it's mandarin psychology to keep mandarism alive), and then a man bent with the need to <u>write</u> having to cap in hand it and getting a cold sniff and a hand-out like a soup kitchen. It's all an act—what happens outside the study—and you have to get into it. Something tells me it was getting into the money side of the act (freedom and guarantees) that made people think The Love Pavilion was a winner financially—because here was a chap who'd been in the lit. swim suddenly getting out of it. The only reason they could think of was that I thought I'd written a bestseller, so while it didn't become a bestseller it sold streets ahead of anything I'd done and spread me into translations, etc., of which I'd only ever had Swedish before […] a publisher who has an author always trusts in God and Lords—because in heaven and Lords, authors are thought to play the game.[36] I hate all this personal stuff, this "partnership" attitude that only works one way—the publisher's. They're hard as nails when it comes to taking someone else's author, but if one of their own shows signs of rebellion their eyes get big and soft like night creatures starving in the woods […].

How can one cope with all this personal stuff? It's nothing to do with the writing, especially when it turns out that the man who works the personal stuff doesn't see what you're getting at as an author! […] Authors are basically "properties", and their work is merchandise. But between the truth and the effect of the truth being exploited there's this awful psychological cage—which is only there because authors need it and perhaps because publishers and agents die every morning when they wake up and know they can't string two words together when that is all they ever wanted to do […].

Box 13, Folder 1 (McFarlin)
78 Addison Way
To John Willey, William Morrow & Company, USA
27 May 1961

Dear John,

I owe you two letters: the last enclosing the final batch of reviews, which were nice to read. Now I have a cheque from David Higham's which was a surprise, because I thought it would take much longer to work out what I had really earned, or are there further returns to take into account I wonder.

I delayed writing because the rewrite [of *The Birds of Paradise*] was going so well and I hoped to make my letter one of victory. I've rewritten 25,000 words this month, getting up at six because it all seemed so right. Now am not so sure. Actually I'm rather in despair, not because I don't think I can do it but because I'm taking so long. It's the most difficult book I've ever written and the first three sections go on standing up however many times I read them. Still, this is, emotionally, my problem: but I hate the delay. Even up to last night (after a hair-tearing day last Tuesday) I told David H[igham] who rang and asked how things were going, that I expected to finish this week, more or less to time, and then get the whole thing typed professionally and sent off. But last night that nasty little worm started wriggling. You can't buck it. You can't pretend it isn't there. All I am determined is that when it is first read it shall be as I want it to be, and not a compromise with the overall intention of the book. Another distracting thing is that I suspect I have laid the foundation stone for three or four other books, and I have always sneered at sequences à la Proust, Snow and Durrell. But there is so damned much to all the people. This is what makes it exciting to me and also nerve wracking: to make it stand up on its own, single-novel feat, with no smell of family epic about it. I cut, cut, cut all the time, and extend, extend: looking all the time for the periphery of the circle in whose centre the end lies. As you see, John, I am almost inarticulate about it....

Please bear with me. The answer will drill its way into my bone head sooner or later. Sooner, it must be. I fancy I'm psychologically no great shakes in this role of full-time professional writer. But I wouldn't change it for the world. Hope you won't want to!

Ever,

Box 6, Folder 13 (McFarlin)
78 Addison Way
From a letter to Gerald Hanley
n.d., [July 1961]

My Dear Gerry,

[...] Have begun to hate town, going up there on business. Sometimes fear I'll become an alcoholic. When I'm in town I have to drink in order not to notice people's blank faces and to forget that amongst them mine is blank too. While waiting for people's reactions to <u>The Birds of Paradise</u> I went on a terrible bender, not because I was worried what people would think but because I suddenly found I didn't care, the book was over, finished with, and it was all peanuts, basically. The awful thing is that at a certain stage my mind seems to go blank (I mean during one of these alcoholic sessions). I remember being in a dreary drinking club, which must have been about 5.30 p.m., and there are flashes of being refused admittance to the Gargoyle or thrown out of the Mandrake, but nothing is really clear until I nearly got arrested at 3 a.m. on Haverstock Hill on suspicion of trying to pinch a car. Actually I was walking home, moneyless, all the way from the West End, and was looking for a place to kip. The police patrol car ended up by giving me a lift to the Whitestone Pond, at which place I more or less came to. How bloody silly and juvenile, and dirty somehow, to be staggering blind drunk in public at the age of forty one for no good reason—I mean no one had told me I'd got cancer or that I couldn't write for toffee or that my wife had left me, or that one of my daughters had been raped by a White South African.

Ah well, enough of this! The trouble with living in the West is that there is no frontier to cross to freedom [...].

Yours ever,

Box 13, Folder 1 (McFarlin)
78 Addison Way
To Adèle Dogan Horwitz, William Morrow & Company, USA
25 July 1961

Dear Adèle,

How quick you were to let me know your reactions to <u>The Birds</u>. I am most grateful. I haven't yet taken in fully what your various suggestions are going to mean, as I must compare the notes page by page;

but, as always, you strike chords. I think, on reflection, on investigation, you may well prove to have a point, as they say, about this vagueness, these ifs, perhapses and must have beens. Needless to say I was aware, at the time, of the danger of too many of them. A good thing you didn't read the drafts as they went along! It was always a question of balancing what I thought would have been the truth of Conway's memory and knowledge with the need to make impact. I am ready to be persuaded that I haven't achieved quite the balance hoped for.

This is to be a short letter. I'd have sent a cable if I'd been sure whether to find you in New York or Toronto. What I want, in this letter, to say is how grateful I am to you for your overall reaction and comprehension, for your ending to the first paragraph of your letter[37] which vindicates my method and approach in the way that John's reaction to the illusion business vindicates my <u>thoughts</u> (which you do, too).

Glancing (in the sense of reading carefully but not having time to consider carefully) at the detailed notes I have a feeling that we shan't part company on much, if anything; perhaps only part company over the Dora/Krishi section—and then only, I think, because from a practical point of view I don't believe I shall be able to cope, within the context of the rest of the book. The trouble about this damned book is that shift an emphasis in one place and the whole structure begins (to my mind anyway) to topple. It's the trouble I had in the process of composition. When I say shift an emphasis I mean shift an emphasis in <u>presentation</u>. Perhaps I don't know what I mean. It's all instinctive, really. The main thing is that everyone so far has accepted the book in the spirit it's presented in—quite apart from the deeply encouraging things said about this part or that part. I was fascinated by your reaction to the section on page 287. It nearly came out at one moment, when I had the blue pencil. A certain pride in it made me keep it in, even though I am suspicious always of passages <u>I</u> like more than I feel I should. But of course that passage sums up the whole approach (Conway's) to his recollections, so even though I hoped the rest of the book illustrated what that passage said I thought I'd treat myself, and let it stand. How glad I am that I did!

The Anne Conway sequence is, actually, what I call my occidental style. It has appeared in earlier books, not quite so honed down. When I write about England it comes out, somehow. The new novel [*The Bender*] is, I think, about England; but who can be sure. The Birds of Paradise was originally to be acted out in Spain by Bill and Dora. But it wouldn't work that way because presently I saw that Bill and Dora never had an adult affair, only that childhood one in Tradura. Anyway the new book, "The Careerist", or "Novel with Hero" (tentative titles) is churning away inside (not very fast and not at all clearly) and is Greater London Contemporary in manner (like the drawing room at Four Birches)! Unless I see suddenly that I should be writing quite a different book that has been worrying me for several months (almost years) and all of which I have at present is this picture of a man walking (riding?)—leaving, anyway, a town (village?) on his way to do something that has to do with his wayward brother. All I know is that he is watched in silence by the inhabitants of this (town, village, hamlet). Where is it? When was it? Is the brother as bad as I think other people think he is? Fascinating, this dumb charade business. Sutton walking across an open space with a kris, a woman (who became Dora) appearing at a doorway (a hut, which became Conway's hut in Manoba) and saying something to Bill which suggested something important had come to an end. What had come to an end of course was Conway's illusion and everyone's illusion of their usefulness, but it took time to discover that this is what I meant!

Anyway, thanks many times, Adèle, for your rapid and sympathetic reading, your long and detailed and so soon to arrive letter. I'll be a little while before I can reply in similar detail. I expect I shall await Maurice [Temple Smith]'s return from France, because as John [Willey] may have told you, all I've had from him so far is an enthusiastic telegram sent on the eve of his vacation. When he comes back he may have the odd reservation to coincide with your own; not that I set one off against the other. It's a question of garnering all the opinions and then sitting down to think what it means in terms of Mr. Conway.

How nice to have publishers such as mine (I mean Morrow!). Love, and best wishes to you both in Richmond, VA.

Box 2, Folder 12 (McFarlin)
78 Addison Way
To Miss Cecilia Brown[38]
23 August 1961

Dear Miss Brown,

As promised I'm now dropping you a line to set out all the details about the cats and the various things you will want to know....

FOOD: Just to confirm. We shall leave all the implements on the kitchen table. We heat water in a kettle and soak a thick (3 inch) slice of bread, pour the water away and add two tins of kit-e-cat, mash it all up into an awful pink mess and then divide it on to three tin plates. The only other thing to do then is to renew their bowl of drinking water.

The Cats

SOOTY: She is the boss cat, the sensible one of the family. She is all black (with wisp of white bow tie).

MINTY: Her sister. Black and white. Alert and tense. Will occasionally demand attention.

MING: Poor skinny Ming, we refer to her as. She stayed out all night in the rain as a kitten, when her sister was killed on the road, and has never grown much bigger. She is the light tortoise-shell who looks as much like an owl as a cat. Her feet get cold, and she demands attention quite often.

ROTA: The ginger neuter, very nervous and highly strung, but big and heavy. Has had veterinary treatment for trouble in left ear which seems now to be cleared up and shouldn't cause any bother that can't wait until we are back.

CHLOE: The foundling. She is the thicker furred, darker tortoiseshell, with three yellow paws. Has always been conscious of her position as a stray amongst a family of hand-picked cats. Is affectionate but not one to push herself forward.

BARON: The full male Russian Blue. Will be the first into the cupboard if a dog gets into the garden. Has a strong voice which he uses often. His autumn season is not yet upon us, so he shouldn't cause any bother, and will probably be scared stiff of you. If you leave him to himself he will get used to you and "come round" probably. When he "comes round" he is a bit of a pest, and very heavy.

BEAUTY: The sister of Baron, female Russian blue. At heart she is not Beauty but Beast. Energetic, agile, naughty; she cannot bear to see the others resting peacefully. Looks upon herself as someone to stir up some interest, get things moving.

ROLL CALL: When giving the meal a call of "Minty, Sooty, Rota, Ming!" should bring them all running, although you may find they arrive one by one as soon as they hear the saucepans. Sometimes one or two of them are absent on important business, like stalking birds or investigating other people's larders. There will probably be days when they don't all arrive, but don't worry because they come in later and eat what is left. You may also find on the following day that the plates aren't quite empty, and that will mean that the slaughter of birds in the woods has been successful. On the other hand, since they will be alone most of the time they'll probably eat to fill in time.

Box 7, Folder 19 (McFarlin)
78 Addison Way
To David Higham, David Higham Associates
24 August 1961

My Dear David,

I don't know whether you are back in the office this coming week or the week after, but as Penny and I are off to do host and hostess duty at that Summer School in Derby tomorrow (back Monday Sep. 4) I must get this letter off now. It is an expansion (or maybe a contraction) of the letter I wrote on July 28, which just missed you.

At long last Maurice [Temple Smith] finally rang me on Tuesday of this week to say he was ready to talk about the book and Adèle [Dogan]'s points.[39] I went round and had supper with them last night. I think Maurice is more concerned these days with his interior decorating; it was not the most convivial evening I've had. I'll tell you all about it one day. However, the main point is that I don't seem to be any further forward. I expect it was a mistake to show him Adèle's long American comments. He told me he had made pencil notes in the margins but when I looked at Adèle's notes when I got home I found that the only pencil notes in the margins were the ones I had made myself a month ago.

In the brief and yet too long and rather uncomfortable hour in his more or less naked living room (prior to an uncomfortable couple of hours in the dining room when Jean [Temple Smith] also suggested what was wrong with the book) he confirmed what he said in his telegram prior to his trip abroad, e.g., that it was the best thing I'd done and they'd publish with enthusiasm whether I altered a word or no. After that nothing nice was said about the book at all, and he admitted he was going back on his previous word to keep the book out of my clutches so that I shouldn't be tempted to rewrite anything. I gather that, like Adèle, he finds a lack of tension in book four. He wanted Conway to find out something new about his father from Krishi, so that book Four could have more immediacy. He hinted, too, that he'd have liked something more sparkling as between the man Conway and the woman Dora, but dropped this when I explained that that was how the book originally ended before I rewrote it twice.

It would be perfectly possible to carry out his final suggestion, which was that in Jundapur, Conway (knowing nothing at this stage about his father's outburst over the betrayal of Gopalakand) should learn from Krishi that his father had gone down fighting; that Krishi, faced with integration, should have gone to see Conway Senior (who would have to turn out to have been a kind of father-figure-cum-popular-hero to Krishi); that he should seek Conway Senior's advice and so become privy to Conway's outburst at the private conference between the State Department and the ruler of Gopalakand. I have explained to Maurice the various political and practical and geographical reasons for Krishi not being any longer directly connected to Sir Robert Conway, so the only answer was that introduction of this personal, perhaps irrational approach of Krishi's to Conway Sr.

It would be perfectly possible. It would mean what from my point of view at this later stage, would be a fairly major re-think. I have written to John Willey today asking the bare question: What is John's personal opinion of Adèle's opinion that Book Four lacks tension? If he agrees with her the problem looms larger. If you agree that Book Four lacks tension it looms larger than ever—and that is really what I'm writing about—to find out whether you have similar reservations, and to ask your opinion of Adèle's letter and notes in general (but not in detail, because that means checking page by page). I enclose her letter, etc.

My own feeling is that I wrote the book, I did my best, everyone cheered like billio by phone and cable and telegram, and that I must let the book stand or fall as it is written. It is two months since Maurice had the book. I know he has been away for a fortnight during that time. But two months is enough time to make me forget the bloody birds and be thinking of something else. We fixed on March publication. Last night he talked about April and finally about July. I can't afford to have it held up like that, but want it to come out in March. I don't believe that any alterations I make at this stage are going to make any difference to sales or reviews. If Iris Murdoch can get away with A Severed Head can't I get away with The Birds of Paradise? I reckon I did all my sweat on it when I finished it on March 1st and summoned up the courage to chuck the last 100 pages away then, and rewrite them twice. But I felt that's what I owed everyone including myself, because I'd had the cheek to try and be a full time professional novelist. This bitter little tirade isn't directed against Adèle, who, bless her, even if she had reservations, wrote about them straight away and in detail. It's really directed against Maurice who seems to me now to have only two attitudes—the off hand and the high hand, chiefly off hand. Quite frankly, I think it's an awful nerve to have kept me hanging about for two months, without even an apology. It was bad enough having the first reaction from his fraught taut little wife, bad enough to have a telegram instead of a phone call, but for nearly a month to elapse between his return and our eventual meeting, and then to get home and find he's mistaken my pencil notes for his own so that I've either got to ask him again for specific answers or ignore the whole thing, strikes me as the last straw.

And there's also an annoyance about the <u>Pavilion</u>. When I saw him in the spring he was talking about the possibility of a 2,000 reprint later on, because (as I gathered) the book was doing so well, and there was little doubt it would sell out its 18,000. Now I've got the statements for the six months ended March 31st, and the total sale is only just over 14,000. When I asked him on the phone what had happened since, he said they hadn't quite sold 15,000. I can't remember whether that includes 1,000 damaged, but it certainly means, in my opinion, that they won't get over 15,000. God knows why publishers go on adding noughts to their figures just for fun—or why, for that matter, authors go on believing them when they give verbal reports.

I'm glad, very glad, you kept us free of an option, David, because Maurice and I aren't, I think ever going to spark. If we go on at all it will be increasingly on a once removed basis. The fault is partly mine, I know. If I believed passionately in a book after I'd finished it I could probably make him spark by sparking myself; but I don't believe passionately in them. I think I'm learning to feel strongly (if not passionately) that I've done my best with them, but that's all. It's a fairly new feeling, though, and it illuminates the other feeling I have that Maurice treats every book as it comes along much as he'd treat a first novel from an unknown author, trying to get it <u>right</u>, and off to a good start. Haven't I started yet...? Aren't I to be allowed my funny idiosyncratic little ways, like putting un-climaxes into un-novels? This morning I feel very badly that I want to move somewhere where they'll treat me like a sixth former, where I can stick my hands in my pockets and wear the top button of my coat undone. Better still, somewhere I'll be treated like an Inspector of Schools.

On our way back from the pub up the road Jean called to Maurice from the room in which she was interviewing the new German maid,

"Do you want a whisky?" To which Maurice called in reply, "No, I've had a beer", and led me firmly upstairs. Ah well. It is, as Krishi said of Rajput hospitality, all part of <u>jannu</u>.

I apologise for the length of this letter, remembering too well the sigh with which <u>I</u> greeted this sort of thing on my morning desk. Don't feel it necessary to reply except at leisure, unless you're not back until September, in which case a certain urgency arises. In case you are back next week and want to lighten the burden of life at Derby my address is, from Aug 25 to Sept 1—c/o the Writers' Summer School, The Hayes, Swanwick, Nr. Derbyshire, Tel No. Leabrooks 484. After Sep 1st we spend a couple of days in and around Lincolnshire, address unknown, but that's weekend anyway.

Of course I've got the odds and ends of factual things still to sort out, having postponed doing anything about them until we'd settled the main problems if there were going to be any, so when I return to London, I'll have a bit to do on the book, although (assuming I finally decide to do nothing major) that needn't hold Maurice up from getting his copy of the book moving in some productive way. Nothing at all has happened to it, so far as I know. I don't think anyone else at E & S has even read it yet. He left it at home when he went on holiday, and I think it has been there ever since. The copy I have here is eventually due to go to Ragnar [Svanström], and that of course I'll do through Sheila [Watson]. I don't expect it will be ready to go to Sweden until she is back from Spain.

Love to you all from us both,

Ever,

Box 20, Folder 19 (McFarlin)
78 Addison Way
To Miss Violet Wilkinson[40]
13 September 1961

Dear Miss Wilkinson,

Thank you so much for your nice letter, which E & S have forwarded to me this morning. It was good of you to think of writing to me care of them. I don't think they actually keep a record of fan letters passing through, but it must make a mental mark.

And your letter has been very encouraging to me in itself. I'm sure I'm not a man's writer in the sense usually meant, but I do certainly appear to have been given that label. Saxby is a character a reader either likes or dislikes intensely, so I've found. On the whole I think I failed to explore him properly, even within the limits imposed by a first-person narration.

But what mostly encourages me about your letter is the way you have reacted to this business of form and shape which, to me, is all important in any art or craft. Your reaction to this confirms what I felt when we talked that evening—that you have a creative writer's mind and eye—and, I suspect, the right amount of determination. Perhaps determination comes first always. It is constantly being challenged, not only by the circumstances facing you but by the circumstances of the work itself. The first word goes down on a blank page, and a challenge exists because a relationship has been set up (just as it is by the first brush stroke an artist makes on his canvas); a two-level relationship and a two-level challenge. There is the technical problem of how to go about it, and the moral problem of whether you can or should. Where there's a relationship there must, I suppose, always be a challenge implicit in it. Fascinating. But then dragging ideas out of the air and forming them into pictures must be fascinating; otherwise we shouldn't both want to do it, but till the soil, chop wood, keep our homes dry and our families warm.

Note. The missing word you point out isn't really missing.[41] Thinking about it I believe this telescoped slang use is of Irish derivation; but I'm not sure. I only know it is sometimes used in this way, giving more pith, somehow, more force. Thank you again for writing. I shall look forward to hearing from you in the not too distant future that your own work has borne fruit; and then, as I said in Derby, I'll be very glad to help in any way I can. Thank you, too, for keeping confidence.

With kind regards,

Yours sincerely,

Box 1, Folder 6 (McFarlin)
78 Addison Way
From a letter to Miss E. M. Almedingen, Shrewsbury
13 September 1961

My dear Chris,

[…] The Birds of Paradise finally went to press last week after a disagreeable two months of waiting for people to come back from holiday to find out if everyone agreed about this or that minor alteration. It is due out next March or April, and I have now started on the novel (in a dickering sort of way) that you kindly agreed I might dedicate to you, Chris.[42] I wish I had been able to make "your" book The Birds of Paradise, but I owed my American publisher a debt of very practical gratitude. Without them I couldn't have set up on my own. The one I'm playing with now mayn't be your sort of book—except at its heart; and that is mainly what matters. Anyway, I hope it "works". For it I come away from the East and into London.

[…] I seem to be out of touch with so much of my past, at the moment, and time goes so quickly. Today someone called Maureen Owen from The Evening Standard is supposed to be coming to interview us as a family. I never see that paper but gather she does a weekly article about families, and that it comes out on Tuesdays. I expect she'll be interested in the cats and domestic arrangements, and scarcely notice that there are also books.

[…] Our home decorating is all but finished, but we still lack curtains at the windows, and the chairs in the living room are only temporary while we await delivery of the stuff we want. We've turned the dining room (that little box) into a garden room—that is to say we've got white garden furniture in it and our old pink bedroom carpet died to a tone they call Woodland Glen. The walls are Chinese blue and the ceiling is Samurai blue—so at least in our garden the war between China and Japan is in a state of truce. In my study there's a lovely blush red geranium that's really Spanish—the cutting having been spirited by Penny through the customs. It bloomed last week and reminds me of that hard but happy country.

We all send our love—the children go back to school tomorrow and are glooming about the house. But give them a day and they'll be full of beans again.

Ever,

Box 38, Folder 3 (Scott Archives, HRC-UT)
78 Addison Way
From a letter to John Willey, William Morrow & Company, USA
27 September 1961
[Handwritten across the top: "Not sent, carbon destroyed" in Scott's handwriting]

Dear John,

[…] I hope that the amended copy of <u>The Birds</u> manuscript reached New York safely. It was supposed to go from Dean Street by airmail and should therefore have been with you a couple of weeks ago, I think. I had a nice letter from Adèle [Dogan] in Richmond the other day containing an interesting account of a drive-in movie, and I'm dropping her a line at the office because I believe she'll be with you now. Meanwhile I'm waiting to hear from E & S about a definite English publication date. Maurice [Temple Smith] seems to want to make it April, but I'm trying to explain to him why I think April is a bad month, especially the Thursday before Good Friday! Anyway, John, directly it is settled I'll be letting you know officially so that you can fix a tentative date for your own edition. Either with this letter, or with Adèle's or separately, I shall be sending a copy of the Author's note and acknowledgments as it is to appear in the English edition. You may fancy that such a long libel disclaimer is unnecessary for America; but I leave it to you. Over here it is partly my author's joke, although serious, too.

I have begun the new novel: about 10,000 words exist. But you know what can happen to those. It is something new for me, set in London. The atmosphere is turning out funny-sad or sad-funny. It may be called "The Careerist", or it may be called "The Bender". Is Bender an American expression too? It means tying one on (if I've got the right idiom).

I think I want it to turn out shortish (80,000), swift, crammed with stuff but essentially simple in outline. It is about having Power, being a force: about the subtle or perhaps not so subtle distinction between doing a job and having a career. It is also about the curious levels of class, high and low, which most middle-class English people have roots in or connexions with. It is about wanting love and wanting work, loving with honour and doing an honourable job. And about why this is virtually impossible; and how funny that is, and also awful. "If you are not required", one of the characters, a Lady Butterfield, confides to her journal, "it is imperative to be hated". The action develops mainly through George Lisle-Spruce. He was christened Spruce, but his lower class mother was a Lisle. The hyphen was all his own work. As a family the Spruces spent most of their time sucking up to Lady Butterfield (the daughter of a butcher) who married a distant cousin Roderick Butterfield, late of the Bengal and Orissa Horse, but gone into business and knighted for disservices to the nation. George, the eldest of three sons, was left the income from a sum of trust money—not enough to live on in any sort of style but too much to provide an incentive, in the absence of any other, to work. The money comes from the Butterfields. When he dies it will go to his eldest surviving child, failing which to the eldest surviving child of his younger brother, hardworking accountant Tim, or his youngest brother Guy, aged only twenty or so, a tyro dramatist of the Theatre Workshop school. George, when we first meet him, is recently divorced, has no issues, knows, after a "wretched affair with a test tube" that he has been sterile since an attack of the mumps at the age of puberty. He owes Tim two hundred pounds. "The twin causes of my ruination are money and sex". Even in a thing as personal to a man as his own ruin he has not struck an individual note. "A man must always live under the threat of illicit fatherhood". "There were amongst them, George thought retro-spectively, women who came to him only symbolically, to consider in tranquillity the obscurity of their situation, which his sterility, taking nine months to prove, underlined". "In time people would have no further need to meet face to face. Smedley's could feed you by post. You could say all that you had to say about yourself (which was the only reason for what was called conversation) on postcards and the telephone; and in memoirs you left behind when you died. In your memoirs you put down all the things you would not even dare to write on a postcard or say on the telephone. And in time, because you saw no other human face, your own face would be revealed. It would come out of its lair like a naked animal, attracted by the sun and a feeling of repose, and no longer ashamed of having no fur".

Our friend George, of course, is the man who wants to say Yes but can only see reasons for saying No. When he posts a letter he feels he is engaging in an act of charity (pillar boxes all over London, standing on the curb like scarlet paupers, their mouths open, dumb, patient and hungry. But when he puts four pence into a telephone he feels he is engaging in an act of combat. The two hundred pounds he owes Tim, which he has no hope of paying back, is weighing on his conscience. The loan dates from the time Tim got him out of a jam in the days when George Lisle-Spruce was called Silky Spruce by his friends in the Sloane Street drinking club. He is also beginning to see Lady Butterfield (his so-called Aunt Clara) as The Enemy. She puts him on to a girl called Anina ("She is living with your brother Guy at the moment, but I judge them quite unsuited".) His first sight of Anina in Lady Butterfield's salon— "When he entered Lady B's salon the first thing he noticed was a girl riding on the back of Aunt Clara's black panther. He knew the panther of old but the girl was a stranger. The panther, so the story went, was shot by Colonel Butterfield when he was Lieutenant Butterfield of the Bengal and Orissa Horse (circa 1912). It was mounted on a mahogany plinth, legs striding, head lowered and turned a few degrees to the left as if some alien sound had come from that side of the jungle track down which it padded, its yellow eyes glazed by eternity into the likeness of the hunger it had been seeking to assuage when it encountered an Uncle Roderick dressed in topee and shorts and little brown moustache: the last being it was destined to look at upon earth before every one but itself came to a sudden end. George had always been sorry for the panther, not least because in the Butterfield museum it was given no marked pride of place. It should have been near the fire in winter and by the window in summer, but it stood in the shadows cast by escritoire and chaise-lounge. If he had not been in the habit of looking for it directly he entered the room he might not have noticed the girl as soon as he did; although she, too, was as strange a visitor to St. John's Wood as the black panther. He was not sure, either, at first glance, whether she was real or wax work. She sat upright and still, side-saddled, with her hands twisting the panther's ears. Her hair, the colour of ripening corn, was piled in a stack above her brow. Sheaves of it fell down her neck. Her face was clown white, even the lips: all, indeed, but the eyes which were pencilled into a shape that reminded him of pictures he had seen of the eyes of the Nepalese painted on the walls of temples to remind the poor and lowly that they were constantly watched. The girl, below this curiously European disarray, wore a peacock blue sari and gold sandals, and was staring ahead of her in a direction which brought their glances together; not, he felt, because she was inquisitive or even wanted to look at him, but for an entirely geometrical reason which has something to do with fixed angles or the shortest distance between two points being a straight line. "My dear George", Lady Butterfield said, emerging from a small group of men and women who were gathered round the Adam fireplace holding little glasses of martini as if they were at home with the Borgias, "I am so delighted to see you again". She offered her Elizabeth Arden cheek. Kissing it always made him feel like licentious soldiery come to rest after an afternoon's street fighting. In a room such as this with women such as these, he was always aware of bristle, perspiration and the incongruity of worsted. What on earth did women mean, he wondered, when they talked about the nice smell of men? You could never smell another man yourself. You would only hope that you did not smell as everything about you conspired to suggest you might.

Her real name was Annie McBride, but she had changed it to Anina. "You aren't as good looking as Guy", she said, "but you have an interesting face. It is the face of a little boy". She stared at him through her bleak, lamasery eyes. "A starveling", she said. "Man, it's like, way out there, in Hungerville".

"Can I get you a drink?"

"They invited you. You come. It's up to them. For why should you act bearer? I ride the ole black panther. He takes me ways I want to go and that's no crappy old wood, St. Johns, St. John's style wood, but dark black wood, full of thought trees and crazy-notion creepers. Like I'm twisted with this thing". She dug her fingers into the black, busby-smelling ears. "Man", she chanted, "is it like uphill all the way? Yay yay yay. It is to the very end".

Anina is Anglo-Indian. 10 years ago she would have tried to pass, in India, for white. But she's too young. I haven't worked out her exact background. Actually she was left on the cutting floor when I was editing Birds of Paradise, but I knew she was destined to play a part sooner or later, and this is it; because George has got to feel guilty about Guy, too, even though he despises Guy's careerism (sitting on steps with Lord Russell in order to feel in on the act of the contemporary drama-tists, and to get his picture in the papers (just discernible behind John Osborne's and Sheila Delaney's). Anina is white-skinned, even under the thick white coffee-bar mask. Her kookie talk is the equivalent of what would have been her pseudo-memsahib talk in the days of the Raj; vaguely effective on the surface, but not quite right. George also feels guilty about Tim (hardworking Tim, who pays rates and taxes, has nearly grown-up children with teen-age problems and is, unknown to George just yet, wrestling with the moral implications of thirty pieces of silver, which will buy the consumer goods he needs, but leave his senior and near-to-retirement partner in the accountancy practice in a difficult situation. Tim is being enticed by the board of directors of their one big cli-ent for whom he has done a brilliant job of financial organisation. Here again the career motif comes in. He doesn't like the company he's being invited to join, as financial controller, but what the hell, he's not all that keen on his senior partner, old stick-in-the-mud Wallingford, of Bartle, Wallingford. The point is, of course, that he doesn't love accounts. He's only doing a job so he might as well have a career and save his mar-riage as well, because Sarah is looking restless and somehow beaten by all this lack of consumer goods. I think when George discovers Tim's problems he stops thinking of murdering old Lady Butterfield and starts thinking of committing suicide, because then <u>Tim</u> will enjoy the income from the Butterfield trust money, and Tim's daughter (the eldest, a girl of seventeen who is probably pregnant from the summer holiday spent with a ton-up boy) will come into the lump sum which will mean it won't matter about her having a baby and not being married. The ton-up boy is prepared to marry her, and Sarah, hysterical though the thought makes her (because she never quite saw her son-in-law in a leather jacket and crash helmet) wants her to marry him to save her name. Tim isn't sure, but can't work out whether he's thinking of Gillian's happiness or his own social position (leather jacket and crash helmet). Only Gillian knows and all she can say, being of her Age, when asked if she wants to marry Click Clayton, is "I don't mind". In any case it will mean expulsion from the convent school when she appears for the first time dressed for gym and four months gone.

The idea of murdering Lady Butterfield, by the way, comes into George's mind when he begins to see that she is typical of the faceless class, the establishment (butcher's daughter and all) which recognises that only force and power count. He sees that all his life has played into her hands by following the sucking-up policy laid down in his lower middle class original upbringing. From the idea of murdering Lady Butterfield he moves (I think) to this idea of suicide. To help Tim (who as his younger brother, and subject to colds, etc., but now much fitter than himself, was part of his charge, his social obligation even as a child).

And so: the bender, one tied on, a drunk, a party, to get up courage or to look death in the face before he embraces it. Naturally when he has reached the point where all that remains is to go and cut his throat on Hampstead Heath (not far from Tim's house) his courage fails. And he is picked up at three o'clock in the morning by a police car on Haverstock Hill, accused of trying to steal a car because he has been watched trying all the door handles (he wanted a place to sleep). What saves him is his accent. He doesn't realise this until after it is all over and the police have given him a lift as far as the Whitestone pond. He had said, "Yes, I've tried door handles, but not to pinch the cars". He used the word pinch on purpose, because he was talking to the police. But the words didn't matter. The voice which had been so carefully trained over years and years to fit in with Lady Butterfield—that is all that counted. He had power and force, and the police respected it. He was not, they knew, a man who would pinch a car. He is not, either, a man who will defy another kind of power and kill himself. In the early stages of the bender he decides to ring up God because the telephone is the most powerful instrument of all. He dials G, O, D, 1961—but gets the engaged signal. Now on Hampstead Heath he just says, "Gentle Jesus, speak to your servant". He says something else, too, but I haven't quite worked out what it is because the totality of the book hasn't emerged, only this set of construction lines that leads me to Haverstock Hill in the small hours of a September morning.

And of course I've used this letter as a form of clarification, so if you think it sounds mad just forget it and think of all the dreary stages it has to go through yet before I decide that it is working. I might just add that Haverstock Hill is a personal experience! Even your most respectable authors have their moments.

Best to you all.

Ever,

Box 18, Folder 19 (McFarlin)
78 Addison Way
To Muriel Spark
9 November 1961

My Dear Mu,

Carol told me you rang the other evening to ask how things were going, and would be out all the following day. I meant to get a line off to you yesterday but didn't manage it. Actually I'd tried several times to sit down and write out a letter headed WHAT I WANT! But the more I thought out the words the less real they became, and presently I decided that I just didn't know what I wanted and that any approach to Macmillan in <u>detail</u> would go off at half cock, which is the last thing one wants. I don't know whether there was a lot of trauma involved, and some annoyance at the way on the Sunday before pubn they just didn't announce Miss Brodie, let alone in a splash way, as they should have done. They made up a bit last Sunday, but their adverts were at the bottom of the page and somehow without weight. However, that is the sort of thing a publisher can, I suppose, always be trained to do! (I mean get right.)

Actually I had a very traumatic week last week. I have a feeling it's something to do with this new novel The Bender, not really wanting to write it, but having to, and also knowing it may be the best thing I've done in spite of it being worked out tremendously quickly for me (page 145 of typescript already, but of course there is always the shadow of a snag round the corner). But mixed up with it all is a kind of anger at having to worry about publishers and a half belief that I'm being silly and hysterical. Then there's the puritan thing about not wasting the past, and a move[43] is a kind of waste. Anyway, I spent most of the week before we met a bit drunk and most of last week very drunk and only working on the book in rare moments of sobriety, until I pulled myself up short quite suddenly. That was last Thursday, and since Thursday I have tried to adopt a cold sober approach to it all. It happened last Thursday because on the Wednesday I suppose I was drinking from about 10.30 in the morning, just breathing in gin, and it not really having any obvious effect! Round about 11.30 Kay [Dick] rang me to say that the night before the Temple Smiths had been round and Jean had been having a row with Maurice because he always left her alone while he read manuscripts and it was bad enough not being taken out for that but when it came to not being taken out because he was being taken out by a woman author, that was the last straw. Apparently Maurice was booked to go out with this woman author on the Thursday and she said, Now who can I get to take me out. And she said, I know, Paul can take me out. Ring up Paul and tell him he's got to take me out.

Kay said that they did dial the number (but by this time Maurice had arrived at Flask Walk too and put his hand on the phone to stop it ringing because he obviously didn't like it and it was nearly midnight).

Well, I heard all about this on the Wednesday morning, from Kay, and it made me a bit annoyed when I thought of the number of times I haven't been taken out by my publisher, and I mean the idea! Being asked to take his wife out because she was lonely. So I just laughed and Kay laughed, and that was that, and I poured another gin and tried again to write the letter saying WHAT I WANT! Then at midday the phone rang, and it was David Higham really telling me nothing except that John Braine had sold film rights to his new novel for £30,000.[44] So after that I had several gins and we rang up the Epicure and Penny and I went up there because the day was suddenly the wrong shape, and I was ashamed of being jealous of John Braine's £30,000. After the Epicure we went to Marshall's and bought Penny a Hardy Amies coat just to make us feel better, only I suppose it made us feel worse in the end because the children wanted new slippers or bed jackets or satchels, I forget which! Anyway, in the evening Penny had to meet an old friend at the local pub, and I went with her, had one with them, and promised to pick them up later. And on the way back I thought I'd beard the Temple Smiths in their den (knowing it was the day after Jean would be alone and wanting to be taken out to dinner). When I got there she said, Oh Lord, has Kay been talking to you, and I pretended to know nothing, and went upstairs, and was drunk, and there wasn't any drink in the house, so Maurice went out and got a bottle of wine because my drunkenness wasn't the sort you notice, and while he was away I asked Jean what she meant by Kay talking to me, and she told me the whole thing that I already knew, and was very embarrassed and yet not embarrassed, otherwise she wouldn't have told me, would she? So being a perfect gent I said, well of course I'll take you out. And that made me madder than ever because I hadn't reckoned on the story coming out. I hadn't reckoned on landing myself with the wife of the publisher I thought I was going to leave, I mean land myself with her for a whole evening while Maurice took another E & S author out who was supposed to be very pretty and sexy. I mean it made me wish I was pretty and sexy too, I mean the way Maurice would want to take me out to The Caprice and sign a contract for £30,000 on the spot. Because if he signed a contract for £30,000 on the spot Carol and Sally would be able to have new bed jackets or slippers or satchels or whatever it is they haven't got instead of Penny's new Hardy Amies coat which I don't think she likes now that she's got it but is too kind to say.

Well, back comes Maurice with this bottle of burgundy which I know is death to me, which seems appropriate, so I drink most of it and begin to tell him that I don't think we ever have sparked together and he doesn't turn a hair, and you can't tell whether he minds or doesn't mind, and by this time it's nearly time for me to go and collect Penny in the car and take Penny and Joyce to Liverpool Street, and I find I can't remember some of the things I said to Maurice who didn't know I was as drunk as a coot (it not showing), but there is a faint feeling of a bit of the barrier being broken away, until I come out and get in the car and know that all I've got out of it is the heavy end of a dinner the following night for my publisher's wife who is lonely in her house in Christchurch Hill.

So there I am back in the pub, and only Penny knows I'm as drunk as a coot, and Joyce buys me a double gin on top of the burgundy, and then I think I buy her one and we drive very fast to Liverpool Street, so fast that it is early for her train and time for more double gins. And I drive home and leave Penny at the door to go in and get the midnight tea and drive round to the garage[45] and as I open the garage doors and switch on the light there is this feeling of This is What The End is like, rather sordid and cold and all damp brick. And so I back the car in and close the doors and leave the engine running and wonder how long it is before the carbon monoxide poison begins to work.

And then of course I begin to get plain bloody scared and the Puritan in me says Get out of this bloody car, Scott, and go and write your novel, and then a very curious thing happens. There's a wind on a still night and the garage door swings wide open, so that I nearly jump out of my skin, and get away from that awful place very quickly. And in the morning when I wake up the trauma is over and I sit down and work, and work well and in the evening I take out Mrs. Temple Smith and tell her I'm thinking of leaving her husband—and I spend three hours telling her all kinds of things, and she tells me all about his stiff upper-lipped family and how she never can stand the way his emotions never show on his face, but loves him like anything, and he loves her, and it's a splendidly loyal evening during which she drinks wine and I drink water because she is pregnant and I don't want anyway to be drunk and drive Mrs. Temple Smith and her baby into a telegraph pole. And the next day Maurice rings and says we must meet and I say yes, and he says he'll collect me on Monday evening and we'll go out to dinner. And when it is six o'clock on the Monday evening and pouring with rain and I think how swish it is to have your publisher call for you in his car, he rings and says he's ricked his back and would I mind going round to them for supper? So I say no, I don't mind, and walk round to the garage (15 minutes) in the rain and come back and have a hot shower in order not to have pneumonia, and change and drive over and spend a long time there telling him why I'm thinking of leaving him, and what it might be that I might want from him if I decide to stay, which is to say a guarantee of £4000 a year for three years against all my writing income. And he says he will put that up to Mr. Alan White who hasn't got a face but is the head of the group, and of course I already know it would have to go to Mr. Alan White who doesn't recognize me when he sees me at parties because I'm only one of E & S's better authors. And I fight down my trauma, and aren't drunk, and remember the swinging door in the garage, and say that I don't want him to put anything up because I'm only telling him what it is I <u>might</u> want if I stay.

And that, dear patient Mu (if you've read as far as this) is my private confession to you. I mean I haven't of course even told Penny about the swinging door in the garage, which swung open as if someone with a lot of wind and force had yanked it back and no nonsense to let the carbon monoxide out.

You see for a moment it is right that I do not <u>know</u> WHAT I WANT, except to write a good book called <u>The Bender,</u> and to go on writing other books that might be good and called something else, and to see that Carol and Sally have satchels and dressing gowns and bedroom slippers or whatever it is they want and Penny has a Hardy Amies coat that she likes and doesn't just pretend she likes; and to go on seeing my friends without leaning on them for help that only I can give myself or get from a garage door.

I have only had a pint of beer today!

My love, as always: and please drop me a line presently to let me know that you understand?

Box 13, Folder 2 (McFarlin)
78 Addison Way
To John Willey, William Morrow & Company, USA
11 November 1961

Dear John,

Many thanks for your two letters, November 1 and November 6. You'll be glad to hear (as I've written to Adèle [Dogan] this morning) that the returned mss reached me safe and sound in this morning's mail. Many thanks.

Did I mention our actual anniversary date when I told you about our 20th celebration? Like you and Fern we were married on an October 23rd. And if that is not an omen of togetherness I don't know what is. And congratulations, too.

By the way, is Sam[46] about to come over here? David Higham rang me about a week ago to ask if I knew what has happened to him, because he's just got a letter (which had been delayed in the mail, asking whether November 1st or something was all right for them to meet. David rang the Connaught but was told a trip had been cancelled or postponed. Not, I hope, through Sam's or Janet's illness or anything like that.

Thank you for all the facts and figures about the financial situation and for confirming that the unearned balance won't get set off against quarterly payments, which is my cue to seek your comments about something confidential. I mean I haven't talked to David [Higham] yet about it. In brief I have been going through an agonising reappraisal of my position at E & S, details of the reasons for which I won't bore you with. I say "agonising" not only because it is the cant phrase but because of the mixture of emotion: hard-headed business, temptations from elsewhere, puritan conscience about continuing to build upon existing foundations. Let me say at once that E & S propose to fly the <u>Birds</u> from just as high a mast as the <u>Pavilion,</u> so sour grapes isn't it. But sometimes one feels like part of the fixtures and fittings and there is only Maurice [Temple Smith] there (remote as he is) with whom I can spark (and as often as not the plugs are damp. Come to think of it Maurice is rather like Conway Senior!). I know I can walk into Michael Joseph tomorrow and sign up. I can walk into Macmillan and sign up. And Secker I think unless Fred [Warburg] has changed his mind in the last year. Hodder too, but their list would be a disadvantage for me when it came to lit. editors and some reviewers. In fact, I suppose I could walk in anywhere and get taken on. This of course is almost the best reason in the world for staying where I am, if you see what I mean. Anyway, my agonising reappraisal led me only a few days ago to tackle Maurice personally and in private and per-haps more ultimate good will come of that talk than would come of going where the grass looks greener from the field you're in. It has never been a case of <u>terms,</u> but of overall attitude and part of the trouble is that when Maurice first met me he was a very new boy and I was an established E & S younger novelist and a director of a leading firm of agents. He finds it difficult to adjust and realise that when I go in now as an author, I need reminding that other people think I'm better than I know I am. The other part of the trouble is that Maurice's power is limited, even if in the end he gets his own way about most things, and limited not from within but from without. I told him straight out that I was thinking of going and he felt all the right things and said most of them. I told him why I wanted to go and why I didn't want to go and that if I went I would just be hard about it and make it expensive for someone, and that if I stayed I might want to make it expensive for the E & S group. I told him that it had always struck me as ridiculous that a British author should have to go to an American publisher for the money to buy his freedom to write. He said he agreed but that at the time there wasn't anything he could have done about it. He said how much do you want, and I told him what I might want, and he said he would put it up to Alan White and didn't fall backwards off his seat. So I told him no, he wasn't to put it up because it wasn't a request yet and that in any case I'd not talked to David about it, let alone to William Morrow, who were more than just my American publishers. I also said that if I decided to make it a request I'd want him to see what existed of the novel in progress (and that I think would be so in the case of moving to another house: I mean showing them the current goods first) because I wanted any arrangement to be on the basis of what is known and not of what is anticipated.

I wonder whether any of this is making sense to you. I think what I'm trying to do is rationalise my position, but at the same time not count on anything: not count for instance on The Birds of Paradise having an easy commercial and critical passage over here, let alone do anything exotic in America. There's something a bit wrong with my work. I talked to M[aurice] about this and asked him to be honest. He put it rather well. He said he always expected me to do something really terrific and that what I did do was streets ahead of most of the things that got real acclaim but that there was a kind of membrane in the books, the final membrane I might never break through but he thought I would, and if I did, well there we were, perhaps part of lit. hist. and read fifty years from now, or maybe he said a hundred.[47] Now, I don't know whether this is M[aurice]'s original idea or something someone in London has said to him and it is no good wishing he had said it earlier because that's the kind of thing that can only be said to you when you're ready to take it, which I was because between the mood of agonising reappraisal and seeing Maurice there was a rather clear-headed mood which stopped me jumping straight into Macmillan (where Muriel Spark is very anxious for me to join her and where it is known I would be expensive but it makes no difference). I don't think I can stop being ridiculously ambitious, but I can stop being neurotically ambitious, I think. I don't think the membrane was broken through in The Birds (neither does Maurice although he thinks it was broken through much more nearly than ever before) and there's no real reason to suppose that it will be broken through in The Bender, although it is novel number seven and luck might work. I see my job now as wholly devoted to the business of trying to break through it and the three years that began on April 1st 1960 and seemed to possess their own magic now seem pretty irrelevant. I think I know that they are in a sense also irrelevant to you, and that the three could be extended to five with no change in the rhythm of anyone's breathing. But what there is of my reputation is almost wholly English at the moment and I do wonder whether an English publisher (either E & S or someone else, whoever will play) shouldn't therefore be making the investment (which is a nicer way of saying taking the risk!). As a business relationship that alternative could never be as warming to me as the one we have and have so far made to work with what I look upon as almost unlooked for success.

What it comes to is this: it would help my thinking over the next few weeks if presently I could have your views; I mean about my asking David to negotiate a three-year banking arrangement over here that would end the present one. It is still time that I want and security and the money to indulge what William Conway called habits of comfort and English publishers aren't exactly standing in the bread line.

I hope I've put this all down right.

Ever yours,

Box 3, Folder 21 (McFarlin)
78 Addison Way
To Kay Collier [Kay Dick]
21 November 1961

Kay my dear,

What a week. Now Penny is in bed with a kind of 'flu—actually since Saturday. Tomorrow I have to speak at the National Book League, and before that attend the private view of the exhibition of the Royal Society of Portrait Painters (195 Piccadilly) in which that portrait of me hangs. Fame—elusive—depends from a picture rail.

Today you go down to see your mother. I hope all is much better than you will be imagining. I think of you, anyway, which is perhaps why, especially today, I write to you at last about Sunday,[48] which I finished at the weekend and have since been thinking about between chores.

It is impossible to judge it by itself, I think. It is immensely civilized, beautifully written, constructed with a skill which I suppose only another writer will really understand and admire. From the point of view of the common reader it produces, as skill always does, compulsive readability (now a cant phrase, although I have a feeling I invented it some time ago).

When I tried to read it in manuscript you may remember I came unstuck round about the beginning of part two; unstuck because I had been working on the same lines of construction. If and when you ever read <u>The Birds</u> I hope you will see what it is that makes them and <u>Sunday</u> similar in attack, otherwise you'll just think I was swinging the lead. But now, after some months of divorce from the bloody birds I do not come unstuck at all. The Geneva section is in very fine counterpoint to prayers and sleep. The four parts fold into each other with beautiful precision, and the sense there is of <u>growing</u> gives the novel the air of being a living organism. So that what is <u>not</u> said becomes just as important (and visible) as what is said. This, I think you'd agree, is the mark of a big writer.

And yet I think you <u>just</u> fail to deal the knockout blow. But that is what I mean about it being impossible to judge one book in a series of seven. There is only the appearance of the knockout blow not coming; and I think that is because Sunday's romance turns out to be curiously unworthy of Sunday—of the Sunday we have come to know. I can't equate my Sunday with the silly and rather desperate little girl who chased a silly and unpleasant man through the streets of Cambridge. The book is <u>major</u> but Sunday's romance turns out to be minor; shop girl, landlady's daughter stuff. Which no doubt is <u>true</u>. Perhaps the technical problem of giving it an air of final grandeur is insoluble in the first 90,000 words or so. And yet, again (I'm thinking aloud to you) what was it that changes Sunday from this silly desperate little girl into almost the likeness of a grand dame. One feels the need to know so much more about young Sunday in Cambridge. (Is this developed in the rest of the series?) There should, I am convinced, be a kind of magnificence in Sunday in that last few moments in the hotel. Or am I melodramatising? And of course, in one sense, the book isn't really about Sunday at all, it is about Cass (and that feeling emerges very strong in the last section). I know that by the time the last part is under way Cass is seeing her mother as a fake (and also being cruel as only the young can be cruel), but to counterbalance this Sunday I think had to emerge as, indeed, a fake, a silly fake, but with sufficient evidence of the kind of dignity (which allied to cunning and knowledge and experience and assumed fluffiness attracted men of the world) that would make her last comment on the subject of Luke immensely moving. It had to be moving for us to be utterly sympathetic towards Cass as well.

I am explaining all this very badly; but I was not <u>knocked</u> by that last scene in the hotel. Not because you didn't handle it beautifully, but because the <u>facts</u> didn't provide a basis for catharsis to set in. Luke is a ghastly asocial creature with none of the warmth I should have thought Sunday had to find in a man to respond to him at all. What <u>was</u> it that attracted her to him? One can almost see that if she had had a bad experience with a man like Luke she would thereafter only like men of whom she could say, "He is very <u>kind</u> to us." What was she looking for when she chased Luke at the age of eighteen or whatever it was? There are layers of Sunday not uncovered.

But of course all this carping is, in a way, no more than proof of the extent to which Sunday lives. If she did not come so splendidly to life one would not bother. But Claire, for instance, has her cathartic moment. That is a classic scene. Full of faded splendour and a kind of grandeur in the midst of the sordid. My Sunday is absolutely the kind of woman Claire would like, different in approach to life as they are. But what is it Claire would have seen in a Sunday who chased Luke through the streets of Cambridge?

I think what I wanted Sunday to say right at the end was something to the effect of: What did I ever see in Luke? Because I think that <u>is</u> what she thinks. She is such a different person from the 18 year-old girl, but Luke is clearly just the same deadbeat bastard with his sights set selfishly on a life of selfishness. If <u>we</u> could see Sunday's romance torn to shreds in front of her middle-aged eyes, and if we could see that Cass sees it, and <u>know</u> that Sunday sees it, hear her admit it, or even not admit it but say this Sundayish thing about Luke not wanting to compromise her, but be found presently by Cass in tears, or staring into space, I believe that might have produced the effect I was waiting for.

But perhaps not. I don't know. I can, in the last count, only admit that I felt a lack of something right at the end and give my reasons as lucidly as I can. And I have to admit that I <u>know</u> what you show happening is the likely, true to life thing. But there is this small misty patch on the mirror you hold up to it. And how insignificant that patch probably is in terms of the whole.

Bless you, meanwhile.⁴⁹

Box 13, Folder 2 (McFarlin)
78 Addison Way
To John Willey, William Morrow & Company, USA
27 November 1961

Dear John,

My last letter was very badly expressed, hasty and perhaps even ill advised. So please ignore it. I meant well but reading the letter over last night it didn't sound especially like that. I hope very much that you didn't take it ill.

Yours ever,

Box 7, Folder 20 (McFarlin)
78 Addison Way
From a letter to David Bolt, David Higham Associates
5 December 1961

My Dear David,

[…] I want, very badly, to go to India next year. I am seeing Jean [Leroy] tomorrow for lunch and shall be talking to her about it, too. I realise that you could sit down and write a popular history of the Gurkhas in Cheltenham, but that is not the way I would do it, if I did it; and I expect in any case the kind of contract I'd want would be on unpopular terms, so I'm not sanguine of anything coming of it. However, who knows, several arrangements in several directions might produce the desired end of a return passage—the real object of which is, of course, fictional. The rest of this letter will make more sense to the other David [Higham] than it will to you who haven't yet had the opportunity of reading <u>The Birds of Paradise</u>.

Before <u>Birds</u> was finished I said, in a talk with Maurice [Temple Smith], that at times I felt I was laying the foundations for several further novels about the same characters. I asked M[aurice] to comment on this when the book was finished but he has never done so and I myself haven't been convinced, so it hasn't been of much consequence. But bubbling away now in the back of my mind is the feeling of a big scale novel about the British power and influence; for this is something that continues to excite me. Every few weeks I review non-fiction on the subject for the TLS. I know that David feels I have scraped the bottom of my barrel on India—and he is absolutely right in the sense of a barrel of personal experience—although in <u>Birds</u> I was beginning to skim off some of the cream of that compulsive interest that goes beyond personal experience.[50]

Meanwhile my sad-funny London novel which when David last heard about it was going so well has suffered a block which might only be mechanical. On the other hand, it might be psychological. The trouble may be that as a writer I'm only extended when I take something seriously. I can't take anything that happens in London seriously! At least, not at the moment, or in that way. To breathe fresh air east of Suez might unbung all kinds of barrels.

Yours ever,

Box 18, Folder 19 (McFarlin)
78 Addison Way
From a letter to Muriel Spark
25 February 1962

My Dearest Mu,

Your letter of the 21st only reached me yesterday morning (Saturday), but as it so happened I knew I'd be seeing Bill Smith at the same party yesterday evening, so it came at just the right time.

First. I and Penny are absolutely delighted that you would like to come and only hope that when the time comes it will fit in without causing disruption, and only causing pleasure.[51]

Second. Bill too is naturally delighted, and is absolutely ready to keep the door held open. Lecturers do sometimes have to cancel without a great deal of notice. I expect what Bill will do is include you officially (i.e., in the programme that is eventually printed) and that you will be approached by the nice secretary Marjorie Harris about which day you prefer and which time of day, etc. so that everything is set for you to come and perform. If they have to find a substitute at the last moment, well—we shall all be disappointed but it can be faced and dealt with without feeling that they have been let down.

Third. Bill rose at once to the idea of your reading stories and then answering questions. He said, as a matter of fact, that he has heard you do this, and was most impressed (I think at something to do with John O'London's) not only by the way you handled the questions but also with the way you read. So it can be in the nature of a lark for you. Actually I am all for this kind of platform performance at places like Swanwick where too easily the lecturers get stodgy and the audience—although respectful always—bored. When I lectured I did so in 2 parts, 1st an off-beat story of the stone age and the beginnings of creative story (!) following by the somewhat sardonic survey of modern developments in the business of writing. It was a spoof, but I think people liked it, because I was inviting them to sit back and enjoy themselves and not learn anything noticeable!

Anyway, the prospect of having you at Swanwick is marvellous. Please do try and let it germinate in your mind as something you are going to do: and then there is more likelihood of your being there. And don't forget that you can either stay whole time, part time, or just for the night.

Mu dear, E & S are giving me a publication party on Monday April 9th (Pub date) [of *The Birds of Paradise*] to mark pub and the <u>Choice</u> business. Naturally you are at the very top of my list of personal guests, so please do come. I don't know what they have in mind for afterwards (they ought really to take Penny and me on to dinner, I suppose) but perhaps we can extend it ourselves in some way. I've no idea how big or small the party is, but they asked me to give them a list of people I wanted to invite, and I'm making it jolly big—all the people who have sort of helped and encouraged over the last ten years and more, plus people like my accountant (he's yours too) and my bank manager! I might also make it the occasion for Carol's debut into lit. party world, because she has a boyfriend who wants to be a writer. He's only 15 but looks 18 and takes them both to X cert films. So if I decide Carol should have a look at the lit. world she'll be escorted. It makes me feel not old but faintly distinguished even to be considering bringing a daughter out.

Anyway, an official invitation will issue directly in the next few weeks. I do hope it doesn't coincide with your first night, or with anything you've got to do other than come. […]

Love,

Box 4, Folder 10 (McFarlin)
78 Addison Way
To Maurice Temple Smith, Eyre & Spottiswoode, Ltd.
25 February 1962

Dear Maurice,

Many thanks for the Daniel George piece. He doesn't quite make it, but it serves its turn, I think. When one thinks about it remarks like "by far the best he has written but not the best he will write" are pretty silly. How does he know it isn't? The penalty for making the new book better than the last is to be thought of as "steadily improving", which suggests faintly amateur status. I mention this because even our staunch friend Whitefriar has fallen for this line (see this week's Publishers circular or Smith's News or whatever it is). It traces back to

Pamela Snow, reviewing <u>A Male Child</u> in <u>The Bookman:</u> "a distinguished, grave and original novel by a writer who gets better with each book he writes".

Perhaps all critics are Chinese. "It is better to travel than to arrive". But I suggest it is an attitude to be attacked gently, wherever it is possible, otherwise I shall likely be labelled permanently "Promising".... What is faintly silly is that I believe reviewers do <u>think</u> of me as established but the impression they pass on to the public is somewhat less than that.

Random thoughts on a cold morning.

Box 4, Folder 10 (McFarlin)
78 Addison Way
From a letter to Charles Friend, Eyre & Spottiswoode, Ltd.[52]
8 March 1962

Dear Charles,

[...] Many thanks for your letter of the 6th and for confirming the total sale [of *The Chinese Love Pavilion*] to 30 Sept last at 14,100 [...].

Believe it or not, I am interested in the mechanism of the trade. True, I like my publisher to be optimistic. I have enough of pessimism sitting here at the desk wondering often why I bother—on at least 3 occasions I threw the mss of <u>The Birds of Paradise</u> on to a high shelf saying: Drivel. Rubbish. That book'll kill me. It has always been so and will go on being so. As a member of society the only excuse (it seems to me) for putting a lot of words on masses of paper and expecting people to pay to read them later is that the words are important, and too often they seem spectacularly useless. So optimism and enthusiasm from the publisher is the necessary leaven in this unrisen bread. But those two things said and done there is this third matter: the blessed relief of dealing with facts, of how things are, of how it works, who does what and why in the places where you get connected to the people who might be glad you sat at your desk writing like a fool. There are some authors who don't want to know, and others who only want to know what sounds good, and others who jump to conclusions if you say so much as good morn-ing to them; so no wonder if there has grown up a publisher-feeling that the less an author is let into the total secret the better. But I want to know, because (a) I write what I want to write and (b) want to be read by as many who are likely so that (c) I can afford to go on writing what I want to write. And to me the trade is the mechanism to achieve this happy state of affairs through, and unlike the motor car engine which always defeats me in the end, it is a mechanism made up of people who presumably do things for reasons and have methods and motives which aren't mysteries to them, and are nice to know about because it is awful to feel that between yourself and the achievement of your end is an amorphous mass of mystique.

[…] I expect your immediate reaction is that if every author felt like this you'd spend all your time putting them in pictures which, by virtue of that, would quickly become non-existent, and they'd spend all their time being put into them; and that it was pretty difficult anyway to put people into pictures that weren't by any means clear even to yourselves. (And there are, I know, always the imponderables: like why do people like this book and not that one? Or who reads books anyway?) But per-haps for the time being it is enough if you know that I'd like to know because I feel it's part of my job to know even if that's because knowing only spreads the load of disappointments in store.

Cheers,

Box 10, Folder 2 (McFarlin)
78 Addison Way
From a letter to Mollie Hamilton [M. M. Kaye]
20 April 1962

Dear Mollie,

Many thanks indeed for your nice letter, which I was so glad to have. Yes, we shall be off to Spain in September, providing certain things hap-pen in relation to a new contract about to be negotiated![53] Living entirely on proceeds from writing isn't all that easy, and I've had quite a dollop from <u>The Birds</u> in advance, in expectation as it were. Somehow it is the book you're working on, not the one just published, that you have to rely on for security. Interesting situation!

I'm very sorry to hear you've been in the wars. Don't worry too much about its kick-back effects and the effect of <u>those</u> effects on the novel. If you could <u>adopt</u> a kind of detached attitude to the work and not worry about the detached attitude imposed by the kick-back, I think you'd beat the latter. What I'd do is pick the mss up regularly and say, Fancy that, a novel I was writing. Well, well. Then read bits and say: How good it will be when I decide to work on it again. Suddenly you will break through the shell and be in there mixed up with the yolk. And that will be the best sort of getting-well operation. The thing I've trained myself to do now is to worry like stink for a few days and then shrug my shoulders and say, so what? It stinks. And put it away. Then it doesn't stink. And down it comes until the next time.

The writer's home away from home (at Swanwick in Derbyshire) is (I think) Aug 17–24. Are you thinking of coming? I don't advise it! Unless you come as a lecturer or are on the committee, it must be hell. During the war they kept German POWs there; Von Werra was there.[54] But didn't escape. Nobody could.

<u>Passage to India</u>? God, that book is like a train terminus none of the fly-boy lit crits will allow you to go beyond. I mean we're all of us stuck with it, if we write about India. It's jolly nice of you to think <u>The Birds</u> might outlast it but they won't. <u>The Birmingham Post</u> doesn't think so. And did you see the flash boy's piece in <u>The New Statesman</u>? It was headed "Ruined Lads," and said it was a study in ruined masculinity. Funny, directly you start talking about people who regret being unable to do a decent honourable job of work they think you're talking about sex. A Freudian slip showing somewhere.

[…] Best wishes, Mollie, to you and <u>Trade Winds</u>. Ragnar [Svanström][55] was asking after you the other day. He has made a remarkable recovery from that lung operation (cancer I suspect). Why not drop him a line?

                    Yours ever,

Box 20, Folder 19 (McFarlin)
78 Addison Way
To Violet Wilkinson
7 May 1962

Dear Miss Wilkinson,

I am so very sorry to hear about the rheumatoid arthritis. I do hope that this lessens, indeed clears right up (although I'm not sure how easy it is to clear), and that we see you this year at Swanwick. I'm also sorry to hear—or gather, rather—that you are feeling discouraged about writing. The only thing I can say is this: never consider a book in terms of paying propositions for publishers. That is <u>their</u> worry. Writing it and believing in it is, of course, yours alone, and no one can <u>help</u> you to believe in it unless you show it to them and they say: Yes, this is good. But I appreciate that to show it to anyone proves a subconscious-at-least belief in the book you have to have yourself.

I can't begin to answer your long and interesting letter in anything like the detail you've put into both letter, thought and reading of text. So I shan't even try. And how could I be affronted? To publish a book is to offer it to everyone who cares to read it, and the relationship set up then between reader and writer is a relationship between free thinking and feeling people, each entitled to his and her view, and entitled to express it.

One of the reasons I can't begin to answer you, though, is that once a book is finished it is, for me, finished in practically every sense. I can never read a book through once I've passed the proofs. A book is a kind of total vision, I suppose, and having had it and mapped it, the life goes out of it. You drain its substance away in words and leave scarcely a shadow for yourself. Who is Conway? Who is Cranston? I no longer know. I knew at the time. I knew very well. Now I don't. It's as simple as that—and to discuss them and the situations surrounding them is to discuss people and situations which no longer quite exist. Perhaps this indicates a failure somewhere. Perhaps it is simply due to the fact that since finishing it I have been intimately mixed up with a totally different set of people and totally different complex of situation (the new novel, just finished), and can no longer whip up interest in Tradura, Jundapur and Manoba. After a time something rises to the surface and remains. I believe, for instance, much more now in the existence of Craig and Ramsay in The Mark of the Warrior—and in the existence of Tom Brent and Teena Chang and Saxby in The Chinese Love Pavilion. It is like, from a distance, suddenly finding yourself able to look back upon a period of your own life and finding that it is a period, with its special flavour and meaning and actuality. But of course most of the detail has gone. But it has emerged with its own period, personality and significance. In a year or two's time perhaps I shall find this happening with Conway.

What I think I ought to say, though, is this: writing novels I play largely by ear. I don't mean from the technical point of view. I think I know what I'm doing, and why I'm doing it. I think I'm reading the notes, indeed setting them out to a design, to a plan. But the thing that, as it were, makes the music for me is entirely intuitive.

You analyse The Birds intellectually. And why not? It is a compliment, in any case. And if The Birds is worth anything it ought to be capable of intellectual analysis. But not by myself. I do not believe, really, that the things that people do and the kind of people they are can ever be proven. And Conway, you know, was quite aware, all the time, of his Oedipus complex. But. And it is a large and clearly set out but: Conway knew his complex could only be designated Oedipus in a world "which found it easier to reduce a man's life to two brand words on a label". Oedipus complex. That's the label. And he accepts it as a label. But with that gentle aside about the total weight of evidence.

I think, at the moment, that I can only meet your questions with one answer—which I'm sure is going to be difficult to frame. But here goes. The Birds of Paradise is an attempt to give a picture, an impression, a sense, a feeling of that curious and restless little worm in men and women which reminds them of the mystery that remains behind when everything else seems to have been explained and pigeon holed. When what is romantic has been seen through, what is real has been accepted;

when the genes have played their part and environment has played its part. It hoped, I think, to be a picture of a man saying: This is how things were and this is how things are. And then a look of incomprehension falls on his face because how things were and how things are suggest a total emptiness he is nowhere near feeling. Directly he puts it into words, though, the emptiness he doesn't feel is somewhat banal in definition. He can only link it to a sense of duty. "When there's not duty to go back to, going back becomes a duty in itself".

The world can put Conway into a pigeon hole. He can put himself into one. The truth of the matter is, though, that there's <u>no</u> pigeon hole. But there <u>is</u> Conway. He simply won't be analysed out of existence. Please don't misunderstand me, or think I'm hitting at you because you've tried to analyse him. I'm hitting more, perhaps, at the school which is so terribly <u>sure</u>, so <u>slick</u> with analysis, the people who say, "So and so is false because—"—the whole set-up which, in literature alone, can lead to such sad exhibitions as the Leavis-Snow kerfuffle.[56] Leavis and Snow are supremely unimportant in a certain sense. But literature isn't. Snow is as much to blame as Leavis. Everyone is looking for some kind of proof of what is fundamentally insoluble (as I see it)—the key to a door when they don't even know where the door is. Nobody does.

Hope this makes some kind of negative sense. I suppose, as a writer, I deal in negatives. But then I never see any positives clearly enough for them to excite me. And God knows <u>The Birds of Paradise</u> is full, full of faults and passages that could be proved to be false if it is the intention to prove them so. I could probably do it myself! But I hope there is some truth in the feeling I have that a work of art (if, if, if one is producing that sort of work and who can tell) <u>can</u> be the sum of its imperfections.

Thank you for writing to me. This kind of communication is important. If you can come to Swanwick I hope we'll have a bit of time together.

Meanwhile try and get rid of that rheumatoid-arthritis. With best wishes and kind regards from us both,

Yours sincerely,

Box 13, Folder 4 (McFarlin)
78 Addison Way
To Adèle Dogan Horwitz, William Morrow & Company, USA
7 June 1962

Dear Adèle,

Yours of the 1st just arrived. Many thanks indeed. I'm delighted that you like the book [*The Bender*] so much. We'll go into the "cons" in due course. Yours is now the second American reaction I've had—Ivan von Auw wrote David H[igham] that he thought it "quite terrific"—so I'm heartened a lot. In making the departure from the old Indian scene I had fears of being found "too British" in this one.

Anina, by the way, is a refugee from The Birds of Paradise. She was originally Krishi's girlfriend at the Jundapur palace (when they were all grown up). She used to sit on a stuffed black panther, twist its ears and stare into space when what she called "Allah Reshershy and all that jazz" (K, Dora and Bill[57] remembering things past) got too much for her. I was, as you can tell, reluctant to lose her from Jundapur, but she didn't really fit, and once I'd got up the courage to cut her out (putting her carefully on one side to see what, later, she might fit into) everything became clear for the end of The Birds. Then, suddenly, I saw that she lived in Camden Town all the time, and was a natural for George's brother Guy.

Glad, too, that you like Gillian, who is almost my favourite.

But, oh, oh, I'm so fond of Aunt Ada. David H. thinks the Ada Lisle sections are very very fine. And isn't it odd—I thought, well, at least Ada Lisle will have a kind of meaning in America. Shows how wrong one can be!

Anyway, Adèle, blessings on you for reading it so quickly. I work it out that you can only have had it at the earliest on 30th or 31st May (judging from Ivan's letter), and there you are writing to me on the 1st. Now I await John [Willey]'s personal reactions. Please ask him not to hold up writing about the book in the mistaken belief that what I first want to hear about is the result of his business discussions with Ivan.

And apropos the latter, I hope they aren't being blown up into a kind of treaty conference! But John knows my feelings.

Love, and thanks,

Box 8, Folder 3 (McFarlin)
78 Addison Way
From a letter to David Higham, David Higham Associates
19 June 1962

My Dear David,

First of all, many thanks for the splendid lunch. I think I forgot to say so at the time!

I've studied M's [Maurice Temple Smith's] letter carefully. And come back to the point I half saw over lunch, e.g., that unless E & S guarantee a specific sum as a non-returnable advance on each book there's not a great deal of point in guaranteeing a total sum, since they were guaranteeing £2500 a year for 3 years in the first place and anything earned under that was non-returnable. The £7500 is whittled down now not by £2400 but by, say, £1500 (i.e., the balance of the known amounts securing on past books). Past books are unlikely to earn much more than the "known" amounts, unless The Birds of Paradise is selling much better in the trade edition than we think, so—disregarding for the moment any "advances" on each book or on all—E & S are guaranteeing about £6000 on the next three as a lump, in any event.

The crux of the matter lies in Maurice's words, "By further splitting the advance into equal amounts for each book we would give Paul no greater security but we would face an additional risk ourselves".

In their risk lies my security. I don't think we should depart from the good old-fashioned principle that each book is worth its basic salt. And I think that only by getting the publisher to say what valuation he puts on the basic salt of each of the next three books can we get anywhere near judging the difference, if any, between one publisher's belief in the future and another's.

I wonder whether you'd talk to M[aurice] on the telephone about this and try and get him to say what his best offer would be for an advance on each book? At the same time perhaps you'd tell him I feel the time may have come for us to have a heart to heart together? [...]

Ever,

Box 13, Folder 4 (McFarlin)
78 Addison Way
To John Willey, William Morrow & Company, USA
27 June 1962

Dear John,

Been somewhat at sixes and sevens and scarcely remember whether I thanked you for the advance copy that came by airmail. Yes, I think I did. I seem to recall mentioning how much I liked the look of the whole thing. Anyway the remaining copies are here now, and handsome they look in a row. I was delighted to hear from Sam that he liked The Bender, too. And another letter from Adèle, promising me shortly her editorial memorandum.

John, I'm moving to Secker and Warburg with The Bender. My old friend Roland [Gant] is there, and he and Fred [Warburg] are both wild about the book. Not that in all the recent months they hadn't made it very plain they'd like me to join them in any case. And finally I decided, and the contract is all signed and sealed. It's for my next 3 books and everything is splendid moneywise, and enthusiasm-wise, too. When it finally came to it I found that the first time in all the ten years I've been at E & S that I asked them to stick their necks out a bit for me there was an element of wariness and caution. So that was that from my point of view. Secker and W volunteered better royalties, a guarantee of £2000 on each novel, and £500 free contribution to the expenses of a trip to India or elsewhere as may be mutually agreed. This, with monies still to accrue at E & S (the bulk of my Birds of Paradise money) gives me £2000 a year for 4 years, plus £500 plus about £400 for a trip abroad when the time is ripe. The total amount of money at E & S worked out about the same, but they wouldn't guarantee a definite sum for each novel. And there was a lot of Arab marketplace bargaining about how much of my accruing moneys from the past should be released and how much held against the future. Broadly E & S would have paid me £2500 a year for 3 years; and although I drop £500 a year on the Secker arrangement it is for 4 years instead of 3, and with that first-rate guarantee per novel, non-returnable, or with unearned advances set off against the next book. So all in all I hardly think anyone can blame me, particularly as I detected a much hotter enthusiasm for the book on Fred's and Roland's part. And the whole idea of ending the banking arrangement with you was to get a British publisher to stick his neck out (just as you all stuck yours out 2 ½ years ago when I'd hardly sold a copy in the States).

Anyway, John, with the new deal at Secker, and the new arrangement with Morrow, I couldn't be happier or more settled in my mind about the future; so hope—whatever your reservations may be about such a move—you'll all wish me luck.

Best regards to you all,

Box 4, Folder 10 (McFarlin)
78 Addison Way
To Maurice Temple Smith, Eyre & Spottiswoode, Ltd.
30 June 1962

Dear Maurice,

Many thanks for your letter.

I am delighted with my Secker arrangements and nothing can detract from that, but it was sad having to move from the firm I've been with for something like twelve years; especially sad—for me anyway—that one of the main factors in the business of coming unstuck should have been terms and conditions, which I never had expected. However, a disagreement over what is fair and reasonable, although the swiftest and most conclusive, is the least damaging in the long run since it leaves no lingeringly unpleasant aftertaste of personal disagreement.

From my point of view E & S, with the first six books on their list, are still, in one sense, my publishers. My hope is that some of these at least will prove to have a continuing value although that, I know, will depend on the success of the work I do with Secker & Warburg. But meanwhile they form a tentative link between past and future.

As for the personal note you strike in your letter, well yes, this—as David [Higham] has told you, I think—exactly corresponds with my own feelings, and I am glad you feel the same.

Yours ever,

Box 13, Folder 5 (McFarlin)
78 Addison Way
To John Willey, William Morrow & Company, USA
19 September 1962

Dear John,

Many thanks indeed for your kind telegram. To have answered it would have meant a journey to the Telegrafos, which was just too hot to make! But it made my day to be remembered so far from home—and to hear that the review had appeared in <u>Time</u> magazine, and had been good. I shall look forward to seeing a cutting whenever you can send one along to me.

The advance sale sounds promising enough. Let us hope that this time it is added to rather than subtracted from my returns. And of course I look forward as well to hearing what the NAL [New American Library] decide.

We reached home yesterday evening, rather exhausted and—in my case—suffering from a cold which I think I caught in Spain doing La Twist[58] and working up a sweat. As we drove back through France the cold emerged into something recognisable as one, until on the boat at Dover there wasn't any doubt. All our friends seem to have come back with colds this year, so I can't complain.

Am not yet back into my right mind, if you know what I mean. The girls are glooming about the house complaining about having to go back to school tomorrow. And I face a pile of unanswered (and partly unanswerable) correspondence—including a letter from someone I've never heard of who asks me to recommend books on archaeology for a friend of hers who is interested in that sort of thing. Why pick on me?

This year I went to the bulls, accompanied by Carol and Señor Justus whose lotus-eating job is to control what traffic there is in Tamariu (a line of cars parked for 2 weeks solid). Unfortunately Sr. Justus's English wasn't good enough to explain the finer points of the corrida. One of the matadors was Antonio Ordonez, who is supposed to be a maestro. None of the people sitting near me (mostly Spaniards) seemed to be able to tell me which matador <u>was</u> Ordonez. One of the picadors fell off his horse. Another one left his pic in the bull. I fancy the whole thing is somewhat overrated. I found that the best way of sitting tight through 6 bulls was to pretend that it was the same bull who came out six times. The other main point of interest for me was to notice how <u>old</u> the matador's assistants look. Poor chaps. They've been at it for years—like in that Hemingway story. Wizened little old men in dancing pumps with violet-coloured bags under their eyes, on sallow skins, hating the crowd, hating the bulls, hating the matador, wishing they could be armed and blindfolded like the old nags (that try to look as if they're walking on in Don Quixote).

I'll drop you another line when I've come to my workaday sense; but meanwhile many thanks again for your cable. I do hope <u>The Birds</u> are getting something of a hand.

Yours ever,

Box 13, Folder 5 (McFarlin)
78 Addison Way
To John Willey, William Morrow & Company, USA
3 October 1962

Dear John,

Of course I haven't crossed you off my list. I knew full well why there was a certain silence—i.e., that you were wanting very much to write some good news when you answered my letter, and this depended upon how the reviews came in, and how the NAL reacted.

I suppose I should be a bit depressed—and in one sense I suppose I am. Clearly I'm not breaking through into that enclosed world of interested literary response, presided over by distinguished lit. editors and top reviewers. And clearly my sort of book does need that kind of benediction if the public is to have its curiosity aroused. And of course I am deeply sorry that NAL have said No, because that denies us the financial compensation. I'm not sanguine about a sale in that direction now, and I'm sure you're not. So—one gets stripped to the bone, in a way. No bad thing....

As we all know, a writer should only write what he wants to write—and this is how it has always been with me and how it will always be. But we live in society—ideas and opinions are spurs to creative organisation. Your thoughts and comments would never be wasted on me even if I seemed, in effect, to have disregarded them. How rich or significant or plain interesting a figure—for instance—was Anina? She keeps impinging in various guises.... Adèle described her as a sublime creature, and I think you agreed. Certainly, as I said, she keeps impinging upon all this potential material (London), which has all kinds of vague working titles such as "The Careerist", or even, simply, "The Marriage"—and I begin to wonder whether (with my controlled affection for the symbol) I haven't sloughed off the artefact symbol and found the mining tool (which the symbol has always represented to me) in the shape of a person, Anina, who is a romantic and a realist—but may also be a bore!

Yours ever,

Box 20, Folder 28 (McFarlin)
78 Addison Way
William G. Smith, Chairman, Swanwick Writers' Summer School
13 December 1962

Dear Bill,
Writers' Summer School, 1963

We have never thanked you and the committee properly for the kind invitation to be host and hostess again at next year's school—but as you know we haven't been sure whether we could come.

I have now fixed with Morrow in America that the new novel won't be published there until very late September or early October. The idea is that this time I should try to be in New York at the time, or immediately after publication. My trip to India is most unlikely to be before January of 1964. This means that we ought to be free in August and as we've decided not to go abroad for a holiday this year; we're thinking in terms of doing our stint at Derby[59] and then continuing on from there to wherever we decide to go.

The other thing we had to consider was my failure last year to keep my head above the water at Swanwick. This may not have been especially noticeable, because Penny kept things running smoothly for both of us. I think that the main trouble, for me, lies in the feeling that as "Host" there are duties to members as well as to lecturers, whereas in actual fact one spends a great deal of time trying to pass from point a to point b without being "caught", simply because if you're caught a lecturer stands in danger of being left high and dry somewhere.

I'm sure there isn't much that can be done to get over this situation— but last year I was particularly sensitive to the feeling in the school at large that the "host" was unapproachable and acting like a VIP. This year Penny and I would very much appreciate the programme note making it quite clear that we are Host and Hostess to the Lecturers and that X & Y are Host and Hostess to Members. In fact Members Host and Hostess should take precedence in the programme note.

The duties of speakers' host are fairly simple. It may be thought that it isn't necessary for the host to meet the speakers personally at the station or at the entrance; but that initial meeting (particularly at the station) is the whole basis of the relationship the speaker then has with the school. Simple as the duties are, they do call for a bit of thought—not necessarily rewarding because as we all know the third-rate people always need more looking after than the first rate.

Top Table and Room X. Last year Penny and I were never really certain to what extent we were responsible for dishing out and clearing away. Dishing out and clearing away, being physical acts, often provide a blessed relief from small talk with speakers who would prefer anyway to disappear for a while into a quiet corner and work out what's hit them. But there ought to be a clear ruling on this. Host and Hostess are sometimes thought of as members of the committee and sometimes not. In the early days of the school when the speakers are arriving in droves my own feeling is that dishing out and clearing away are <u>not</u> duties the speakers' host and hostess have time or opportunity for—but in the absence of a ruling the host and hostess, in failing to dish out or clear away, are apt to feel they have got out of something. In room X, too, I think there is a tendency to think of it not as a common room but as the host and hostess' drawing room. Male members of the committee anyway should never be backward about looking after themselves in the matter of drinks. Perhaps this excessive politeness is the result of some earlier experiences of a host and hostess who thought of the bottles as personal possessions. But serving and replenishing drinks for upwards of 30 people when there is a VIP speaker intent on telling you the story of her life (which has happened at least once) is a chore <u>we</u> are only too willing to be helped with.

There may be a few other small points that ought to be clarified but these are all I can think of just off hand, and the main thing, anyway, in our opinion, is to make it as clear as possible to members, through the programme note, that there <u>is</u> a difference between Members' and Speakers' host and hostess. We are there to put the speakers at their ease, and their ease should be a guide to the state of our poor feet. It would help if, in the vinery, one didn't keep intercepting glances which say, "Why aren't you doing your job and chatting us up?"

That said, let me also say that we do very much appreciate the invitation to Swanwick for a third time running, and the inclusion in the invitation of the children is by no means taken for granted.

I'm sending a copy of this letter to Marjorie [Harris],[60] so that she's in the picture.

Our love to you both,

Ever,

Box 3, Folder 2 (McFarlin)
78 Addison Way
From a letter to John Adams, Country Life
27 December 1962

Dear Mr. Adams,

[…] Pretty reluctantly, I have come to the conclusion that I'm not successfully combining the Country Life job with work on my own new book. All the work I have done on it since beginning it in September has had to be scrapped. This is not at all an unusual experience for me, and the temptation is to believe that once I've begun again, on the right foot, I could carry on with the reviewing, but I think I must accept the fact that the moment has come to concentrate.

I am anxious to break the back of the new novel by August, because apart from a holiday with the family towards the end of that month there is also a plan for me to be in New York in late September and early October for the American publication of the book that comes out here in the spring. There is also another plan, rather more tentative but still to be reckoned with, for a trip to India in January 1964, and if that comes off I am left, after August, with only November and December to put what I hope would be the finishing touches to the new book […].

The only fair thing at the moment is for me to ask you to release me under the arrangement we have to one month's notice […]. I really am very sorry to begin the new year with a negative resolution!

With kind regards,

                       Yours sincerely,

Box 10, Folder 16 (McFarlin)
78 Addison Way
From a letter to Magnus Lindberg, Sweden[61]
8 January 1963

Dear Mr. Lindberg,

Many thanks for your letter of January 3rd. I am delighted to have a letter from the translator of <u>The Birds of Paradise</u>, and will do my best to answer the questions you have asked.[62]

Page:

31   Suraj-ud-Daula is the name of the Indian prince who imprisoned about 180 Europeans in an underground dungeon lighted only by one small, barred window. In the morning only a few of the Europeans came out alive. The dungeon was known as the Black Hole of Calcutta (time: 18th Century).

32   Bidis. A hand-made Indian cigarette smoked by peasants and poor people.

37   Nimbopani. a drink like lime juice, non-alcoholic.

57   Chota pegs. Small measure of alcoholic drink. Chota means "small", peg means "measure".

158   Subedar. An Indian officer, holding the Viceroy's commission, and therefore of lower rank than an Indian or a European holding the King's Commission. There is no equivalent rank in the British Army. Viceroy's commissioned officers (Jemadars, Subedars, and Subedar Majors) came—in rank—between senior warrant officers (e.g., Sergeant Majors) and junior subalterns (e.g., Lieutenants).

209   Koi-hai. Meaning in Hindi or Urdu is—"Anybody there?" Its constant use by Europeans in India as a means of summoning servants led to its attachment to Europeans as a satirical nickname. A Koi-hai would be a man thought of as typically Colonial. A Blimp. A Reactionary.

227   Jannu. Literally = knowledge. In this case used by Krishi in its applied sense = social code. Rajput Jannu means the Rajput code of behaviour, which puts hospitality to strangers high on the list of social and religious priorities. Desirable behaviour in a good Rajput.

Political Department. This was a specialised branch of the Indian Civil Service, which came directly under the jurisdiction of the <u>Viceroy</u>, who was the King-Emperor's representative. Since the independent Indian States were not <u>ruled</u> by the Crown, they could not come under the ordinary Indian Government and Civil Service. The King-Emperor was the paramount power; however, the Viceroy had responsibility for advising and guiding the States. He did this through this special department. Political Service is also a valid description. The Political Department recruited its members both from the Indian Army and from the Indian Civil Service. To get into it at all you had to be either an Army Officer or a Civil Servant. On Independence and Partition in 1947, the Political Department became known as the States Department of the Indian Government, and was then responsible for the gradual integration of the States into the constitutional framework of the new Republic. It has now, I think, entirely ceased to exist, since the States are absorbed into provinces. During the British rule, though, the Political Department was entirely separate from the Indian government and its Civil Service. Its head was answerable only to the Viceroy. This led, as the book shows, to that strange dichotomy of the principle in British rule. Through his Central, provincial governments the Viceroy applied the policy of leading British India to democratic self-rule. Through his political department he upheld, on behalf of the British crown, the theory of autocratic self government for ruling Princes. Only a very <u>bad</u> Indian Prince would be deposed. Mysore is a good example. Years ago the Crown took the state over and much later re-instated a ruler there. Mysore was often pointed out as a proof that an Indian Prince could rule well, but its modernisation and democratic government was chiefly the result of the period of direct rule by the Crown. The political point I'm making in the book is that the British, years ago, should have adopted a policy of easing the Princes out of their autocratic seats of authority and of uniting the country democratically.

[…] I hope these answers are clear enough. Please do not hesitate to write to me again if there is anything you are still unsure of. And meanwhile I send my best thanks and kind regards.

Yours sincerely,

Box 3, Folder 23 (McFarlin)
78 Addison Way
From a letter to Dr. A. Dohm, Germany[63]
23 January 1963

Dear Dr. Dohm,

Thank you very much for your letter of the 20th. Since my last letter to you, the Swedish translator has also written to me with questions very similar to yours: so perhaps it simply is that this is the only novel I have ever written that puzzles translators!

[…] In the passage you question ("thanks for my father") there is a very slight element of irony in Conway's reference to his father. What he is really saying is that his father was a man of common sense and foresight, whereas, truth to tell, he partly wishes this had not been so, because he never had the opportunity to fulfil boyhood ambitions of a romantic life in India. He thanks his father for organising his life in such a way that he grew up to have money and leisure. He thanks his father for saving him from the discomfort of life in the East and from the possible dangers of going mad from too much sun and too much liquor. But deep in his heart he regrets never having had experienced the splendid things which he believed would have compensated him for the discomforts. He is not blaming his father. He does not really think his father is guilty of anything. He is genuinely paying tribute to his father's common sense. But his heart does not quite agree with his head. He sees the irony of this. So "thanks" has a faintly ironic note.

In the next paragraph, of course, he acknowledged the fact that even if his father had not denied him the opportunity of a life in India, even if his father had forced him to follow in his footsteps, history would have taken a hand, and denied him what his father didn't. India's independence would have put an end to a colonial career—UNLESS he had been the kind of man who believed the sun could never set on the Empire and had gone to places where the native population was still treated as inferior, e.g., Kenya, Rhodesia. In this context by all means think of "a Welensky" as "Welenskys", as "opponents to native independence", as "reactionaries"....

All best wishes,

Yours sincerely,

Box 13, Folder 5 (McFarlin)
78 Addison Way
From a letter to John Willey, William Morrow & Company, USA
30 January 1963

Dear John,

[…] Since writing you, the situation has changed a bit. I've abandoned "The Careerist" book, because I felt finally that I was simply repeating myself, and that the scope of the book was too narrow. Having come to that decision, and shelved about 20,000 words, I not only felt better but knew I was ready to do what I've called to myself for some years my Spanish book [*The Corrida at San Feliu*]. And that is under way and extending me properly. I shan't tell you anything about it, though! It means, however, that instead of holidaying in England we shall all go back to Catalonia again in early September, by which time it would be nice to think I had the book in draft so that—refreshed by the holiday and the immediately following trip to New York, I could spend the rest of the autumn rewriting, correcting and getting it ready generally for submission. That would leave me free to go off to India in January or February 1964—a trip that might be just as good for "The Careerist" as for anything else […].

Our best to you all.

Box 10, Folder 16 (McFarlin)
78 Addison Way
From a letter to Mr. Magnus Lindberg, Sweden
25 March 1963

Dear Mr. Lindberg:

Many thanks for your letter. I'm sorry to hear that you have been in hospital, but I'm glad it was for nothing serious. I'm also very glad to hear that you have been asked to translate <u>The Bender</u>, having finished <u>The Birds of Paradise</u>, and I am most grateful to you for the very kind things that you say about both books. I've not yet heard from Norstedt about the possibility of their publishing <u>The Bender</u> first, but I'm sure that whatever decision they come to will be the right one.

The difficulties of translating <u>The Bender</u> must be enormous, and I will do my best now, and in the future, to help you in any way you need, so please never hesitate to write to me whenever a question arises, however trivial. I am at a loss, for the moment, to suggest an alternative title for the Swedish edition. My feeling is that as you work through the book, translating into Swedish, you will probably think of a word, or words, that epitomise the whole. Bender of course <u>does</u> mean reveller, and in English The Reveller would have been a per- fectly adequate alternative title. (Actually I mean that Bender means Revel). You can go on a bender purely for fun, or from <u>angst</u>. George, for all his easy going and happy disposition, is a very anguished man. Gay dog, therefore is the wrong feeling; as you have recognised for yourself. Presently, as I think about it, I may be more helpful than I can be at the moment. It is a question of thinking about all the different reasons one would go out and get drunk in this day and age. Originally there was a subtitle (<u>The Bender: A Sad Comedy</u>). It is comic, but is also sad. What kind of a title does "A Sad Comedy" become in Swed- ish? Certainly one will not find the right title simply by working on synonyms in English for Bender. To go on a bender has almost come to mean, in English, to go on the kind of drinking spree that will strip the drinker down to his inner nakedness […].

<u>The Bender</u> is a lyric, a poem, a sad little pavane for a middle-aged man who (like William Conway in <u>The Birds of Paradise</u>) did not feel that there was a real place for him in the modern world. However, he lacked William's stoical upbringing, and never had a chance to see the birds of paradise. But the birds are there, in his sad little sitting room in Bayswater: and when he decided to end his life and drive a stolen car to crash into a tree trunk for Gillian's sake, he was looking for the birds. He is the only character in the book, apart from Anina, who knows,

subconsciously, that birds of paradise exist. Anina knows it. She wanted to be a poet. "But the talent did not occur except in bottles, which are soon empty".

Box 6, Folder 4 (McFarlin)
78 Addison Way
To Peter Green
25 April 1963

My Dear Peter,

I was glad to get your letter.[64] Most of the time I realised that you must have been up to your ears in some sort of work crisis; but occasionally I did wonder whether I'd offended you in some way.[65] One has so few real friends in this bloody racket that it was a relief to me to hear from you and to know that all was well. When I gave up agency I think you were the only one who went out of his way to put me on to the kind of necessary job that spread a bit of butter on the bread. It's always been much appreciated (TLS, Bookman, Book Soc, that Bates interview on TV, our interview on TV. The TLS thing in particular has been a real help. Old Crook[66] is the kind of chap I liked working for—and the whole feeling of being persona grata there has been encouraging).

I can't tell you how glad I am you're breaking away. I knew it would happen one day, because it had to. It was knowing it would happen that really made the Hodder thing impossible for me, although I felt like all kinds of heel when I turned it down. But I don't really go for the set-up, and the set-up minus Green would have been downright scary. And I was convinced that one day the set-up would indeed be minus Green.

It's the only thing to do, isn't it? To try and make the writing work by itself. And for you that old Greek Island is going to be right. I'm sure you feel it. Damn the whole sordid wheels-within-wheels mess. You have to keep as clear of it as you can or—I suppose—make the wheels turn only for yourself, which I think neither of us has the temperament to do.

I won't burden you with too long a letter; and no answer needed. I wish like hell I had the facility to do only half the amount of work you have been doing (and as I always said maintaining the highest standards)—if I did I'd take you up like a shot on that friendly offer to try and steer the DT [*Daily Telegraph*] my way. It's a horrible temptation, and God knows I need the money; but this—to put it crudely—is my shit-or-bust year (or maybe 18 months). When I contracted with Secker and Morrow I spread my known earnings (knowing providing one delivers) over as many years as possible, and in doing so cut my assured income to the bare necessity, hoping to make up on reviewing and reading. The important thing was the four years of freedom from going back to a job. This is why I continued with Country Life, and accepted everything Arthur Crook wanted me to do; and read mss until they were dropping out of my ears. This was all right for a bit, because I'd finished The Bender and hadn't started the new one. Came the end of 1962, when I had started, and I had to give myself a long straight look in the mirror (which as Anina said is a very very serious business and no way to end up looking like the Mona Lisa) and accept the fact that I was either dumb, bone-idle or mixed-up. So I gave Country Life notice, and asked Arthur to hold off. And of course the novel then began to work. I had vague hopes of The Bender making some good money, but as far as I can tell it's not going to. Not being a fashionable novelist the reviews, good as they were, simply weren't long enough to convey to the readers what the hell the book was about. Secker are very pleased, and they had a jolly good subscription; but as you and I know, if you don't have snob value the cash customers buy Mankowitz or the Kama Sutra. Tony Godwin[67] made an offer both I and Secker thought insulting. I don't know what is going to happen paperback wise.

Having promised Country Life I'd stand in when [Richard] Church and [Geoffrey] Grigson (my successor) went on holiday I'm faced with a five-week stint at the end of May (which will help pay for Spain, where I have to go re the new novel, so am making it the holiday with family). I'm trying to get the new novel at least nearly home and dry by the end of August (leaving the big corrida scene—the book isn't really about those old Hemingway bulls by the way, as maybe I needn't even say—until I get back). Then in October, Morrow paying my fare bless them, I go to New York for 10 days to be there when they publish The Bender, hoping that at least they'll have some sort of proper success with me. And in February I really am more or less set to the Indian trip—Secker contributing. But all this means a tight money string, a tighter time string. But I think what I've decided is that if The Bender goes down the drain then it would be sensible for me to a) go to India and b) come home in mid-1964 and think seriously whether I'm kidding myself I can make the writing work and keep the family in reasonable comfort. If it can't work by itself I think it would be wrong to bolster it up with journalism—journalism I haven't really an aptitude for. It might be better to seek a job in publishing (the only thing I know) and write a novel every five years, risking the danger of becoming a tired old chap who hates the young authors he helps to get published!

As you'll see (apart from seeing I am after all burdening you with a long letter) I'm in a somewhat pessimistic mood, which judging from the reviews and from Secker's present enthusiasm is entirely unjustified. And I expect when the new novel is finished I'll be as starry-eyed about the future as I was when I finished The Bender. So we go on from short year to short year, dragging along a reputation that always seems to increase but never casts its shadow in front of us. But the RSL[68] thing I suppose I can take as a pointer to the fact that gradually the work is beginning to make sense to other people. Clearly I must be patient. I don't lack confidence in what I can do, only in what is going to happen to it. And being patient and not lacking confidence in myself seems to involve cutting my short-term throat about reviewing (the new novel is horribly difficult). But I'm grateful to you as ever, Peter, for the suggestions. Since you're already dropped a word at DT [*Daily Telegraph*] perhaps they are vaguely waiting for an idea of my reaction? If it comes up and you need to say anything I think the answer is that I'd have loved to do it, and perhaps they could bear me in mind for the future, but that at the moment I can't do it because of these several travel plans (which would make me an unsatisfactory regular contributor), the Country Life stint in May and June, etc. Looks as if one of those pesterers will get it.

Finally, for what you say about <u>The Bender</u>; this has cheered me up a lot. If you think that about it, then I know the book was a success after all.

As I said, no need to reply to this; but of course uppermost in my mind is the hope that before you go, you and Lal could have supper with us either here or in town or failing that, that you and I could meet if only for a drink, but preferably a meal. A postcard or a phone call (out all day next Tuesday) would suffice.

Blessing on all the Greens great and small,
Love from both to both,

Box 8, Folder 6 (McFarlin)
78 Addison Way
To David Higham, David Higham Associates, Ltd.
3 June 1963

My Dear David,

I wonder whether in either your or Jean [Leroy]'s or Sheila [Watson]'s departments there is any old material of mine such as carbon typescripts, stereotypes of radio/tv adaptations, page proofs? I hardly imagine there is, but I'd be most grateful if a casual check could be made. The University of Texas's department of Humanities is interested in opening negotiations for the purchase of original and pre-publication material, and apparently anything remotely connected with the preparation of work is relevant. I seem foolishly to have got rid of everything I ever had to do with the first two novels, and apart from a copy of [Donald] McWhinnie's adaptation for radio of <u>The Mark of the Warrior</u> I seem to have got rid of my play adaptations as well. I did certainly have a clear out of a couple of years ago but thought I'd kept basic things like that. Never mind. I expect when I hear what kind of price they are prepared to pay at this stage I'll prefer to wait for a few years. (I suppose it's just possible Maurice [Temple Smith] might still have something?)

I don't imagine anything very interesting is developing on the film front and I've been thinking about McWhinnie (for stage adaptation) and also the possibility of <u>The Bender</u> being adapted for television. However, I wouldn't be at all interested in doing anything of that kind myself, but I'd be grateful if you'd think about the pros and cons of sending a copy of the book to Donald either direct or through MV and/or to the television people. Donald seems to have had a flop with his Shaw production[69] and may be on the lookout for something new. I expect steps in this direction will depend on Richard's view of cinema possibilities. But I mention these things simply to get them out of my mind, so that I can get on with the new book.

Ever,

Box 8, Folder 6 (McFarlin)
78 Addison Way
To Monica Preston, David Higham Associates, Ltd.[70]
10 June 1963

My Dear Monica,

Many thanks indeed for the prompt cheques. Must say Secker pay up like gents!

Yes, the dinner was very nice. There were some photos but only of the very distinguished people. Penny and I were very small fry. All the same I think we looked nice, and my little row of four medals wasn't put to shame. There were some without any, and others of course with those classy things hanging round their necks (CBEs etc), so I thought the old Burma Star, etc., was just about the happy medium. Penny decided against the mink and there wasn't any Russian sable.[71] The stole that went best with her swish frock (turquoise blue with gold embroidery) turned out to be an ordinary dyed musquash, but it looked jolly nice. Often at those dinners that cost 2 guineas a crack you find you have to pay for drinks, but not in this case. It was all in. Aperitif (whisky if you had the common to ask for it, which Penny did), sherry with the consommé, white wine with the salmon, and red with the duck montmorency. Strawberries and cream followed by coffee and brandy and some mercifully short speeches. Evelyn Waugh made the crack of the evening.

As he was invested with the Companion of Literature scroll he said he thought they were all the kind of companions (looking round the room) who would never meet again except <u>perhaps</u> in heaven. (He's a Catholic). Sachie[72] stood in for Dame Edith and Stephen Spender stood in for Aldous Huxley who was subpoenaed as a witness in an embezzlement case in Los Angeles.

After the dinner they sent round the Skinners gold plate finger basin for us to wash the mess off. We all retired in good and respectable order at about 10.30. Christopher Hibbert was there with his nice wife.

Mr. Lindbergh rang yesterday.[73] We're picking him up at the flat on Tuesday next, about 6.45, and then just driving them a bit out of London to have something to eat at a pub. I thought the cock at Cockfosters would be a good idea. Saves all the washing up, too. Is there a special bell to ring at the flat?

Box 19, Folder 20 (McFarlin)
78 Addison Way
To The Editor, <u>The Times</u>
6 July 1963

Sir,

I was interested in the statement by Mr. F. M. Gardner, borough librarian of Luton (your issue of 6 July) that novelists of the calibre of Dickens, Thackeray, George Eliot, Trollope, Wells and Bennett "belong to the past" and that we cannot today name "one great 'popular' writer whose influence transcends all barriers of class and education".

That the novel was once a medium whose influence transcended many of those barriers can, I suppose, be admitted, so long as we add "to a greater degree than at present". It is difficult, I know, to think of a modern literary equivalent to a whole family weeping over the death of Little Nell. They have probably been grieving instead over Martha Longhurst.[74]

Modern mass media and wider education have fragmented and not unified the public view of what it wants, from where, in the form of entertainment. Tastes have sharpened, not broadened. Reading a novel always was and still is a leisurely business. Mr. Gardner seems to think that if the novels were of a higher calibre more people would read them. I don't think that is true, although I believe more people read them than he realises. The public libraries are by no means the main outlet for established writers.

I think the truth is that people will only read the novels they want to read, and writers will go on writing the novels they want to write—regretting perhaps that their influence is limited but not letting it bother them too much or change their own notions of what a novel should be—and that the future will show there to have been novelists writing today whose work is at least as good as that of the authors Mr. Gardner mentions, even though they did not succeed in becoming household names in the way their predecessors did. But then households have changed, and if Dickens were writing today he would be hard put to it to become a name in those households where the competition from other types of entertainer is strong.

Yours faithfully,

Box 1, Folder 4 (McFarlin)
78 Addison Way
To Sri Prem Manaktala, Allied Publishers Private Ltd., Bombay
24 July 1963

Dear Mr. Manaktala,[75]

Mr. Alewyn Birch of Heinemann has written to me to tell me of your very kind and friendly response to his inquiries about my visit to India next year, a trip that I have planned for many years now. It becomes possible at last because Secker & Warburg (to whom I moved recently from Eyre & Spottiswoode) are contributing towards the cost of it. Even so, it has been difficult to determine the duration of my visit. My budget will have limitations and I really have no idea of present costs, although I am warned that in the major cities some hotel prices can be high enough to be prohibitive for someone like an author travelling on his own resources.

For that reason, among others, I asked Mr. Birch whether he would be kind enough to inquire to what extent I could expect to pay my way on a rather different basis than the average tourist. The other reason was, of course, that I am <u>not</u> anxious to stay in luxurious hotels, but to be modest in the towns and simple in the country.

The itinerary I have worked out is as follows: First of all, to fly from London to Bombay, and then from Bombay to Madres (staying for perhaps a week in Bombay). In Madras, I may have the opportunity still of going to see an old friend in a village some 200 miles north of that city. I told him so many times that I hoped to be coming to India, and he invited me so many times to stay with him and his family in his village, that eventually I became embarrassed having to tell him I couldn't come to India after all. It is now two or three years since we exchanged letters, but I shall write to him presently, and then I shall know whether I can add this visit to my itinerary while in Madras. But in any case I want to see Madras, and the surrounding country, because when I was in India between 1943 and 1946 I never travelled as far south.

From Madras, I propose to fly up to Calcutta (where there may also be an old friend from my army days: both these friends I mention are, of course, Indians). While I'm in Calcutta it would be tempting to go out to Ranchi for a few days—and also in the other direction to Comilla and Agartarla, but on the whole it is the India I haven't seen that I want to see this time. That being so, towns that I missed seeing are on the itinerary. I should fly from Calcutta to Benares, to Agra, to Lucknow, perhaps to Cawnpore, staying perhaps a few days in each place. I should then fly to Jaipur, via Delhi, then back to Delhi, which would be the last place on my itinerary. I can stop off at all these places, for very little increase in the overall fare from London, so long as I arrange to do so in advance. From Delhi I am hoping to fly back to London via Tashkent, Samarkand and Moscow and Stockholm.

So, to summarise, I see my Indian Trip based broadly on the following centres: Bombay, Madras, Calcutta, Benares, Agra, Lucknow, Jaipur, Delhi. I am hoping that my budget will allow me to spend two months in India, and a fortnight between Delhi and Stockholm.

The length of the stay in each centre, the number of excursions from those centres, and the total length of the visit, will naturally be dictated by cost. I should plan to leave London about the middle of February, which means I would leave India about the middle of April, if I spend two months there.

Although the object of the trip is to "'recharge the batteries", to give me material for future books, I am not coming with any particular book in mind; neither am I coming as a journalist with a commission from a newspaper. I suppose it is always possible that later some editor may want to make an arrangement to have first look at any article I decide to write, or to discuss ideas for articles, but I think of myself, in coming back to India, as a private person who happens to be a writer and is therefore interested in seeing places and meeting people: Indians, Europeans, Eurasians, Americans, Chinese (the un-armed kind!) and British.

I am deeply touched by the remarks in your letter, which Mr. Birch has quoted to me; and while I don't want to impose unreasonably on people's kindness and hospitality, I shall be most grateful for help and assistance. For a man who, over here, has some reputation for knowing something about India, you will find me extremely ignorant in reality. I am conscious that Indians who have read any of my novels that have an Indian background will have found many faults, errors of fact, and misconceptions—although not, I hope, prejudices.

If while I'm in India, there is anything you think I could usefully do to help young writers, students, anybody, I hope you will call on me; and I hope that I shall also have the pleasure of meeting you and your colleagues.

Again, with many thanks,

Yours sincerely,[76]

Box 3, Folder 25 (McFarlin)
78 Addison Way
From a letter to B. V. V. Narayana Dass[77]
24 September 1963

Dear Narayanji,

Thank you very much indeed for your letter, which has reached me safely, forwarded by Eyre & Spottiswoode. The reason for my long silence is this: so many times I said that I was coming to India, only to have to tell you later that I wasn't, that eventually I said to myself, "I shall not write to Narayanji until I can say I am coming to India in such and such a month". Unfortunately months, years have gone by. But by a strange coincidence your letter has reached me just at the time when I was planning to write to you, because God and health willing I am coming to India for a couple of months next year [...].

There is, of course, nothing I should like more than to come and see you and your family in Timmapuram. Perhaps when you reply you would let me know whether you will be at home in the end of February and March, and whether there is anywhere nearby that I could stay for a few days [...].

Yours very sincerely,[78]

Box 17, Folder 17 (McFarlin)
The Players, New York
To Penny Scott
23 October 1963—letter No. 2[79]

Darling,

I was collected about mid day Saturday by Helen King[80] (she comes from the South, & talks like that). The train journey took about an hour & John & Fern [Willey] met us in the car & took us to a hotel out in the country called The Fox Hill. V nice. Thought Fern was a bit preoccupied. (She is at her best when she is out with other people & not having to think of being hostess.) We then drove back to their place, stopped at a supermarket & bought 25¢ worth of ice from a machine. J's & F's house not large, but v. well decorated & furnished, split level. Lovely but wildish garden. In the evening some v. nice Americans came to a buffet supper & we went to bed I suppose about midnight. Morning was fairly relaxed. We had blueberry muffins. We then drove to a stately home on Long Island Sound, the home of one of the owners, Larry Hughes, who has an English wife called Rose (granddaughter of the painter John Sargent). We had barbecued steak. It was really awfully nice, & Rose was sweet (not much English accent left). Rose drove us round the beaches & we picked up stones. Then Fern drove us home, going past Stratford (replica of the old Shakespearean Globe Theatre). I had a real impression of American domestic living. Finally we drove along what is called the Merritt Parkway. Wonderful sunset. And everywhere the trees had these marvellous colours. On the train back we were able (Helen King & I) to have dinner so didn't arrive home starving. All this will come out best in talk. Don't seem to be able to think when I've got a pen in my hand.

Had thought of sending you a cable once I was on the boat, but you can assume that if I <u>don't</u> get on it, or it is held up, you'd get a cable then. I keep thinking of that lovely Friday morning, getting into a taxi & asking for Pier 40 & then knowing that this whole little waking nightmare is over. I can hardly tell you how much this place depresses & weighs on me. My tummy is begun to feel queasy with nervous tension, & I am also tired of the expression that comes over the faces of shop assistants & waitresses, etc., when I have to open my mouth & speak English! They mostly pretend to love it, but I think they find it funnier than they quite want to show. Conversation (except <u>in</u> publishing company) trails away & I am reminded now that this was how Dr. Fleishman, my cabin mate, reacted. It is as if suddenly they distrust you deeply (or not being as they are). The friendliness is only on the surface. Perhaps that is too much of an easy generalisation to be true, but it is such a cold city that New Yorkers must insulate themselves in some way. And perhaps there is a reserve in English people that we aren't aware of but which they always manage to come up against, because of their different approach to casual encounters.

Hope you won't mind if I don't bring anything back. It wouldn't be something I bought with any pleasure. Maybe there will be something on the boat (although I hope to goodness my cabin for 3 isn't going to be the last straw!). Will try to write again, darling, to tell you about the party. Nearly over now. Thinking of you all the time.

Love to all,

Box 1, Folder 8 (McFarlin)
78 Addison Way
Miss E. M. Almedingen, Brookleaze
9 November 1963

My dear Chris,

Many thanks for your picture postcard and for your card of the 11th of last month. I've now been back from New York for a week, and just getting down to clearing up my correspondence. I meant to send you a postcard from New York, and carefully took your address with me, but it was a city that depressed me so much I couldn't bring myself to send any souvenirs of it to anyone. Everyone was very kind and generous (and I did spend a pleasant weekend out in Connecticut) but New York, after a brief, initial excitement, was like a trap; unreal and monstrous. Towards the end I had fantasies of not being allowed to leave, and a series of awful nightmares.

You, on the other hand, must be having a wonderful time in Switzerland. I hope you are having a really good rest, and that the eye is now better and not spoiling your enjoyment.

I sailed on a Dutch ship, the Rotterdam, and on the return journey (same boat each way) we had Tito [Marshall of Czechoslovakia] aboard. It seems the reason for our being late leaving New York was that a hoaxer had phoned to say there was a bomb on board. None of us knew this was the reason, but Penny heard it on the news that night, and so was not really happy until I walked in through the door one week later. Because of Tito the boat was escorted out of the Hudson by four police helicopters, 2 police launches and a US coast guard cutter. This kept away all but two of the bravest seagulls. I should have preferred the seagulls. They are so much a part of arrivals and departures at sea.

Our love to you, and wishes for a splendid holiday and safe journey home.

Ever,

Box 10, Folder 7 (McFarlin)
78 Addison Way
To John Bryan, Knightsbridge Films, Ltd.
24 November 1963

Dear Mr. Bryan,

Although we met on what a few hours later turned out to be an unhappy day,[81] I must write and thank you for an excellent lunch and a most enjoyable talk (not least about Henry and Becket).

After I left you it struck me that if I have any valuable contribution to make to the translation of <u>The Chinese Love Pavilion</u> into a screenplay it will be by thinking less in terms of a film and more in terms of what I might do if I were rewriting the novel; and as in the next week or so we are both agreed to go through the book again I thought you might be interested in an idea that has occurred to me and will certainly influence my own rereading.

The imagery of the book is the imagery of flowers. I did less work on this than I should have done. Clearly (and I say clearly because it seems clear to me) Saxby was not a rich drifter but a dedicated, eccentric botanist; and Brent was not an embryo-romantic working on land reclamation but a young man studying botany who came under Saxby's influence before the war, in Malaya. He worked with him in the field for at least a year before being caught up in the hostilities. As a young man of early military age he went home in 1939, joined up, went through several campaigns, was wounded in Burma, and in 1945 was in India lecturing in Field craft at an Officers' Training School. When Turner (Force 136) sends for him in connexion with the Saxby affair (work out reasons why he sends for him) he turns up in Kuala Lumpur as a man ostensibly more devoted to the arts and theories of warfare than to plant gathering which he treats, on the surface anyway, with a certain irony, as a harmless but useless occupation he was foolish enough as a young man who knew nothing of the ways of the violent world to think important.

As an ex-active soldier (with a shattered shoulder and more or less useless arm) he is glad to be out of India and its peace-time atmosphere, and back in what still ranks as a theatre of war. He is, initially, at home in the atmosphere of Major Reid's headquarters. He is a man who has long ago learned to control his feelings, but you can see the pleasure, the sense of security, just below the surface when, for instance, he sits down for the first time at the hurricane-lamp lit table. But presently he realises that Reid and his officers look down on him as a man from GHQ, a desk wallah. He is half pleased, half resentful, when Holmes happens to see his wound and their attitude towards him changes. He is shocked, later, by their callous attitude to killing bandits (and is present when MacAndrews shoots the unidentified Chinese who is bathing in the jungle-pool). He has made the mistake of forgetting that his own experience of hostilities was with an army that always faced defeat. The army he is with now is different, being victorious, cocksure, intolerant. In six months it has swept through Burma. Malaya has been liberated without the firing of a single shot. The atom bomb is the symbol of power.

The pride Brent has taken in himself as a good soldier and a fine instructor starts to strip away. He was a good soldier only in adversity. (The psychology of an army facing defeat is always different from the psychology of a victorious army. It is the difference between a sense of preservation, and a sense of destruction, of getting even.) When he is stripped of his pride, what is left is the reality of his wound. Perhaps it is Teena's apparent acceptance of it (which is to say her professionally simulated lack of distaste for it) that makes it easier for him to persuade himself he is falling in love with her.

And of course, remove the soldier, the soldiering experience, and you uncover the young man who accompanied Saxby through the Malayan jungles, looking for rare orchids. Perhaps, even as he walks to Turner's office, his attention is taken not only by Japanese soldiers sweeping the yard but by some comparatively rare flower that he has not seen for many years. And of course there must be plants in the garden of madness, and flowers in the rooms of <u>The Pavilion</u> that rekindle his interest and subtly alter the attitude he has to the job he has been give by Turner, to try and track down Saxby. Perhaps, in the crudest possible terms, the search for Saxby becomes a search by Brent for his own lost innocence? One that becomes increasingly agonising to him as the threat to Teena's life develops?

When I first worked on the novel I had always imagined a longer and more telling meeting between Saxby and Brent, one at which Sutton was also present (Sutton representing a man, a boy, at a half-way mark of corruption)—but the novel didn't work out in that way. However, rethinking the novel in terms easier to convey visually, there must probably be a major confrontation, not only to clarify Saxby's motivation but to leave Brent in the acute psychological state that leads him later to perform the symbolic act of throwing away his gun and equipment and walking unarmed into the open space where Reid eventually kills Saxby's Chinese disciple.

If eventually it is thought that this re-moulding of the basis of the Saxby-Brent relationship is viable, then the Saxby-Brent confrontation may prove the biggest problem. And the screenwriter would have to do some homework, some botanical homework. I have often found that such fact-finding missions yield information that supports and extends the original imagery. If the burning of the house of flowers is to mean anything, then the flower imagery must be paramount. In the novel as it stands it means less than it should.

This letter is already far longer than I intended, so I will cut it short while it still leaves enough questions unanswered by off-the-cuff solutions.

With kind regards,

Yours sincerely,

Endnotes

1. Scott's American editors at William Morrow, John Willey and Adèle Dogan Horwitz, figure prominently in the letters from this period on, as do his American agents at Harold Ober Associates, Dorothy Olding and Ivan von Auw.
2. The editors at Secker and Warburg were Fred Warburg, David Farrer, and Roland Gant.
3. From series 2 in the Paul Scott collection.
4. In 1965, at the invitation of the school's president Vivian Stuart, Scott was invited to deliver the opening address at the school. His topic was "Aspects of Writing." In 1967 he delivered the closing speech of the session: "Method: The Mystery and the Mechanics." His final presentation to the school was in 1975. See Scott, *My Appointment with the Muse*, for transcripts of the 1965 and 1967 speeches.
5. Under the pen name Elizabeth Avery, Penny Scott published *The Margaret Days* (1959), *The Marigold Summer* (1960), *Nurse Has Four Cases* (1961), and *Sister Bollard* (1963). Later, she wrote were several unpublished works: one that was untitled about a young girl named Nellie (completed in 1963), "Eliza Rowen" (circulated in 1966), "The Probationer" (completed in 1971), "Back to Nursing" (circulated in 1972), and "The Foster Child."
6. The working title of the manuscript was in fact "The Phoenix Nightingale," with *Sister Bollard* the eventual published title.
7. To the revisions of *The Chinese Love Pavilion*.
8. Reid commanded the Indian rifle company that was stationed in Bukit Kallang in Malaya, the setting of *The Chinese Love Pavilion*.
9. Refers to the radio script adaptation of Scott's novel. The stage version of *The Mark of the Warrior* was broadcast in June of 1960.
10. This is typical of Scott's grueling pace of publishing a novel every eighteen to twenty-four months, beginning a new novel (*The Birds of Paradise*) even before the newly completed one was published (*The Chinese Love Pavilion*). Not until the production of the *Raj Quartet* did this pace slow.
11. Characters in *The Birds of Paradise*.
12. In a letter dated 5 June 1960, Mr. Rolton had requested the exact lines (quoted at the beginning of Scott's letter from the radio broadcast) and offered reflections on the idea of illusion versus truth (McFarlin 16:6).
13. *The Mark of the Warrior*.
14. Of *Books and Bookmen*.

15. In 1961 Eyre and Spottiswoode published Baron's *The Road to Barcelona*. Scott evidently saw the prepublication manuscript, because the idea for the family vacation in Tamariu, Spain (on the Costa Brava), was inspired by the book. The chapter "To the Spanish Frontier" describes the route the Scotts took in April of 1961, driving down through the south of France towards Spain, through the Perpignan and the Pyrenees mountains, down to Palafrugell, and then to the coast itself. Note courtesy of Sally Scott.

16. Dorothy Olding (1910–1997), also of Harold Ober Associates.

17. Originally a client of Scott's, Russian-born Edith Martha (Christine) Almedingen (1898–1971) published poems, novels, children's stories, poems, biographies, histories, and an autobiography. Almedingen and Scott shared a mutual admiration. Scott characterized Almedingen as "a writer of tremendous warmth in which there is not a hint of sentimentality" (letter to Robert Lusty dated 13 March 1957; DHA-HRC 263:3).

18. Abbreviation for "hire-purchase," or buying on the installment plan.

19. Earlier in the month, the New American Library bought the paperback rights to *Pavilion* for $17,500, half of which was Scott's share.

20. *Pavilion* was, in fact, Scott's greatest commercial success to date.

21. Dorothy Eden (1912–1982), who wrote also under the name of Mary Paradise, published novels in the gothic genre.

22. Kuala Lumpur in Malaysia.

23. Refers to Edith Sitwell (1887–1964), a British poet and critic, and Margaret "Storm" Jameson (1891–1986), the author of some forty-five novels and works of literary criticism and a regular fiction reviewer for the *London Sunday Times*.

24. On 6 October, Almedingen had written, "There is nothing of Kipling or Conrad in you. [...] Yours is a gift which is wholly your own. Perhaps Dostoevsky alone achieved that precious blending of brutality and tenderness which comes alive in the Pavilion, and at what well did you learn that deed qua deeds mean little enough, that man's most important business was being, not doing, that being—how true—must be rooted in love. I think it is because of that quality that the most trivial detail is alive—& nothing jars, nothing is too light or too heavy, not a single transgression is made against the well-nigh incredible unity of the whole, and nothing is leadenly codified because life never is, though we do try to imagine it is. My dear friend, when I put it down [...] I had nothing to say except 'thank you' [...]" (McFarlin 1:5).

25. Almedingen responded to Scott, "You can't lose faith—not just because you owe it to yourself or to all of us, who love you & understand you— beginning with Penny, but because you & your God are so deeply involved

one with the other [...]. Yes, I did know about 'this wretchedness'—which—anyway—should never by pried into—but the general landscape—and that's where your integrity comes alive in your work. Don't dismiss it as a paradox [...] your strength is in that 'wretchedness'—in so many ways—one of those being that, hurt yourself you don't hurt back though <u>that</u> might cancel out the hurt done to you" (McFarlin 1:5).

26. The Scotts shared the same wedding anniversary date with John and Fern Willey.

27. Refers to the novelists and critics Christine Brooke-Rose (b. 1923) and Evelyn Waugh (1903–1966). It might also refer to Alfred Duggan (1903–1964), a novelist and critic and the stepson of George Nathaniel Cruzon, the former viceroy of India.

28. Founded in 1948, the Writers' Summer School in Derbyshire was open to both amateur and professional writers. Scott first spoke there in 1959, and for the next two years the entire family attended.

29. Deutschbok-Gemeinschaft.

30. On December 5, Willey responded that although a novel a year would be ideal, "we would be poor publishers indeed if we did not realize that serious fiction sets its own pace" (McFarlin 12:20).

31. Higham (1895–1978) was first Scott's employer at Pearn, Pollinger and Higham, then his agent beginning in June of 1952. Scott was the godfather of Higham's son Ben.

32. Scott would write to Gerald Hanley that same day, "I realised, in writing the long last section of <u>The Birds of Paradise,</u> how unlike <u>me</u> a lot of my previous work has been. I mean, as a person, I do get some laughs, but all my work has been so bloody serious and Sunday school. But the Bs of P, although serious and terrible (I mean to me) is also (I mean to me) in so many places terribly funny, and <u>clean.</u> All of which probably means it's a stinkeroo [...]" (McFarlin 6:13).

33. *The Journey Homeward*, published in 1961.

34. Scott's aunt, the youngest of the siblings on Frances Scott's side. She died on 4 September 1971.

35. The reference is to the family's first new car, a Ford Anglia.

36. "Lords" is a play on words—that is, Lords Cricket Ground. Note courtesy of Sally Scott.

37. Dogan wrote on 22 July, "The best thing of all—at least to me—is the rationale you give to reflection, illustrating the dimension it can give to our lives, showing where meaning may be, and how many different meanings there can be" (McFarlin 13:1).

38. An elderly neighbor who routinely stayed with the cats while the Scotts went on vacation. Note courtesy of Carol Scott.

39. Regarding *The Birds of Paradise*.

40. Wilkinson attended the Writers' Summer School in Swanwick the month before, where she met Scott.

41. Wilkinson mentioned a line from *The Chinese Love Pavilion*: "I'll bloody murder you," thinking that "well" or "near" had been left out after "bloody" (McFarlin 20:19).

42. Once Almedingen had read a draft of *The Bender*, she refused the dedication in a letter dated 29 September 1962: "I must refuse the great honour you have offered me. This refusal is not coloured by the least reflection on the book as such—it is based on my consciousness that the themes & my own self, as expressed in my novel, seem to inhabit different worlds. Fully conscious of the beauty of your English, I none the less felt its whole alien quality both of language & thought. I admit that, in actuality, lives Pico della Mirandola's image of truth, has myriads of aspects & that no author can honestly deal with any except those which allowed his own inner but—but—and I fear you will have to forgive me again & again—<u>do</u> George & all his others really belong to *your* truth? I could not tell—but with a friend of your stature, candour should be the only acceptable coin" (McFarlin 1:7). Two years before writing this, Almedingen had praised Scott as a novelist who "has not betrayed his soul" (McFarlin 1:5), but she felt differently about this novel. Scott's friendship with Almedingen did not recover (Spurling 261); he dedicated *The Bender* to his agent, David Higham.

43. Scott's contract with Eyre and Spottiswoode was ending, and he was deciding between renegotiating with them or moving to another publisher.

44. Braine's *Room at the Top* (1957). Scott had recruited Braine to Pearn, Pollinger and Higham and placed *Room at the Top* with Eyre and Spottiswoode.

45. Scott rented a lock-up garage about half a mile from the house. Note courtesy of Sally Scott.

46. Throughout his correspondence, "Sam" of William Morrow is John T. Lawrence (d. 1998), the president of Morrow.

47. On 29 November, Willey affirmed Maurice Temple Smith's assessment and formulated a cause: "I think it lies in your technique, the stance, the point of view, that you take toward the telling of a novel. Everything of yours that I have read is told in the mood of remembrance of things past. You stage scenes, to be sure, with the most loving attention to detail, do everything to make them come vividly alive; but always there is the knowledge

in the reader's mind that these actions are, in truth, past and done with, and the narrator is remembering them if not in tranquility, at least in a later and philosophical turn of mind. I think this is where the feeling of the membrane between the reader and the novel comes into play. The remedy, it seems to me, however difficult it might prove at first, is to overcome this lack of immediacy. This would be a matter of letting present action really take over in your novels—of putting your characters into a setting, letting them look up and down, forward and back, and get involved before our eyes, rather than meditating on how they came to be where they are as if their lives were over" (McFarlin 13:2).

48. *Sunday* (1962) was a portrait of Collier's mother, who never told Kay the name of her real father.

49. Scott declined to review the book for *Books & Bookmen* as he had promised, a decision that prompted Collier to write that she was "personally hurt" by this: "Still I suppose this teaches one just another unpleasant lesson about human relationships. [...] I am stunned in a sense, fully realizing now that one has to work only for oneself and never never expect anything of anyone" (McFarlin 3:21). In August of 1962, Scott wrote to Gerald Hanley, "I'll drop a note to Kay before I go. I've not seen her for several months. She was going through a crisis, and I didn't feel I could stand getting involved in it" (McFarlin 6:13). There is a gap in the letters from Scott to Collier between 1962 and 1966. The correspondence from Collier indicates an ongoing though tumultuous friendship. In April of 1962, she borrowed money from Scott. On 11 June 1963, she wrote, "I'm truly sorry for chucking you out after Kathleen [Farrell]'s party. I'm not asking you to forgive me now, because what one does, however stupid, one just does, drunk or sober, and the only good one can struggle to get out of bad is to learn from it. But still, and even so, I do want you to know how unhappy I was afterwards, about what I had done, and that I know it was really quite undeserved and unjustifiable. Tell Penny that I did enjoy meeting her and you too. I hope we can meet again in more sober circumstances, or if equally drunken ones, at least joyfully so. Kathleen too will no doubt pass on to you my sincere apologies at the next opportunity. With very best wishes, Kay (Collier)" (McFarlin 3:22).

In July of 1963, Collier attempted suicide, later calling it "a rash and vain gesture"; Kathleen Farrell (her then-former partner) called it "an action to get her back" (McFarlin 3:22). In a letter to Peter Green dated 19 June 1963, Scott wrote, "Poor old Kay Dick nearly kicked the bucket the other day. Took an overdose of sleepers. (She and KF had parted last year; you probably knew.) She was rushed to New End Hospital. Haven't seen her. Seems she was violent. Just sent flowers. Most of the people I've spoken to feel best left alone now to find her own way home, as it were" (McFarlin 6:3).

In August of 1964, Collier wrote to Scott, "Don't bother to answer this: I do realize that to some of my friends my attempted suicide was a sickness they could not bear to be brought in touch with even indirectly" (McFarlin 3.22).

50. Years before, in 1958, his friend Peter Green had also questioned the wisdom of revisiting India as a setting when he had listened to the broadcast of *Sahibs and Memsahibs*: "Here we were again, gnawing round the Far East military gone, time 1943; men in uniform, special conditions [...]. To date A MALE CHILD has been your unquestioned masterpiece. Why you returned to the Far East again I'm not sure. Because AMC wasn't generally understood? Because the creation of it revealed things to you which were alarming, or disturbing?" (McFarlin 6:3).

51. The Scotts were hosting the Writers' Summer School in Swanwick and invited Spark to be the scheduled lecturer on the short story.

52. The senior editor at Eyre and Spottiswoode.

53. Involved paperback rights to Scott's last three novels.

54. Franz von Werra (1914–1941) was a German World War II fighter pilot who was shot down over England and captured. He was believed to be the only Axis prisoner of war to succeed in escaping.

55. A translator at Norstedt & Söner in Sweden. Scott's business relationship with Svanström began in 1957, when *A Male Child* was published in Sweden, followed by *The Mark of the Warrior* (1958), *The Chinese Love Pavilion* (1960), *The Birds of Paradise* (1962), *The Bender* (1962), and *The Corrida at San Feliu* (1964).

56. In his 1962 Richmond Lecture, and in a subsequent book review for *The Spectator*, Frank R. Leavis had attacked C. P. Snow's argument that the lack of communication between the two cultures of science and the humanities would lead to a failure in solving the world's problems. Leavis called Snow a "public relations man" for the scientific community.

57. Krishi, Dora, and William Conway, characters in *The Birds of Paradise*.

58. The twist was a popular dance in Spain and the United Kingdom as well as in the United States.

59. The site of the Writers' Summer School.

60. The secretary of the writing school.

61. Scott's Swedish translator.

62. What follows are three pages of explanation and definitions of terms such as "drip-dry suit" and "tricel dress." I am including only the terms from Indian culture.

63. Dohn translated *The Birds of Paradise* into German.

64. Green had resigned from Hodder and Stoughton, sold his home, and moved his family to Greece in May of 1963.

65. Scott was worried that his decision to move to Secker and Warburg rather than Hodder and Stoughton (where Green was working) had disappointed his friend.

66. Arthur Crook (1912–2005) was the editor of the *Times Literary Supplement* and later the chairman and president of the Royal Literary Fund.

67. Anthony Godwin (1920–1976) was an editor for Penguin Books.

68. Scott had been elected a fellow to the Royal Society of Literature.

69. McWhinnie was directing George Bernard Shaw's *The Doctor's Dilemma* at the Theatre Royal in Haymarket.

70. Preston was the company secretary of DHA.

71. The Scotts rented evening dress from Moss Brothers for such occasions. Note courtesy of Sally Scott.

72. Sacherverell Sitwell, one of Dame Edith's brothers.

73. Magnus Lindbergh, Scott's Swedish translator. He and his wife, Grunilla, were in London for a brief visit.

74. A longstanding character played by Lynne Carol in the TV serial *Coronation Street* who had died unexpectedly in a recent episode. Note courtesy of Sally Scott.

75. Manaktala was the managing director of Allied Publishers in Bombay, who distributed books for the Heinemann group.

76. In a letter dated 27 December 1963, P. C. Manaktala arranged for Scott to be the guest of Dorothy Ganapathy in Bombay. In a letter dated 30 December 1963, Scott wrote that because of visa issues and his plans to stop off in Moscow, he has postponed his trip to India and was now leaving London on 24 February 1964 and arriving in Bombay the next day. In his response of 11 January 1964, Manaktala sent contact information for Ganapathy but also recommended that Scott contact P. L. Kumar, in Madras, who had agreed to Scott's staying with him (McFarlin 1:4).

77. Dass had served with Scott in India. When Scott first was posted to Comilla, Dass was a naik in rank, but Scott promoted him to havildar and put him in charge of the stock-control system. In a letter to Ralph King dated 17 July 1985, Scott described Dass as "a sturdy rather silent little Madrassi, who subsequently was in charge of my stock-control system, and every morning

wrote up that blackboard I had a 1010 section tent at Imphal (Tulihall, rather) to show how much POL and IT and BT comp we had available, so that a glance at the board, and a glance at the demands, showed what the transport and collection problems might be at the end of the day" (McFarlin 10:7). After the war, Dass had repeatedly invited Scott to his home; the 1964 trip was the first time this visit could be arranged.

78. In December of 1963, Dass provided directions to the village nearest his home: "ELLURU is on the main line of Calcutta-Madras Railway Route. On either way, you can catch the Madras Mail and safely come over to Elluru Station. ELLURU is nearly 305 miles from Madras or—720 miles from Calcutta. If you catch the mail at Madras by 7.30 P.M. you will get down at Elluru on the next morning by 7.15 A. M [...]. My village is 22 miles from ELLURU and there is Bus Service every half-an-hour" (McFarlin 3:25).

79. Scott's American publisher William Morrow paid for Scott to travel to New York on the publication of *The Bender*. Although he met with friend Muriel Spark and agents Dorothy Olding and Ivan von Auw, and enjoyed a weekend in Connecticut with John and Fern Willey, he was very homesick. He wrote this letter to Penny on their anniversary.

80. Helen King (1913–1989) was a senior editor and the vice president of William Morrow.

81. The day President John F. Kennedy was assassinated in the United States.

SECTION 4

INDIA RETURNED
(1964–1965)

In early 1964, Heinemann financed a trip to India, which Paul Scott felt he needed to "recharge" (McFarlin 1:4) his knowledge and love of India. P. C. Manaktala, the managing director of Allied Publishers (Heinemann's distributors in India), arranged for Scott to stay in the home of Draupadi (Dorothy) Ganapathy in Bombay, the Rajput daughter of a lawyer and the widow of a medical officer of health. They would remain friends for the rest of Scott's life. Through Ganapathy, Scott was introduced to Homi and Nurgiz Banker as well as Nello and Cuckoo Mukherjee, with whom he would correspond for many years. After a visit to Madras, where he stayed with P. L. Kumar, Scott journeyed to Timmapuram, a village in Andhra Pradesh—the home of B. V. V. Narayana Dass,[1] Scott's havildar during the war. His letters to Penny (at least two per day) describe his "culture shock" with rural India—an emotional/psychological state that was exacerbated by an amoebic infection. Despite his host's generous hospitality, Scott fabricated a ruse to cut his visit short, blaming a painful leg condition. Ironically, when he reached Calcutta, he was plagued by sciatic pain, which prompted him to cancel his planned stops in Moscow and Stockholm on his return trip to England. During his final days in Calcutta, he met Neil Ghosh (the product of a public education in England) and his partner Caroline Davies, as well as Dulal Nag Chaudhuri (a nuclear physicist) and his wife Dipali, a classically trained singer.

Scott returned to London on 9 April and in June, at the promptings of Roland Gant, arranged for treatment in Paris for amoebiasis, which he had contracted in India during the war without being diagnosed. By June, the treatment helped to cure some of the symptoms that had interfered with Scott's ability to write: lassitude, depression, insomnia, mood swings, and lack of concentration. The entire family would be treated for the infection three months later.

The ten days Scott spent in Timmapuram in 1964 became a watershed experience. Because his plans included visiting bustling, big cities and spending a great deal of time with strangers who had agreed to put him up for a few days, Scott counted on his reunion with Narayana Dass to serve as an emotional and artistic respite. "I have reasons for wanting a bit of rustication—apart from the fact that I shall hope to put down a few things on paper, and a village seems the ideal place in which to do it" (McFarlin 10:2). He hoped that "Mr. Dass's village is a real relaxation" (McFarlin 17:19).

Dass came from a military family. Both his father and his grandfather had served in the British Army. Dass himself had served under Scott at Tulihall as a naik, in charge of the stock-control system for military supplies:

> Every morning [he] wrote up that blackboard … to show how much POL and IT and BT comp we had available, so that a glance at the board, and a glance at the demands, showed what the transport and collection problems might be at the end of the day. (McFarlin 10:7)

Scott promoted Dass to havildar, not realizing "the extra 'face' I'd given him back home in his village. Now he is head of the village council—a man of relative wealth, with a house instead of a hut, a rice mill, and a dowry" (McFarlin 15:17). Between 1946 and 1963, Dass faithfully wrote to Scott. In one letter, he wrote,

> I am always anxious to hear from you often and I am sorry that your time is so precious that I am not getting replies often. Apart from our relation of Master and servant, a close friendship has been formed during our service together. Your cheerful attitude, kind heart, and considerate affection will always be before my thoughts, and I will be joyful over the cheerful memories. (McFarlin 3:25)

Scott, however, proved to be an undependable correspondent.

> I told him so many times that I hoped to be coming to India, and he invited me so many times to stay with him and his family in his village, that eventually I became embarrassed having to tell him I couldn't come to India after all. (McFarlin 1:4)

Unlike his first exposure to India during the war, Scott carefully documented his reactions and perceptions during the 1964 trip in his letters home to his wife, Penny. I have included as many of those as possible because of their importance in understanding Scott's reaction to what he called this "primitive" side of India as well as what that experience revealed about Scott and, by extension, about the British who were living in India. Scott's letters to Penny create a kind of diary, an immediate, textual tablet upon which his reactions are imprinted. In an odd way, Scott had been right. His village experience provided him with an opportunity to write, but not (as he had hoped) from inspiration but from a kind of desperate self-defense. Instead of a pristine tropical paradise, he found primitive conditions (such as having to empty his bowels in the rice fields). He expected to enjoy talk of the good old days with a long-time friend, but neither he nor Dass could reframe their friendship outside of their military past ("he still calls me sir … and I have no one to talk to"). The village children's watchful eyes made him feel like a specimen ("oh god how they stare"). The roles of the women in Dass's home made him feel both elevated (being waited on) and unclean (having his feet washed "for the re-entry"). Yet the touching signs of hospitality, such as jasmine placed on the table and on his bed, made him feel all the more guilty for inventing an excuse to leave early. "How I long for England," he wrote to his wife. And then, to allay her concern, he added, "Don't worry about these miserable letters. It's my safety valve, to complain" (McFarlin 18:1).

Timmapuram would be revisited in his later letters and, of course, in *The Jewel in the Crown*. Scott spoke eloquently in April of 1966 to his American agent Dorothy Olding of the humor, the magic, and the horror of contemporary India. But he was extremely critical of his own protective instincts:

> So devastating is the actual experience of having to live in these primitive conditions (not helped by a form of dysentery, and a lame leg) that there were times when I suspected I had been got there for some awful purpose that would only be revealed when I announced that it was time for me to go. This is a form of what you call cultural shock. In my case it was the greater because I'm not the type of person who responds favourably to "sahibism". I do not like being treated like a sort of Roman Emperor. To have got the most out of this visit, I should have enjoyed wearing what I call my Sahib's face [...] being superimposed over my own (I hope) liberal one, and hated it, but certainly needed it as an item of protective colouring. (McFarlin 15:17)

Ironically, Scott would discover such isolationism not in political conservatives such as Enoch Powell[2] but under his own liberal skin. In Scott's heart festered the "fear of the strange and alien, of losing one's sense of identity [...] what causes like to cling to like" (*My Appointment* 95–96). He understood that kind of fear because he had experienced it while he was in India. "India always did, still does and probably always will bring out the Enoch in me" (95), he confessed. Having experienced that same protective, insular instinct, Scott foresaw its consequences: if England were successful in forgetting its past, then paternalism would give way to ignorance, and "one of the first fruits of ignorance is prejudice" (119, 121).

Scott represented his own reactions differently to Dass, of course, after his return to England. With Dass, he reminisced about his trip:

> I also am getting back to normal health, and beginning to do some work, but I think often of the time I spent with you in your village, and of the kindness of your family [...]. Please tell your elder daughter and members of the family that I still have the garland of jasmine that they gave me on the last night I spent in your home. It is dried and faded now, of course, but it hangs in my study. Also the garland given to me by the priest at the temple. I often think of the happy days spent in your village. (McFarlin 3:26)

Dass replied,

> Our intimacy is such that I feel that I always see you in my imagination as if you are moving in my house. It has been very hot ever since you left this place, as there has been no adequate rain till now [...]. I cannot forget the companionship of the English friend. (McFarlin 3:26)

Although the two friends would correspond through 1974, they would never again meet. Scott continued to write fondly to Dass of his memories of their time together, although his more honest response to his experience in Timmapuram vacillated between discomfort and enjoyment. But this is clear: from 1964 on, he could not write about anything or anywhere else, because in a small village in Timmapuram, Scott gained a sense of himself he had never had achieved before, a sense he could not maintain apart from India.

I have also included Scott's letters from India to Penny to illuminate a more personal feature. Whatever "membrane" existed in his early novels, whatever "English reserve" might have characterized his personal manner, when Scott put his pen to paper, he could (it seems) comfortably and completely express his mind and his heart. These letters to Penny reveal longing, loneliness, affection—an intimacy to be admired. Penny was his lifeline to all he loved and understood. As he told his mother's caregiver, "I do not feel divisible from my wife & family" (McFarlin 16:1).

By the fall of 1964, Scott's elder daughter, Carol, had left school and was enrolled in a stage management course at the Tavistock Repertory Theatre. His younger daughter, Sally, had passed all of her GCE ordinary-level examinations and was about to start her A-level studies, with a view to going to a university. All seemed well. Scott felt "an expanding sense of freedom for the future" (McFarlin 13:7) as he tackled his next book: *The Jewel in the Crown.*

WORKS CITED

Scott, Paul. *My Appointment with the Muse*. Ed. Shelley Reece. London: Heinemann, 1986. Print.

Box 10, Folder 18 (McFarlin)
78 Addison Way
To Mr. and Mrs. Magnus Lindberg, Sweden
4 January 1964

Dear Magnus and Grunilla,

Many thanks for your lovely calendar, and Christmas Greetings. Penny and I send our Best Wishes for the New Year.

I am off on my Indian trip on February the 24th and fly from Delhi to Moscow on April 17, and from Moscow to Stockholm on April 27th. Penny will not be able to join me in Stockholm, and I can only manage a few days there. I shall probably fly back to London on Saturday May 2nd. I am in touch now with Ragnar Svanström, who said he would arrange my accommodation. I hope it will be possible to see you both in Stockholm during that time, though. I wish I could spend longer, but both time and money will be in short supply by the time I arrive! I wanted to go to Samarkand on my way to Moscow, but at the moment no airline, British, Indian, Polish or Russian, has Samarkand on its 1964 schedule. However, I may be able to arrange it in Delhi. My biggest problem will be clothing. I shall be in India during the build up of the hot weather, but Moscow in April, I imagine, is pretty cold, and I suppose Sweden is only just beginning to warm up. I shall have to buy some warm clothes in Delhi, obviously, so I shall probably look like a refugee from the Steppes of Central Asia by the time I reach Stockholm.

I have finished my new novel,[3] just, and delivered it to my British publisher and agent, both of whom seem to be enthusiastic, so I am relieved, and can concentrate on plans for my tour. In India I hope to live for a couple of weeks with an old Indian friend in a village, where there are rice fields and jungles full of parrots, and the sea not far off. During the next few weeks I shall become a human pincushion, being inoculated for (or rather against) every kind of plague you can think of.

Ever yours,

Box 18, Folder 7 (McFarlin)
78 Addison Way
To Roland Gant, Secker & Warburg, Ltd.
4 January 1964

My Dear Roland,

So glad and relieved you like the <u>Corrida</u> book. I promised to drop you a line about the possibility of libel.

First of all, in this book, I have taken no steps to check for accidental libel, e.g., through use of names such as Clipsby-Smith, Edward Thornhill. Playa de Faro is really Tamariu, the little bay where Penny and I have spent summer holidays these last four years. Antonio and Carmen Rojas are based on some people who run a little bar called the Bar Royal. Their name is Burgos, and they are known as Miguel and Maria. Miguel was an officer in the Republican Army (so he told me) and was in jail for four years. I don't think the portrait of the Rojas's is libellous of them, though.

There <u>is</u> a villa up on the hill, and of course it is white; but it isn't called the Vora La Mar, and I have no idea who lives there. I've never been beyond the gate marked Prohibido el paso. There is a resort further down the coast called Playa d'Aro. Faro means lighthouse. Beyond the bay of Tamariu there is the lighthouse San Sebastian, which overlooks the bays of Calella and Llafranch. Playa de Faro might well be recognisable as Tamariu, but apart from the Rojas's there is no attempt to characterise any of the people living here. Lola, Domingo and Miguel are entirely imaginary.

The main point to consider is that of the corrida that took place in San Feliu on Sunday September the 9th, 1962. The year has to be 1962 because it was in that October that a lot of people lost their lives in the floods that ended a record dry summer. I enclose a bill-poster which shows that the other matadors, apart from Ordonez, were Bienvenida and the South American (Colombian) Pepe Cacares. I have had them visually in mind when describing the corrida. An aficionado or anyone who kept data of corridas would be able to say that the "Senior" matador, with his expanding waistline, is Bienvenida, and the South American with the pink suit is Cacares. But whether any of the remarks made about them in the long corrida chapter are derogatory in the legal sense I wouldn't know. There is no intention to libel those two matadors. I have simply used them because they are the ones I saw with Ordonez and for once, in a novel, I felt it necessary to base an incident four-square on an actual experience. I don't think Ordonez is libelled. As we both know criticism of matadors is often pretty crude (e.g., Hemingway on Ortega in <u>Death in the Afternoon</u>). All matadors at some time in their careers are likely to bungle, especially with the estoque. I don't know whether exception could be taken to a suggestion that they bungled on an occasion when they didn't. I do not remember any of the details of the corrida at San Feliu on that particular Sunday, because it was the first one I ever saw, and I knew nothing of what to look for. I have a pretty clear impression, though, of Bienvenida making a mess of his first bull, of Ordonez being disappointing and of Cacares having a good afternoon. My own feeling is that <u>if</u> someone wanted to identify Bienvenida and Cacares, the only difficulty comes in the section where Thornhill is discussing the reasons for the change of expression on the senior matador's face.

I got most of my technical information from Barnaby Conrad's Encyclopedia, e.g., the story of Civilon. Before I began writing the book I reread <u>Death in the A[fternoon]</u>. I have also referred to a book published by Faber—<u>The Running of the Bulls</u>—and to a book called <u>The Horn and the Sword</u>. I am inclined in an author's note, when acknowledging the assistance given me by the Natural History Museum (in connexion with Leopards) to acknowledge Conrad, just as I acknowledged a man called Menon (the Indian States Minister) in <u>The Birds of Paradise</u>, because although works of non-fiction—in the sense that they record fact and general knowledge—are anyone's source materials, and although you don't expect a bibliography in a novel, it seems only fair to give credit where it is due. If you agree, then, I will draft a short note of acknowledgments.

Hope Fred [Warburg] likes it.

Ever,

Box 16, Folder 1 (McFarlin)
78 Addison Way
To Mrs. Gladys Roche[4]
5 January 1964

Dear Mrs. Gladys Roche,

Thank you for your letter. As I am uncertain of the address on Roderick Road perhaps you would post the enclosed card for me, adding the number if necessary.

Although your letter implies a moral judgment I appreciate your reasons for writing it. I imagine, too, that it is you who telephoned & spoke to my wife when I was abroad in October.

I did, of course, receive the card from my mother. If it had been sent to all of us here I'm sure it would have been responded to, but it was sent to me alone & I do not feel divisible from my wife & family in this way. In responding to it now, at your request, I must be honest with you & tell you that my heart is not in it because its receipt can, I think, only aggravate the sense she has of that divisibility, & in the long run such an aggravation would be more harmful to her than otherwise. Since the death of her second husband she has, as I know from my brother, been completely on her own, & it is only natural that her thoughts should move acutely to the idea of reconciliation. But rec[onciliation] with whom? With me alone?

I hope this letter will not encourage you to believe that there are further steps you can take in regard to the estrangement, or do not expect a reply. Since you have a professional although voluntary interest, tho', I have left the envelope enclosing the card unsealed, so that you may have no doubt about sealing & posting it.

Yours,

Box 10, Folder 2 (McFarlin)
78 Addison Way
From a letter to Mollie Hamilton [M. M. Kaye]
15 January 1964

Dear Mollie,

Many thanks for your long and interesting letter. First of all, though, congratulations on <u>Trade Wind</u>. After a short bout of 'flu just before Christmas I stayed in bed a day longer than was strictly necessary because I began to read and was caught up in it. The narrative flows at a fine pace and I think the whole atmosphere was extremely well captured. I won't pretend I liked it better than <u>Shadow of the Moon</u>—but then of course India is India and Zanzibar is Zanzibar (or rather was until a few days ago) and my heart was not in it to the extent that it was in <u>Shadow</u>. All the same, the construction and juxtaposition of scenes seemed first rate to me, and the characters were alive as soon as they appeared. What will you do next? India? Long ago you had an idea for a novel about China in the thirties. I wonder whether that still excites you as an idea. My recollection is that John Guest threw cold water on it because he thought no one would be interested in so recent a picture of a China that has disappeared. I wonder whether he is wrong. <u>I'd</u> be interested.

You may well be right about the time I propose to spend in that village (yes, it really is a village). But I have reasons for wanting a bit of rustication—apart from the fact that I shall hope to put down a few things on paper, and a village seems the ideal place in which to do it. He's going to lay on some cock fighting for my entertainment. Haven't the heart to tell him I don't really want to see such a thing. But then it's a bit like going or not going to the bulls in Spain. In the end I went. That's virtually what the new novel is about. Not that I contemplate a novel about cock fighting.

[…] I expect when it comes to it I shall only be able to afford a week in the village. When you start plotting 2 months into days and weeks you are shocked to discover how short a time it is. If the Bharatpur you mention is the one near Agra I shall be in that region end of March early April. It would be marvellous to meet HH [His Highness]. He sounds splendid. It's awfully kind of you to offer to write to him, and to Neil Ghosh. I leave here on February 24th and in Bombay I am being put up by someone called Mrs. Dorothy Ganapathy, 3 Queens Court, Queen's Road, Fort, Bombay 1 (an arrangement made by Mr. Manaktala, managing director of Allied Publishers in Bombay who distribute books for the Heinemann group, and who is being very cooperative about putting me on to places where I can stay cheaply but in comfort—at least that is how he describes it). From Bombay I shall fly to Madras to contact whoever in the Allied Publishers office there Mr. Manaktala introduces me to.

[…] Next time you write, do let me know if there's anything I can do for you in India.

Ever,

Box 13, Folder 7 (McFarlin)
78 Addison Way
From a letter to John Willey, William Morrow & Company, USA
25 January 1964

Dear John,

Your wonderful letter of the 22nd was a joy to have, and a tremendous relief. I feared everyone was basically not going to like this new book. Time and again during its composition I thought: Why do I expect to get away with a thing like this? I could already hear the critics talking about the author scraping the bottom of the barrel, emptying a rag-bag, etc. But I always had to go back to it, and pursue all that material to its (to me) logical conclusion; and in the end, in myself, I felt encouraged at the thought that I'd not consciously compromised anywhere. Now I'm rewarded, not only by your warm response to the things the novel is about, but by what you say about the wedding of structure and sense. You pay me ample compliments on the level of the writing, too. What I think happened—and I do believe myself that the writing is the best I've done—what I think happened is that the complexities of the structure gave the words themselves a kind of liberation, so that the simplest phrases, an almost vernacular attack on the reader, somehow worked. I felt I'd broken through that little barrier that up to then had stood between me and my material. Another new thing for me, too; although I feared people weren't going to like it, in a curious way I wasn't worried. I didn't build up my usual neurosis about hearing from people what they thought. I got rid of the book, emotionally, directly it was finished. The nice things people are saying about it at the moment are acting on me in a different way than usual, too. In the old days if people said, yes, this is a good novel, I used to rush back to my copy of the mss and dip into it and think, Yes, I suppose they're right; how clever I am! Now I feed on compliments in a new way. Every time someone says how good they think The Corrida is I feel an expanding sense of freedom for the future. I think what I mean here is that at last I feel I've proved to myself that "I can write". And that the joy of writing lies not in what has been done but in what remains to be done, next year, and the year after. Hope I've explained this in a way that makes sense to you, and doesn't fill you with apprehension that I'm set on a course of self-conscious experiment and wilful "difficult" writing.

By now I expect you've heard from Dorothy Olding that she too is enthusiastic; her letter reached me an hour or two before your own. She thinks there may be an even chance of magazine extracts, and has written to David [Higham] for a second copy. I have no spare at home, only the finally revised ts from which the top copies and carbons were typed, but I think David is releasing his one office copy for Dorothy.

At Seckers, Roland [&] Nadia [Gant], Fred [&] Pamela [Warburg], and David Farrer are all enthusiastic. So is a young man of 23 called Giles Gordon, who is in charge of jackets, etc. David Higham also v. keen, and his 25 year-old assistant, Jacqueline Korn. Roland showed a mss to Arthur Coleridge, who is the Readers' Digest man here (Digest Books). Nothing doing, naturally, for RD (it was a long shot of Roland's) but Coleridge read over to Roland a v. enthusiastic report he'd had. I mention these responses because they cover a wide field of age levels, and perhaps bear out your own instinctive feeling that the book may well appeal to a great many people at different levels. It would be nice if this turned out to be so, so that I could get off the ground in the States, and so repay Morrow for their long and loyal and enthusiastic support. Incidentally, we shall naturally never know the full value of the contribution my trip to the States made to The Corrida. When I left London I was actually in one of the periodical fits of despair about it. When I got back I just tackled it from page 280 approx. to the end, and was through writing on December 7, so if that is any guide my Morrow-sponsored journey at least hastened the turning of the key in the last lock that was keeping me out of the last section of the book.

Oh dear, you're right about Uncle James. Born in 1885 he would be 19, not 17, when Edward arrived from China, in 1904. In my calculations I had failed to notice that the disaster to Edward's parents took place 2 years after E was born in 1902. I think this alters just the 2 references (can't quote page numbers because my own ts is a rough), but the first would be "The youngest child, the robust James, was now 19" and the second ref on the next page would be altered to "He was 17 years my senior—a youth of 19 jealous of a boy of 2." The subsequent ref is, I think correct, i.e., in 1920 he would have been 35 as stated […].

BBC television, by the way, are contracting for a 75-minute dramatic adaptation of <u>The Bender</u>. Since I'm off to India I shan't be tempted to ask to do the adaptation myself. It's for the new BBC channel, channel 2. I met the young adapter the other day, and thought we saw eye to eye.[5] As for the film of The CLP, have had two talks with the producer and the director, but am still not anticipating the project getting even to the draft script stage.

Title. People here seem to have become used to it, and Fred has always liked it. I think its interest lies in the promise it seems to hold out of a story. I mean obviously something happens at the Corrida at San Feliu. But I am aware of the drawbacks. Unfortunately I have no alternatives to suggest. Perhaps something magical will come to your or Adèle's mind.

Must stop now. Many many thanks for all that you feel and say about the book. Now my cup of contentment is full. Love to Fern and you from Penny and me.

Ever,

Box 5, Folder 1 (McFarlin)
78 Addison Way
To Dorothy Ganapathy[6]
27 January 1964

Dear Mrs. Ganapathy,

Thank you very much for your kind letter of the 23rd. I'm glad that you liked <u>The Birds of Paradise</u>. I'm afraid, though, that there must be a number of mistakes in it that someone who really knows the country will have noticed. That is the kind of thing that will be interesting to talk about.

I don't think I shall be disappointed. I realise how much the country must have changed; but most change is good and all change is exciting. I'm already impatient to be off, and to see for myself.

It is most kind of you to think of having a dinner party for me. Thank you very much. Thank you, too, for letting me know it isn't necessary to bother about a dinner jacket. Even though coming by air automatically cuts down the amount of luggage you can bring I had already decided to travel as light as possible, so I will stick to that and hope not to look too crumpled. As for food I am actually looking forward tremendously to eating real curry again. Over here, on the few occasions when I've had it, it hasn't particularly agreed with me, but the climate is wrong. I hope that when I'm back in India I shall enjoy Indian food just as much as I used to.

It is kind of Mr. Manaktala to be arranging for me to be met by car at the airport. When I have full details from BOAC[7] I will write to him and let him know the flight number and exact time of arrival. Meanwhile, many thanks again for your letter. It is nice to know that I shall be staying with someone who has read some of the things I've written.

With kind regards,

Yours sincerely,

Box 13, Folder 7 (McFarlin)
78 Addison Way
To John Willey, William Morrow & Company, USA
4 February 1964

Dear John,

Spasseeba for your letter or rather pisymo. Real horrorshow and helmeet, like I dig it tovarishch way out to Petersville.

I got my visa the day after we met. Looked into my travel agent on the way home and was told that I'd been summoned to the consulate. When I got there Mr. Kutuzov (I forgot to ask him whether he was really the <u>War and Peace</u> general) said it was the consul himself who wanted to see me. So I was ushered in and sat beneath a portrait of Nikita, was given a glass of vodka (10.30 a.m.), and then we discussed the weather in London and Moscow, what I was to do in India. I was left alone for a few minutes, but forgot to take that opportunity to look at the papers on the consul's desk; so maybe they thought I was safe. They gave me my visa, which I can't read for toffee, so perhaps it says Arrest on sight. On my way out, Mr. Kutuzov asked me for the title of my last novel so that he could go out and buy one to read. So of course I said I'd send him a copy. He asked me whether I would autograph it. So now he has an auto-graphed copy of <u>The Bender</u>, and it's the salt mines for me, no doubt. How absurd it is that even at such a friendly meeting these thoughts should arise.

Spasseeba for the proof, too. You are so bloody industrious and eru-dite, I feel like an 18th century dilettante.

Thought you'd be interested in this example of Indian-English, from the man I'm going to stay with in a village 300 miles north of Madras. His English has fallen off in the last 18 years, but he always had a streak of poetry in him, and that's still there:

"Please determine even when your are in London to stay for a long time in my village. You must stay for one month in my home. It will be summer when you come to India. But it will be cool in my village. There are very big trees in my village. We have table-electric fans in my home. When you come to my home we will both go to the next village in a double bullock cart; when the bullock cart is going—garland of brass belts to necks of the bulls, which will give sweet sound."

Thanks and again, our best to you both,

                              Ever,

Box 18, Folder 1 (McFarlin)
Bombay
To Penny Scott
27 February 1964, 10.40 p.m.

Darling,

Most extraordinary hospitality. Every day something is arranged for me, the party yesterday was a great success. Today Dorothy G[anapathy] (who is kindness itself) took me to see a high official of the State Bank, a Parsee, called (like happy families) Mr. Banker. This evening he took us, with his wife, for a sunset drive to Malabar Hill, to the hanging gardens. On our way back we stopped in at the modern flat of his daughter & son-in-law that looked like an advertisement for interior decorations. (This part of Malabar, steep hills, tall modern apartment bldgs like hinterland of Tamariu). Tomorrow, DG, Mrs. Banker & I are going to Elephant Island to see the temple carvings. In the evening to an amateur production of Chekov's <u>Uncle Vanya</u> & back here for dinner with the Mukherjees, whom I've not met yet. Saturday we dine at the Manaktalas, Sunday the Manaktalas take us to lunch at Juhu Beach to an hotel called "Sun & Sand". I am allowed, so far, to pay for nothing, except the occasional taxi, & of course to supply my own rations of drink. Tomorrow is the Festival of Holi, when we may get spattered with coloured ink & chalk, so I shall be wearing the coffee-stained shirt. Haven't had time, since that initial impact, to feel lost. Only still slightly deaf in right ear. I expect it will be OK by the time I'm due to get on the plane to Madras. Many thanks for your post-Plaidy letter. Glad you got a lift home from Monica & Bob [Preston] & that the party was enjoyable, in spite of this & that. Keep exchanging cards with people, so goodness knows who will ring us unexpectedly over the next few years! (Good thing I had those cards printed. They are still used out here, as I suspected.) I shan't finish this letter until tomorrow. It's a holiday & I shan't be able to buy any more [postal] forms until Saturday, & I want to jot down my impressions of Elephanta some time during tomorrow. Am <u>very</u> comfortable. The bath water works again (most of the time). It's not <u>too</u> hot & there are no flies or mosquitoes. It is probably a good thing that I've made Bombay my first port of call. It breaks you in gently. Only the beggars remind you of the India that lies inland. It is awful to give them nothing, but if you hand to one you would be surrounded. Life in Bombay otherwise very civilized—& of course on the whole <u>not</u> what I came to see, but it will do for a beginning. Goodnight, darling. Shall finish this tomorrow.

3 p.m. Friday 28th. The trip to Elephanta was fine. The temple, hewn out of solid rock, is certainly an extraordinary sight. I took some colour pictures, but suspect they will look rather dull. Had a sleepless night, worrying about the trip & how things are at home. Each approaching stage of the journey looks so impossible, & different even if it's not impossible! But in daylight there's not time to get too hot under the collar. Didn't get spattered with any colour this morning, so still have clean clothes. The boat trip to Elephanta Island took an hour. We went with a conducted party & had a guide to explain all the carvings. There were 120 steps up to the temple. We could have gone up in chairs carried by four porters, but only a couple of Americans did that. It was quite a climb but worth it. All that part of Bombay, I mean that kind of thing, you would love. Still a bit deaf in right ear, but no other ills yet, touch wood. Dorothy G. facially, looks like Sybil Thorndike, but she's a small woman. Only worn her sari once. European clothes otherwise. Daughter of a knight (Indian). Dorothy is the name her Indian convent school knew her by & it has stuck, but she is pure Rajput. Think we're having Chinese food with Mr. & Mrs. Banker on Monday. Dorothy G has travelled over most of Europe & has been places I don't suppose we shall ever go. As far as Japan, but never yet to America. She is known personally to Nehru, so you will understand the level. She says if anything goes wrong with my plans I can always come back to Bombay. I am resting now, after lunch & before tea & date to see <u>Uncle Vanya</u> with the Mukherjees. Saw a snake charmer on the island today, near the gateway of India, playing this flute while his mongoose sniffed the basket. Yesterday evening saw the entrance to The Towers of Silence, but no one is allowed in, not even the Parsees, unless they are carried in dead. I suppose that gradually everything I'm seeing & doing

will fall into some kind of pattern—but can't sort it out at the moment. May not write for another 2 days, so don't worry. Meanwhile, my love darling—P.

Box 18, Folder 1 (McFarlin)
Bombay
From a letter to Penny Scott
1 March 1964

Darling,
[…] Last night, after attending a flower show in the afternoon, we had buffet supper at the Manaktalas, who today took us in the car to Aasey Milk Colony (gorgeous flowers) & a fabulous hotel on Luhu Beach, called "Sun 'n Sand." Afterwards at D[orothy] G[anapathy]'s request we called on an English friend who lives there & who had read <u>The Birds of P</u> & wanted to meet me. But he had two frightful examples of the new English memsahib visiting. The air was icy, with me, too, because I came with Indians. It made my blood boil. You have to see this kind of thing to believe that it is possible. The commercial English here (& that's all they are) are even <u>allowed</u> to have a club to which Indians are not admitted. It's just like the old days. Some of the English work for <u>Indian</u> firms, too! What is as awful is that Indians like the Manaktalas & Ganapathy just accept the situation philosophically, & their attitude & generosity to one never wavers. One of these 2 memsahibs wasn't even what used to be called pukka. The air of boredom and superiority was ridiculous, unbelievable. Well, I must not get hot under the collar. They were the first English I've met. But I don't think they were isolated examples.
[…] My love to the girls, too.

Box 18, Folder 1 (McFarlin)
Madras
To Penny Scott
5 March 1964

Darling,

It's ten in the morning. Hope by now (4.30 a.m. your time) you've got to sleep after Carol's party![8] Wrote for a time last night, but the posts don't go from here until tomorrow morning, today being Sunday. The faint reserve which at first made me wonder to what extent the Kumars really liked my being here has completely vanished & in their different way (from Bombay) they are equally friendly & hospitable. This morning at 12 there is the beer party. Every night I'm booked to accompany them to parties. Met a nice man last night (an Indian) & talked to him about the British (average British) attitude. He at once said that tomorrow, Monday, he will send a car to take me over to the factory where he is a director. He said I would then have the opportunity of observing the different & subtle ways that racial prejudice in a partly owned British firm works. This man, about my age, had a very good English friend whom he knew in England. Now that friend has come out to India & they are no longer friends because the Englishman has been caught up in the European Colony. Sorry to keep harping on this subject in my letters but it really amazes me.

Yesterday Mr. Ullal took me in his car to Mahabalipuram, the place where there is a temple on the edge of the sea. It was a wonderful place. Inside the temple (a room only) you come across the shrine of the Sleeping Vishnu (a god)—a large reclining figure in a dim little cell. The temple was built in AD 600 & it is said that there used to be 7 temples in a straight line—& all but 1 of them swallowed by the sea. Also in Mahabalipuram there are more of these amazing carvings out of solid rock—& a rather sad sight, a hill with huge boulders, which the inhabitants had begun to carve & than abandoned because of an invasion. We drank milk through straws out of huge green coconuts. On the journey there were lovely emerald green rice fields & women bending & planting the rice plants in other fields (like the description in The Corrida at San Feliu). I think you would love the countryside as much as I do (so much like Spain in many places) & it is only the cities & towns that you would need some time to get used to. Had a nice letter from Mr. Churamani of Allied Publishers in Calcutta, asking me for dates & times of arrival & talking about my prospective <u>hosts</u> in Calcutta <u>and</u> Benares. I don't suppose that in the end I shall spend much less than I imagined even with this free hospitality—because there will be presents & large tips to the servants. All I can say is that if I were living in hotels I'd be broke in short time! It's so hot I have to take a taxi even to go ½ mile & here we are 3 miles outside Madras. I get my shirts & underwear laundered every day by the woman here & the bearer gets my khaki trousers (I bought 2 pairs to replace the torn ones) ironed each morning. I bought Dass a Parker pen (it cost £11, but I felt I had to give him a rich present). Bangles & a doll for the children (& sweets still to buy). I got a small Chanel No. 5 in Bahrein for Mrs. Dass. Shall have to give Mr. Kumar something quite expensive I think. I mean 3 or 4 pounds. They are setting up a new home in Delhi. I may see them there. That PP&H author Monica Felton[9] has been out of Madras, but I've had a telegram from her saying she's back 7.30 a.m. Thursday morning & wants v. much to see me. So I shall see her before I depart for Elluru on Thursday evening. David Higham will remember her, if you mention her to him. She is a large woman, once chairman of the Stevenage New Town Committee & got into trouble in UK for visiting the wrong side of the front in the Korean War. All my love Darling & to the girls.

B[10] xxxx

Box 18, Folder 1 (McFarlin)
Madras
To Penny Scott
5 March 1964, 7.40 p.m.

Darling,
    Have just realised that the way these aerogrammes unstick my date & time & place have often been concealed! This letter follows the one I've just finished acknowledging receipt of the 2 lovely long typed letters dated last Friday & Saturday. And again I repeat—next Tuesday p.m. go by train to Elluru where Mr. Dass will meet me early Wed morning. And on Mar 26 fly from Hyderabad to Calcutta, via Madras. Shall now

postpone completing this letter until I've relaxed & read over again your long typed ones (v. poor reading light here). I worked it out that when you started typing them I was just watching the close of the play Uncle Vanya. Now at last can begin making that kind of connexion in my mind. Often look at my watch, deduct 5½ hours & say "The girls will have gone to school." "HG [Honey Girl] will be getting up" or "Now it's Restolling!"

11 p.m. After dinner. All abed except me. Quiet evening chatting about Hindu philosophy & family life in general. The Kumars are very nice, but not so easy to know as the people of cosmopolitan Bombay. Their daughter's marriage was "arranged". Now she feels herself better intellectually equipped than her husband, & blames them. Can see her point, but also understand their feelings of disappointment & worry &, I suppose, self reproach. Kumar is a great fan of the musical Hair & London Palladium in particular. Have told him when next in London, etc. If this holiday doesn't cost so much as it might there are obviously going to be repercussions when one by one they all turn up in London!! Think you would like them all, tho! I wonder whether this Sat you are going to R's & N's [Roland and Nadia Gant's]. Hope so. Chat & sociability helps to pass the time. Quite agree you should take them to L'Epicure. Hope they can come & that you all have a marvellous time. Yes, it's odd, but the jets are not silent, not really. The quietest is the Caravelle, which has the engines in the tail like a rocket. I came to Madras on it. V. Comfortable & my ears are now more or less normal.

Sometimes I wish I could describe everything to you so that you could get a real idea of it—but it is impossible. Hope Eric didn't accept Carol's proposal! I mean we can't afford a marriage, not one with 3000 lights in the trees (see my letter last night in Bombay). Sorry about her health trouble & hope it, and Sally's health, are better. Have written a line to Bug because I sent a letter to Keek for her birthday. Hope the card arrived. Did Sally's visit to the Palladium show come off? Tell her if it did Mr. Kumar would be jealous. Incidentally, all these Indians should be prefaced Shri (or Sri) not Mr. It's like Esq. So—c/o Sri xyz. I believe it means a lot to them. But, like Esq., although you put it on the envelope you write

"Dear Mr. xyz". My voucher for 15% reduction on air-conditioned coach is made out to Shri Paul Mark Scott. The Air India people are marvellous. They are the only international airline that makes a profit too, even tho' they are noted for service. The girls in the office are terribly efficient & helpful, cool & charming as they look in their saris. There is a store here (relic of British days) called Spenars. Like Harrods with Victorian Gothic architecture & electric fans & sell almost everything. Am going there tomorrow for my cigarettes & small presents for the Dass family. You would go mad in the silk shops. The colours are fabulous. So, alas, are the prices! But I hope to find something before I leave here.

Love, darling

B xxxx

Box 18, Folder 1 (McFarlin)
Timmapuram
To Penny Scott
11 March 1964, 12.30 p.m.

Darling,

Three letters from you (Thur Mar 5) awaiting my arrival here. Many thanks. Glad all is OK. I got in to Elluru Station after a comfortable air-conditioned journey from Madras overnight. Dass was waiting for me. How strange it all is here. Am feeling a bit lost & unable to describe it. My main worry is that the loo is 50 yards down the road—but I have a torchlight for night time. The bath is simply an open-air enclosure in the courtyard. The house is simple but comfortable & reasonably cool. I hope I can settle down. Trouble is I probably need about 2 crates of gin, but only have one bottle! Our Austrian snapshots are on the wall here, framed & looking down at me, so that gives me a link with home & civilisation as I knew it! Carol & Sally are there too! Seem to have been given the whole house, bedroom & sitting room. I have to wear bare feet, tho', because this is really a Hindu house. The four daughters are sweet. The baby died about 3 weeks ago. The four came in and made namaste,[11] more or less like the King of Siam's daughter. I haven't met the wife yet. I'm about to have lunch, probably alone. Wonder what it will be like? Wonder indeed whether I shall be able to manage 2 weeks? The kindness & hospitality are the same as ever, but basically this is primitive. There are hens brooding on turkey's eggs in 2 of the back rooms. The shaded patio at the front is charming, tho'. If only there were a <u>bar</u> & a loo next to my room. Bathing in the enclosure is fun. Huge brass urns of water, & a bale to scoop & pour it over yourself. Joss sticks burning in a quadruple vase of roses on my table. Imagine that house in Spain that we might look into. Similar atmosphere, but small & probably cleaner. A huge electric fan for my comfort just being put on. At Elluru, went in cycle tongas to bus stop. There I was sat down in a chair practically in the middle of the road, chief source of attraction until it was time to get into the bus.

3.30 p.m. After lunch served to me alone by No. 1 daughter with comings & goings by Mr. Dass, I rested until now. This letter is my link with everything familiar & dear to me. The strangeness here persists. Have a bit of a headache from the mounting heat. The food was good but purely village Indian; goat's meat curry & rice & dhal & peppered eggs. How I long for the civilised comfort of the Kumars', let alone of Bombay. I suspect I'll have to cut the visit short, but have no real life line to Madras again with the Kumars packing to leave. It will probably be a question of leaving for Hyderabad earlier than intended & staying in an hotel there. Village children keep coming to peer at the strange apparition of an Englishman sitting at a table writing letters!! One more chore, darling. MRS. KUMAR gave me 50 rupees to cover the cost of the following from England: Supply of NESTLE COLORTINT, NO. 30, BLUE GREY made by LEMUR LTD. & distributed by Fassett & Johnson LS, ECI. Also for what she described in a way I interpreted as a stretch-nylon girdle that was v. small but expanded. Shouldn't think it would be one with suspenders. I know they don't wear stockings. If you can get these things & send them to her (MRS. P. L. KUMAR, c/o SRI R. N. SACHDEN, 65 Sunder Nagar, New Delhi) I'd be grateful. 50 rupees = 75/ = £3.15–0). She will have to pay duty, even if they are member gift, but if the shop sending them fills in the correct price she will only have to pay the right amount of duty. Again a big store should be able to deal with the whole operation, providing you can find one that sells that special colour rinse. Don't panic or rush over this. They aren't in Delhi for several weeks yet. I'll keep my copy of the details of what she wants until you're able to acknowledge this letter. I think by the time you get this letter, better more or less start writing me at the Allied Publishers Calcutta address, especially if there are important things, but I'd appreciate the odd letter here until March 24, in case I can stay the course. If I leave for Hyderabad shall try to stay at the Ritz Hotel there. Have seen v. little of the village as yet. The bus from Elluru stops right outside this little house. Continue another sheet.

LOVE, DARLING.

B. xxxx

Box 18, Folder 1 (McFarlin)
Timmapuram
From a letter to Penny Scott
11 March 1964, 3.45 p.m.

My Darling,

[…] I look at my surroundings sometimes & feel I was MAD! to come here. At other moments I think well it is an experience & perhaps presently the compensation will become apparent.

Am devastated to hear there's been snow at home. I find it difficult even to imagine it! Incidentally, never saw a paper in Madras & shan't see one here, so any interesting news of Europe or USA always welcome. Additional letter from Adèle waiting me here, but I can't seem to take it in as about anything real. Just been brought a cup of tea by Mr. Dass. It tastes a bit odd. Probably goat's milk. My bare feet are being bitten by ants! Oh, dear. It would be funny if only, just for a moment <u>you</u> were here to see it all with me & then whisk me away. I guess my time here is rationed in accordance with my stockpile of cigarettes. It's amusing when you think that of <u>all</u> the tour, this village sojourn seemed the most promising, almost halcyon. I suppose I should have known better. Poor Dass. I'm sure he is as anxious as hell to do everything right & to make me comfortable & welcome, but he still calls me sir & treats me as an officer & I have no one to talk to, so know what it must be like for you when the girls have gone to school. On the other hand you can always go to the shops at Temple F & talk in English.[12] Here they only speak Telegu so I can't even speak my rusty almost non-existent Hindi. Dass of course speaks English, but he doesn't always understand what I say. Sorry if this letter & the previous one are a bit miserable, because you will be worried about Timmapuram for longer than I will. I mean I shall know before you do whether I can stand it or whether I've got to go. If only Dorothy G[anapathy] were in Madras I could turn up there at midnight & get a bed. I expect it will take 3 days to book a train in any direction, too. My plan is—if I can't take it—to sham illness, & need of an air-conditioned room somewhere. The lizards on the walls here are not transparent, & they are bigger! Presently shall have to make the long journey to the loo! I read your letters over and over, but they don't sink in. Hope I'm not overlooking some important point. I hope Carol's party was a great success. The Ames both sound fun. Wonder whether you took R & N[13] to L'Epicure last night? Shall now write to Churamani in Calcutta, telling him I may be departing here & arrive in Calcutta unexpectedly! Actually would give anything to be on the train or plane now. Well, no one made me come, so there's only me to blame. All my love, darling, & don't worry. I shall do what I find necessary. Meanwhile thinking of you & the girls all the time.

Love B. xxxx

xxx

Box 18, Folder 1 (McFarlin)
Timmapuram
To Penny Scott
12 March 1964, 8.30 a.m.

My Darling,

Have written Allied Publishers in Madras to telegraph me to return & proceed to Calcutta soonest re lecture tour! So maybe sometime next week I shall get the message, then 3 days wait for train booking, & I may be off before the weekend after this coming one. This letter is the 3rd from Timmapuram. It will probably get the same collection as the 2 I wrote & posted yesterday evening. The "P.O." is simply a box. Last night I slept in the open under a tree, with Dass in a bed nearby to see I came to no harm. It was wonderfully cool & I was glad to get out of the house because the room was v. hot & when I stirred my d/gown a lizard scuttled out of the pocket! Outside, a few yards from the road I slept intermittently to the sound of munching cows & buffalo, & bullock carts creaking & tinkling through the night. Very romantic & supportable if only the loo were within hailing distance. The ritual is clean but troublesome. A water pot (but I use paper as well)—then coming back in, shoes off & wash feet in courtyard. Was shaved (no soap) & massaged this morning by the barber. V. relaxing but the whole of the village children stood & watched. Shaved under armpits too, & had toe nails cut with a kind of scalpel. Then a warm water bath, coffee & some kind of whey dish, which has set the old tummy going. Shall start on my course of entero-vioform[14] this morning & hope it does the trick (just swallowed the first two!). (I have a 5-day course & can get more of the same tablets in any major city, e.g., Hyderabad. Mr. Dass, knowing my tum was upset, offered me castor oil. Oh Lord!). So much hope that the post this morning will give me some letters. Last night walked a mile (in the evening) to Mr. Dass's fields & then a mile back. At fleeting moments I think perhaps I'm making mountains out of molehills, but inwardly I know that the whole visit, however long or short it turns out to be, will live in my memory as the plan of someone who needed his brains tested. Only have 5 more of these air forms, & can't get any more except 20 miles away in Elluru. Hope they will last me until I can go in there to book my train. In Madras I used to long for relaxation because we were always going off to parties. Now I'd go mad for a party! And to speak fluent English. Have just had an interruption with about 6 children all wanting English lessons. "I am writing a letter to my home in England. They are watching me while I write it. They will go with me to the Post Office & help me to put the letter in the box. The Post Office will send the letter to England. I wish the Post Office would send me instead of the letter." Darling, all my Love, & kisses to the girls. Will be writing again soon with some news from swinging Timmapuram.

Love,

B xxxx

Box 18, Folder 1 (McFarlin)
Timmapuram
To Penny Scott
12 March 1964, 4.40 p.m.

My Darling,

Closed my last letter by saying just going loowards. Now back. Very liquid, what there was of it. Told Dass I'm not well. Will only eat curds tonight & try to get up courage to broach subject of departure. I think most of the unwellness is due to worry about how to get away. Or may be the effect of the entero-vioform, which began by making me feel well. Drinking a cup of over-sweet tea & sitting in front of fan at moment, having had a cold cup to try & cool down. If only there were a telephone in Timma[puram]. I could try to ring the sister of a friend of the Kumars who lives in Elluru & ask her to take me in. Don't worry about all this. I work it out of my system a bit by writing it all down. Maybe by the time you get these (worrying) letters I shall have wired you that I'm in Hyderabad. If I can get to Hyderabad I shall wire Chura- mani in Calcutta & then try to re-fix my flight dates. It will mean a small cancellation—or—booking fee charge, but will be worth it to get to Calcutta with Churamani who is an old friend of Dorothy Ganapa- thy's & responsible for getting me fixed up with her in Bombay. But I tell you that the loo here, apart from being 50 yards (perhaps 100) away, is a squatter. My back doesn't take kindly to it. Just an added difficulty! Actually went into the fields this morning (dawn) as it was fresher there. Also the radio is put on for my benefit all day practically—mostly mournful music. The small children always peeping in. I gave them an English lesson last night, so every time I look at them they seem to want more. They are v. sweet, but oh God how they stare. There is one staring at me now, just resting in the doorway. No wonder the old 19th century English became eccentric. Now there is a whole gang collected around me, actually leaning on the table. Have had to tell them "to go as I'm not well". Feel awful doing things like that. Begin to feel I'm probably the first white face that any of them has seen. Probably, am, come to think of it. Well, it is certainly an experience, darling. When I'm fed, the elder daughter stands against the wall <u>behind</u>, waiting for me to finish. Not been allowed to see the wife yet, but was introduced to her unmarried sister last night. The self-effacement of these village women is most embarrassing. Makes you feel like some kind of slave owner. The daughter is sometimes made by Dass to pour the water on my feet for the re-entry into the "clean" part of the house. Just been called out to see a man climbing a palm to tap it for toddy. He goes up with the end of a looped rope woven of fibre. His feet are hobbled with another rope so that they are always a certain width apart. He attaches a bowl against the cut he makes in the bark (just where the branches form out, & covers the pot with a mat so that the bats don't drink the toddy at night. The bowl is big, but will only be ¼ full in the morning. It is 5.30, so have poured myself a gin & soda. The soda bottles make an explosion when you open them. Seem to be running out of ink. Hope Mr. Dass has got some more & I don't have to go to Elluru to get it!!! Thanks for news of cost of starter, another repair! of nice Victor Vauxhall.[15] Feel I love him at the moment. After all the work you put in on the house it must look lovely. Only hope the party didn't spoil it. Dreamed last night that Sally came home & had proudly cut her hair off quite short. Then today your letter about Alice in Wonderland. How odd. Wonder whether she <u>has</u> now cut her hair off?[16]

Got fresh ink. Sweet little boy been learning English. Taught him to say how do you do. Always feel better after gin! Wonder whether main trouble is lack of easy sociability. Gin has settled tummy, at least temporarily. Dass just switched on neon light. Curious mixture of current & primitive. All my love, Darling, honey—

B. xxxx

Box 18, Folder 1 (McFarlin)
Timmapuram
To Penny Scott
13 March 1964, 6.30 a.m.

My Darling,

In spite of all the moans in my previous 5 letters from here, decided last night that providing my tum settles, I must stick it out as a kind of duty. I expect Dass would lose face forever if the Sahib exited after a couple of days only. Shall at least wait for the telegram from Madras I've asked Mr. Ullal to send. I've worked it out that it is midday onwards until about 6 that I feel worse: the heat. Evenings & early mornings pass pleasantly enough & no longer feel that the curiosity of the people is resentful curiosity. Today Mr. Dass is going to take me to a couple of interesting & quite famous temples. When I'm doing something I feel less worried about things. After I'd finished my letter No. 5 was caught up in quite a long English lesson session with about 6 small boys, & found myself enjoying it. Also for supper only had curds & rice. This morning tum is not so fluttery. I still long for a lovely private loo, tho'. Have just had some quite good coffee that has made me want to go again! I suppose it is all a question of mind over matter.

While I give these English lessons the elder daughter & unmarried sister come in & hang about in background. Every time they find themselves in the corner of my eye they retreat. They obviously want to join in the lesson, but it would be more than my life is worth to pay them any direct attention! The best pupil (aged 12) is Dass's nephew, Balarama Krishna. Expect he will come this morning to go with me to the post box & post all these letters (4, 5 & 6)—as yesterday we posted nos. 2 & 3—marching rather proudly by my side, holding the letters & putting them in the box. I have a specimen of his handwriting. He can read & write, but is too shy to speak, except v. hesitantly in answer to questions: What is this? This is a letter, etc. Have taught them to shake hands & say, "how do you do?" which they find terribly funny. When

I was shaved yesterday (water & razor only, quite clean) I was also massaged with coconut oil. Makes skin feel very good. Head massage entailed having it used like an Indian drum, but no headache resulted. I expect the performance will be repeated this morning at about 8 a.m. This house of Dass's looks more & more Spanish. Slept last night in the courtyard, because out in the road <u>was</u> a bit chilly towards dawn. No more lizards in pockets, but plenty on walls. They are incredibly swift when pouncing on small flies, etc. No mosquitoes here that I can see. As long as I think positive thoughts I may settle & be reasonably happy & once I've <u>fixed</u> my train departure date, even if for a week ahead, it will seem like a basic security. All my Love Darling, & kisses to you all.

B xxxx

Box 18, Folder 1 (McFarlin)
Timmapuram
To Penny Scott
13 March 1964, 2.45 p.m.

My Darling,

Afternoon again, v. hot, tummy much better but flies bothersome as I try to write this letter. So suppose am in for another afternoon of brooding & escape fantasies! This morning 3 young English-speaking gents from next village arrived to pay their respects. Hearing I was here, their "hearts were inspirited to greet me". One tried to present me with his fountain pen. They live in the place where's a temple. Dass is showing me this evening, so have to call at their home. Another hour or two of awkward conversation with 3 pairs of eyes fixed on me, hoping to hear me speak the next magical words in real English. Very touching, really, but oh for some real relaxation. Maybe on Monday shall get my pre-arranged telegram. No post today as yet; it comes early afternoon, so guess today is a blank day. Anyway you wouldn't have been able to write me last Saturday, Keek's birthday,[17] so can't really expect to hear until tomorrow at earliest. The letters seem to take 6 days. I got your Friday letters yesterday, Thursday. Went on tour of village this morning about 11 a.m., with Mr. Dass as guide. Followed of course by increasingly large gang of children. Entered two "houses" & had glass of buttermilk in one, praying that it wasn't full of germs. Somewhere, say 200 miles away in Hyderabad, there is civilisation! Mr. Dass has a huge old safe in my room. Have put my important papers, passports, etc. & some money in it, thus exchanging one worry for another. Before I worried about someone entering the house & pinching stuff. Now I worry about Mr. Dass losing the keys & having to wait for a week before it can be blown open. Of course I am constantly asked <u>why</u> I'm not eating meat. No matter how many times I explain my tummy is upset they always query my eating & of course I feel I'm insulting Mrs. Dass's cooking. Still haven't met her. I suppose she slaves away all day in the kitchen preparing food I don't eat & then gets angry with her husband! I think some of the villagers think I've come to take Dass back into the army. He was the only man here to join up. But then his father & grandfather were soldiers (Viceroy's Commissioned officers) such as Abraham Sofaer[18] played in that TV play. My best suit (tropical) is hanging to get out the packing creases—I only unpacked it this morning in the excess of enthusiasm for the idea of shaking it out. But wish I were in a place where there was once again daily need to wear it. Wonder if it is still snowing in London? This village not a bit as I imagined it. The shady trees are few & far between. Had imagined something lusher, more interesting vegetation. The house itself is pleasant enough, but I'm sure he said he had <u>six</u> or <u>4</u> electric fans in it. There is only one, & one knows it costs of lot of money to run. Any more thoughts about our holiday, Darling? If your mind is in anything like the state of mine you won't be able to think about it at all, except as something (in my case) wonderful to contemplate. Never, never shall I voluntarily go away alone again. My chart is beginning to look a bit fuller with days crossed out, but there still seems (is) an age to go.

All my love, darling,

B xxxx

Box 18, Folder 1 (McFarlin)
Timmapuram
To Penny Scott
14 March 1964, 6.45 a.m.

My Darling,

My, just see how early I get up! Just before six. Thank goodness for entero-vioform. Much better from that point of view. And it is definitely in the hot airless hours after lunch that I am plagued by these thoughts that I can't stand it here & must get away. Enjoyed last night. We walked a couple of miles to this temple. The 3 young English speakers met us on the outskirts of the village. Then we went to the temple & climbed about 100 steps to the entrance. I was allowed in, not only to the courtyard but into the inner sanctum where a Brahmin Priest performed puja over us. Given coconut milk (as in communion, but poured into the cupped hands). Was garlanded & given a red puja mark on forehead. It was of course due to Dass & his efforts that I was allowed to participate. All a bit weird, but interesting. On entering the inner sanctuary you ring a bell, to draw the attention of the god to the fact that you are entering (Vishnu in his case, the purifier). Then you enter a kind of catacomb with little openings in the walls in which the images are. Finally line up round kind of barrier of tubular metal (like getting a place in a bus queue stand). The main shrine is then in front of you. The priest says something to the god, then comes around with the coconut milk. After that he comes round with a tray of coconut pieces & flowers & distributes (I was given the main portion). Then he takes a gold headpiece, holds it over your head (the shape of a fez or flower pot) &, I suppose, blesses you. Then you go to the Kali shrine, the black goddess who destroys evil spirits, etc., to get the red mark & this time a silver headpiece is held over your head. The temple was high up & there was a panoramic view from its ramparts. They are all built on the walled courtyard principle with the main shrine in the middle & smaller ones round the walls, etc. Then we went to the little house of the English speaker. He is a village-level official. He goes round the area trying to teach farmers up-to-date methods. Came back on the dirty old Indian bus.

Dass turned on the wireless & guess what was playing: "The Hippy Hippy Shake", & then Nat King Cole! Dass's little cowherd (looking like a 7 year-old Sabu) presents me with flowers every day. Met another nephew of Dass's who is having exam soon to try to get into an Indian University to study as a doctor. So you see the curious mixture of people who live in a village. The little girls, even at age 4 or so, efface themselves like the elder female counterpart & it is always the boys alone who troop in ready for an English lesson. As I said earlier, older girls like Dass's elder daughter & unmarried sister, come into the room & listen to the lessons. Sometimes they prompt the small boys, but if you turn round towards them they retreat. Tomorrow I believe we are having the ride in the bullock cart. The bullocks are white, well fed & have lovely bluish eyes made up like Sally's. Yesterday evening on way to temple saw 2 parrots flying home.

Earlier I'd mentioned the concern here because I don't eat "enough". Yesterday thought I'd pleased them by asking for another cup of tea. Dass said yes of course. ¼ hour later found that they had used the last of the milk & that the daughter then had to go & milk the goat especially. Felt awful, especially when I realised milk is precious & not fresh on tap from bottles.

Writing letter No. 7 (a miserable one) I said I couldn't expect a letter yesterday, and your No. 1 of Sunday (post party) arrived about an hour after I'd sealed mine. Glad the party was fab, & that there was a well-trained "slave" gang to clean up & "strike the set". Looking forward to No. 2, continuation which will tell me what extent you did London & if you went to Nadia [Gant]'s? You asked recently about the new aerogrammes. When you buy them they are the same texture as those at home, so it is the heat on this end that affects them, makes them like parchment. On other hand must be something different in the paper, because yours don't change in texture.

Are all the cats OK? Glad it has stopped snowing (your last letter). When you (if you) start in the garden, don't overdo things in a fit of enthusiasm and put your back out. My back is still rather painful, but maybe it will be better when I leave here. Barber just arrived, so must have my soapless shave! All my love, darling, & to the girls.

B. xxxx

Box 18, Folder 1 (McFarlin)
Timmapuram
From a letter to Penny Scott
14 March 1964, 3.15 p.m.

Darling,

[…] Not so depressed this afternoon here, but it remains the worst part of the day. Flies, heat, boredom, apprehension, homesickness. Your letters always make it worse (the homesickness), but please don't stop sending them. My back (base & spine) is troublesome. I don't think my petty ailments here are properly understood. Of course they are used to sickness, etc., it is all part of the pattern of life. One day I shall probably look back on the visit & be glad not to have missed it. It's a good reminder, too, of the reasons why the English always made themselves v. comfortable & would have no truck with "customs." Have temporarily stopped my entero-vioform because they seem to have done the trick & I don't want to waste the ones that are left. Earliest I can get my "telegram" requiring my presence elsewhere is Monday afternoon. I think once the telegram reaches Ellum, it is treated like a letter & just comes in the post with everything else. So shall plan here to go to Ellum on Monday or Tuesday to book Hyderabad sometime next weekend. But, as I hope actually to book earlier as the result of the telegram. You were quite right when you told me to arrange a good line of retreat. If the Kumars hadn't been packing up their home I could always have told them I might be back. So it was fate, I suppose, that they were going & I couldn't pre-arrange something with them. Wrote Fred & Pamela [Warburg] today telling them I heard them on the wireless. Wasn't that silly?! I mean silly to hear them in this wilderness. Also wrote the Maharajah & Mrs. Ganapathy who sent me a long letter full of that charming Indian slang "doi", "bashing off to a party" (meaning dash off to a party!) She is the kind of woman who if she lived in Madras & knew of my predicament here would hire a car & drive to fetch me. Darling, shall continue to write over the postless weekend so that when you do next hear it will be more than one letter. Gin almost gone. Another reason to bash off to Hyderabad (the wet

capital of this dry state). Now it's 4 p.m., the most breathless moment of
the day. So shall close, thinking of you & the girls. As always, lying on
my bed in shorts, swatting the flies & thinking I'd better have my brain
tested when I get home. My Love, darling.

B. xxxx

Box 18, Folder 1 (McFarlin)
Timmapuram
From a letter to Penny Scott
17 March 1964, 8.30 a.m.

My Darling,

Lots of letters to write this morning. Was in Elluru most of yesterday
to book my passage to Hyderabad on Thursday evening & came home
to find 3 letters from you and the long typed one. (Incidentally I still
lack the one that told me all about how you spent Keek's birthday party
evening but gather from ref to cold, & Nadia & R shivering, that you
went to Napier Road). First quite right not to send the Lindt. & quite
right not to cable. Don't try to do any more re D. Ganapathy. I will tell
her about the drive, so proving that the Spirit was willing, & will think
of something presently, or when I get home. Thanks for news about cats
& car. Good if George can run it on a special license arrangement. It is
still insured because I never suspended ins. officially. Oh about Ruth,
too.[19] I wrote her from Madras & had a reply yesterday. Pl thank her for
her letter re birthday. Will try [to] write both girls when I'm settled in
Hyderabad. Odd about the Cashmores.[20] Was I supposed to say goodbye
to them? Re stain. Is the diverting a preliminary to the main wall alterations, I wonder?

Re British & self-preservation. You are partly right. Living here I am
reminded how essential it is for the European's peace of mind to make
himself comfortable & to insist on his own ways & customs. But that
is no excuse for the British who live in sophisticated India where the
Indians' ways are as cultured as our own. In London that kind of Indian
can go anywhere, live in the Dorchester or Claridges. Only in their own

country are they treated as "black" populations. I don't mean there isn't a great deal of social mingling, there has to be, because the English and Indians have to trade & run business. But at the push, the old prejudices work. Basically it is due to fear. I experience it myself here. Sometimes it is stark terror. Elluru yesterday was ghastly. I could feel my "Sahib's face" getting fixed like a mask & I found myself thinking Havildar (not Mr. Dass) should not expect his commander to subject himself to this squalor. Timmapuram was like heaven in comparison when we got back. Anyway, whole thing has given me an idea for a short novel. To give you an idea of Elluru, while waiting in the crowded bus, a leper came begging outside the window.

[…] All my love, darling,

B. xxxx

Box 18, Folder 1 (McFarlin)
Timmapuram
To Penny Scott
17 March 1964, 3.30 p.m.

My Darling,

No post this afternoon, unless it is late being sorted & delivered. This morning I wrote you giving you my Calcutta address & confirming I am leaving here day after tomorrow to reach Hyderabad on Friday morning where I have wired the Ritz Hotel to keep a room for me. Hope they have one so that I don't have to spend the day searching for accommodation. Anyway with today ½ gone, only one more <u>complete</u> day to get through here. I shall be leaving at 3 p.m. on Thursday. Shall just miss the day's postal delivery, I'm afraid. Waiting for the post & writing to you are my main pre-occupations here. Like being a recruit in the army. After 2 small glasses of alcohol Mr. Dass begins to shout. His favourite expression then is, "Sir, I am feeling some intoxication". Last night he told me that his wife & daughter were quarrelling with him, saying "Why were you fighting Captain Sahib, & not letting him eat his curry". He <u>was</u> shouting more than usual last night, & it <u>was</u> difficult to answer his questions & eat at the same time. A bit wearing, too, because he was shouting about religion. He plans when older to become a missionary. He sees all religions as equal.

My back seems much better today. It really was a trial especially in loo matters. The most pleasant part of the day's routine is the evening bath—an open air enclosure, with an electric light bulb just providing sufficient illumination & these huge brass bowls or buckets—all with hot & the other cold water & a scoop to pour it over the poor sticky old body. Then we sit on the veranda & drink a little & talk about the army & all the old personalities, so many of whom I've forgotten. Seems I must have been bad tempered in Singapore—gave some troublesome men a special drill, running up & down with huge parachute bales on their backs. Every time they passed the door of my office they had to salute. The NCO in charge of the drill, when told he could dismiss them, reported that they were still being bolshie & demanded to do some more drill. Apparently I said they could either dismiss right away or carry on until nightfall. So they dismissed! Only vaguely remember that. Dass particularly remembers that I was the only officer in corp who insisted on the senior NCOs having a separate mess from the men. The idea was, of course, to give the NCOs a sense of self-importance & it seems the mess was much appreciated & boasted about, & it kept the NCOs from being too familiar with the men under them. Most of my recollections are of course to do with what went on in the officers' mess, things Dass had no knowledge of—so there is the interesting difference in levels of memory. He reminded me how on the boat going to Malaya I saw some British soldiers deliberately spitting into the Indian soldiers' fresh water supply & of the awful row that ensued. All I remember really is the trouble I had, commanding the only Indian troops in that boat & trying to make the British NCOs realise that my men were human beings too & sailing in far worse accommodation (the worst in the boat) than their English counterparts. Ah well, funny days, long ago & far away & I find myself not a bit nostalgic for them. Present life so much more satisfying. Should hate to be back to all that artificiality, that spurious business of being "in things", etc.

The other evening went 4 miles down the road to see a cock fight. It was held in the grounds & under the auspices of the local "maharajah"— not really a maharajah, I reckon, but anyway someone rather like Krishi in The Birds of Paradise. The palace & grounds, tho', were in ruins practically. Empty cages dotted around where the maharajah's father used to keep tigers. All gone now. Dass says the maharajah is very rich tho', but prefers to live as he does. His sons are uneducated & just laze away all day. The cock fighting is really illegal. I had to sit practically in the ring. But having become used to bulls, cocks were feeble substitutes. Lots of material in that place for a story, probably. The maharajah greeted me, made them give me a chair, & then disappeared. He was wearing baggy old trousers & a shirt hanging out. Did not feel inclined to address him as Your Highness, so perhaps he felt insulted. Think at most he is a Rajah, and not H. H. The palace was only a largish house.

Dass never says, "Yes, sir" but always "yes sir, yes sir", said v. loud & rapidly. Dorothy G[anapathy] has sent me an enormous expensive book about Indian sculpture, for my birthday. So you see it is quite impossible to keep up with the Jones's. Dass has promised to pack & send it to London via ordinary sea mail. Maybe I'll reach home before it. Do you realize, Darling, that today, 17th, is only one calendar month away from my departure from India? That's more like it, as far as I'm concerned—actually to see a bit of daylight emerging re homecoming. If the rest of my time in India is as nerve wracking as this last week, shall seriously think of cancelling Russia & flying straight home on grounds my constitution won't stand it. Hope I don't weaken in that way, tho! Shall be more satisfied to reach home, having gone through it all.[21]

My Love, darling, & to the girls

B. xxxx

Box 18, Folder 1 (McFarlin)
Timmapuram
To Penny Scott
18 March 1964, 8.15 a.m.

My Darling,

My last full day here. Going for bullock-cart ride this morning and also believe there is some ghastly bus trip planned as a special treat! There are jasmine flowers on my table this morning. Got my laundry back OK & the older daughter herself did me a drip-dry shirt & handkerchief yesterday so shall leave here fairly up to date on washing. Still haven't seen Mrs. Dass! Wonder whether she'll be presented at the last moment? Is it an insult to <u>ask</u> to see her? Or an insult <u>not</u> to ask? Heaven knows.

Now of course am suffering anxiety re train & hotel! No post yesterday (I wrote you about 3 p.m. Letter will go out with this one at mid day). Back almost better, thank goodness. Went to inspect the uncle's fields last night (evening). Another scary walk back in the dark! Also saw the rice mill at work. By general standards the Dass family is pretty well off, I suppose. One lot of fields cost him 15,000 rupees (over £1000). He sold some of his wife's jewellery to pay for it, he tells me. With 4 daughters to provide dowries for, of course, he must be a bit worried about [the] future. Hope he hasn't run away with the idea that <u>I</u> can contribute to anything. You can never tell really what is expected. People still come just to stare at me, but am used to it now, so it doesn't bother me so much. Keep your fingers crossed for me that by the time you read this letter I have a flush "toilet" within a step or two of my bedroom. Directly I have that amenity don't suppose I shall want to go. Here I have to go all the time. Psychological, I expect. Darling, will close now & send all my love, & to the girls.

B. xxxx

Just had stomach-turning looking breakfast placed in front of me!!!

Box 18, Folder 1 (McFarlin)
Timmapuram
From a letter to Penny Scott
18 March 1964, 6 p.m.

My Darling,

This afternoon your two letters of Friday 13th arrived (posted Sat. 14th). You'd just had mine of the prev. Mon & Tuesday, & told me about

Sheila Watson passing you in the street, etc., also about sleepless night. Tonight, fingers crossed, my last night here. After bullock cart ride this morning have done washing, pleading unwellness (partly true). Have gargled with TCP in case I've got a cold or something. The constant humidity & heat leads you to take risks from fans, etc. I'm just praying that come Monday I'll be OK & not <u>stuck</u> here with feverish chill. How awful! The boys have just brought in a baby bleating goat. Well, at other times I suppose I'd find it interesting. Before I go tomorrow at 3 shall try like anything to get the postman to check whether there is anything for me.

[…] This place is a kind of nightmare, basically, only one never wakes up from it. This afternoon had fantasy of cancelling the whole of the rest of trip & flying home. Am still v. much wondering whether I can cope with that Russian cold after this awful heat. If you want an excuse to put off Nadia [Gant] in Paris you could always tell her I'm seriously considering flying <u>home</u> from Delhi instead of to Moscow. But don't let us raise our own hopes about it too much. If Calcutta onwards is civilized may feel more like tackling the whole town. Isn't it absurd? One is <u>paid</u> for, to come away on this theoretically marvellous tour. But oh, the loneliness & homesickness. Never, never again. If they ever want me to go away, shall stipulate <u>double</u> tickets. Not that I'd dream of making you swallow India. Think now we should <u>all</u> have gone to Spain on the £500. But then, how long would it have lasted? Perhaps 6 weeks. So why didn't we? The whole summer holiday. I was mad. This trip isn't wasted, but think of all kinds of ways in which it could have been better.

Darling, thanks for agreeing re present sending. Glad you like Harrods. Wondering seriously whether there is anything in <u>this</u> country worth bringing home. After all, what would you do with a sari. Fabulous ones for £20, but £20 at Harrods a better buy? How is the diamond & ruby ring? You've not mentioned it recently. If it's lost or stolen please tell me, so that I can get used to the idea. What would you like to do when I get home? Just be at home or do something glam? Like a weekend at the Compliant Angler?[22] How I long for England. Don't worry about these miserable letters. It's my safety valve, to complain. In one way it is much worse for you, & I know it. Only you <u>do</u> have a LOO!!! See that Ruby has been sentenced & is to appeal. And Cypress is all quiet for the moment. Shortly Mr. Dass will join me & start shouting about god. Oh dear. Thought the bullock cart ride had done for my back again, but it seems to be OK after all. Wonder whether it is now warmer in England? Can't even imagine what it's like to feel cold. Darling, shall write again in the morning, & put both then together. Hope they turn up at the same time. All my Love, & to the girls, & try to get better sleep.

B. xxxx

Actually, I suppose, Timmapuram is very FUNNY!!!

Box 18, Folder 1 (McFarlin)
Ritz Hotel Hyderabad
From a letter to Penny Scott
20 March 1964, 2.30 p.m.

My Darling,

Here I am safe & sound & luxurious after a truly nightmare journey from Timmapuram. Got here about 10:30 a.m. V. swish. 30 rupees a day all in = £2.5.0, but beer costs about 8/- a bottle! Even as I was at the reception desk, a <u>call</u> came though for me from a friend of Mr. Ullal's. After a bath & a beer I went to his factory & he took me out to Chinese lunch. Didn't care for him much, but <u>anyone</u> to talk to in a civilized manner. Was brought back here in the firm's car—meant to rest but instead must write you in hope letter will be posted today. <u>Also</u> when I got back letter from Mr. Ullal inviting me to stay with him in Madras or go to a friend of Monica Felton. So before I close this letter shall ring airline people to see if I can get a plane on Monday or Tuesday to Madras—& also ring Ullal to tell him. He says he will meet me at airport. How kind & thoughtful everyone is.

Just before we <u>tried</u> to leave Timmapuram at 2 p.m. the postman brought yr two letters of Thursday—which was lovely. And odd, because the day before I'd had your two of Friday. Then we sat on the roadside on chairs under a tree from 2 p.m. until 3:30 waiting for bus. At Elluru,

5 p.m., they didn't know whether I had managed to get a booking on the Express (which started miles away in Puni). So settled for the passenger. At last minute Dass whisked me into town to have our picture taken. I was nearly screaming with frustration, fear of missing the train. I made it alright because the train was late. I was the <u>only</u> 1st class passenger in a <u>whole</u> empty carriage. "Guard your life & your property, sir", Mr. Dass said. So I grinned & locked everything. Train left about 6:30. About 10 p.m. it was 25 miles down the line at a junction. Guard came. "Lock up, sir. Do not answer if anyone knocks". Got off & went to see what was happening re Express. It had arrived. <u>Got a sleeping berth.</u> Safe at last. But no pillows, no sheet. Just me in my filthy trousers & shirt & 3 silent Indians asleep in dhotis. By contrast here I have water & loo, loo, loo, & fan, & carpet & desk & laundry & people ringing me up & writing me inviting me to Madras. And food that doesn't make me want to vomit. Sorry about the last 10 days' tale of woe, but really was often near the end of tether, afraid for health & of <u>snakes</u>. "Do not walk there, sir", Mr. Dass said one night—walking me back in the dark w/out lights, "at such times, in such places, snakes creep"!!! Poor Dass & family. They did their level best & sent respects very seriously to you & the girls & repeated the invitation to stay there. When I'm in Calcutta I'll send them your best wishes […].

All my love to all the family,

B. xxxx

Box 18, Folder 1 (McFarlin)
Ritz Hotel Hyderabad
To Penny Scott
21 March 1964, 11 a.m.

My Darling,

Just back from shopping run in kind of private taxi, 8 rupees and short sight-seeing trip round town. The place is full of old palaces that belonged to the Nizam family. Some are gone to ruin, others used by State as offices & museums. The old Nizam only has 7 palaces left,

poor chap. He was (is) you may remember the Muslim ruler of a virtually Hindu State. There are only mosques, no Hindu temples. Present
Muslim population—35 people. India took Hyderabad by force in 1948,
when Nizam threatened either to join Pakistan or retain sovereignty
(another kind of thing mentioned in <u>The Birds of Paradise</u>). Now he is
Nizam in name only. In his day the discrepancy between the richness of
the palaces (10,000 servants) & the surrounding squalor must have been
awful. The <u>only</u> decent buildings are palaces, ex-palaces. The roads are
very wide, tho', made so just to accommodate the princely processions
of elephants, etc. This hotel very peaceful this morning. I sat in an enormous lounge, alone, working under the fan, drinking a lime juice & soda
& occasionally looking out to the terrace beyond, which in Hyderabad
is just a vista of flatness & distant lake, close by—the roofs of some
new apartment bldg. The hotel is built on a hill, & was called in the old
days The Hill Fort Palace. Got 200 Players No. 3 (my favourite in India)
29 rupees = £2-3.0—about same as UK. The airlines booking office is
only 5 mins. drive away, so shan't have far to go, come Tuesday morning.
Feel rested & less anxious now. Think I've been in need of time & place
to myself where I can catch my breath, & just let my mind go blank. No
doubt, but in this world you have to pay for peace & quiet & comfort.
Suddenly the hotel feels more friendly to me—I mean this place itself.
It's always a question of getting to know the ropes & the layout before
you can truly relax. Should spend rest of this morning writing letters.
I owe the girls one each especially. Shall also look through my diary/
address book to see if there is someone I ought to write to at this stage.

Not mid day yet but the sky is already puny-blue with heat haze. No
sound here except distant aircraft, sparrows. Until now, in India, the
constant sound of the crows has been the most noticeable—enormous
blue-black creatures with long gun-metal beaks. Close to you they look
a bit like Minty when she has her head on one side, inquiringly. In Timmapuram there were turkeys as well as hens. In the house there were two
broody hens sitting on turkey eggs. Wonder if they will have a shock
when they see what they've been hatching? That place always seems far
away. Don't regret having <u>been</u>, now that I've got away. I kept thinking,

too, how awful if we had both gone there, expecting the kind of rest & peace I was expecting only to find that truly primitive surrounding. Awful thing is, of course, that the Dass family, comparatively, lives in luxury. Oh, I met the wife finally, when I took colour pictures—but could hardly tell her from the other women in the household. This business of women being tied to the kitchen is very odd—but then Dass only twice ate at the same time & in the same room as I did, & then was when we had chicken pulao, the only thing I could eat with relish. So it's no surprise that the women had to treat me as if I were their master. Dass, by the way, was very critical of my smoking. "Sir, I think you smoke very severely." "Sir, I think you are spoiling your health." Felt often like saying, "If I don't smoke I shall scream." Must have smoked nearly 50 a day there, & was afraid of running out & going mad! Re loo: Kulkar told me last night that he knew young Indians in London who hardly ate anything for a week because they couldn't stand the "horror" of the pedestal with water in it. But then my point was I had to go so often & in full view of people as I walked to the place (& I had to take the tissue secretly, so as not to outrage them).

I hope there aren't too many things you've written me about that I've failed to comment on, or answer. In one letter (last Friday's or Thursday's) you referred to letter about long talk with Roland [Gant]. Wonder whether that was in the missing letter re how you spent Keek's party evening? Noted the south of France. Maybe we'd better make it Spain, some other part of the Costa Brava? Really don't know, do you darling? It's nearly mid day, or 6.30 with you, Sat morning. Tomorrow you'll be closer, only 4½ hours behind our time, although I believe Calcutta is 1 hour ahead of rest of India.[23]

All my Love Darling,

B xxxx

Box 10, Folder 2 (McFarlin)
78 Addison Way
To Mollie Hamilton [M. M. Kaye]
17 April 1964

Dear Mollie,

My trip was cut short in Calcutta because of a dreary sciatica in the right leg, which what with the drug and the heat was rapidly becoming useless. I got to Agra as far as the office of Indian Airways only to find that some fool either there or in BOAC had marked my ticket with the wrong time and the plane had left 3 hours before. On the way out, cursing to high heaven, and not being nippy on my feet, my bad foot was run over by one of those slap-happy Calcutta cyclists. So I called it a day. I only missed a week of India and had already decided to cut out Moscow.

HH [His Highness] of Bharatpur had wired me suddenly not to arrive in Bharatpur before April 12 at the earliest, by which time I was definitely scheduled for my last 4 days in Delhi, so it's extremely unlikely we could have met anyway. I had hoped (and indeed planned with him) to see him when I was in Agra on April 7th and 8th. I had to give the toy pistol to a small boy in Calcutta, because it couldn't have gone through the post. I've written HH explaining.

The x-rays I had to have in Cal showed that I had something called asymmetry of the lumbarsacral diarthrodal, which basically means I haven't got a space where a space should be, and is supposed to mean also that as I get older and the bones contract I have to be careful not to move in certain ways (e.g., packing a suitcase) in case I nip one of the five roots of the sciatic nerve, which I did in Madras, about 5 weeks ago. The doctor here also comes up with the pleasant news that the lower knob of the spine shows some arthritis.

Anyway, I had a pretty marvellous time, even tho' in the end it was an effort to walk 100 yards along Chowringhee! Glad I spent nearly all my time in the south, on what was new ground for me. I now have a built in excuse to go back and see the north. In the south there is prohibition, and that produces some interesting social pressures among westernised Indians. I lived entirely with Indian families (laid on for me by Allied Publishers). Of course I was out there 2 months too late from the climate point of view. It was 103 in Calcutta and 99% humidity—much higher than normal for the time of the year. But if it hadn't been for the leg and the drug I had to take I don't think I'd have cared. Hyderabad is a curious city. There's nothing architecturally of note except old palaces. The poor old Nizam only has 7 left.

At the moment am neither in London nor India. You probably felt the same. Neil Ghosh[24] was very kind. He and Caroline Davies (the Australian girl) turned up at midnight to meet me on Good Friday at Cal. The Madras plane was 2½ hours late. I split my Calcutta time between Heils and some nice people called Nag, out in Behala (about 7 miles from the centre). He is a nuclear physicist at the University and she a classical Indian singer and teacher.

Ever,

Box 3, Folder 26 (McFarlin)
78 Addison Way
To B. V. V. Narayana Dass
8 May 1964

My Dear Narayanji,

The coloured pictures I took of you and your family have all come out very well in the form of coloured slides (for use in a projector on to a screen) but Kodak in London say that they should also make good colour prints, so they are being processed at the moment, and I should get them back in about 2 weeks. I have remembered to ask for a print each for the five boys (of the two groups of them that I took). The toddy tapper was on a black and white film, and that hasn't been printed yet, but I hope to have it in time to send along with the coloured pictures.

Since returning home my elder daughter, Carol, has been in hospital with glandular fever, but she came out yesterday, and is much better. My family were of course very happy to see the pictures of you and your family, and thought the colours of the ladies' saris very beautiful.

I also am getting back to normal health, and beginning to do some work, but I think often of the time I spent with you in your village, and of the kindness of your family.

I will write a longer letter when the photographs arrive from Kodak. I shall send them to you by airmail, and hope they will arrive safely, and without too much delay. I'll write a separate letter at the time I send them, so that you will know they are on the way.

With kind regards, and best wishes to your wife and daughters, and relations.

Sincerely yours,[25]

Box 4, Folder 15 (McFarlin)
78 Addison Way
From a letter to Dr. G. E. Farreras, Paris
20 June 1964

Dear Dr. Farreras,

I am bringing my family to Paris on Wednesday, August 26th, that is to say myself, my wife, and our two daughters Carol (aged 17½) and Sally (aged 16).[26] Would it be possible to fix appointments, for the four of us, with Dr. Dao and with yourself for Thursday, August 27th […]. I think that it is very likely that my wife has caught amoebiasis from me at some time during the last 20 years. As neither of us speaks French and consultation may be difficult my wife is preparing a report on her medical history, which Mr. Roland Gant has kindly offered to translate into French […]. I myself continue to feel in excellent health, following your treatment.

With kind regards,

Sincerely yours,

Box 3, Folder 26 (McFarlin)
78 Addison Way
From a letter to B. V. V. Narayana Dass
28 June 1964

Dear Narayanji,

[…] I myself haven't been well either. I have been to Paris to see a doctor there who specialises in tropical diseases. He diagnosed that I had a thing called amoebiasis, and had had it for 20 years. Going back to India had increased the symptoms. Anyway, I had a long series of injections, and am now back home and feeling better. I have to go back to Paris in September to have another check [...].

Please tell your elder daughter and members of the family that I still have the garland of jasmine that they gave me on the last night I spent in your home. It is dried and faded now, of course, but it hangs in my study. Also the garland given to me by the priest at the temple. I often think of the happy days spent in your village. I wish that I had been in better health. I am afraid that I put your household to a lot of trouble, cooking and looking after me.

I shall write more later. Meanwhile my kindest regards to you and your family,

Box 10, Folder 2 (McFarlin)
78 Addison Way
From a letter to Mollie Hamilton [M. M. Kaye]
16 August 1964

Dear Mollie,

Hope this eventually finds you. I'm not sure of your present address; anyway you're probably in Spain or somewhere. And I'm off on holiday to Paris on the 25th, so no urgency.

Am beginning work on my India novel, and have chosen 1942 for the background. I find myself awfully forgetful—or perhaps just plain ignorant—about certain things, and I wondered then whether you or Goff could put me right.

I have this imaginary civil and military cantonment, Mayapore (I may change the name), which is also the headquarters of a District, in other words there are the Deputy Commissioner, the Deputy Superintendent of Police, and the District and Sessions Judge—on the civil side. On the service side I envisage a few units of Indian and British, perhaps a holding battalion or training depot. Where my memory fails me utterly is over the more permanent military staff. Am I right in thinking of a Station Commander (or commandant) who would be responsible for troop administration in the station, would in fact be the senior military officer—and therefore the man to whom the Deputy Commissioner would have to apply in the case of aid to the civil power? Or would he be <u>Area</u> Commander? (Wasn't that a different thing?) If he is Station Commander would his rank be full colonel, or higher? I want him as a full colonel, therefore outranking any battalion commander who may be in Mayapore. And I want him to be responsible for the conduct of the troops when called out in aid. If he <u>is</u> station commander, what kind of staff would he have? Am I right in thinking the unit commanders in the district would be responsible to him for general administration and discipline, but of course not to him, but to formation commanders (in another part of the province) for training and internal admin, etc?

You see what happens in Mayapore, in August 1942 (after Mr. Gandhi is arrested and the Congress Party's civil disobedience campaign goes into operation) is that the Deputy Commissioner has to admit that he has lost control and therefore calls in Colonel X—who rules the town for several days (with results not unlike those effected by poor old General Dyer in Amritsar, 23 years earlier). I have my Colonel X pretty clearly in mind as a character, but I have yet to fit him into an authentic role. This, for me, is a sort of period novel. I'm having to do all kinds of research into things like Missions and civil administration, and now military. This is only for background details, but I do want to get them as right as possible. The book really is about different people, an Indian woman called Lady Chatterjee and an English girl called Daphne Manners. [...]

Ever,

Box 16, Folder 2 (McFarlin)
78 Addison Way
To N. K. D. Purkayastha
23 September 1964

My Dear Nimu,

I have just returned home from Paris to find your letter of 2 September waiting for me, and hasten to answer it in the hope that it reaches you before you leave again on the 30th. If not, I'm sure your wife will forward it to you. It was a great sorrow to me to come to Calcutta and not be able to see you again. Your wife and your brother and sister-in-law, and Nag, and your little son, all greeted me with great kindness, though, and I was pleased to be in your home, and to feel in touch with you again. I would have seen your family again but unfortunately I was unwell and had to see a doctor and have an x-ray for my leg. I have also been unwell again since returning to England, which is why I have had to be in Paris. Apparently ever since I was in India in 1943 I have had a tropical infection, which returning to India made worse. Now, though, I have had a series of injections and feel well again, although the course of cure takes about 2 years. If ever I return to India it will have to be with a case full of medicines!

Your wife and Mrs. Nag gave a wonderful present for me to bring home to my wife, a sari. I know that my wife has written to thank them, but I do so again now—and for the sweetmeats for my own children.

From Calcutta I was supposed to go on to Agra, Benares, and Delhi, and then return to England from Delhi via Moscow and Sweden. But all that fell through, which was annoying, but couldn't be helped. Anyway I was glad to be in Calcutta. It is still my favourite Indian city, in spite of what some people think about it. I thought that Nag looked just the same, except for the fact that he was a bit fatter! I expect he told you that I now have a lot of grey hair. I wonder how you are looking? Very smart in your Jemadar's uniform.

Glad to hear that you had a letter from Narayana Dass. I think I was a lot of trouble to his wife when I stayed in his village, because my illness was beginning and I couldn't eat much. I think she thought it was because I didn't like Indian food, but during the whole of the 2 months I was in India I only had 2 European meals, because I don't like European food out of Europe. Dass has 3 very nice daughters—one now of marriage-able age. I think she is to marry a man from Bangalore some time next year, if the plans materialise.

Please give my kindest regards and thanks to your wife, Mr. and Mrs. Nag and Mr. and Mrs. Hiren Roy. And of course, to you, I send my very sincere good wishes.

Box 11, Folder 19 (McFarlin)
78 Addison Way
To Arthur Warne, Maw Ellis Warne & Co.
3 October 1964

Dear Arthur,

A few weeks ago you raised the question of our elder daughter's full-time education. I wasn't able to answer it fully at the time, because we hadn't had her GCE[27] result and weren't sure what she'd be doing.

Just before we went on holiday at the end of August we had the news she had failed, so I wrote to the Head of the full-time cramming college she'd been going to and told him she'd not be coming back this term. Back now, she is doing a course in Stage Managership at the Tavistock Repertory Theatre in Islington—for which a small fee is paid. She is also doing an evening course of shorthand-typing. The stage managing course is evenings only (as is the shorthand typing), but as the season progresses and she becomes involved in practical work with productions, the number of evenings and hours spent will increase. I'm not sure where this leaves us. She is not doing a job in the sense of earning any money, and won't be, so far as I can see, for some time to come.

The younger daughter, Sally, passed all eleven of her GCE levels, six with first grades (monstrous child!) so goes into the sixth form for the two-year A level course, after which we hope she will be able to go to University.

Is my Children's Tax allowance affected in relation to Carol? We have realised, too, that we have to get in touch with the Family Allowance people to tell them the situation. I expect our 8/- a week for Sally will therefore be withdrawn.

Yours ever,

Box 13, Folder 8 (McFarlin)
78 Addison Way
From a letter to John Willey, William Morrow & Company, USA
18 October 1964

Dear John,

[...] Life has been a bit hectic over here, what with the election,[28] and the news about Roland [Gant] leaving Secker to take over the editorial chair at Heinemann—which I'm sure you know about. I think he goes at the beginning of the year. This is rather a blow to me personally, although we can obviously continue to be associated, since Secker is an associated company, but I had always had hopes of Roland eventually inheriting Secker. I'm glad for him, but sorry for me. Heinemann is a much more powerful position for him. I rather think he was in a cleft stick over the decision. If he'd refused the Heinemann organisation would, I suppose, have marked him off as a man without real ambition—and that would probably have meant a disappointment for him at Secker when the time came for Fred [Warburg] to retire—which after all can't be many years away.

What a shake up, internationally. K[hrushchev] gone from the Kremlin, the Tories from Downing Street, Mr. Jenkins from the White House, a bomb in Asia and Roland [Gant] leaving Secker. On election day I was up at 5.30 a.m., working on behalf of the Liberals, and got to bed at 2 a.m. the following day. We've had a liberal council in this area for a number of years, but failed to send our candidate to the House in this election. The Tory majority was halved, though, from 16,000 to 8,000.

A year ago this weekend I was with you in Norwalk. The weather is sunny as it was then. My best to you all,

                                        Ever,

Box 5, Folder 1 (McFarlin)
78 Addison Way
To Dorothy Ganapathy
23 October 1964

My Dear Dorothy,

So many thanks for your letter (of the 19th) and also for your Diwali greeting card, which came in the same post this morning. I send my own greetings to you for the festival (November 5 this year? That's our Guy

Fawkes night, too, of course). First I must say how angry I was at that tale of the Harpy Mem. Just like the time before. I shall be wary of a call. Trouble is, about a week ago my publisher rang and said he'd had a letter from a Mrs. Mukherjee, saying she'd got my book and wanted to write to me, so could she have my address. I said, of course, naturally; and only afterwards wondered why Cuckoo couldn't have rung you up and asked for it. I supposed poor Cuckoo had undertaken to let these Davidson people know it, and couldn't get out of it. It's sweet of her to send me a tie, and I suppose if they call I shall have to cope, unless I can think of some splendid off-the-cuff excuse (e.g., that I've taken not to wearing shirts with collars!) or can't receive people between November and August. But you did absolutely right, Dorothy. Those awful women think they can get away with murder. That business at Sun and Sand, calling on Mr. Tipton, wasn't the last experience I had during my trip of such women. And wives think they're memsahibs, too. I used to observe them with a mixture of disgust and amusement in the air-conditioned coffee room of Spencer's in Madras. When giving their order to the waiter they never <u>looked</u> at him, never said thank you, or gave any indication of being aware that their coffee didn't come out of the air, the moment they said "Coffee!" At home, of course, they would put up with being called "dear" by the waitress, and think nothing of it. Unless of course they were serving the coffee themselves, and calling the customers "dear". When I was with you, and we had that business with Mr. Tipton's lady dragon, you tried to pretend that it was an isolated case; but I could tell it wasn't, and my meetings, subsequently, with English people confirmed it, and confirmed my suspicions of the kind of thing Indians are still having to put up with in the name of Technical Progress, or whatever it's supposed to be called. If the Davidsons turn up here, of course, she will probably be as nice as pie, and if I'm cool I shall be, curiously, in the wrong. English social manners are very circumscribing! I shall feel I want to strangle her with the tie. Shall report in due course.

I have mislaid that letter you so kindly sent me in Paris (I love hearing from my friends when I'm away from home). I don't think I commented on the news you told me about Mr. Manaktala and Mr. Churamani.

I liked them both, and am sorry to think of Manaktala no longer connected to Allied. But glad for C, who I know was a bit browned off
with Calcutta. Incidentally, when I got home the other day there was my
overcoat, waiting for me. I haven't opened the parcel yet because I shall
only do so when I can send it straight round to the cleaner. It must look
a mess, parcelled up all that time. But I'm sure it's the right coat, and
I'm glad, because I didn't want to have to buy another. Thought of you
a lot in Paris—walking past the Sorbonne, and all the places I imagined
you'd have been. Did you ever go to the flower market on the Ile de la
Cite? There was a Son et Lumiere performance at Notre Dame—very
impressive.

Look after yourself, Dorothy, and don't go around getting fevers
again. I shall (just have) hold Ganesh to send you luck.

Will write again soon. Please let me know directly the book arrives.[29]
The press has been very good, except in The Observer, where an old
"friend" of mine called John Davenport tore me to shreds in 6 lines or
so. Have you read Naipaul's book on his return to India? An Area of
Darkness. Very good press over here, but I don't like the sound of it.
Daily Telegraph wanted me to review it but I was off to Paris.

Love as ever,

Box 4, Folder 15 (McFarlin)
78 Addison Way
From a letter to Kathleen Farrell
27 October 1964

My Dear Kathleen,

[…] On the whole I've begun to hate the slavery and actual physical
act of writing. It's much better when it goes on in my head. When I put
pen to paper I find it so difficult to believe. It's all a question of finding the formula—the meeting point of idea, form and development.
Wish I could just go on with well-tried formulas. On the whole people
hate it when you do something different. They feel you've let them
down in some curious way. Curiously I think a lot of people will never

quite forgive me for catching them on the hop with <u>The Bender</u>. I mean I think that tho' they may have liked it they didn't think <u>I</u> should have written it.

All well. Just off to Paris again for a few days tomorrow night.

Love,

Box 9, Folder 12 (McFarlin)
78 Addison Way
To Mr. Charles Alva Hoyt, Bennet College, NY
14 December 1964

Dear Mr. Hoyt,

That was kind of you to send me, through Morrow, a preview of your piece about <u>The Corrida at San Feliu</u>, for the Louisville <u>Courier-Journal</u>. I much appreciate it, and am gladdened, of course, by what you say.

Naturally enough a number of reviewers have mentioned an initial fear that I was just pasting bits and pieces together. I don't think, though, that any of them in the end seriously accused me of doing that. I was prepared for it, though. In fact there were times when the book was such a puzzle to me that I even accused myself of doing a scissors and paste job. However, of the pieces that make up the text as it stands only the two short pieces, "The Arrival at Playa de Faro" and "The Arrival in Mahwar" had origins prior to the origin of the book itself. But even those two are part and parcel of the overall scheme, in fact you could say the genesis of it. I wrote the "Playa de Faro" paragraphs about 5 years ago; and some years later some passages similar to the Mahwar passages. In each case I was attempting a story about two people turning up in disgrace. The idea of this did actually come to me in Spain. So you could say that I was really acting out Edward Thornhill without quite knowing it. When Edward Thornhill finally emerged as a fictional persona of the narration, those two earlier pieces fitted into place. Although even then I didn't use them in the first version of the novel, which got to round about page 140 before I scrapped it and started again. In the first version a young man arrived to interview Thornhill—and Thornhill told him the details of a story that he was writing. In the final version this became the self-contained "Leopard Mountain". And of course for the final version the complete story "The First Betrayal" had to be written from scratch, and the two arrival pieces rewritten to fit them to Thornhill's experience. It was a fascinating exercise in the awful business of suspending one's own disbelief in fiction, and at the same time getting away from the limiting factor of the "I" narrator. Even in a third-person narration there is an extra character off stage, one who never appears—the person who is telling the story.

I hope this letter doesn't bore you. I only write it to try to repay your courtesy in sending me your review.

All best wishes,

Sincerely yours,

Box 12, Folder 12 (McFarlin)
78 Addison Way
To Valerie Meidlinger[30]
28 December 1964

Dear Mrs. Meidlinger,

Thank you very much for your kind letter of the 17th, which was forwarded by Eyre & Spottiswoode. It reached me on Christmas Eve.

I am only too glad to hear from anyone who has got some pleasure out of what I have written—particularly from <u>The Corrida at San Feliu</u>. My publishers told me that their South African agent had reported immense difficulty getting the bookshops to take it, and that only a review in <u>Time</u> had made them change their minds. So you can imagine how pleased I was to hear from a reader in Johannesburg, especially from one who obviously enjoyed the book in the way it was supposed to be enjoyed.

I was never actually in Johannesburg, but years ago I spent a couple of months in South Africa, in Cape Province. When I received your letter I thought, from the writing on the envelope, that it was from someone I knew years ago in Rondebosch, from whom I haven't heard for a very long time. The handwriting, in fact, is really identical. So even before

I opened your letter I felt that I had received a Christmas present from an old friend. Opening it I was touched to realise that it was from a stranger.

I doubt that I shall ever return to South Africa. If I did, I'm afraid I should probably be deported within a short space of time. Even in India—to which I returned this year after a long absence—I seemed to say the wrong things to the Europeans. Perhaps it is as well—when I was in South Africa I was much younger, naturally, and perhaps more thoughtless, and responded mainly to the tremendous beauty of the place, and the immense sense of well being which that particular climate fills you with, and it is a memory that probably ought not to be spoiled. Which may be what I had in mind when speaking of curiosity as destructive.

I'm afraid that if you read all my books you will be disappointed. Once I have corrected the proofs I never read them again. Sometimes I have tried, but find that I have grown out of them. The furthest back you should go is The Birds of Paradise—with the possible exception of an earlier one called The Mark of the Warrior, which I still have a certain affection for.

I am sorry to hear that you have been ill. I hope that when this letter reaches you, you will have put the hospital behind you.

I am sure, by the way, that you are right about your son. Knocking about one half of the world anyway, I have been struck by the thought that some people are bigger than their country, some countries bigger than their people, and some countries and people which seem strangely complementary. South Africa, curiously enough, is in the latter category. I think that one day this will be proved in the best possible way.

Thank you for writing.

Yours very sincerely,

Box 18, Folder 8 (McFarlin)
78 Addison Way
To Fredric J. Warburg, Martin Secker & Warburg, Ltd.
10 February 1965

My Dear Fred,

Thank you for that letter—couched in such generous terms. David [Higham], of course, told me several days ago that the transfer to Heinemann had been agreed in principle, but I thought I would delay writing to you until all the details were ironed out—a process which from the sidelines looks complicated but which I suppose the accountants will find fairly easy. However, you have got in first with a letter, which gives me the opportunity to say how much I appreciate the friendly way you and your colleagues—and particularly you—have met a request which was not easy to make.[31]

Just what combination of circumstances it is that leads to an author doing well on one list and not on another I simply don't know. From my point of view it remains a mark of distinction to be a Secker author. At the same time it has begun to look as if I'm simply not cut out to be one. The reception of the last two novels was disappointing for both of us, and I have been fairly acutely conscious of the actual loss to the firm. My own loss has been one of confidence, not—fortunately—in my ability to write but in the fortunes attending the result. Perhaps Roland [Gant]'s move to Heinemann has been the happy solution to what increasingly looked to me like an insoluble because perplexing situation. Without his move, to a firm within the group, well—as you say—there could have been no question but that each side would see the contract through. Perhaps the new novel would have reversed the trend, and we should all then have been happy. But after two failures I think it is true to say that the smell of failure somehow persists, and another failure would have left the future looking pretty black, from my point of view as a full-time professional writer. Unfortunately, in this kind of situation, there is so often a cumulative effect. I really don't know what kind of reversal of fortune can be looked for in a change of publisher. There can certainly be no magic in change for change's sake. But perhaps the new combination will prove to be the fortunate one. If it isn't then for me it will be a case of the famous agonizing reappraisal. By then I shall have had six years of freedom to devote to writing, and considering the kind of books I write, I suppose that's not too bad. If the new combination is the fortunate one, then at least I shan't be leaving behind, at the end of the contract, the sour taste of unearned balances.

The one thing in this odd business that I am sure about is this: that I don't for a moment regret leaving Eyre & Spottiswoode. As a middle-aged novelist I felt that at least I should indulge myself in the luxury of working with a man who spoke the same language as myself, and of course it is true that I came to Secker because Roland came there. There are moves he could have made that would not have found me joining him. And I should like to make it clear, Fred, that I haven't sought to follow him to Heinemann simply for the sake of following him. This is why earlier in this now too-long letter I referred to his move as possibly a happy solution to a perplexing situation. What I have been after in this business of assigning the contract is a way of transferring the investment—the subsidy if you like—from you who entered into it willingly and have so far found it doesn't work, to someone who will enter it just as willingly and may find it works. Clearly, this could not have been done outside the group. One of the bonuses of the transfer is that I continue to work with Roland. The other bonus is in the thought that (always assuming the Secker and Heinemann accountants don't come to blows) our all too brief association can end with each of us knowing we did our best and, for me, without any guilty feeling about money. Perhaps I shall have to transfer the guilty feeling about money to my association with Heinemann, but I put my trust—and it's all I can do—in the rough magic of the new formula.

There is one thing I should very much like: if you, and David [Farrer] and Roland would all have lunch with me presently. I suggest Tuesday, March 2nd. Not only because it is far enough away to make the three-some (foursome) likely, because it is Shrove Tuesday and we can have pancakes. 1 p.m., at the Epicure?

Ever,

Box 5, Folder 15 (McFarlin)
78 Addison Way
To Doctor Howard B. Gotlieb, Chief of Reference and Special Collections
Boston University Libraries
15 February 1965

Dear Doctor Gotlieb,

Thank you very much for your letter of December 17th, which has been a long time in the mails and has only just reached me. It is good of you to think of me in connexion with your plans for a collection of original material. I am, naturally enough, extremely flattered that you should do so. I should like to thank you, also, for the personal note on which you end your letter.

Last year the University of Texas acquired practically all the material that was available. The exception was the manuscript of my last novel, <u>The Corrida at San Feliu</u>, which is at present lodged at the bank complete with all working notes, proofs, etc. And of course some time this year there will be the manuscript of the novel I'm at present working on. I don't know whether the University of Texas will eventually wish to add this material to the collection they already have, but when the time comes for me to dispose of it, I think I shall have to discuss it with them first, although I am not under any actual obligation to do so.

I thought I should let you know what the position currently is. As for correspondence: Texas do have a few of my letters—perhaps a dozen in all—but otherwise my files, such as they are, are still intact, and I suppose that one day, once they were sorted out, there might be something worth preserving.

I am sorry that my immediate response to your very kind inquiry can't be more cooperative. May I ask you whether I should continue to bear your interest in mind? I am keen to ensure that from time to time original material is safely deposited and preserved, and I suppose an ideal arrangement is for that to be done all under one roof. This may not always prove possible, however, and I should be grateful if you would tell me whether, from your point of view, a Texas collection rules out one in Boston as well.

With kind regards,

Yours sincerely,

Box 8, Folder 10 (McFarlin)
78 Addison Way
To Miss Jean Leroy, David Higham Associates, Ltd.
19 March 1965

My Dear Jean,

Here, signed, is the BBC agreement for the schools broadcast extract from <u>The Birds of Paradise,</u> which was nice to hear about. I also agreed to the reprinting of the extract in the programme pamphlet and the fee of five guineas. I don't know whether that becomes an anthology right within the meaning of my E & S contract. (They have no interest in the actual broadcasting of extracts.)

Kay Fuller came long the other day with Peter Duval Smith, and they recorded about 30 minutes or more of tape interview.[32] I don't really know how it went, but they seemed pleased. The questions were not all that original!

You ask how we all are. Carol has been doing a course in stage management at the Tavistock Rep in Islington, and was given the job of stage managing that Russian play <u>A Million for a Smile</u>, which got a good write up in <u>The Times</u>. She has an interview at RADA this week, in the hope of being accepted for their 12-month stage management course; and in the summer hopes to go with the Tavistock to Arles to put on <u>A Winter's Tale</u> in the old Roman arena. I'm glad she's so keen on theatre, but especially glad that she doesn't want to be Sarah Bernhardt. Sally is hard at work for her A levels, and goes to Florence with the nuns at Easter. The girls of course plan to slip out of the back door while the nuns are asleep and go haring off on the back of Lambrettas. Penny and I are simply drudging. The first 100,000 words of the new novel are finished. Only another 50,000 to go!

Love,

Box 3, Folder 26 (McFarlin)
78 Addison Way
From a letter to B. V. V. Narayana Dass
20 March 1965

My Dear Narayanji,

[…] Yes, it is a year now since I was in Timmapuram. I have often thought of my pleasant stay in your village, and of all the kindness of yourself and your family. It is a pity that I was not in very good health at that time. I'm afraid I gave your family a lot of trouble […]. Do you still have […] the same barber? I remember sitting on the veranda of your house in the morning, being shaved by him. At first I was astonished that he should shave without using soap, but presently realized that soap was unnecessary. It was very soothing and refreshing […]. With kindest regards,

Very sincerely,[33]

Box 2, Folder 12 (McFarlin)
78 Addison Way
From a letter to Mr. Nicholas G. Brownrigg, Albuquerque, NM
12 May 1965

Dear Mr. Brownrigg,

[…] You ask about my earlier books. The blurbs on the back of The Corrida are—I believe, accurate in the sense that they are lifted out of favourable reviews, and not snipped out of bad ones. You might like The Birds of Paradise. The Bender is what I call a sad comedy, and hardly a novel at all because I wasn't extending myself technically. But I enjoyed writing it, and wanted to do a book about modern London for once. Don't bother with any of the others, with the possible exception of an earlier novel called The Mark of the Warrior. These three, and The Corrida, are the only ones I can still look in the face. Although I must confess that by "look in the face" I only mean think about. Once

I've corrected the page proofs of a novel I feel it's dead, and I never read it again.

Incidentally, I believe that the only thing Thornhill and I had in common is the mounting hysteria, as a book nears completion, the nightmare of the mss being lost or destroyed, which has led me (as it led Thornhill) to put it in the boot of the car if I go out for a day! (leaving at home the holograph, but that seldom bears much resemblance to the typescript). I have to keep a typescript up to date because after a week or two I can't decipher my own handwriting. It's the ts that carries all the corrections. It ends up looking like a scissors and paste job.

Thank you for writing to me. All best wishes,

Sincerely,

Box 13, Folder 9 (McFarlin)
78 Addison Way
To John Willey, William Morrow & Company, USA
19 June 1965

Dear John,

Many thanks for yours of the 15th. I contacted Helen [King] yesterday at the Connaught and we've fixed June 29 for an evening together. I'll wait and see what the weather is like before deciding what we'll do. She sounded in her usual good form and grateful to Greece for having given her some sunshine (precious little of it here).

Tomorrow I drive early to London airport to meet my Bombay hostess [Dorothy Ganapathy], who is spending a month or two in Europe. By Bombay hostess I mean the woman who volunteered to put a roof over my head when Allied Publishers were wondering whatever to do with me when I arrived. To her a lot is owed—and the new novel will be dedicated to her. Of Rajput origins she was educated in London and Paris. Maybe if the mood is right I'll get her to meet Helen.

John, your letter is a great encouragement. I wrote to people here at the same time I wrote you, but such cold water was thrown on the idea of delivering only 4 or 5/7ths that I lost heart, and have sat on the type-script, which (with 4 carbons) looks like the leaning tower of Pisa.[34] And the longer I sit on it, the more it leans. I'm not sure now what the typist will deliver next week, part 6, I suppose. I've not sent anything off to you yet, because I can't cope with the postal complexities. At this end the feeling was that unless the whole was delivered at once it wouldn't be possible to tell whether it was "too long", so I decided to take nothing up to London at all, but wait until the whole was here at N.W.11. Then they can read it and distribute it.

Point is, please take your time reading it. It wasn't written to be read in a night, or even in a fortnight. It either works as it is written or doesn't work at all. It may be an awful mess, or it may be good. It certainly isn't casual. Nothing is on its way to you yet, but don't let that worry you. Perhaps you'd really prefer to have the whole thing in one batch. Be that as it may, whenever and however it arrives, please read it at the pace you want to read it. Because that's the pace of the impression I want to hear about eventually. Once I've got it out of the house I have a couple of lectures to prepare and some reviewing to do, so I shan't be minus an occupation.

If you're writing to Helen please ask her to try to remember to ask me the story of the Monk who went around saying "Would you like to see what I can do with my cherry red lips and my lily white hands?" Maybe she knows the answer already. But every so often I fall off my chair, thinking about it.

Our love to Fern: and please tell her she'd better bring you over next year, or else.

Carol, who is working 12 hours a day at her Stage Management course at RADA[35] is dressing the American student presently playing the Helen Hays part of The Glass Menagerie. Dressing, lighting, scene shifting, panatrope: even a line in a Restoration Play, which I now know myself because she rehearses it on the landing, between bedroom and bathroom: "Madam, Mr. Medley sends to know whether a visit would not be troublesome this afternoon". Question: Is Mr. Medley an agent? And is Madam the editress of LHT? (or is he an edit<u>or</u>).

Ever,

Box 9, Folder 8 (McFarlin)
78 Addison Way
To Nell Higham[36]
29 June 1965

My Dear Nell,

Something David said on the phone today suggests it might be useful if I explain our Indians in advance. The darker-skinned one is Mrs. Broome. She is married to an Englishman, Mr. Justice Broome, and lives in Allahabad. (There are two Eurasian daughters presently over here, but neither will be at the party—at least I don't think so). Mr. Justice Broome is in India still. Mrs. Broome is known as Agnes, or Aggie—the name she got at her first (convent) school in India.

The lighter skinned one is her sister, Dorothy. Dorothy was my hostess in Bombay—a dear woman; about 55 or so. A widow, once married to a chap called Ganapathy (pronounced Gunner-putty), who was in the IMS (Health Office Bombay). He died years ago. She has no children. Dorothy Ganapathy (friend of a man in the Allied Publishers, Ltd.) is the daughter of a Rajput called, I think, Sir Hari Singh Gaur, who founded the university at Saugor, in India. She was educated in England and at the Sorbonne. Much more cosmopolitan than Aggie—smokes and drinks. Aggie drinks but doesn't smoke. Fluent English, of course, in both cases.

We're both looking forward enormously to seeing you again. Ragnar Svanström and Roland and Nadia will be here, and—if we can get him, Gerry Hanley. I hope Carol will get home in time to say hello before the party ends. She's working night and day at RADA, at the Vanbrugh Theatre, and if she turns up, won't do so until about 11.30, wearing jeans, a dirty shirt, and bare feet covered in paint. Sally will be here, but will have to disappear to do homework!

Love,

Box 13, Folder 8 (McFarlin)
78 Addison Way
To John Willey, William Morrow & Company, USA
22 July 1965

Dear John,

As I've said to Sam, in a letter this morning, I can no longer put off replying to your letter of the 9th (having received yours of the 19th), thanking you both for the specially bound copy of The Corrida. I've delayed because the damned mails are slow, and the book itself hasn't arrived yet. It probably will, a few hours after I've posted this. But I was touched that he and you should have sent me a present like this.

You, David Higham, Dorothy Olding and Roland Gant, have all come independently to the same conclusion. The Brigadier must be reduced in rank, as it were, although he must necessarily remain, as you have adjudged. Excisions in Reid must also necessarily lead to reductions in White. We might thus lose 50 pages or so? What we must retain is Reid's picture of Mayapore (a delightful station), which is in juxtaposition to that of young Kumar's ("nothing in it that isn't ugly"); also his standing as a man of grand emotions, whose son is a prisoner, whose wife is dying, who is utterly committed to the British administrative illusion of India as somewhere curious and beautiful. Additionally, there are certain vital plotting sections in Reid (particularly in regard to the characterisation of White, and more important still, District Superintendent of police, Merrick). But you have sensed all this. You have sensed everything it was intended should be sensed. But then you always do. I have delayed my decision until hearing from you, knowing that you would balance an antipathy to Reid (whose name, spelled backwards, comes out more or less as Dyer—the General who massacred 300 odd unarmed Indian civilians in the Jallianwallah Bagh in 1919, scarcely a year after the end of a war in which the Indians died in hundreds, if not thousands. It must have been thousands)—balance an antipathy to Reid (as part of the novel), with a sympathy for the general run of what the novel is really about. Colour, and invisibility. I do remember that

Jim Finkenstaedt was concerned with Civil Rights,[37] but had no particular idea that he had reduced the problem to the one it took me a return to India to realise was the vital one.

I am pretty tired, John, after 900 odd pages. Can you (and I have asked Roland to do the same)—give chapter and verse of the places in Part 6 where your ordinary attention loses focus? I don't mean literally chapter and verse, but, by and large, solid sections where things go wrong? For once, writing a novel, I have relied upon what I think I have learned about automatic technique. I have also reduced the narrator to a mere physical nothing, as you may have noticed, but left him, somehow, in charge. Between whiles I have tried to get under the skin of the individual people. Reid, being a species that is abrupt in life but expansive on paper (so much committed to the pursuit of the wrong and the irrelevant) has probably led me, as an organiser of the material, astray. But I honestly can't feel it, or see it. I can only agree to wise decisions. And I am sure they are wise. At least I am sure now. The whole thing is too important to me to allow firing at half cock.

If I have left unanswered so many of your warming comments, it is because, warmed, any kind of comment induces a kind of extraneous chill.

So thanks. And cheers.

Ever,

Box 20, Folder 31 (McFarlin)
78 Addison Way
To Miss Alex Stuart[38]
30 August 1965

My Dear Vivian,

From Derbyshire we went straight down to Sussex, and have only just got back, so this is the reason why I haven't replied earlier to your kind letter.

The main thing, from my point of view, was to give a speech that wouldn't disappoint you and Marjorie [Harris], and the second thing to stay for as long as was reasonably possible. I'm not sure now that we should have stayed after the Monday or the Tuesday. Preserving an air of detachment is pretty wearing. Also capable of misinterpretation. Stay long enough, preserving such an air and the opposition seizes imaginary chances: e.g., to state, in my case, that the choice of PS as opening speaker was theirs (a statement never made to my face).

By Thursday I was literally shaking with controlled hysteria, and saw Swanwick as the kind of place where one could fall dead of a thrombosis on the main staircase! However, we survived. Just!

Re Gerald.[39] Yes, I agree. I didn't attend the business meeting, as you know, but apart from the brief exchange at lunch on the Tuesday, when he commiserated with me over the fact that my speech was over everybody's head, he never said a thing to me, or to Penny or to the girls, that wasn't just by way of pleasant conversation. I imagine that things would have been different if I'd boobed on Sunday morning; but all the same I found his general attitude curiously moving.

Thanks, too, for your postcard. Don't imagine JOL or T&T will actually approach me. If they do I shan't let them have it. Not because I'd be anything but grateful to you for suggesting they publish the opening talk, but because I think of it as written for speaking, rather than reading, and in a special context at that.

Love, and thanks, from us all,

Box 5, Folder 2 (McFarlin)
78 Addison Way
From a letter to Dorothy Ganapathy
11 September 1965

Dorothy my dear,

[…] Although it was sad to see you leave London I'm glad that you went on the day you did,[40] because you were back in our beloved India before all the awful things began to happen, and you would have been miserable, I think, still to be in London, when there are so many reasons for Indians to be in India at the moment. The whole thing is terribly sad, and reminds me of what Lady Manners said in one of those letters she wrote to Lili Chatterjee: "I have decided to leave Rawalpindi. I refuse to live in a place whose people at the stroke of a pen will be turned into enemies of India—the country my husband tried to serve—and you can count on it that 'enemy' isn't overstating the case. The creation of Pakistan is our crowning failure. I can't bear it. They should never have got rid of Wavell. Our only justification for two hundred years of power was unification. But we've divided one composite nation into two and everyone at home goes round saying [how] swell the new Viceroy is for 'getting it all sorted out so quickly".

[…] Penny is hard at work on her book,[41] and I am thinking about the next one, and also wondering when and how I shall make the journey back. Wish I were (sometimes) a newspaper correspondent. Then I could force my way to India, to comment on the hostilities, although my comments would probably please no one in this country….

Love,

Box 14, Folder 9 (McFarlin)
78 Addison Way
To Dipali Nag[42]
11 September 1965

My Dear Dipali,

Very many thanks for your letter of the 10th of August, which was waiting for me on my recent return home from holiday. The verses from the two ragas of the rains will, I think, be very useful for the next book in my sequence.

Meanwhile I'd be very grateful if you could advise me about the following. (I may have asked the first question earlier, but can't remember clearly.)

1. Here, in typescript, is how I have set out the two verses of the raga of the young bride leaving home:

> Dooliya le ao re more babul ke kaharwa.
> Chali han sajan ke des. Sanga ki sakha
> sabe bicchud gayee hai apne ri apne ghar jaun.

(Oh, my father's servants, bring my palanquin.
I am going to the land of my husband. All my
companions are scattered. They have gone to
different homes.)

(A morning raga.
Translated by Dipali Nag).

As you see I've made no attempt to punctuate or divide into line the
Hindi version. As I want to make it look right in print, and as I shall get
galley proofs sometime in November, I expect, I should be glad to have
your comments about punctuation and division.

2. Is the Urdu word for temple <u>mandir</u> (or mandal)?

3. Is it roughly correct to say that the full course of training for a
singer of Indian classical music is 8 years, or am I confusing it with classical dancing?

4. Is there another name for the goddess of rain, apart from Indira?
Sorry to burden you with these—especially at this moment when there
must be a lot to worry and think about (I mean re India/Pakistan). Was
hoping to hear that Dulal managed to meet those friends of mine in Sweden, but the last I heard from them he'd not been in touch. Maybe he
returned directly to India from Moscow? Had also hoped he might be in
London for a day or two on his way back, either before we went away on
holiday or after we came back. Mrs. Ganapathy, who joined us at supper
that night when Dulal was in town on his way to Moscow, flew back to
Bombay last Sunday.

Hope all is well with you, and that Dulal has enjoyed his trip.

Love,

Box 5, Folder 2 (McFarlin)
78 Addison Way
To Dorothy Ganapathy
18 September 1965

Dorothy my dear,

What a week! Rain, Crises. The news of India. I've not made up my mind, yet, what people over here really think about things. The growing impression I have from the papers <u>we</u> take (the <u>Times</u>, <u>The Daily Mail</u>, <u>The Observer</u>, the <u>Sunday Times</u>) is that liberal opinion is definitely on the side of India. But what is so interesting (historically) is that although there is an obvious and increasing feeling of responsibility, no one has yet traced that responsibility back to the failure of the British to consolidate and unify. No one has yet had the courage to say that Divide and Rule has come full circle. At best, on the man-in-the-street side, there is a faded idea of paternalism gone wrong. I expect the Koi-Hais[43] in Cheltenham are talking about the Muslims of Pakistan as if they were still the favoured blue-eyed boys. (There always was, on that level, a preference for the warrior Muslims—but this is not what opposition-thought identifies itself with.) The other day, in the Tory <u>Daily Mail</u>, there was a large photograph of Ganapatu being immersed, and a short article which was definitely on the side of India. What the English have never liked about Pakistan is the idea of an embryo-autocracy (they created it themselves, but, no matter). Where Wilson is caught is on the pincers of the Labour Mystique. Labour, after all (so they think) <u>freed</u> India. (All this is in my book, you know.) Labour now hates to think that it "allowed" Independence for its own political ends. We now have a Labour Paternalism, instead of a Tory one. They obviously imagine that they are in a paternalistic position vis-à-vis India. When they see "the children squabbling" they get out the big stick. They get it out by saying "no pocket money, and no sweets this week". (I am thinking aloud on paper.) And of course, broadly, they (we, the west) are not interested in India qua India, or in Pakistan qua Pakistan. We are interested in Total World Peace. We are afraid of China, and Russia, and France, and USA. We don't <u>look</u> at the war between India and Pakistan except in this broader sense. If we look at it too closely we see our responsibility. We pretend it's not necessary to look at it closely because a conflagration in the Indian subcontinent is globally dangerous. What is clear to me is that in the end India must be reunited. Pakistan always was an impossible concept (politically and morally). If reunification can only be brought about by war, so be it, but let us hope the Chinese and the Russians don't extend the conflict artificially. One has to live in the world as it is. This is why it is always so difficult to erase mistakes. The mistakes contribute to the total wrongness of the world, but you can't adjust the world by attempting to erase the mistakes. The total area of commitment (of human commitment) is always larger than the area of the mistake. In a way, I think this is what Shastri sees, too, and why he extended the silly Kashmir dispute by unofficially invading "Pakistan". It was the action of a big man. History might say he was mistaken, but he can never again be called small. We (myself included) tremble at the thought of what all this could lead to. There are such terrifying weapons available in the world that one has always to admire courage. I think Shastri has shown great <u>moral</u> courage. Perhaps this is the answer to the threat of hydrogen war: to bluff it. To defy it. And at the same time (from India's point of view) to defy the west. Has it yet struck you that the war with Pakistan is really an extension of getting rid of <u>us</u>? I'm sure Wavell is smiling in his grave, whereas Mountbatten is probably wearing a puzzled frown. What also will presently become notable to us, over here, if the situation continues as it is, is the lack (so far as we know) of communal war. If this situation does continue, and Indian Muslims remain Indian nationals, in 100 years time British historians will be taking credit for having solved the communal problem by turning it artificially into a national one!

Enough of all this. Family News. Carol has been selected with one other first-term (now second-term) RADA student to stage manage the new RADA production of <u>Hamlet</u> (directed by John Fernald). This means that in her third term (January, 1966) she will go with the production to Boston and Arizona for a 6-week tour. RADA provide the basic expenses (board and lodging) but I expect she will ask me for some pocket money and some new clothes. She is cockahoop (so are we) because in their second term Stage management pupils normally only became ASMs (Assistant Stage Managers) whereas she and a boy called Mike are made DSMs (Deputy Stage Managers), which in student terms means doing all the stage management work, and putting on the production. And touring the States! We all send loads of love, as always. More news presently.

Box 19, Folder 11 (McFarlin)
78 Addison Way
To Arthur Thompson[44]
21 September 1965

Dear Arthur,

Monica [Preston] gave me your new address some weeks ago, and I've been meaning to write to you, to say hello, and (latterly) to say I have my fingers crossed for you about the film deal David [Higham] told me about the other day. I won't tempt fate by saying anything more, but I hope you'll let me know the outcome.

I am, of course, most upset to hear Monica's own news of her retirement.[45] I'm sure you feel the same. I have known her since 1946—four years before I joined PP&H as it was—in the days when I was an accountant and secretary myself for a group of doomed publishers. Of all the agents' accountants I had to deal with then, it was only with Monica that I established a personal friendship. She was tough, which I admired, but human, which I found, in those days (and still do) a fairly rare quality. What I knew, from the other side of the fence, was that it was always the PP&H royalty statements that got priority attention from me. Without her, this would not have been so, I don't suppose. And of course, after all these years, from the writing side of the fence, and as an ex-colleague on the board, I know the extent of my personal loss. For me, receiving money from DHA will never be quite the same again, even if the amounts double or treble. But I suppose we have to let the times and the tides move us on with them.

I have in mind the formation of a sort of small, select Parting Gift for Monica committee—formed from among those of her author-friends whom I know. Those of us who can afford it will probably want to give her a present, and it struck me that if we joined forces we might be able to give her something more lasting than a bunch of flowers. At the moment I'm thinking of me, you, Gerald Hanley, Dorothy Eden, Jean Plaidy, Mary Patchett, James Hadley Chase. I shall drop a line to Gerry and also to Dorothy Eden (who knows Plaidy and Patchett). I'll have to extract Hadley Chase's address from DHA without the reason being known. Would you be willing to come in on such a scheme?[46]

Penny and I both send love to you and Dodo.

Ever,

Box 5, Folder 2 (McFarlin)
78 Addison Way
From a letter to Dorothy Ganapathy
3 October 1965

Dorothy, my dear,

[…] I'm afraid there is no doubt—we have antagonised India for, perhaps, the last time. The go-slow, or holding back of materials already paid for, not to mention the threat of general withholding of supplies, is something that is unforgivable. It shows how far the Labour government has moved from its old liberal principles. What I find so devastating is that not once has any influential voice been raised over here, pointing out that Britain's part in the partition of India places the burden of moral responsibility for hostilities on her shoulders. For ages now I have described to myself and to others the creation of Pakistan as our crowning failure. That everyone over here in a position of responsibility has ignored this shows, perhaps, the depth of bad conscience we have. No more of this. I am too upset to talk much about it […].

I can't remember whether I told you that I had planned, for some time, to make the next book one that examined the British attitude to Muslims and Hindus. History seems to have overtaken me. But just as the rebellion of 1942 was the background to The Jewel, I anticipated making the time of the partition the background to the next. The third and last novel (because I have been thinking in terms of a trilogy) would be modern India. And that would probably mean making the main background one of the aftermath of the present hostilities. My overall object is, of course, to examine the effects of the whole British connexion. You know where my sympathies lie, so no more said....

Love as ever,

Box 5, Folder 2 (McFarlin)
78 Addison Way
From a letter to Dorothy Ganapathy
6 October 1965

My Dear Dorothy,

[...] This is just to tell you something, so that you can hear it from me direct. Although I know there was some disagreeableness for you, when you were over here, I didn't feel I could let Agnes[47] leave England without bidding her bon voyage. So I rang the Hendon number yesterday, but found that they had left [...]. Ruby told me where Agnes was, and I got in touch with her by phone. I invited the Seths with her and Indira for next Monday, just for a few drinks and a bite to eat. Hope you understand why I felt I should do this [...].

My love, as always,

Box 4, Folder 17 (McFarlin)
78 Addison Way
From a letter to Monica Felton
18 October 1965

Dear Monica,

[...] I have just had a terrible slap in the face from an Indian I thought was unlikely to confuse British policy with friendship.[48] Still trying to work out what I did wrong. The level of emotionalism must be at a boiling point [...].

I may be coming to India again in the not too distant future. My publishers seem pleased with the new novel, and will help me with fares, etc., but I'm not sure when or where I shall go. Have the feeling that if I arrived in India now nobody would speak to me, or tell me anything! The book doesn't appear until next July, I think. They seem to want to make it a summer novel. By which time I shall have forgotten it or learned to hate it, and be in the midst of the next.

If you have anything interesting to tell me about India that you're prepared to share with me, do write me. As a result of this slap in the face I suddenly feel cut off—as if I'm wearing the clothes of an old koi-hai who never was!

As ever,

Box 16, Folder 9 (McFarlin)
78 Addison Way
To Mr. Keith C. Roy, Merck Sharp & Dohme of India Limited, Bombay, India[49]
22 October 1965

My Dear Keith,

Many thanks for your letter. I look forward to hearing from you when you're in London, and to seeing you again—if that is possible.

I ought to tell you, though (because Dorothy [Ganapathy] mentioned in a letter that she was sending a few things to us, by you), that because of something I have done since her return to India she no longer counts me as one of her friends and has made it clear that she wants nothing more to do with me. In the circumstances, as I hope you'll understand, neither Penny nor I could take the gifts she sent before I roused her anger. I don't know in what degree, if at all, the emotional climate in India at the moment has contributed to her attitude—but in any event it is most distressing. Only the thought that you might ring me, completely unaware of the situation, which would turn out to be an embarrassment for both of us, forces me to mention a subject I'd much prefer to forget, although that of course is hardly possible.

All the same, please do ring if you still feel you would like to.

As ever,

Box 6, Folder 4 (McFarlin)
78 Addison Way
To Peter Green
26 October 1965

My Dear Peter,

Very many thanks for your long letter. Jolly nice to hear from you again, and of all the family doings. The new magnum opus sounds marvellous—although doing that sort of thing would kill me (I mean all that research). Glad you liked what there was of my Times piece. Jock[50] was furious about Wardle. I wrote to him checking on your address, but didn't tell him I was reviewing the book myself. Personally, I am fed up with the Sundays, and every so often promise myself that I'll save money by giving them up entirely, but there is a horrid fascination which stops me doing so. You should have seen the killing job our old friend John Davenport did on my own last novel in The Observer.[51] Trouble was Secker brought it out in August (because of the threatened election), and it happened to coincide with a week when at last JD had been given some more novels. They appeared as novels in brief. Gerald Hanley told me later that he'd met John and John was all of a tizzy—not at the thought of having cut my throat in print but at the thought that he's probably been wrong about the book! The other reviews were very respectable. I read most of them in Paris, sitting on the edge of the pond in the Tuileries, dabbling my feet. It was a very hot day.

Actually my little affair with Secker didn't work. So when Roland Gant became editorial director of Heinemann there was a mutual agreement to transfer me lock stock and barrel to Heinemann, who took over the existing contract and are just making a new one. The new novel is horribly long and will be out next summer. It's so long since we were in touch I can't even remember whether you knew I'd gone from E & S. The last book they did was The Birds of Paradise. Secker did The Bender (my sad comedy about London) and The Corrida at San Feliu.

I think Arthur [Crook] told me on the phone one day that he'd visited you. He and I have only met once, strange to say. I was at one of those stuffed shirt do's given by the RSL [Royal Society of Literature] to present scrolls to the blessed: Waugh, Huxley (Spender standing in) and Edith S[itwell] (Sachie standing in). Saw Arthur's name on the table list, so sought him out and introduced myself. That must have been in 1963. I must say I prefer the anonymity racket. Reviewing under my own name makes me feel like a performing monkey—but the obvious disadvantage is that no one finally remembers you exist, except from book to book as it were, and the Sunday boys get younger and younger.

Looking back over the past few years I wonder about muffed chances. I threw up Country Life, which was regular bread and butter, because the regularity of it became stifling and I found I couldn't write my own stuff. They come back to me, summer time, when Church or Grigson are on holiday, and the money seems so easy just for five weeks that I wonder why I gave it up. At some stage or another, David Holloway asked me if I'd like to join his fiction panel—and I declined, because I was then just finishing a book, going to New York, and later to India, but asked him to keep me in mind if a vacancy arose later. I did drop him a line last year, suggesting I occasionally did some non-fiction, but nothing came forth—although I'm told he was looking for me when I was on holiday this summer. And there was a blank period early this year when even Arthur seemed to have forgotten I was here—but that seems to have righted itself. I think my future largely depends now on what happens to my mammoth novel (about the Indian rebellion of 1942). I think I am capable of seeing through the next couple of years, by which time Carol should be earning some kind of living in the theatre, and Sally should be in mid-academic stream. Once they have flown we shan't live here—unless by then I have been forced back into a job. If the latter, I shan't ever regret the attempt to make writing work, and to make it work by itself, scarcely supported by anything except the occasional mss reading, and the thinly scattered TLS and Times reviewing. The old itch to be part of the junior literary establishment fades away in middle age (although it tickles badly from time to time, when you watch the parade of clever girls and boys banging drums and marching to switched-on glory).

It would be nice if you and Lal were back here—but I wouldn't wish it on you for the world. It's an increasingly nasty civilisation. There are more ¾ submerged Smethwicks than we normally realise. I think the next election will be fought on such grounds.

Bookseller. Surely. I'll parcel it up and send it off. Merry Christmas reading! Meanwhile, lots of love from us both to you both,

Ever,

Box 5, Folder 2 (McFarlin)
78 Addison Way
From a letter to Dorothy Ganapathy
7 December 1965

Dear Dorothy,

[…] I never answered your last letter to me because I did not know how to, and in any case I judged from it that you wanted nothing more to do with me. I'm not answering it now, but do have to write. This does not mean that you have to write back.

In your last letter to me you said nothing about the dedication of my new book—although I might read into your letter a withdrawal from the position my request to dedicate, your acceptance, and the book itself, established between us on mutual ground. Since I never make a dedication in a frivolous way, then whatever happens subsequently between me and the person I have dedicated to (between us, or to us) the dedication, so far as I am concerned, stands. It may be a source of puzzlement (what went wrong?) but can never be a source of regret.

I shall be correcting galley proofs of The Jewel in the Crown quite soon, providing the printers do as they have said, and I intend to leave the dedication exactly as it was in the manuscript you read. The only thing that would make me remove it now would be a direct request from you to do so. I should be sorry, but I should comply because half the point of a dedication is lost if it becomes a source of regret or irritation to the other person.

That is why, you see, you need not answer.[52]

Yours,

ENDNOTES

1. Scott referred in his letters to "Dass" in 1964, but in later years he used "Doss." The Tulsa archives catalogue his letters under "Doss," whereas Hilary Spurling used "Dass."
2. Powell (1912–1998) was a Conservative Party member of Parliament, known in the 1960s for his reactionary stance toward immigrants from the former colonies, describing them as strangers and aliens who would only contaminate British culture.
3. *The Corrida at San Feliu.*
4. In the autumn of 1958, the newly widowed Frances Scott moved into Addison Way. The subsequent weeks were filled with tension as Frances battled Penny for the love and attention of Paul and his daughters until Paul ordered his mother to leave. Frances then married Arthur Pridmore, the father of Peter Scott's wife, Eileen. Some years later, Pridmore also died, leaving Frances widowed for a second time. Scott had not spoken to his mother in years at this point, nor had he answered any of her letters that were addressed only to him. Gladys Roche was a welfare volunteer who visited Scott's mother—who was now nearly blind and deaf—on a weekly basis. On 2 January 1964, she wrote to Scott, telling him how much his mother grieved because she never saw or heard from him. Roche added, "I have a family and grandchildren, and I know how broken hearted I would be if one of my sons treated me as you do her" (McFarlin 16:1).
5. In July of 1964, a play based on The Bender was (in Scott's words penned to Dipali Nag on 4 July) "performed and canned" (canned as in recorded, "put in the can"). The actress playing Anina was not half Indian, but Lady Butterfield did talk into a tape recorder. On 17 August, Scott wrote to Dipali Nag that the actor who played George Lisle-Spruce was very good. He wrote, "People seemed to think the play came over well, but I wasn't so sure" (McFarlin 14:9).
6. According to Scott, "Mrs. Ganapathy is [...] a daughter of the late Sir Hari Singh Gour, founder of Saugar University in India, sister-in-law of the English High Court Judge in Allahabad who stayed in the country after Independence" (McFarlin 5:7).
7. Stands for "British Overseas Air Corporation," now British Airways.
8. Carol's seventeenth birthday.
9. According to Spurling, Felton was a novelist and political maverick who condemned the atrocities that were committed by British troops during the

Korean War and was subsequently ostracized by the British press. She then moved to Madras, and there Scott renewed their friendship during his 1964 trip (Spurling 291–292).

10. Scott's routine sign-off in his letters to his wife was "B," short for "Honey Boy" (Penny was "Honey Girl")—nicknames for each other from their early years of marriage.

11. A traditional greeting often accompanied by pressing the hands together in front of the chest. The word literally means "I bow to you," but the gesture itself could be sufficient.

12. Temple Fortune on Finchley Road, a local shopping area near the Scott home. Note courtesy of Sally Scott.

13. Roland and Nadia Gant.

14. Medication Scott took with him as a topical anti-infective, intestinal antiamoebic.

15. The family car, a Vauxhall Victor.

16. Penny had written about Sally playing Alice in the school play. She did have her waist-length hair cut to shoulder length.

17. "Keek" or "Kiki" was the Scotts' nickname for Carol. Sally was nicknamed "Bug."

18. Sofaer (1896–1988) was a Burmese-born actor of British and American films and television.

19. Scott's aunt, Ruth Mark, the unmarried sister of his mother, Frances.

20. Neighbors to the Scotts. Paul Cashmore (known to the family as "P" or "Pee") would later marry Sally Scott.

21. In fact, Scott cancelled both the Moscow and Sweden visits. See his letter to Mollie Hamilton dated 17 April 1964.

22. A hotel and restaurant at Henley on the Thames, named after Isaac Walton's 1653 book.

23. Scott stayed in Calcutta from 27 March to 4 April, when he traveled to Agra, then Delhi. On 9 April, he flew back to London.

24. Ghosh, educated in English public schools, was the prototype for Hari Kumar.

25. Dass replied on 22 June 1964, "Our intimacy is such that I feel that I always see you in my imagination as if you are moving in my house" (McFarlin 3.26).

26. Scott had suffered from amoebiasis since the war, but it had been diagnosed only recently. His symptoms included acute stomach pain, cold in the lumbar regions, irritability, lassitude, and a chronic inability to finish anything (Spurling 264). The entire family had contracted the infection, and physicians in France (not Britain) were able to treat the condition.

27. The General Certificate Examination (now the GCSE, the General Certificate of Secondary Education). The ordinary O levels are taken when the student is sixteen; if he or she is successful, he or she can then continue to study at the sixth form. At the age of eighteen, the student then takes A-level exams to determine his or her university acceptance.

28. Refers to the general election held on 15 October, which gave the Labour Party, under Harold Wilson, a narrow majority.

29. A copy of *The Corrida at San Feliu.*

30. Meidlinger, a white woman living in Johannesburg, had previously read *The Birds of Paradise* and told Scott that she was "highly stimulated by the shock of meeting you ... I mean your writing and this your mind". In reading *The Corrida at San Feliu*, she could "relax and get to know you". She wrote that she had read *Corrida* nearly in one sitting: "It was like listening to the music of Bach". In speaking of the apartheid regime, she said, "This is a country where a thinking human being can know of love and hate, tenderness & cruelty so intense as be almost unbearable." She would have liked to meet Scott in England, but her passport had been revoked by the South African government (McFarlin 12:12).

31. Warburg's letter of the eighth of February notes that Secker and Warburg released Scott from his third contracted novel because of Roland Gant's transfer to Heinemann, but also because of Secker and Warburg's "failure to sell a reasonable number of copies of the two novels we were privileged to publish [...]. I hope you will no more hold this against us than we hold against you the fact that the two books of yours which we published did not turn out to be sellers" (McFarlin 18:8).

32. For the BBC.

33. After this letter, Scott did not write to Dass again until 15 July 1968. He apparently sent a signed copy of *The Jewel in the Crown* to Dass and wondered if it arrived. "I have of course been hoping to come to India again, ever since my last visit, in 1964. But that has so far not been possible, and in the last year with my wife unwell I have been unable to make any plans of that kind. But I do hope that it won't be long before I can return to another tour" (McFarlin 3:26). Scott's last letter to Dass is dated 14 October 1968, when he sent a copy of *The Day of the Scorpion*. Dass continued to write through 6 April 1974. Scott didn't tell him of his trips to India in 1969 and 1971.

34. The typescript is *The Jewel in the Crown.*

35. The Royal Academy of Dramatic Art.

36. The wife of David Higham, Scott's British agent.

37. Finkenstaedt was the vice president of William Morrow and the husband of Rose L. H. Finkenstaedt, who worked with Malcolm X and the civil rights movement in the United States. Note courtesy of Sally Scott.
38. Vivian Stuart (1914–1986) was a member of the Society of Authors and the Institute of Journalists. She served as a chairperson of the Swanwick Summer Writers' School (Derbyshire) from 1965 through 1967. Under the pseudonyms Vivian Stuart, Alex Stuart, Barbara Allen, Fiona Finlay, V. A. Stuart, William Stuart Long, and Robyn Stuart, she published numerous novels and several books on naval history.
39. Gerald Pollinger of Pearn, Pollinger & Higham served on the summer school's committee. Scott refused to act as a host at the 1965 school because he didn't want to be ordered around by Pollinger. In a letter dated 20 September 1964, Scott wrote, "We have no liking for each other [… and] it seems to me ridiculous that Pollinger should be on a committee of a school for writers. It is rather like me being on a committee for a school for scientists" (McFarlin 19:3).
40. On 6 September, the Indian army had invaded West Pakistan to start the second Indo-Pakistan War.
41. Entitled "Eliza Rowen," which was circulated in 1966 but never published.
42. Dipali Nag (1922–2009) was a classical Indian singer and teacher. Her husband, Dulul, was a nuclear physicist at the university. Scott stayed with them when he visited Calcutta.
43. "Koi-Hai" was originally how members of the Raj would call their Indian servants. The term later referred to a long-term European resident of India.
44. Thompson (1917–1975) published nineteen novels under the pen name Francis Clifford. Scott was his agent while he was at David Higham Associates. The "film deal" Scott referred to was for Thompson's novel *The Naked Runner*; it was released in 1966 starring Frank Sinatra.
45. Monica Preston, the secretary at David Higham Associates.
46. The list of contributors eventually included Scott, Dorothy Eden, Mary Patchett, Francis Clifford, Eleanor Hibbert, James Hadley Chase, Bruce Marshall, and John Braine. Scott hadn't heard from Gerald Hanley as of yet—26 October 1965—but Hanley eventually bought in as of 10 November 1965. For a gift, they settled on a canteen of Swedish cutlery from Liberty's.
47. Dorothy's sister, Agnes Broome, was married to an Englishman, Mr. Justice Broome. The couple lived in Allahabad but was visiting London at the same time that Dorothy was there. The sisters had a falling out during their visit, and Dorothy thought that Scott had taken sides with her sister, thus proving himself a disloyal friend.

48. Dorothy Ganapathy had written on 11 October 1965 that Scott had been "disloyal to your 'so called friend.'" His behavior she found to be "British," marked by "disloyalty, dishonour & expediency." She ended the letter, "Before I close I want to tell you & thank you for opening my eyes to your complete disregard of my feelings & your complete disloyalty. You have found good British friends with the Broomes. Good luck to you—D. Ganapathy" (McFarlin 5:1).

49. Scott conferred with Mr. Roy on several matters, including who could be imprisoned under section 144 of the Criminal Procedure Code in India during World War II and the history of the Indian National Army (the INA), which was comprised of Indian troops who, captured by the Japanese, opted to fight against the British.

50. John Murray of John Murray Publishers Ltd.

51. Refers to Davenport's review of *The Corrida at San Feliu*.

52. Ganapathy responded to Scott as if all were well and did not mention their previous conflict. *Jewel* was dedicated to her.

FIGURE 1. Paul Scott in World War II.

FIGURE 2. Paul and Penny Scott on their wedding day.

FIGURE 3. Penny Scott.

FIGURE 4. Paul Scott.

FIGURE 5. Paul Scott.

Index of Recipients

Note. Only the first page of each letter is cited.

Subject Index

Lightning Source UK Ltd.
Milton Keynes UK
UKHW03n0822010518
321884UK00001B/14/P